# ATRA-ḪASĪS

## THE BABYLONIAN STORY OF THE FLOOD

# ATRA-ḪASĪS

# THE BABYLONIAN STORY OF THE FLOOD

BY

W. G. LAMBERT

AND

A. R. MILLARD

*with*

THE SUMERIAN FLOOD STORY

BY

M. CIVIL

OXFORD

AT THE CLARENDON PRESS

1969

*Oxford University Press, Ely House, London W. 1*
GLASGOW NEW YORK TORONTO MELBOURNE WELLINGTON
CAPE TOWN SALISBURY IBADAN NAIROBI LUSAKA ADDIS ABABA
BOMBAY CALCUTTA MADRAS KARACHI LAHORE DACCA
KUALA LUMPUR SINGAPORE HONG KONG TOKYO



PRINTED IN GREAT BRITAIN

# PREFACE

THE following is the history of the present volume. Lambert, in preparing a still [1968] unpublished corpus of Babylonian creation myths first planned to include the earlier portion of *Atra-ḫasīs*, and with this in view he re-copied the tablet known here (see pp. 40–1) under the symbol **E**, and identified among the copies of the late Dr. F. W. Geers in Chicago the fragments J–N and K 8562. At that time Miss E. Reiner made known to him her identification of K 6634 and K 13863. This material with the other then published fragment of Tablet I he prepared for publication. However, meanwhile the big Old Babylonian tablets **A** and $\mathbf{C}_1$ had come to light in the British Museum, and Millard was invited to copy them for publication in a *CT* volume, to which Lambert would also contribute his copies. Dr. R. D. Barnett, Keeper of the Department of Western Asiatic Antiquities, British Museum, who initiated this plan, also suggested that the two authors should co-operate on a critical edition of the epic. The *CT* volume, no. 46, appeared in 1965; the present volume marks the fruition of the second part of this plan. Millard made a first draft of the edition, contributing the initial decipherment of **A** and $\mathbf{C}_1$. He also first worked on **D**, which F. R. Kraus had identified in Istanbul. The final manuscript is largely the work of Lambert, except for the Glossary, which is largely the work of Millard. The copies and collations on pls. I–XI are the work of Lambert. All the original tablets have been either copied or collated for this edition, except that **B** has been read from photographs with the aid of collations supplied by J. J. Finkelstein; x and y have been copied from photographs since the originals cannot be located.

While this is a scholarly edition, the Introduction has been written with the needs in view of those who are not cuneiform scholars. In doing their work the authors have enjoyed the co-operation of numerous scholars. Professor J. J. Finkelstein not only supplied collations of **B**, as mentioned above, but also made known to us privately the results of his work on the epic. He first read the vital sign *arḫu* in I 280–1 and grasped the sense of *palû* in I 282. Other suggestions of his that we have adopted are mentioned in the appropriate philological notes. Professor R. Frankena generously allowed us to see a rough copy of **D** that he had made. D. Kennedy collated **D** for us. J. Nougayrol sent us his copy of 𝕳 before it had appeared. Professor Benno Landsberger has been consulted on various points, and suggestions of his are noted in due place. Professor O. R. Gurney read the final draft of the manuscript and suggested improvements. Mrs. A. R. Millard and Professor J. Emerton read the Introduction and contributed to its clarity. Permission to copy and publish **D** has been given by Mesdames Kızılyay and Çığ, curators of Near Eastern antiquities in the Archaeological Museums, Istanbul, who rendered every assistance in our work. The Deutsche Orient-Gesellschaft gave its permission for the publication of x and y from the Babylon Photos. The Musée d'Art et d'Histoire, Geneva, consented to the recopying and republication of $\mathbf{C}_2$, and Mlle Dunand facilitated the work. The Trustees of the British Museum have allowed the publication of K 14697 and the collation of the other tablets in their collections. For all this help and co-operation the authors express their gratitude. Thanks are also due to the craftsmen of the Clarendon Press for a difficult but well-executed piece of printing.

W. G. LAMBERT
A. R. MILLARD

*April 1968*

## POSTSCRIPT

Thanks are due to Professor W. von Soden, who sent a list of corrections and suggestions while the book was in proofs. These have been adopted where possible. A lengthy article by G. Pettinato, 'Die Bestrafung des Menschengeschlechts durch die Sintflut' appeared in *Orientalia*, N.S. 37. 165–200, too late to be used. Its main contention is that 'noise' (*rigmum, ḫubūrum*) in the Epic means or implies 'evil conduct', so that Enlil did not destroy the human race for mere noise. The idea is not well founded philologically, and depends too much on preconceptions about that mythological being, 'der orientalische Mensch'. Attention is drawn to Addenda on pp. xi and 172.

*October 1968*

# CONTENTS

# ABBREVIATIONS AND REFERENCES

## I. TABLET SIGNATURES

British Museum, London
- BM British Museum
- Bu Budge
- DT Daily Telegraph
- K Kuyunjik
- Rm Rassam
- Sm Smith
- Th Thompson

Vorderasiatisches Museum, Berlin
- BE Babylon Expedition
- VAT Vorderasiatische Abteilung, Tontafel

Oriental Institute, University of Chicago
- A Asiatic

University Museum, Philadelphia
- CBS Catalogue of the Babylonian Section

Musée d'Art et d'Histoire, Geneva: MAH

Library of J. Pierpont Morgan, New York
- MLC Morgan Library Catalogue

Archaeological Museums, Istanbul: Ni(ppur)

Musée National Syrien, Damascus
- RS Ras Shamra

Ashmolean Museum, Oxford
- W-B Weld-Blundell

## II. PUBLICATIONS CITED BY INITIALS

| | |
|---|---|
| *AbB* | F. R. Kraus *et al.*, *Altbabylonische Briefe* |
| *ABRT* | J. A. Craig, *Assyrian and Babylonian Religious Texts* |
| *AfO* | *Archiv für Orientforschung* |
| *AHw* | W. von Soden, *Akkadisches Handwörterbuch* |
| *AJSL* | *American Journal of Semitic Languages and Literatures* |
| *AL* | F. Delitzsch, *Assyrische Lesestücke* |
| *AMT* | R. Campbell Thompson, *Assyrian Medical Texts* |
| *AnBib* | *Analecta Biblica* |
| *ANET* | J. B. Pritchard (ed.), *Ancient Near Eastern Texts* |
| *AnSt* | *Anatolian Studies* |
| *ARM* | *Archives royales de Mari* (texts in transliteration) |
| *ArOr* | *Archiv Orientální* |
| *AS* | *Assyriological Studies* |
| *BA* | *Beiträge zur Assyrologie* |
| *BAM* | F. Köcher, *Die babylonisch-assyrische Medizin* |
| *BBR* | H. Zimmern, *Beiträge zur Kenntnis der babylonischen Religion* |
| *BBSt* | L. W. King, *Babylonian Boundary Stones* |

| | |
|---|---|
| *BE* | *The Babylonian Expedition of the University of Pennsylvania* |
| *BIN* | *Babylonian Inscriptions in the Collection of James B. Nies* |
| *BiOr* | *Bibliotheca Orientalis* |
| *BRM* | *Babylonian Records in the Library of J. Pierpont Morgan* |
| *BSGW* | *Berichte der Sächsischen Gesellschaft der Wissenschaften* (Leipzig) |
| *BWL* | W. G. Lambert, *Babylonian Wisdom Literature* |
| *CAD* | I. J. Gelb, B. Landsberger, A. L. Oppenheim, E. Reiner, *The Assyrian Dictionary of the Oriental Institute of the University of Chicago* |
| *CT* | *Cuneiform Texts from Babylonian Tablets in the British Museum* |
| *GAG* | W. von Soden, *Grundriss der akkadischen Grammatik* |
| *GSG* | A. Poebel, *Grundzüge der sumerischen Grammatik* |
| *JAOS* | *Journal of the American Oriental Society* |
| *JCS* | *Journal of Cuneiform Studies* |
| *JNES* | *Journal of Near Eastern Studies* |
| *JRAS* | *Journal of the Royal Asiatic Society* |
| *JSS* | *Journal of Semitic Studies* |
| *JTVI* | *Journal of the Transactions of the Victoria Institute* |
| *KAR* | E. Ebeling, *Keilschrifttexte aus Assur religiösen Inhalts*, i, ii (= *WVDOG* 28, 34) |
| *KAV* | O. Schroeder, *Keilschrifttexte aus Assur verschiedenen Inhalts* (= *WVDOG* 35) |
| *KBo* | H. H. Figulla *et al.*, *Keilschrifttexte aus Boghazköi*, i–vi (= *WVDOG* 30, 36) |
| *LKA* | E. Ebeling, *Literarische Keilschrifttexte aus Assur* |
| *LTBA* | *Die lexikalischen Tafelserien der Babylonier und Assyrer in den Berliner Museen*, i (L. Matouš), ii (W. von Soden) |
| *MAD* | *Materials for the Assyrian Dictionary*, i–iii (I. J. Gelb) |
| *MAOG* | *Mitteilungen der altorientalischen Gesellschaft* |
| *MBI* | G. A. Barton, *Miscellaneous Babylonian Inscriptions* |
| *MIO* | *Mitteilungen des Instituts für Orientforschung* |
| *MSL* | B. Landsberger *et al.*, *Materialien zum sumerischen Lexikon* |
| *OLZ* | *Orientalistische Literaturzeitung* |
| *Or* | *Orientalia* |
| *PBS* | *Publications of the Babylonian Section, University Museum, University of Pennsylvania* |
| *PSBA* | *Proceedings of the Society of Biblical Archaeology* |
| *R* | H. C. Rawlinson *et al.*, *The Cuneiform Inscriptions of Western Asia* |
| *RA* | *Revue d'Assyriologie* |
| *Rit. acc.* | F. Thureau-Dangin, *Rituels accadiens* |
| *RLA* | E. Ebeling *et al.*, *Reallexikon der Assyriologie* |
| *RT* | *Recueil de Travaux relatifs à la philologie et à l'archéologie égyptiennes et assyriennes* |
| *SBH* | G. Reisner, *Sumerisch-babylonische Hymnen* |
| *SBP* | S. H. Langdon, *Sumerian and Babylonian Psalms* |
| *SEM* | E. Chiera, *Sumerian Epics and Myths* |
| *SGL* | A. Falkenstein, J. J. Van Dijk, *Sumerische Götterlieder*, i, ii |
| *ŠL* | A. Deimel, *Šumerisches Lexikon* |
| *SLT* | E. Chiera, *Sumerian Lexical Texts* |
| *STC* | L. W. King, *The Seven Tablets of Creation* |
| *STT* | O. R. Gurney, *The Sultantepe Tablets* |
| *STVC* | E. Chiera, *Sumerian Texts of Varied Contents* |
| *TCL* | *Musée du Louvre, Département des antiquités orientales, Textes cunéiformes* |

*UET* *Publications of the Joint Expedition of the British Museum and of the University Museum, University of Pennsylvania, Philadelphia, to Mesopotamia, Ur Excavations, Texts*
*VAB* *Vorderasiatische Bibliothek*
*VAS* *Vorderasiatische Schriftdenkmäler*
*WVDOG* *Wissenschaftliche Veröffentlichungen der deutschen Orient-Gesellschaft*
*WZKM* *Wiener Zeitschrift für die Kunde des Morgenlandes*
*YBT* *Yale Oriental Series, Babylonian Texts*
*YOR* *Yale Oriental Series, Researches*
*ZA* *Zeitschrift für Assyriologie*
*ZDMG* *Zeitschrift der deutschen morgenländischen Gesellschaft*

## III. CITATIONS FROM AKKADIAN AND OTHER ANCIENT TEXTS

Except where otherwise stated, quotations from the following works follow the line numbering of the following editions:

*Aḥiqar* A. Cowley, *Aramaic Papyri*
*Code of Hammurabi* A. Deimel, E. Bergmann, A. Pohl, and R. Follet, *Codex Ḫammurabi*[3]
*Enūma Eliš* W. G. Lambert, *Babylonian Creation Myths* (forthcoming)
*Erimḫuš* Unpublished edition of B. Landsberger, quoted by permission
*Erra* F. Gössmann, *Das Era-Epos*
*Gilgameš* R. Campbell Thompson, *The Epic of Gilgamish*, supplemented from *CT* 46. 16–35
*Šurpu* E. Reiner, *Šurpu* (*AfO*, Beiheft 11)

# ADDENDUM TO TABLET I

AFTER the proofs had been corrected K 10097 was identified and joined to columns ii and iii of S. It supplies the ends of nine lines of ii after a gap of about seven lines from the previously known part. They are so numbered in the transliteration below,

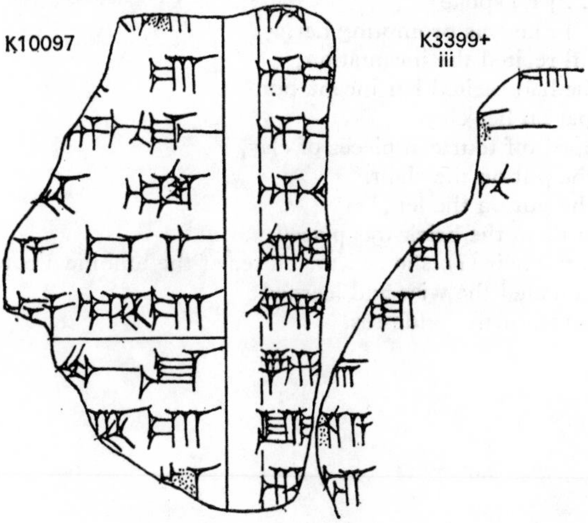

and the parallel lines from the main recension are added in brackets. It appears that the Assyrian Recension abbreviated this section. The portion of iii on K 10097 restores part or whole of the first eight lines of the previously known portion, and supplies traces of one preceding line, which is here numbered 0 to save renumbering the rest. Since the spitting in line 4 is put after the recitation of the incantation, whereas in the main recension it comes twenty lines before (I. 233–4, 253–4), it is possible that the whole process described in the main recension was condensed.

ii 22 . . . ] × ×
23 . . . $^{d}$*e*]*n-líl* (125)
24 . . . ] *an-nu-gal* (127)
25 . . . E]N *tāḫazi*(KA×ERÍN) (129)
26 . . . *ig-ra*]*-a* giš.lá (130)
27 . . . *b*]*āb* $^{d}$*en-líl* (133 ?)

---

28 . . . *a*]*-bu-šu* (136)
29 . . . ] $^{d}$*en-líl* (137)
30 . . . ] ×

Note: If 25 should be restored [*man-nu-um-ma b*]*ēl tāḫazi*, the same could be done for I. 128–9 and 140–1 in the main recension.

iii 0 *a-n*[*a* . . .
1 AN × [ . . . . $^{d}$]*é-a is-sà-qar*
2 AN × [ . . . ] × *ú-šám*$^{\text{šá-am}}$*-na-ši*
3 $^{d}$*be-l*[*et-ilī*$^{\text{meš}}$ *tam*]*-nu ši-ip-ta*
*iš-tu-ma tam-nu-ú ši-pa-sa*
4 *ru-t*[*a ta*]*-ta-di eli ṭí-iṭ-ṭí-šá*
5 14 *kí-*[*ir*]*-ṣi tàk-ri-iṣ*
7 *kí-ir-ṣi ana imitti*(zag) *taš-ku-un*
6 7 *kí-ir-ṣi ana šumēli*(gùb) *taš-ku-un*
*ina be-ru-šu-nu i-ta-di libittu*
7 *tep-da-a ap-pa-ri ba-ti!-iq a-bu-un-na-te tep-te-ši*
8 *tal-si-ma er-še-te mu-te-te*
9 [7] ⸢*ù*⸣ 7 *šà-su-ra-ti*

0 To [. . .
1 . . [ . . . . ] Ea spoke
2 . . [ . . . ] . he was prompting her.
3 Bēlet-[ilī] recited the incantation;
After she had recited her incantation
4 [She] spat on her clay.
5 She nipped off fourteen pieces of clay,
Seven she put on the right,
6 Seven she put on the left,
Between them the brick was placed.
7 She . . . the hair (?), she . . . the cutter of the umbilical cord.
8 She summoned the wise and learned
9 Twice seven birth-goddesses.

# INTRODUCTION

THE *Atra-ḫasīs* epic is one literary form of Sumero-Babylonian traditions about the creation and early history of man. For some 1,500 years during which Babylonian civilization flourished it was copied on clay tablets, but as Babylon sank under the eastward flood of Hellenism that followed Alexander the Great it was lost. All that remained for two millennia were some related Hebrew traditions worked into the Book of Genesis and a synopsis of material similar to it that Berossus, a Babylonian priest about the time of Alexander, had put into Greek, though this work did not survive for long, and in Europe it has been known only from excerpts, occasionally garbled, quoted by Greek and Latin writers at second or even third hand.[1]

Its recovery began in the middle of the nineteenth century A.D. when European diplomats, travellers, and savants began serious exploration of the mounds covering the ancient cities of Mesopotamia.[2] The sites of Assyria first attracted attention, since they yielded big, showy reliefs that could adorn the galleries of Western museums, and British and French interests were competing to secure prior rights to dig, which at that time automatically conferred the right to carry away anything found. The mounds yielded clay tablets inscribed in cuneiform script, which at first attracted little attention, but fortunately the decipherment of the script was proceeding apace as the early excavators were finding more of these objects, and they were then assigned a proper importance.

Kuyunjik, which covers part of ancient Nineveh, is the only site which need be mentioned here. Paul Émile Botta, French Vice-Consul at Mosul, first dug there for some weeks in 1842/3, but found few of the results then expected. British interests were furthered by Austin Henry Layard, supported at first from the private resources of the British ambassador in Istanbul, Sir Stratford Canning. Layard secured rights to dig, and this created a nice problem at Kuyunjik, which was solved by a gentlemen's agreement; the French considered one sector of the mound theirs, and the British the other sector. This arrangement lasted until Layard finally left

[1] For the editions of Berossus see p. 135.

[2] For further information on the beginnings of Mesopotamian archaeology and the decipherment of the cuneiform script the following are recommended: the early chapters of R. W. Rogers, *History of Babylon and Assyria*; E. A. Wallis Budge, *The Rise and Progress of Assyriology*; Seton Lloyd, *Foundations in the Dust*; S. A. Pallis, *The Antiquity of Iraq*, chs. II and III.

the country in 1851. Spasmodic digging had taken place, and toward the end the palace of Sennacherib and two chambers rich in cuneiform tablets had been found.

The local Arabs were on the British side. Botta, abetted by a particularly brutal local pasha, had ridden roughshod over the rights of a local gentleman who held a lease on Kuyunjik from the Turkish Government, while Layard had voluntarily paid some compensation to the man. Also, after Layard's departure, British interests were served by Hormuzd Rassam, a Christian of local extraction, who well understood the people of the district. During the intervals in official excavations these people had conducted their own explorations of the mounds, and, as always, knew where best to dig. Thus, when in 1852 Victor Place, who was replacing Botta, began work in the French sector the natives were watching just where he dug. When, therefore, Place's trenches were being extended in the direction of a particularly rich spot, they urged Rassam to act. But the place was in the French sector, so Rassam arranged that a select group of workmen should dig there secretly by night. This was done on 20 December 1853. On the next night the diggers struck reliefs, and on the third night they began to expose a large room surrounded by the most magnificent series of Assyrian reliefs ever found. Rassam, considering that like a prospector for gold his claim was now staked, proceeded to work openly by day. The legal position was certainly obscure since both French and British had at various times been given permission to dig at Kuyunjik. What Rassam had dug into was the palace of the last great Assyrian king, Ashurbanipal, and in addition to the reliefs it yielded thousands upon thousands of broken pieces of cuneiform tablets. These were the remains of libraries that were collected under Ashurbanipal's supervision and which had made Nineveh a forerunner of Alexandria, where another royal patron of letters, Ptolemy I, formed a library that excelled all others in the Hellenistic world. Thanks to Layard, Rassam, and others who worked at Kuyunjik after them, practically everything that was recovered from Ashurbanipal's libraries was taken to the British Museum.

In London the work of decipherment was forwarded when the British Museum began to publish texts. The first volume, *Inscriptions in the Cuneiform Character from Assyrian Monuments* by Layard, appeared in 1851 and consisted of Assyrian monumental inscriptions. Other scholars, especially Rawlinson, who had done sterling work in the original decipherment, Birch, an employee of the Museum, Norris, Secretary of the Royal Asiatic Society, and the French Orientalist Oppert, contributed much to the progress of interpretation. About 1857 the British Museum committed itself to publishing a series of volumes of cuneiform texts selected by Rawlinson, though others did much of the work. It was planned to issue ultimately volumes in which the cuneiform plates would be opposite pages of translations, but the difficulties of this were underestimated and only the plates appeared, under the title *The Cuneiform Inscriptions of Western Asia.* Large portions of the monumental inscriptions and similar texts on clay tablets were read with ease, apart from particular obscurities, but much of the religious and literary compositions was not understood. The man who contributed most to their understanding was George Smith. Born in Chelsea of humble parents, at the age of fourteen he was apprenticed to a firm of bank-note engravers. He soon became engrossed in the new discoveries from Mesopotamia, and his interest, arising, like that of many others in his century, from an Old Testament background, was to become his life's work. At first he was just an amateur who stinted himself to buy the books from which he acquired knowledge, but by his frequent visits to the British Museum he attracted the attention of Birch, Keeper of Oriental Antiquities, and gave up his career as an engraver to enter the Museum's service in a lowly capacity. There he was put to work, among other things, sorting the thousands of fragments of tablets from Ashurbanipal's library. It soon became clear that his understanding of the texts was equal to anyone's, and in 1866 at the age of twenty-six he was appointed Assistant in the Department of Oriental Antiquities and worked on the Museum's publications of cuneiform texts. Others knew that works of mythology were preserved, but only George Smith collected and joined enough broken pieces to reconstruct entire episodes, and only he could understand the content. His lack of philological training was made up for by hard work and sheer genius. His fame was assured when, on 3 December 1872, he read a paper to the Society of Biblical Archaeology announcing his discovery of a Babylonian version of the Biblical flood story. The solemnity of the occasion is vouched for by the presence on the platform of such Victorian worthies as W. E. Gladstone and Dean Stanley. In 1876 his book, *The Chaldean Account of Genesis*, was published, in which he gave a general account of all the Babylonian literary texts he had discovered with excerpts in translation. Among them was 'the story of Atarpi', which is now known as the *Epic of Atra-ḫasīs*.

George Smith knew only one copy of this epic, which, as we can now conclude, was made up from three broken pieces. They were far from restoring the whole of the tablet and Smith mistook obverse for reverse, which did not help the matter. However, we must not blame him for this, since the correct choice of sides was only finally settled in 1956. Also, after his premature death in 1876, the three pieces got separated, and though two of them were joined again by 1899, when a transliteration into the Latin alphabet was published with full translation, the third piece remained unidentified for some eighty-five years, was finally published in 1965, but was not joined to the other two until work on the present edition of the epic was almost complete, in 1967. While Smith had translated two portions with remarkable accuracy for his time, he understood nothing of the story as a whole.

The next stage in the recovery of the epic seemed at first unrelated. In 1898 V. Scheil, a French priest, published a fragment of a flood story differing from George Smith's, and dated to the reign of king Ammi-ṣaduqa of Babylon, some thousand years earlier than Ashurbanipal of Assyria.[1] After Scheil had had the fragment it was acquired for the American millionaire John Pierpont Morgan, and to this day it remains in the Morgan collection. In the same year part 6 of *Cuneiform Texts from Babylonian Tablets in the British Museum* appeared, and this contained a mythological fragment of roughly the same date describing the creation of man, copied by T. G. Pinches. The following year Heinrich Zimmern, a German of outstanding ability at comprehending Babylonian and Sumerian texts, composed an article in which he gave the transliterated text of two of Smith's three pieces (as mentioned above), proved that what Scheil and Pinches had published belonged to the same work, and that the hero's name was not to be read Atar-pi, but Atra, or Atar-ḫasīs. Zimmern had made his copy of the London fragments available to a compatriot, Peter Jensen, who was preparing a complete edition of all known Babylonian myths and legends, and he too became aware of Zimmern's conclusions. Thus in 1900 both Zimmern's article and Jensen's book appeared. While they put the study of this epic on a firm footing, the results were scarcely epoch-making. There was an account of the gods' plagues on the human race for its sins, an allusion to the flood, and some lines about the creation of man. Jensen saw clearly that the choice of sides for obverse and reverse was in doubt, so that no firm order of the various preserved extracts was possible. And there the matter rested for half a century. Some new small pieces were published, but they did not alter the situation.

Only in 1956 did the Danish scholar Jørgen Laessøe finally demonstrate

[1] For full bibliographical references to this article and to the other publications mentioned in this and the following paragraph see the Bibliography on pp. 173–4. A list of Mesopotamian kings with dates (where possible) is given by J. Brinkman in the Appendix to A. L. Oppenheim, *Ancient Mesopotamia*. Since dates earlier than 1000 B.C. are still not settled, we have usually accepted Brinkman's as the best available.

the correct sequence,[1] and thereby produce a story. First, man was created, but as the human race multiplied its noise disturbed the most important god, Enlil, who tried out various means of reducing the population. They all failed for one reason or another, so finally a flood was sent to exterminate the lot. Even this, however, was frustrated, for the god Enki warned his favourite Atra-ḫasīs, who built a boat and escaped with his family and a selection of animals. With the sequence established, more text material was needed to fill out the details, and this was soon forthcoming. In 1965 the present writers made available a large quantity of new text in *Cuneiform Texts from Babylonian Tablets in the British Museum*, part 46. It consisted of two large tablets from the same scribe who wrote the fragment that Scheil had published in 1898 (they had been in the British Museum since 1889!), and smaller pieces both Old Babylonian and Late Assyrian. It is this accumulation of new material that justifies the present work, and to it there are added in this volume still more new pieces, both Old and Late Babylonian, so that some two-thirds of the complete work can now be presented.

Just what is the *Epic of Atra-ḫasīs*? With a modern literary work the question could not be put in this way. A work of Dickens, say *Oliver Twist*, will always be that work no matter how many editions it goes through. But the ancient world had no proper titles, no sense of literary rights, and no aversion to what we call plagiarism. Succeeding ages often rewrote old texts to suit new language forms and tastes. With *Atra-ḫasīs* the only 'title' in use was the opening words 'When the gods like man'. At the end of each clay tablet there was usually a colophon giving such details as we expect on a title-page. On the rare occasions when complete tablets are available the colophons usually settle the connections of the text. But where only small fragments survive the question of identification is complex. What is available for *Atra-ḫasīs* is discussed in detail and listed on pp. 31–41, below, but the following summary may be useful.

The main edition used here, since it is the most complete, was copied out in the reign of Ammi-ṣaduqa, great-great-grandson of the famous Hammurabi, by Ku-Aya 'the junior scribe'. There is nothing in the tablets to suggest that Ku-Aya was a mere schoolboy, or that his work is a school exercise. It was an edition in three tablets. Of the other pieces of about the same age two agree very closely with Ku-Aya's text, but others differ considerably and probably belonged to variant editions. Most other pieces are Late Assyrian copies (*c.* 700–650 B.C.), and clearly they do not

[1] However, Sidney Smith anticipated Laessøe in 1925 by roundly asserting that col. ii 'should be v' and col. iii 'should be reckoned col. iv' (*RA* 22, 63, and 67).

all belong to one edition. From this source there is the only other edition which is known to have gone under the title 'When the gods like man'. This is George Smith's 'story of Atarpi', now associated with other pieces, which we call the Assyrian Recension because it shows Assyrian dialectal forms. The story is essentially the same as Ku-Aya's, but it has been substantially rewritten. Corrections from parallel passages, such as are well known in manuscripts of the gospels, occasionally obscure the development of the story. It was written on two tablets, not three. Of the other Assyrian fragments some adhere more or less closely to Ku-Aya's text, but are expanded by the insertion of extra lines; others are clearly different. Since there is no means of knowing if all such pieces belong to what was called 'When the gods like man' we have adopted the practical expedient of including all related text material except that version of the flood story which George Smith discovered and which belongs to the XIth Tablet of the *Epic of Gilgameš*.[1] The Late Babylonian fragments, two in number, differ substantially from the Old Babylonian text, as do both Middle Babylonian texts. The one from Nippur is a piece about the flood. That from Ras Shamra on the Syrian coast dealt only with the flood, omitting all the earlier episodes.

A modern reader must not expect to find our translation immediately appealing or fully intelligible. Literary taste has changed over the past 3,000 years, and, if one may use a musical analogy, to turn from the English classics to *Atra-ḫasīs* will be like turning from Wagner and Chopin to plainsong. The lack of dynamism and lush harmonies may give a first impression that plainsong is just dull. The visual arts can often make an immediate impact, but appreciation of literature and music depends very much on acclimatization. Our text is poetry, but lacks rhyme and metre. The basic unit is the line, which is a unit of sense, and in this text it consists of three or four words, with very few exceptions (certain monosyllabic particles not being counted for this purpose). In Ku-Aya's edition the lines are grouped in couplets (again as a matter of sense), but other recensions are not consistently so arranged. The shortness of the line was a great inhibition to style in the modern sense, but the ancients were content with simplicity of wording. A musical analogy may help again. A simple melody may occur in many styles of music, but Western music since the seventeenth century has developed harmony to an extent that now a musical hack can dress up a simple melody with all kinds of har-

[1] English translations are available by E. A. Speiser in J. B. Pritchard (ed.), *Ancient Near Eastern Texts* 93–6; and by A. Heidel, *The Gilgamesh Epic and Old Testament Parallels*. A detailed scientific bibliography is given in P. Garelli (ed.), *Gilgameš et sa légende*.

monies each of which conveys a particular flavour to the tune. The use of elaborate literary style to dress up thoughts is of course much older than Western harmony—Plato was already a master at it—but the Western tradition, which came down from Greece and Rome, is altogether alien to the ancient Near East. Plenty of literary ability existed there, but its subtleties occur within such stark simplicity of wording that most of it is inevitably lost in translation. There is no scope for that kind of rendering of Cicero's speeches into modern English where the thought of the passage is extracted and re-expressed in another idiom. Apart from modifying some metaphors and putting the words in English order the translator can do little but render word for word. Anything else would not be translation. If, then, our readers find the style of the translation bare and jejune, we must assure them that study of the original is more rewarding. However, in the authors' judgement the literary merit of this work is not outstanding considered within its own world. The content gives it its exceptional interest.

As with the majority of works of Babylonian literature, *Atra-ḫasīs* is anonymous, but one must nevertheless ask what prompted its writing. Our use of 'epic' to describe the text is simply modern Assyriological convention. Similar texts in ancient Mesopotamia were called 'songs' and were therefore 'sung'.[1] What style of singing, chanting, or declaiming may have been used is unknown, though most likely the music came from a stringed instrument. This information conveys nothing, however, about the atmosphere of the occasions on which the 'singing' took place. The Myth and Ritual school[2] has an answer to this question: that many myths sprang out of a cultic environment and served in the cult. As far as Mesopotamia is concerned this is a hasty generalization from one specific example. The *Epic of Creation* is known to have been recited to the statue of the god Marduk in the course of the New Year festival at Babylon at least from *c.* 700 B.C. and perhaps earlier. No other similar cases are known, and even with this one it must be observed that the epilogue to the epic states its purpose as being to educate mankind generally in the greatness of Marduk, with which the content wholly agrees. The cultic use does not seem to have been intended by the author. The same can be concluded about *Atra-ḫasīs*. The advice it freely offers on marriage and midwifery was hardly intended for the loneliness of some dark cella shared only with a cult statue. In this epic there is no express statement of purpose, but the

[1] See the concluding section of the *Erra Myth* (*Iraq* 24. 125) and the last two lines of the *Epic of Creation* (*Enūma Eliš*) in the forthcoming edition of the first-named author.

[2] See S. H. Hooke, *Myth and Ritual*, and *Myth, Ritual and Kingship*.

content gives the impression of having been intended for public recitation (note especially the conclusion), and the Homeric poems offer a fair parallel. Whether a religious aura surrounded the recitation is unknown. Oral performance was necessary since the cumbrous system of cuneiform writing restricted literacy to a small élite of professional scribes, but there is no reason to suppose that only scribes sang epics such as *Atra-ḫasīs* to audiences, whether for edification or entertainment. No doubt there was a class of illiterate story-tellers who had memorized their stock-in-trade. We must therefore suppose that an oral tradition existed alongside the copying of texts on clay, but we can only speculate on how the two traditions may have interacted. The existence of widely differing recensions may be accounted for as arising from oral tradition, which is much more fluid than the written.

The story itself begins in the time conceived by the Babylonians and their Sumerian predecessors when only the gods lived in the universe, and they therefore had to toil for their daily bread. In this particular story the three senior gods, Anu, Enlil and Enki, agreed on their spheres of influence (I. 7–16). Under their conception of the universe like a tiered wedding cake we are told that Anu went up to heaven, Enlil (we are left to infer) remained on the earth, and Enki (also called Ea) went down to the Apsû, a body of water believed to lie beneath the earth, from which springs drew their water. Enlil put the junior gods to work digging the rivers and canals (Babylonian has only one word for both), on which, in historical times the agricultural prosperity depended. However, forty years of such labour proved too much, and the junior gods decided on a showdown with Enlil, set fire to their tools, and surrounded his house (the temple Ekur in Nippur) by night. He was roused by his servants and at once convened an assembly of the major gods. At the suggestion of Anu, Enlil's vizier Nusku was sent out to the rebels to demand an explanation of their conduct. He returned with the answer that the hard labour was too much, so they unanimously decided to defy authority (I. 33–152). With tears (whether from pity or indignation is not clear) Enlil suggested that Anu should return to heaven and there exact exemplary punishment on one of the rebels, but Anu replied that the grievances were well justified (I. 166–81).

At this point the main recension breaks off, but if a fragment of another recension can be taken as the continuation, namely **G**, column ii, then Enki spoke up and presented the same case for the rebels, but added the practical suggestion that man should be created with the help of the mother goddess to take over the hard labour. The main recension sets in again at I. 189 as this suggestion is being made. The gods generally accepted it with alacrity and summoned the mother goddess, variously called Mami, Mama, Nintu, and Bēlet-ilī. While not declining the suggestion she deferred to Enki's superior skill, and so the arrangement was worked out that the two would co-operate in the task. In effect, man was to be made from clay, like a figurine, but mixed with the flesh and blood of a slaughtered god. There is much interesting cultic and anthropological content in lines 206–30, which will be discussed in more detail later. The god slain is called either Wê or Wê-ila, but neither name is known elsewhere. The actual stages of the work are not too clear. From line 231 it appears that the clay was at that point of time mixed, and after the gods spat on it the mother goddess talked as though everything was finished and accordingly she received congratulations and the assignation of her name Bēlet-ilī 'Mistress-of-the-gods' (235–47). However, the work was not over, since in line 241 Enki and the mother goddess proceed to what is called 'the House of Destiny' and there set to work in earnest, helped by fourteen birth goddesses. First Enki trod the clay to mix it, then the mother goddess took fourteen pieces from it which the birth goddesses moulded into seven males and seven females. The latter detail is taken from the Assyrian Recension (obv. iii), since there is a gap in the main recension. The moulded figures were next put into two groups of seven, the males in the one, the females in the other, separated by what is called 'a brick'. This was probably not a single builders' brick, but a brick structure referred to in other Babylonian texts on which women performed their labour, and by bringing in this object the author related the myth to actual births in contemporary society. The next stage in the process is lost, but when the main recension sets in again (271 ff.) the various divine actors are waiting for the end of the gestation period. With the arrival of the tenth month the womb (the formation of which is lost in the preceding gap) breaks open and mankind is born. At this point in the main recension, and a little later in the Assyrian Recension, the mother goddess takes the opportunity to give advice on obstetrics and marriage. After this the text is lost or so incomplete as to give no sense until line 352.

We now pass from myth to legends about early times. The human race multiplied and their noise became such that Enlil—still on the earth—could not sleep. He therefore resolved to reduce their numbers by plague, and Namtara, the god of plague, was commissioned to put this plan into effect. Enki, no doubt fully insulated from the noise in his subterranean abode, and in any case sympathetic to his own creation, was petitioned by Atra-ḫasīs, who, unless he was mentioned in the earlier missing section, is introduced very abruptly in line 364. To understand the narrative properly one needs to know that he was king. Enki gave him instructions for averting the plague. The normal custom of the Babylonians in time of need was to petition their personal gods, just as in the story Atra-ḫasīs approached his personal god Enki. For most Babylonians the personal deity was very minor, but it was his duty, if suitably provided with offerings by his client, to look after the latter as need arose. However, under the divinely sent plague special measures were needed, which were mediated by Atra-ḫasīs to the city elders, and by them to the people. They were all to direct their devotions to Namtara in person, who would be pleased by the unwonted attention and would relax the plague. All this happened and, at the beginning of Tablet II, mankind multiplied once more, Enlil again lost his sleep, and having failed with plague, he now tried famine to reduce the human population. Adad, the storm god, was instructed to withhold his rain. This was done and in the ensuing famine Atra-ḫasīs once more entreated Enki, who repeated his previous advice, which was again successful, and Adad discreetly watered the earth without attracting Enlil's attention.

This second attempt of Enlil covered the first column and the top half of the second column of Tablet II, and the gap between the preserved portions in the main recension can be filled from the Assyrian Recension. From this point onwards to the end the difficulty arises that frequent gaps obscure the development of the story, and especially for the remainder of Tablet II. The Assyrian Recension is as incomplete as the Old Babylonian text, and the use of the two Late Babylonian pieces does not fully restore the narrative. The following reconstruction seems reasonably sure to the present writers. With the relaxation of the drought mankind presumably multiplied (with its noise) so that for the third time Enlil lost his sleep. The only surviving account of what he then ordered is x rev. i, which can be compared with column v of the Assyrian Recension (which contains some of this material conflated with other things) and with backward allusions in later parts of the story. It appears that Enlil was now thoroughly suspicious that some god was deliberately frustrating his plans. He did not, therefore, think up a third method for diminishing the numbers of the human race, but instituted a rigorous renewal of the drought. Since previously the earth had been watered without his knowledge, he set guards at each level of the universe to watch that no breach of his rules occurred. Anu and Adad guarded the heavens. He himself (one Late Babylonian copy substitutes Sin and Nergal) guarded the earth, while Enki supervised the regions below. Thus the drought was resumed. This much was probably contained in the bottom half of Tablet II, column ii, of the main recension, and when, in column iii, we find Atra-ḫasīs absorbed in devotions to Enki, we may be sure that he is disturbed that the renewal of the drought seemed to imply that Enki no longer cared for the human race. Enki, however, did respond to his petitions and communicated with him. The text is very damaged, and breaks off at this point (II. iii and x rev. i), and when it resumes again in II. iv the rigours of the famine are being described. It is possible that the gap between the preserved parts of columns iii and iv of the main recension contained an account of Enki's interrupting the famine a second time, but this seems unlikely. For the moment Enki saw no way out and communicated only his benevolent intentions to Atra-ḫasīs. Just as column iv (and Tablet I of the Assyrian Recension) breaks off it appears that Atra-ḫasīs is making a final desperate plea. Enki did then act, though what he did we can only surmise from his explanation when called to account by Enlil in II. v and x rev. ii. It appears from the Late Babylonian x that a cosmic sea was conceived to exist at the very bottom of the universe, a kind of primeval monster that had been subdued and was held in place by a cosmic bar. The lines describing the actual happening as explained by Enki are broken and very obscure, but perhaps there was some kind of tussle down there and as a result the bar was broken. Somehow in connection with this fish were apparently caught up in a whirlwind and released on starving humanity. Whatever the exact details Enki excused himself to Enlil for this escapade, but the latter was far from satisfied with the course of events and held a council of war in which he laid down that no god must again rescue humanity. Enki's hilarious outburst at this solemn warning (II. vi) hardly reassured Enlil, so a new plan was formed. Enki had used water to frustrate Enlil's plan, so now water would be used to further it. The human race was to be wiped out by a flood, and Enki was bound by an oath, against his wishes, to co-operate. At this point Tablet II ends.

Tablet III contains the flood story and the version known to George Smith from Tablet XI of the *Gilgameš Epic* is in fact largely derived from the account in *Atra-ḫasīs*. One piece of the Assyrian Recension dealing with the flood also survives, and a few small pieces of uncertain connections, but Ku-Aya's text is the main source. As the tablet begins Enki and Atra-ḫasīs are in communication. Apparently the king had received a dream on which he sought more light. (Enki had already found a way around his oath!) In reply Enki addressed the reed hut with the instruction to pull down the house and build a boat. We are to conceive Atra-ḫasīs as living in a reed house such as are still found in southern Mesopotamia, where reeds grow to an enormous height. No doubt the wind might whistle through the reed walls, and Enki seems to have whispered to his devotee in the same way, since it was no longer himself but the wall that transmitted the message. Since reed boats were as common as reed houses, the obvious course was to pull up the bundles of reeds which composed the walls of the house and to fasten them to a wooden framework as a boat. To make it watertight it was thoroughly coated with pitch. The Old Babylonian *Atra-ḫasīs* does not have the midrashic elaboration of *Gilgameš* XI, where the boat is a veritable Titanic with six floors. Indeed, in *Atra-ḫasīs* Enki gives the hero only seven days in which to prepare for the onset of the flood, and, interestingly, sets his water-clock for the seventh night. Atra-ḫasīs now has to explain his actions to the elders. He told them quite truthfully that Enki and Enlil had fallen out, so he, a protégé of the former, could no longer live on the latter's earth. He must, then, be off in his boat to live with his own god. With this explanation the boat was built and loaded with the hero's possessions, and with animals and birds. Before embarking with his family he held a banquet, in which he could not participate, being overcome with horror at the impending destruction. Once aboard, the flood came, and save for those inside, the human race was wiped out. In the event the gods were not pleased. Enki and the mother goddess were sorely grieved at the loss of their creation. The other gods began to find the disadvantages of a world without humans. The toil which men had taken over, digging the rivers and canals, for example, was part of the agricultural process, and, with this interrupted, supplies of food and drink were cut off. The mother goddess wondered how she could have consented to such a scheme, and bitterly blamed Enlil.

The flood lasted for seven days and seven nights, and in the gap at the end of column iv and the beginning of column v the rain must have ceased and the boat come to rest wherever it did. This gap is particularly unfortunate in one respect, that the *Gilgameš Epic* at this point inserts the episode of sending out three birds to ascertain if the waters were subsiding. This is the closest parallel of any Mesopotamian flood story with the Book of Genesis. It would be interesting to know if the Old Babylonian version already contained this item, but while there is room for it, there is no certainty that other items did not fill all the space.

On disembarking, Atra-ḫasīs promptly instituted an offering for the gods, psychologically a good move, since this would powerfully remind them of the advantages of living mortals, and in this condition they would be less likely to take a severe view of the survival of this remnant from what was planned as total destruction. The mother goddess was emphatic in her condemnation of Anu and Enlil and wished to exclude them from partaking of the offering. Using her grief as a pretext, she appropriated some lapis lazuli flies which had been Anu's and insisted that she would wear them as a perpetual reminder of the time when her offspring were floating on the surface of the waters like flies. This is aetiological, to explain actual necklaces of fly-shaped beads around the necks of statues of this goddess in the author's experience. When Enlil discovered what had happened he was furious at yet another frustration of his plans. Of course Enki was blamed, but he excused himself and in the damaged portion of column vi Enlil was presumably prevailed upon to accept the continuance of the human race. He required, however, that Enki and the mother goddess organize them better, no doubt to spare him the noise. Enki accordingly set forth proposals, in which the mother goddess shared. The only preserved portion occurs at the top of column vii, and this concerns women who do not bear children, that is, certain categories of priestesses. It so happens that we know these women best from Old Babylonian Sippar,[1] where Ku-Aya probably worked. Save for the concluding epilogue the rest (perhaps nothing very essential to the plot) is missing.

Purely as a work of literature the present writers view *Atra-ḫasīs* with mixed feelings. The ancient author nowhere shows any real poetic spirit, and the purple passages of *Gilgameš* that grip the modern reader are absent. In Tablet III especially one has the feeling of a second-rate poet. Yet the author has his strengths. There is a simple charm about the way he tells the story of the gods on strike, and there is a real dramatic build-up throughout the story. It opens by setting the scene in a time well known to the first hearers, before man was created. After establishing this common bond the author proceeds to the remarkable episode about the gods refusing to work, which leads on to the creation of man. By insisting on the view that what happened at the first creation of man is repeated with every human birth, the author brings home the relevance of his myth. From this he turns to the main theme: Enlil's desire to extirpate humanity and Enki's countering this plan, which is built up step by step until eventually Enlil does his worst and thereby brings the other gods around to sympathy for Enki's cause. So the story ends with the salvation of man and more about social classes and their functions. It should be remembered that the first hearers of this epic were vitally concerned with many of the issues presented. The sociological system described was that which they actually knew, and they conceived that their existence was really dependent on what Enki and Enlil did.

[1] See R. Harris, *Journal of the Economic and Social History of the Orient* VI. 121–57 and in *Studies Presented to A. Leo Oppenheim* 106–35; J. Renger, *ZA* 58. 110 ff.

To appreciate *Atra-ḫasīs* as a work of literature a translation and a little understanding of the life and history of the author's times are the essentials for the modern reader. It can be read just as one reads a play of Shakespeare, but for scholarly purposes something more is needed. The fullest understanding of, say, Shakespeare's *Julius Caesar* is only possible when the various sources for Roman history available to Shakespeare have been compared, so that one may see how he selected and modified his material, so imparting to it his own stamp. This kind of critical dissection is all the more important with an ancient text from a milieu that knew no literary rights and had no aversion to plagiarism. The wide divergencies between the Old Babylonian copies illustrate how the scribes and editors could take a free hand in rewriting the text. Was the author of *Atra-ḫasīs* merely retelling a traditional story, or was he a creative artist? With so much written material perished and with no surviving oral tradition there can never be a definitive answer to this question, but a review of related materials will at least give some perspective.

The Sumerian epic edited by M. Civil on pp. 138–45 comes closest to *Atra-ḫasīs*. Although only about a third of the text remains, this is sufficient to show that it has roughly the same content. The first column deals with the creation of man, the second with the early history of the human race, the third and fourth (which are consecutive) cover the gods' decision to bring a flood and Enki's divulging this secret to his client, the fifth describes the end of the flood, and the sixth and last column tells how the flood hero was made immortal. Despite the similarity in content, the size is quite different (some 300 Sumerian as opposed to 1,245 Akkadian lines), and the wording nowhere agrees. Furthermore, the relative dates of composition cannot be fixed. In its present form the Sumerian text is hardly much older than the tablet on which it is written (*c.* 1600 B.C.), and this in all probability is the time that the Akkadian *Atra-ḫasīs* was first being written down. It is possible that the Akkadian author knew the Sumerian text, but this cannot be proved, and the various elements of the story are sufficiently well known outside these two texts that one must say that the Akkadian author did not need to know the Sumerian text to write as he did. It is unknown if the Sumerian epic survived the fall of the First Dynasty of Babylon *c.* 1600 B.C. There is a small partly bilingual fragment, *CT* 46. 5, that comes from Ashurbanipal's libraries and might be a late edition of a missing portion of column iii, but another possibility will be mentioned below. It contains the end of a list of antediluvian kings and mentions Enlil and the noise, which, as we know from *Atra-ḫasīs*, led on to the flood.

The only other closely related work of literature is Tablet XI of the

Babylonian *Gilgameš Epic*. This, however, as already remarked, is largely dependent on *Atra-ḫasīs*, though probably on a lost Middle Babylonian edition, since in detail it differs widely from the Old Babylonian text, though there is some identity of wording. For a more comprehensive view of the background of *Atra-ḫasīs* the whole range of cuneiform texts must be combed, and the results can be grouped under three heads: (i) the creation of man, (ii) the early history of man, and (iii) anthropology and sociology.

## (i) *The Creation of Man*

Since W. G. Lambert has a corpus of Babylonian creation myths in an advanced state of preparation, details will not be given here, but only a summary of results. The idea that man was created to relieve the gods of hard labour by supplying them with food and drink was standard among both Sumerians and Babylonians, so the author of *Atra-ḫasīs* was just following a common tradition in the main theme of his opening sections. Only two aspects are new to us from his text. The first is the gods' downing of tools, and perhaps some recent experience in actual life suggested this, whether it was a new composition or something borrowed from an earlier text not available to us. The other original aspect is the author's anthropology, which will be discussed under (iii).

## (ii) *The Early History of Man*[1]

From Berossus it has long been known that the Babylonians had a traditional history beginning with a line of antediluvian kings. In cuneiform the best-known document embodying this tradition is now named the *Sumerian King List*, and a number of more or less complete copies dating from *c.* 1800 to 1600 B.C. have been published. It is a list of dynasties from the earliest times to *c.* 1800. However, only some of the copies contained the antediluvian section, others lacked it. Had this section been an original part of the compilation there is no explanation of its lack from some copies. Contrariwise, had the original text commenced after the flood, there would have been every encouragement to add the antediluvian section to make the work more complete. When, furthermore, it is noted that there were copies of the antediluvian section quite separate from the *King List*, the conclusion becomes inescapable that these kings were at first an independent tradition only secondarily prefixed to the *King List*. This conclusion is confirmed by differences in the way that transference of power

[1] For the literature on this topic and for extracts quoted see the excursus on pp. 25–7.

from one city to another is described in the two documents. Unfortunately no single copy of the original, short form of the *King List* has the opening lines preserved. It has been suggested that it began with what is now column i, line 41, of the longer edition: 'After kingship had come down from heaven, the kingship was in Kish . . .'. This is far from certain, and the importance of this question is that if this conclusion were accepted the original *King List* would have contained no mention of the flood. A pointer in favour of the opposite conclusion, that the opening words were, 'After the flood had swept over the land and kingship had come down from heaven . . .' is contained in a rival king list. For some reason the kings of Lagaš are omitted from the standard list. To compensate for this, there is a list exclusively of kings of Lagaš, and this begins: 'After the flood had raged' (egir a.ma.ru ba.ùr.ra.ta). There is one reasonably certain allusion to the tradition of the flood as contained in the *King List*, in a text naming Išme-Dagan, king of Isin *c.* 1940 B.C.: 'after the flood had raged'. This occurs in a sentence describing the appointment of this king, and not only is the wording identical with that of the two king lists, but the context—kingship—is the same. A less certain allusion occurs in a similar text naming Ur-Ninurta of Isin (*c.* 1900 B.C.). The copy seems corrupt, but the sense can be extracted by comparing a small unidentified Sumerian fragment:

| | |
|---|---|
| In that day, [in that remote] day, | In the primeval day, that day . . .[. |
| In that night, [in that remote] night, | . . night . . night . remote [. . . |
| In that year, [in that remote] year, | In the remote year, the year . . [. . . |
| When the flood (. . . | After the flood had been brought about, |
| Unidentified fragment | Ur-Ninurta |

These lines merely speak of the flood as occurring in the beginning, and though 'bring about' is used of the great flood in Akkadian texts, nothing here connects it, though the allusion no doubt refers to a current version of a flood.

All the material in list form just described is from the first half of the second millennium B.C. So far there is no evidence for this tradition of a great flood among the Sumerians of the third millennium. This, however, is an argument from silence, since very little Sumerian literature has come down to us in third-millennium copies. Most is now available only in copies from the first half of the second millennium. It is not unlikely that the Sumerians did have traditions of destructive floods, since the country is notoriously liable to them, indeed there is some flooding of the rivers every year. Several ancient sites have revealed flood layers separating strata of different civilizations. Presumably at various sites and on several occasions floods did wipe out the existing culture. What we do not know is whether the tradition of a flood in this part of the world reflects one particularly bad experience of this kind in a certain year of early times, or if the literary tradition is more loosely connected with actual events and has telescoped memories of several disasters. (The present writers do not belong to that school which relates flood stories all over the world to one prehistoric cosmic disaster.) These problems, however, are not of special concern here.

The antediluvian section lists from eight to ten kings in several cities ruling for vast periods of time. The best preserved copy of the *Sumerian King List*, the Weld Blundell prism (W-B 444), has eight kings from five cities ruling a total of 241,200 years. The small tablet W-B 62, an independent form of the tradition, offers ten kings from six cities ruling a total of 456,000 years. A small tablet now in California, not quite complete, had either seven or eight kings from four cities, and the seven preserved reigns add up to somewhat over 186,000 years. The five cities of W-B 444 are also given in column ii of the Sumerian flood story. Between this second-millennium material and Berossus only one, or two, documents of the same type survive. Ashurbanipal's libraries have yielded one piece of a related dynastic list: King, *Chronicles* II, pp. 143–5. The first column is all but gone: traces of 'reigned [. . . years]' are visible. From the second column all that remains are the second, third, and fourth kings of the first postdiluvian dynasty as known from the *Sumerian King List*. Column iii is completely gone, but iv has remains of the names of the kings of the First Dynasty of Babylon followed (apparently) by the beginning of the Sea Land Dynasty. What survives from column v is a listing of the small dynasties about 1000 B.C. The sixth and last column has no writing preserved. Quite clearly this document listed kings from before the flood to nearly the time of Ashurbanipal himself, but there is mystery about the first column. It is possible from columns iv and v to calculate that each column must have contained at least some seventy lines. The missing kings of Babylon from the First Dynasty onwards are known independently. If the list contained more than the names and lengths of reign, then more than seventy lines a column has to be assumed. The problem is that the first postdiluvian dynasty did not begin until some little way down the second column. It follows that some eighty lines (or more) were occupied with what preceded this dynasty. It is impossible to stretch out even ten kings for this length of column space. The Ashurbanipal fragment mentioned above, *CT* 46. 5, may offer the solution. It could be part of this dynastic list. It contains the end of a list of nine antediluvian kings, set out in list form, but then suddenly breaks out into literary style mentioning Enlil and the noise. There would be no difficulty in filling a whole column with a literary version of the flood story, especially as it is bilingual, and the Sumerian could still have been taken from the source already suggested. It is misleading to refer to this Late Assyrian copy of the dynastic list as a copy of the *Sumerian King List* on the basis of three names only, but one can consider it a descendant, brought up to date by the addition of further material. Berossus, the last witness, in the second book of his *Babyloniaka*, gave a list of ten kings in three cities reigning 432,000 years.

The idea of the flood as a point of time in world history became generally accepted in ancient Mesopotamia, at least by 1000 B.C., and allusions to it and to the antediluvian kings are not scarce. Ashurbanipal himself professes to have read 'stone inscriptions from before the flood'. The *Epic of Gilgameš*, in its Late Babylonian recension, has a prologue stating that the hero *inter alia* 'brought news from before the flood'. A learned compilation of names for philological analysis (hardly earlier than 1400 B.C.) explains one group: 'These are postdiluvian kings, but not in chronological order'. The names of antediluvian kings occur in omen texts, lists of divine names, and in litanies. The seventh king, according to W-B 444 and Berossus, Enmeduranna (or Enmeduranki) is named in a ritual text which describes him as king of Sippar and patron saint (as it were) of diviners, so that all diviners considered themselves his sons. A related bilingual text describes a king (probably one of the Second Isin Dynasty) as 'distant scion of kingship, seed preserved from before the flood'. The first king, Alulim, is addressed in at least one Babylonian incantation as, 'Alulu, king from before the flood'. Also there survives part of an apocryphal letter alleged to have been written to him by the sage Adapa. The 'sages' (*apkallu*) play an important part in the Babylonian conception of early times. From Sumerian literature to Berossus it is everywhere assumed that the human race was at first and naturally barbarous. Civilization was a gift of the gods, and that is the way to understand kingship coming down from heaven, as quoted above. The gods gave it as an institution for regulating society. Works of Sumerian literature express this concept more precisely as the giving of *mes*.[1] A *me* was the concept of any one of the numerous aspects of organized human life, from sexual intercourse to gold-smithery, and all alike were given to man and had to be respected as divine ordinances. The Babylonians explained that in early time the sages had taught the human

[1] The most interesting expression of this idea occurs in a Sumerian myth only partly translated, see *RA* 55. 186, no. 17.

race what it needed to know. Berossus names eight of them and correlates them with the antediluvian kings. The first, for example, Oannes, emerged daily from the 'Red Sea' for a period. He was fish-like in appearance. In cuneiform Van Dijk has published a list of seven sages (the more usual number) dated by the first seven antediluvian kings. A medical text confirms this picture by stating in the colophon that it is 'according to the old sages from before the flood'. However, the same basic idea had other expressions. An exorcistic text offers a quite different group of seven sages. Only four are named, but not one of these occurs in the other lists. The first is attached to Enmerkar, a postdiluvian king according to the *King List*. The second was born in Kish, of which city no antediluvian dynasty is anywhere recorded. This diversity surely proves that the sages were only fixed in that they had to appear at the beginning of human history. It was a tradition not specifically related to the great flood, but only secondarily and in some cases synchronized with it.

One antediluvian king is named in a third-millennium document. This is Šuruppak, who occurs in one copy of the *King List* only, W-B 62, as an extra generation between Ubār-Tutu and Ziusudra, the flood hero. Suggestions have been made that since this is the dynasty of the town Šuruppak the extra name results from a misreading or misunderstanding of an epithet 'man of Šuruppak' applied to Ubār-Tutu.[1] This view, however, is no longer acceptable, since the source of the extra generation has been identified. A literary work, of which copies contemporary with those of the *King List* are extant, professes to be the teaching of Šuruppak to his son Ziusudra. It consists of admonitions of a quite general kind, and throughout the ancient Near East such moral instruction was often presented as the advice of a father to his son. Early Dynastic fragments of *c.* 2500 B.C. have been identified, but here the son's name is not Ziusudra, but ÚR.AŠ.[2] It is uncertain how these two signs should be pronounced, but it can hardly have been Ziusudra, which contains three well known Sumerian roots. There is, therefore, no certainty that Šuruppak as conceived by the author of the Early Dynastic version of this text was a king (though this is not unlikely) and no assurance at all that the son was the flood hero. *Gilgameš* XI. 13 states that before the flood the gods were in the city Šuruppak. This no doubt reflects a local tradition, but it was not accepted in the Old Babylonian *Atra-ḫasīs*. Here only Enlil remained on earth, and he lived in Ekur, his shrine in Nippur.

The survey of traditions about early history just given is a necessary

[1] H. Zimmern, *ZDMG* 78. 21; T. Jacobsen, *Sumerian King List* 75[32].

[2] M. Civil and R. D. Biggs, *RA* 60. 1–5.

background for a study of *Atra-ḫasīs*. The account of Berossus and what can be gleaned from Ashurbanipal's libraries might suggest that views about the beginnings of human history were fixed and rigid. In fact there was (i) a tradition of sages unrelated to the flood, (ii) another tradition of kings which may have begun after the flood, and (iii) still a third tradition of a succession of kings before the flood. In Berossus all three are combined. In the third tradition as we have listed them (the order has no chronological significance) one would expect the king who survived the flood, Ziusudra in Sumerian, Atra-ḫasīs or Uta-napištim in Akkadian, to be a key figure. Yet curiously in W-B 444 he is missing, and this cannot be explained as due to scribal omission, since the list is summed up, and no king or reign is missing. There has been much speculation on this point, and *Atra-ḫasīs* seems to offer the reason as will become clear.

The loss of most of lines 307–51 from Tablet I is most unfortunate in this connection, since they dealt with the initial organization of the human race after its creation. The only two lines nearly complete, 337–8, show that shrines were being built and canals dug. Presumably the complete text told of mankind's instruction in the arts of civilization, and probably the building of at least one city was described. Also a king must have been appointed. The acute problems are, which city or cities, and which king? Did *Atra-ḫasīs* name the same five cities as the Sumerian flood story, the same in which kings reigned according to the lists? At present there is no way of finding the answers to these questions, though it is very doubtful if a list of kings was given or alluded to. This follows from lines 352–5, as restored a little from the same passus at the beginning of Tablet II. We are told that before the end of 1,200 years the population increased and with it the noise. It is difficult to conceive that this could be anything but the initial growth of the human race, and this excludes anything like eight kings ruling for 241,200 years (as W-B 444 has it), since that was plenty of time both to multiply and to make noise. Even if it is supposed that the gap contained a list of kings, and that during their reigns both reproduction and noise were somehow inhibited, the number 1,200 still suggests that we are not dealing with the tradition of the lists. 1200 is neither a mystical nor a terminal number, unlike 7 or 3,600. The two 1,200-year intervals are part of a chronology of the reign of Atra-ḫasīs. Due to the damaged condition of Tablet II the scheme cannot be followed, but one could have expected another 1,200 years to be interposed at each successive reprieve of humanity. Such a scheme would probably have given a total of 4,800, which is on an altogether different plane from the 36,000 years of W-B 444 or the 64,800 of Berossus. Certainty will not be reached until the gaps are filled, but at present it seems that *Atra-ḫasīs* had its own version of antediluvian history. One king only, Atra-ḫasīs, reigned for a comparatively modest period and he it was who survived the flood. This is the fourth strand that was worked into a common tradition in due course.[1]

### (iii) *Anthropology and Sociology*

The Sumerian view of the world provided a stimulus for a comprehensive view of human society, which has been lacking in many civilizations. All too often thinkers and poets have considered themselves above the world of pots and pans. The Sumerians and their Babylonian successors, as mentioned above, conceived of the human race as originally barbarous, civilized only by the express intervention of the gods. Thus every aspect of civilized life, public or private, important or trivial, was looked on as ideally conforming to a divine pattern. With such a conception there is no such thing as the unmentionable, whether that be an effect of social snobbery or moralizing prudery. Every aspect of society was of divine origin and was worthy of study. This does not of course mean that literature lacks plenty of gods, heroes, kings, wars, and conquests, but even in the traditions of early times the kings are matched by the sages. The former are an aspect of political history, the latter of social history. *Atra-ḫasīs* shows more interest in anthropology and social forms than any other Babylonian epic.

This first shows in the account of man's creation. The author used what was the generally accepted view of this matter among those who wrote in Akkadian, that man was formed from clay mixed with the blood of a slain god. To understand what the author of *Atra-ḫasīs* was achieving in his account one must know not only this fact, but also its implications, though no ancient text formally offers a commentary on the meaning of creation. 'Clay' in this context is the material substance of the human body. This can be learnt from a number of passages that speak of death as a 'returning to clay'.[2] Exactly the same concept is shown in the Hebrew account of man's creation where the penalty for disobedience was laid down: 'You are earth, and to earth you shall return' (Genesis 3:19). The present writers have not found any similar Mesopotamian clue explaining the blood, but this does not mean that speculation is out of place. It is well

[1] A Hittite fragment, *Keilschrifturkunden aus Boghazköi* VIII. 63, names an Atra-ḫasīs, son of Ḫamšā ('Fifty'), who figure in a story involving Kumarbi. A translation is given by H. G. Güterbock, *Kumarbi* 30–1, who rightly comments on p. 93 that there can be no assurance that this Atra-ḫasīs is the flood hero.

[2] *târu ana ṭiṭṭi*: *BWL* 108. 6; *Erra* I. 74; *Gilg.* XI. 118 and 133; *SEM* 117. ii. 7. Note also *ṭiṭṭiš emû/ewûm* in the lexica.

known that many categories of Sumerian and Babylonian texts are in themselves incomplete, and need to be understood in the light of explanations which in the ancient world were no doubt given by word of mouth. In explaining the material substance of the human body one has by no means explained the phenomenon of life, and the problem is as acute today as it has ever been. What is the life element imparted from the parent into its young, whether in animal or human, and how did it arise in the first case? The Hebrew account of creation in Genesis 2 explains that God imparted 'the breath of life' into man, and so animation began. The reality of this is that breathing is an essential accompaniment of life, and at death we 'expire'. No similar doctrine is known among the Babylonians or Sumerians. Instead we may presume that the divine blood was held to supply life to matter. A Hebrew parallel is again helpful: the Pentateuchal laws in a number of respects work on the principle that 'the life is in the blood' (Leviticus 17:11, etc.), and parallels to this idea among other peoples are well known. Hence in all probability the Babylonians conceived of man as matter ('clay') activated by the addition of divine blood.

To this traditional concept the author of *Atra-ḫasīs* has added one item, which occurs in a passage (I. 208–30) full of perplexing phrases. It was a common Mesopotamian view that man had a spirit that survived death, which could, if not properly buried and supplied with offerings, trouble the living. It is this spirit (Bab. *eṭemmu*) that the author is explaining in addition to the usual material aspects of life. No other surviving creation account from Sumerians or Babylonians attempts to explain this. Lines 210–11 (cf. 225–6) mention the slain god's flesh, as well as his blood. Both are mixed in the clay, so that in lines 212–13 this is spoken of as a mixing of god and man. At first this seems a *non sequitur*, since man does not yet exist, but since 'clay' was the material substance of humanity its mixing with the divine flesh and blood could be so described. The statement about the drum in 214 (cf. 227) is quite obscure, see the note ad loc., but the following line is abundantly clear. The flesh of the slain god is the source of the spirit of man. We might have preferred the blood, as not being so material and solid, but in traditional mythology it seems that blood supplied the purely animal life, that ends at death. Lines 216–17 (cf. 229–30) are tantalizingly ambiguous, but they seem to say that living man is a memorial to the slain god, and his spirit (presumably after death) likewise.

The technique of finding a continuing aspect of myth in human life provided the author with his first opportunity for dealing with social institutions. On the assumption that every human birth repeats what happened at the beginning, the mother goddess lays down in the story certain norms of ancient midwifery (I. 289–305). The Babylonian conception of society as conforming to a divine blueprint means that no distinction was made between immutable physiological requirements of the human species and local customs which hardly two civilizations will share. Since there is no freedom of choice in the physiological aspects of birth, the epic concentrates on those matters of local custom which might easily be forgotten: the need to have the birth 'brick' in place for nine days, the marriage celebration of the same length, and the invoking of Ištar (goddess of love) under the name Išḫara during this period.

Enlil's demand for a reorganization of the human race after the flood provided the author with his last chance, but unfortunately most of the section is lost. From what remains it appears that there was a classification of people by marital status, and that the social structure of the author's age is being described. If only it had survived it would have been an important document of social history for the Old Babylonian period.

Under this heading one may also note that the kind of city organization presumed for the reign of Atra-ḫasīs—a king and council of elders—is not peculiar to this text, but is found in other ancient texts, especially Sumerian. This is one constituent of Jacobsen's theory of primitive democracy in early Mesopotamia, but it must be stressed that he uses the term democracy in its classical rather than modern sense.[1]

Thus *Atra-ḫasīs* may be analysed as follows. The plot was traditional, though the author had to choose from variant forms of the tradition, and to blend his selection into a dramatic whole. The careful build-up of the material used, and the interest shown in human life and society clearly compels belief in one author rather than in a traditional story that was worked up over a period of time by successive generations of story-tellers. The freedom of individual scribes to make their own versions does not conflict with this conclusion.

It will be appreciated from what has been written that no precise date of composition can be given. All one can ask is, when roughly was the text written down in more or less the form we know? The earliest surviving copies are from the seventeenth century B.C.—that they are copies is shown by the scribal note 'broken' found in two manuscripts of II. i. 12—and from general knowledge of the history of Babylonian literature the text can hardly have been written down more than one, or at the most

[1] *JNES* 2. 159–72; *ZA* 52. 99 ff.

two centuries earlier. There is hardly a scrap of Semitic literature in cuneiform from the third millennium B.C., and this cannot be explained as an accident of discovery when so many tablets of other content are known from this millennium. Babylonian literature first developed in the early centuries of the second millennium, which are rightly considered its classical period. While Sumerian was still taught in the schools and was used by scribes, Babylonian was the every-day language and despite some literary archaism there is reason to believe that literary idioms and popular speech were closer than at any other time. This was, then, a period comparable with fifth-century Athens, when great poets were competing for the drama prizes in the public theatre. It was an age of much literary creativity.

We have considered *Atra-ḫasīs* in Mesopotamia, and it remains to look at its relationships with other literatures. The only certain parallel occurs in the Book of Genesis. From at least the time of Josephus in the first century A.D. the similarity of Hebrew and Babylonian traditions of the early history of mankind has been noted. Josephus had to depend on Berossus;[1] today with large numbers of cuneiform sources at our disposal the observation is still valid. The first eleven chapters of Genesis begin with creation, and proceed through ten long-lived patriarchs to the flood, in which only the tenth, Noah, is saved, with his family and birds and animals. As the waters were subsiding Noah let out of the ark three birds in turn to discover how far the waters had abated. Even from this brief and inadequate summary it is obvious that the differences are too great to encourage belief in direct connection between *Atra-ḫasīs* and Genesis, but just as obviously there is some kind of involvement in the historical traditions generally of the two peoples. They were put in writing in Babylonia first, since the Old Babylonian period ended several hundred years before Moses, the traditional author of the Pentateuch. One possible explanation is that the origin of these traditions is to be sought in the Tigris–Euphrates valley, and they spread to Syria and Palestine in the Amarna period, *c.* 1400 B.C.[2] It has been mentioned above that a piece of a Babylonian flood story has been found at Ras Shamra, on the coast of Syria, written about this time (see the edition on pp. 131–3). However, the question is very complex and cannot be discussed further here. The Graeco-Roman flood story with Deucalion and Pyrrha as its heroes is not certainly related at all. Unfortunately it is only known from late sources,

[1] See the extracts quoted in the editions of Berossus.

[2] This view is advanced by W. G. Lambert, *Journal of Theological Studies*, N.S. xvi. 287–300.

the fullest form is that in Ovid's *Metamorphoses* from early in the first century A.D.[1] This portrays a succession of ages getting progressively worse, termed gold, silver, etc., until mankind is wiped out for its sins and the chosen pair, saved in a boat, started off the human race again. If one could trace back this story it might of course have antecedents more closely resembling its Mesopotamian counterpart, but in its known forms there is no certain connection.

EXCURSUS

## EARLY HUMAN HISTORY

### (i) The *Sumerian King List*

THE standard edition is that of T. Jacobsen, *AS* 11, who suggested that it was first compiled about 2100 B.C. F. R. Kraus, in *ZA* 50. 29–60, published a little new material and proposed that the date of compilation be in the Isin-Larsa period, *c.* 1900–1800 B.C. M. Rowton, in *JNES* 19. 156 ff., offered arguments in favour of a date *c.* 2100–2000 B.C. New material and appropriate discussions have been offered by: M. Civil, *JCS* 15. 79–80; J. J. Finkelstein, *JCS* 17. 39–51; W. W. Hallo, *JCS* 17. 52–7. The last-named author, loc. cit. 56, has argued that the title nam.lugal in a catalogue of texts from Ur (*UET* VI/1. 123. 25, cf. *RA* 55. 171) proves that the short form of the *King List* began with i. 41. It is difficult to see the logic in the argument, and the more recently published king list of Lagaš (*JCS* 21) begins with what is i. 40 in the *Sumerian King List*.

### (ii) The Sages

The Late Babylonian tablet giving a list of seven sages correlated with the first seven antediluvian kings is published in H. J. Lenzen, *XVIII. vorläufiger Bericht über die von dem Deutschen Archäologischen Institut und der Deutschen Orient-Gesellschaft aus Mitteln der Deutschen Forschungsgemeinschaft unternommenen Ausgrabungen in Uruk-Warka*, pp. 44 ff. The other, quite different version of the seven sages is a bilingual text edited most recently by E. Reiner in *Or.* N.S. 30. 1–11. The sages are specified as antediluvian in a colophon to a medical text: *šá pî apkallē* (NUN.ME$^{meš.e}$) *la-bi-ru-ti šá la-am abūbi* (a.má.ùru), *AMT* 105. 22.

### (iii) Other Allusions to the Flood

(*a*) [egi]r a.ma.ru ùr.ra.ta 'After the flood had raged' (*PBS* X/2. 9 rev. i. 23 = *TCL* 15, pl. XX. 27, cf. W. H. Ph. Römer, *Sumerische*

[1] See art. 'Deukalion' in Pauly–Wissowa, *Real-Encyclopädie*.

'*Königshymnen*' 46. 119–24 for the context). The line occurs in a sentence explaining the appointment of Išme-Dagan by Enlil.

(*b*) and (*c*)

[. . . . .] šà [. . .
an.$^{d}$en.líl.bi.da $^{d}$e[n.ki . . .

| | |
|---|---|
| $u_4$.ri.ta $u_4$.[sù.rá.ri.ta] | $u_4$.ul.li.a.ta $u_4$.bi ba ši? la [. . . |
| $gi_6$.ri.ta $gi_6$.[sù.rá.ri.ta] | $gi_6$ UD ri bi ri $gi_6$ ba sù [. . . |
| mu.ri.ta m[u.sù.rá.ri.ta] | mu.sù.da mu ba ši [. . . |
| $u_4$ a.ma.ru × [. . . | egir a.ma.ru ba.gar.ra.[ta] |
| *STVC* 87 B | *Sumer* XI, pl. XIII. 1–4 |

(*b*) is a fragment from the Old Babylonian period not further identified, (*c*) is the opening passage of a hymn mentioning Ur-Ninurta of Isin. Both passages are saying in effect 'in the beginning', and on this theme in Sumerian texts see Van Dijk, *Acta Orientalia* XXVIII 31 ff., where (*b*) is translated. One may suspect that the text of (*c*) is corrupt.

(*d*) Ashurbanipal: *ḫi-ṭa-ku miḫilti*(gù.sum) *ab-ni šá la-am a-bu-bi šá kak-ku sa-ak-ku bal-lu* 'I study stone inscriptions from before the flood, which are obtuse, obscure and confused' (*VAB* VII. 256 18–19 = F. Lehmann-Haupt, *Šamaššumukin*, pl. XXXV, cf. Th. Bauer, *Das Inschriftenwerk Assurbanipals* 80).

(*e*) Gilgameš: *ub-la ṭè-e-ma šá la-am a-bu-bi* (I. i. 6).

(*f*) Name List: *an-nu-tum* LUGAL-*e šá* EGIR *a-bu-bi a-na sa-dir a-ḫa-meš la sad-ru* (V. *R* 44. i. 20).

(*g*) Bilingual text related to *BBR* 24 (below iv *d*):

. . .] a.ma.ùru.na.an.na.$ke_4$
*li-i-pu ru-ú-qu šá šar-ru-ti z*[*e-r*]*u na-aṣ-ru šá la-am a-bu-bi*
*JCS* 21, "Enmeduranki and Related Matters" i 8

(iv) Mentions of Antediluvian Kings

(*a*) In litanies in which they are equated with Tammuz:

am.me.l[ú.an.na . . .
am.me.gal.an.na [. . .
Cros, *Nouvelles Fouilles de Tello* 211, AO 4346. 1–2 (OB)
am.i.lu.an.na am.me.ga[l.an.na]
*BE* XXX. 1. iii. 8 = 12. ii. 15 (= *PBS* X/2. 15) (OB)
$^{d}$am.me.lu.an.[na . . .
$^{d}$am.me.gal.an.n[a . . .
$^{d}$am.me.sipa.[zi.an.na . . .
K 5044. 5 ff. (LA)

(*b*) In god list as names of Tammuz:

$^{d}$am.m[e.l]u.an.na = $^{d}$dumu.[zi]
$^{d}$[am.me.g]al.an.na = $^{d}$[MIN]
[$^{d}$am.me.si]pa.zi.an.na = $^{d}$[MIN]
*CT* 24. 9, K 11035. 7–9 = *CT* 24. 19. ii (+K 15160) 6–7 = *CT* 25. 7, K 7663+ 7–9 (LA)

(*c*) In omens ('the omen of . . .'):

*am-me-lu-an-na* MAN [. . .
*KAR* 434 rev. (?) 14 (LA)
*e-me-lu-an-[na* . . .
*CT* 30. 10, K 3843+ rev. 8 (LA)

(*d*) In ritual text:

*en-me-dur-an-ki šàr sippari*$^{ki}$
*JCS* 21, "Enmeduranki and Related Matters," ii 1 and 23 (LA)

(*e*) In incantations:

én *a-lu-lu šarru šá la-mu a-bu-bu*
BM 45686 = 81-7-6, 91, i. 19 and 25, ii. 12. (The continuation has nothing relevant to the king.)
én *a-lu-lu šá-nu-ú-um*
BM 45686 = 81-7-6, 91, i. 21. (This is cited in a ritual section in a broken context.) (LB)

(*f*) In an apocryphal letter:

*a-na* $^{m}$*a-lu-lu qí-bi-ma um-ma* $^{m}$*a-da-pa ap-kal-um-ma*
To Alulu speak, thus says Adapa the sage (*STT* 176. 14, LA)

Allusions to a flood brought about by Marduk occur in the *Erra Epic*, I 132–48 and IV 50. However, every detail referred to is either lacking from, or cannot be reconciled with, the various versions of the story of the great flood. Presumably, then, this is another flood.

## A QUOTATION OF *ATRA-ḪASĪS* FOR AN ASSYRIAN KING

ONE of the reports sent by astrologers and incantation priests to advise Late Assyrian kings cites our text. The document, K 761, was published by R. Campbell Thompson, *Reports* No. 243, and was compiled by a Babylonian incantation priest, Bēl-lē'î of the Egibi family (rev. 6: *šá*

$^{md}$*bēl*-DA, *mār* $^{m}$*e-gi-bi* $^{lú}$maš.maš), as advice on a drought. Its various sections are separated by rulings, all of which were omitted by Campbell Thompson. The first two sections (obv. 1–2 and 3–5) quote astrological omens with explanatory glosses. Evidently the conditions stated in these omens were then prevailing, for line 6 includes the words: 'Abundant rain will fall for the king, my lord.' (šèg$^{meš}$ *gap-šu-tu ana šarri be-lí-ia il*-[*la-ku*]). The following section (obv. 7–10) consists of instructions on 'how to make Adad send rain' ($^{d}$*adad* šèg *a-na za-na-n*[*i*]), of which the only preserved detail is the use of šu.íl.la prayers or incantations. The reverse, save for the last line, which gives the compiler's name, is as follows:

1 [(*šá*) $^{d}$*ad*]*ad-ma ši-'-a bāb-šú bi-li ú-p*[*u-un-tú*]
2 ⌜*a*⌝*-na qu-du-mi-šú lil-lik-šum-ma ma-a*[*š-ḫa-tú*]
3 *ni-qu-ú ina še-re-e-ti im-ba-ru li-š*[*á*]*-a*[*z-nin*]
4 *eqlu ki-i šar-ra-qu-tu ma-a-mu liš-š*[*i*]

---

5 *ki-i zu-un-nu ina māt akkadî*$^{ki}$ *i-te-qí-ru an-na-a e*[*p-šá*]

---

1 Seek the door of Adad, bring meal
2 In front of it. The offering of sesame-meal may be pleasing to him,
3 He may rain down a mist in the morning,
4 So that the field will furtively bear water.

---

5 When rain has become scarce in the land of Akkad, do this.

---

The lines quoted are Tablet II. ii. 11–13, 16, and 19 of Ku-Aya's recension with a few variants. *up*[*untu*] for *e-pí-ta*, and *kī šarrāqūtu* for *ki-ma ša-ar-ra-qí-tu* are substitutions of more common words and phrases for less common, a phenomenon also noted in the Assyrian Recension. However, the substitution of 'water' for 'grain' (*šu-a*) in 4 cannot be explained in the same way. Bēl-lē'î may have made the change by accident, or perhaps deliberately, since his point in the use of the line is made clearer thereby. It is similarly uncertain if the four missing lines were already lacking from the text then in use, or if the compiler omitted them to shorten the excerpt.

The significance of this direct quotation is that it reveals the Babylonian priest operating on a principle that is put forward in the epic itself, though in other connections, namely that what was done on divine instigation in the beginning can be repeated at intervals throughout history.[1] The technique whereby Atra-ḫasīs got Adad to send rain could be used again whenever there was a drought.

[1] On this principle in Babylonian thought generally, see W. G. Lambert, *JSS* XIII. 104 ff.

# NOTES ON ORTHOGRAPHY AND GRAMMAR

SINCE *Atra-ḫasīs* is the longest preserved Old Babylonian epic, it is of course of great value for study of orthography and grammar. This statement must be qualified, however, in that linguistically speaking the epic's extent is inadequate to provide the basis for a comprehensive study of its dialect. Serious linguistic work would have to draw on all Old Babylonian literary compositions, and be done with a knowledge of the other contemporary and earlier speech-forms of Akkadian. This falls outside the scope of the present volume, but attention will be drawn to points of interest which occur. Only the Old Babylonian material will be used.

A fundamental observation is that the edition of Ku-Aya is not always consistent, especially in matters of orthography, note the following examples:

| | |
|---|---|
| *ša-ma-i* I. 19; III. iii. 7, 48 | *ti-i-ti-iš* I. 339 |
| *ša-ma-ií* III. ii. 35 | *te-i-tam* II. i. 9 **(B)** |

Normally the syllables qa and pi are written with GA and BI, but examples of the signs *qa* and *pi* occur (I. 11 and III. vi. 40, see notes). Normally Anunnakku is written ᵈ*a-nun-na*, but once ᵈ*a-nun-na-ku* (I. 5, see note), and similarly there is one example of *naššīku* (the title of Ea) against several of *niššīku* (see note on I. 16).

Orthographically the text must be classified as Northern by the rules of A. Goetze, in Neugebauer and Sachs, *Mathematical Cuneiform Texts*, pp. 146–7, though the syllables ṭi/ṭe are often written with the DI-sign, a Southern usage according to Goetze. In a text internally inconsistent a few other individual 'Southern' usages are of no great importance. We have adopted *sqr* rather than *zkr* as the root 'speak' (see note on I. 63), and this creates a variety of 'Southern' forms such as *is-sà-qar* and *sí-iq-ra*. Since these are particularly epic words used in stock formulas they may well have had their own orthographic tradition unrelated to that of Sippar. Mimation throughout is optional. There are two striking sandhi-writings: *bābišatmāni* (I. 69) and *līteddilirtaša* (II. i. 19), on which see the notes.

Several interesting phonological phenomena occur. Twice a doubled consonant is resolved into the glottal stop followed by a single consonant: *u'pur* (= *uppur*, I. 284) and *li'tī*[*lu*] (= *littī*[*lu*], I. 300). Examples elsewhere are very rare, but note $^{d}$*ma-’-me-tum* (*DP* VI. 37. vi. 3), normally written *Mammītum*. The consonant *w* has not completely disappeared. At the beginning of words it may be simply lost, note *ālittum* in III. vii. 2. It is replaced by *m* in the following forms: *ilmû* (I. 113), *i-ta-mu* (I. 366), (*t*)*umaššer* (II. v. 20, vi. 29). These seem to be the earliest occurrences of this *m*, though it is normal in Middle Babylonian. *tisia* for *šisia* is paralleled in Old Babylonian letters (see I. 61 and note), but *šanīttiš*[*ka*], for the normal *tanīttiš*[*ka*], in III. viii. 14 could be a scribal error, see the note. If *burra* (III. vii. 8) is a form of *bukra*, it is without parallel.

In word forms one naturally looks for ‘hymno-epic’ idiom, on which see W. von Soden, *ZA* 40. 163 ff. and 41. 90 ff. A detailed study will be included in W. G. Lambert’s forthcoming *Babylonian Creation Myths*, so the material is quoted here with little or no comment:

| | Ending *-iš* | Ending *-um* |
|---|---|---|
| Alone: | *šikriš* III. iv. 17 | *awīlum* I. 1 |
| | | *kīma šarrāqītu* II. ii. 19 = 33 |
| Construct: | *bābiš atmāni* I. 69 | *simānu šīmti* I. 305 cf. 280 |
| | *aḫriātiš ūmī* I. 214 = 227 | |
| | *bubūtiš nišī tîtiš* [*ilī*] I. 339 | |
| | *pūtiš nāri* II. iii. 26 | |
| Suffixes: | *qātišša* I. 11 | *ba’ūlātuššu* I. 14 |
| | *bābiška* I. 113 | |
| | *tērētiš*[*ka*] III. viii. 12 | |
| | *šanīttiš*[*ka*] III. viii. 14 | |

The only unusual thing here is the ending *-um* with the meaning ‘like’, see the note on I. 1. A less common ending is *-ša* (or *-iša*) for *-šam* (or *-išam*) on *šamêša* (I. 13, 17, see the note) meaning ‘to heaven’. Also in III. i. 37 *mūšišu* seems to have the ending *-šu* or *-išu* = *ana*. The nominative case-ending in the construct state occurs in the following passages:

*naḫbalu tiāmtim* I. 15 (acc.)
*mārū rāmānīka* I. 94, 96 (acc.)
*šipru ilqû* II. iv. 19 (nom./acc.)
*ina ašqulālu šamši* II. vi. 30 (gen.)
*ina birku ālitti* III. vii. 5 (gen.)

A totally unexpected revelation is that the third person fem. precative with *t*-prefix is not *lū taprus*, but *i taprus* (see I. 295 and note on I. S iii. 16). Several difficult uses of the acc. occur, see I. 5, III. vii. 8–9 (perhaps also III. iii. 33) with notes.

# THE MANUSCRIPTS

THE best-preserved edition of the epic, and so the one which is used here as the main recension, is an edition in three tablets from the hand of Ku-Aya[1] in the reign of Ammi-ṣaduqa. One copy of each of the three tablets survives (for details see the list below), and they are dated as follows:

I iti.bára.zag.gar ud.21.kám
mu am-mi-ṣa-du-qá lugal.e
alam.a.ni máš.gaba.tab.ba šu × (×)
ù alam.a.ni šu.silim.ma ⌜ab.di⌝.a

Month Nisan, 21st day, the year when Ammi-ṣaduqa, the king, a statue of himself . . . a kid held at the breast and a statue of himself victorious (?)[2] . . .

II iti.áš.a ud.28.kám
mu am-mi-ṣa-du-qá lugal.e
dūr-am-mi-ṣa-du-qá$^{ki}$
ka.íd.zimbir$^{ki}$.ra.ta
in.ga.an.dím.ma.a

Month Shebat, 28th day, the year when Ammi-ṣaduqa, the king, constructed Dūr-Ammi-ṣaduqa at the mouth of the Sippar canal.

III iti.gud.si.sá [ud. × .kám]
mu am-mi-ṣa-d[u-qá lugal.e]
alam.a.[ni . . .
[×] × [. . .

Month Iyyar [×th day], the year when Ammi-ṣaduqa, [the king], a statue of himself [. . .

[1] Scheil in 1898 (*RT* xx. 55) proposed to read the name either Ellet-Aya or Mullil-Aya, and the former has been generally accepted. This, however, as pointed out by B. Landsberger privately, has no sound basis. J. J. Stamm, in *Die akkadische Namengebung* (*Mitteilungen der vorderasiatisch-aegyptischen Gesellschaft* 44) 301 f., comments that the type kù+divine name is Sumerian; and in the period of the First Dynasty of Babylon one finds not only kù in this type, but also kù.babbar and once a phonetic writing *ka-sa-ap-ištar* (*VAS* 8. 22. 4). No writings **el-le-et-ištar* have been noted. Thus in all probability the scribe was called Kasap-Aya, but since there is no proof, we have used the Sumerian form.

[2] The meaning of šu.silim.di is suggested by *Erimḫuš* I. 6 (*CT* 18. 47, K 214 = *CT* 19. 8, Rm II. 587. 6 = *KBo* I. 44. 6): šu.silim.di = *šit-ru-ṣú* in the context of its group and by the meaning of the elements in šu.silim.di.

Tablet I was thus written (or finished) on the 21st day of the first month of Ammi-ṣaduqa's 12th year (*c.* 1635 B.C.), and Tablet II on the 28th day of the eleventh month of the preceding year. The third tablet is dated in the second month of a year which cannot be certainly ascertained, since the 5th, 12th, 15th, and one other, unidentified year formula of this king begin with mention of a statue. It could well be the same year as that of Tablet I, since they both reached the British Museum together.

The rest of the colophons of these three tablets concerns the number of lines and the scribe:

I
dub.1.kám.ma *i-nu-ma i-lu a-wi-lum*
mu.šid.bi 416
šu kù.$^{d}$a.a dub.sar.tur

II
dub.2.kám.ma *i-nu-ma i-lu a-wi-lum*
[mu.š]id.bi 439
šu kù.$^{d}$a.a dub.sar.tur

III
al.til
dub.3.kám.ma
*i-nu-ma i-lu a-wi-lum*$^{a\text{-}wi\text{-}[lu]}$
⸢mu.šid.bi⸣ 390
šu.nigin 1245
ša 3 tup-pa-t[im]
šu kù.$^{d}$a.a dub.sar.tur

I
Tablet I, 'When the gods like man'
Number of lines: 416
Written by Ku-Aya, the junior scribe

II
Tablet II, 'When the gods like man'
Number of lines: 439
Written by Ku-Aya, the junior scribe

III
Finis
Tablet III, 'When the gods like man'
Number of lines: 390
Total: 1245 for the three tablets
Written by Ku-Aya, the junior scribe

Tablet III, cited here under the symbol **C** (see the list below), results from the combination of two pieces, one in Geneva, the other in London. The way that the two pieces are broken and all other considerations suggest that they are parts of the same tablet and might just touch if they were put together. From the first publication of Tablet II in 1898 by Scheil (*RT* xx. 55) it has been argued that Ku-Aya worked in Sippar. The reason, which has not changed since Scheil wrote (see Finkelstein, *JCS* 11. 83–4) is that the overwhelming majority of tablets from Ammi-ṣaduqa's reign come from Sippar, and the two London tablets, I and III, reached the British Museum in a collection mainly of such material.[1]

The Ku-Aya tablets are written in eight columns of about fifty-five lines each, save for the last one, which is shorter, and each column is numbered consecutively from the top (the wedge for 'ten' is put against each tenth line), then the total is given on the bottom edge under each column. The division of the work into tablets is purely scribal. The author wrote it as an uninterrupted sequence, and other editions divide it differently from Ku-Aya's.

Another copy of Tablet II belonging to the same recension is now in Istanbul (**D**). F. R. Kraus has shown that other tablets in Istanbul which, like this one, bear Nippur numbers, certainly come from Sippar, and in view of the close resemblance of this to **B**, Ku-Aya's Tablet II, he has concluded that this too is from Sippar.[2] The two have the same eight-column format, and where both are preserved they are sign for sign identical, except for ii. 18 (**B** has *na-aš-ša*, but **D** *na-al-ša*) and orthographic variants in i. 9–10, vii. 48, and viii. 36. Other differences are that the text is not broken into columns at exactly the same points; that **D** uses ten-marks on the obverse in the style of Ku-Aya, but neglects to do so on the reverse; and that there is no colophon preserved. It is true that the bottom of the last column is broken away, but even if the date was put there and is thus lost, the number of lines and the name of the scribe, which should have followed close on the last line to conform to Ku-Aya's style, is certainly lacking.

[1] With **B** there is a more direct piece of evidence. Scheil only wrote on its origin that it was 'parmi les découvertes de ma septième campagne en Orient' (*RT* xx. 55, *Revue biblique* 7. 5). However, at the meeting of the Eleventh International Congress of Orientalists held in Paris, 1897, he had said substantially more. The *Actes* of the Congress contain nothing by him, but reports are given by two British scholars who attended, Sayce and King. First, A. H. Sayce, in the Preface to his *Early History of the Hebrews* (1897), p. vii, states: 'At the recent meeting of the Oriental Congress in Paris, Dr. Scheil stated that among the tablets lately brought back from Sippar to the museum at Constantinople is one which contains the . . . story of the flood . . . inscribed in the reign of Ammi-zadok. . . .' L. W. King's *Babylonian Religion and Mythology* (1899), p. 124 says, 'It was found during the excavations that were recently undertaken by the Turkish Government at Abu-Habbah, the site of the ancient city of Sippar.' However, somehow the tablet became Scheil's property (cf. C. H. W. Johns, *Cuneiform Inscriptions* 41), and the informative paragraph in Sayce's book was omitted from the otherwise unchanged second edition of 1899.

[2] F. R. Kraus, *Altbab. Rechtsurkunden aus Nippur* 58; *Edikt* 12–13.

The other Old Babylonian pieces, **E**, **F**, **G**, can be assumed to come from Sippar on the same kind of evidence, but if so they attest the presence of at least three widely different recensions in the one town. **E** has a text which is basically the same as Ku-Aya's, but with many orthographic variants and one more substantial one in I. 295. However, this tablet had six, not eight columns, also there are no ten-marks. **F** is a small fragment with traces from the line-ends of one column and better-preserved beginnings of a second. From these one can see that the couplets were written on a single line in this copy, and its columns must have been very wide. But when allowance has been made for the different format, it is clear that there were recensional differences from Ku-Aya's edition, and the traces from its first column, which should come near the beginning of Tablet I, cannot be identified at all. **G** also offers a widely different recension, and again differently arranged. The tablet has only four columns, two on each side, and a ruling is put after each couplet, which is written over two lines, as in the majority of tablets from all periods. The first line of **G** corresponded with I. 157 of Ku-Aya's edition, and the whole tablet must have contained much less material. If the edition represented by **G** covered the same ground as the main recension, it must have consisted of some eight tablets. However, it may not have contained all the same episodes. Even the few words left in its column i offer variation from Ku-Aya's text. It is not clear if its column ii is to be inserted in a gap in the main recension, or is something differing recensionally from a preserved episode. The traces of its column iii are totally unidentified, which is only explicable as due to its deviation from Ku-Aya's edition.

Of the two Middle Babylonian pieces, one from Ras Shamra (𝕳) and one from Nippur (𝕴), it can only be said that they differed recensionally from Ku-Aya, and 𝕳 covered only the flood.

The fourteen Late Assyrian pieces all come from the Ashurbanipal libraries and are all in Late Assyrian script. Even if some were appropriated by Ashurbanipal from other existing collections there is no reason to suppose that any one is more than a century or so older than he. They are not uniform in any other respect, and they can be divided into three groups. The first, of nine mostly very small pieces (J–R), can be regarded as descendants of Ku-Aya's edition or something similar. That is, they often agree verbally with it, though offering many orthographic and phonetic variants. They do diverge more seriously in places, by way of addition or omission, or in other ways. Thus L omits I. 116–17; before I. 241 P has some lines not in the Old Babylonian text, and the same copy transposes the couplet I. 301–2 between lines 295 and 296; Q has remains of five lines covering I. 413–15; P also has a correction from a parallel passage: cf. its readings in I. 241–3 with the main recension at II. vii. 31–3. Only four of the nine pieces seem to be from the same tablets, J and K, and O and P, and in view of the small extent of these pieces generally one cannot be sure that their recensional connections have been properly assessed. Certainly there is diversity among them, and there was no one text, as in the case of *Gilgameš*, that had been thoroughly worked over and was standard in the late periods. Old Babylonian orthographies remain unchanged, e.g. the use of -*sa*$_6$ in I. 255 P. Also there is no standard format. M turned from obverse to reverse after I. 181; L (a piece from the right-hand side of the complete tablet) did the same at about I. 150; P did so at about I. 275. Ku-Aya's tablet (**A**) does so after I. 227. Thus P could have contained the same number of lines as **A**, but M and L must have been only about two-thirds the length of **A**, so that if they contained all the material from Ku-Aya's edition they probably formed a series of four tablets. Q was no doubt Tablet II of such a series, since its obverse covers the end of Ku-Aya's Tablet I and the beginning of Tablet II, while its reverse overlaps column ii of Tablet II. L obverse has a ruling and some damaged signs just above it that seem to be colophonic. If this is a correct understanding of the traces, L is derived from a series of which one (presumably the first) tablet ended with I. 110.

The second group of Ashurbanipal fragments is formed by V and W. We lump them together because they seem to be unrelated to Ku-Aya's edition, and they may well be unrelated to each other. V, for the little of it preserved, seems to have some relationship to the Old Babylonian **G**.

Somewhere among the eleven Ashurbanipal pieces just dealt with there are no doubt remains of one Ashurbanipal recension of the epic in which it was part of a larger whole. This emerges from the colophon of K 4175+ Sm 57+80–7–19, 184, and 82–3–23, 146 (see *CT* 18. 47 and *RA* 17. 189):

*e-nu-ma i-lu*$_4$ *a-*[*me-lum*]
dub.2.kám.ma me.me [kúr.kú]r *i-li*

This tablet itself contains the bilingual creation myth with the Silbenalphabet alongside, and is given in this colophon as the second in the series which begins with the Silbenalphabet itself in its bilingual version. The catch-line is the opening phrase of *Atra-ḫasīs*, so the epic formed the third, and no doubt also subsequent tablets, in this combined series.[1] The only identified fragment of the bilingual Silbenalphabet from

[1] See B. Landsberger, *AfO Beiheft* I (*Festschrift von Oppenheim*) 177–8; C. J. Gadd, *Iraq* 4. 33–4.

Ashurbanipal's libraries is Th 1905–4–9, 26 = BM 98520 (*RA* 17. 202), and as this could well be from the same scribe who wrote K 4175+, it is probably from Tablet I of this series. On the same basis of script one may wonder if V also comes from the same scribe and so belongs to the series.

The only post-Old Babylonian text of *Atra-ḫasīs* of sufficient extent and of such character to be called a recension is made up by the remaining Ashurbanipal pieces, S, T, and U. George Smith first made the epic known from S, which is now represented under three K-numbers. Smith knew all three as parts of a single tablet, but after his death they got separated, and only in 1967 was K 8562 finally joined to the other two.[1] The small piece T is almost certainly the concluding fragment of the same tablet. Script, clay, and content lead to this supposition, and the line of colophon[2] therefore identifies it as Tablet I of *Atra-ḫasīs*. Along with the three joined pieces it covers Tablet I of the main recension and the first half of Tablet II, so obviously it was a two-tablet edition, and reason will be offered shortly for taking U as the only surviving piece of the second and last tablet in this edition. For reasons which will become apparent, this can be called the Assyrian Recension. The format of Tablet I is one of six columns.

The most striking feature of this recension, as already observed by Laessøe, is the occurrence of Assyrian dialect forms (the corresponding word of the main recension, where preserved, is given in brackets):

Third person fem. *t-*

| | |
|---|---|
| S iii. 3 | *tam-nu-u* (*ittanandi*) |
| iii. 5 | *tàk-ri-iṣ* (*uktarriṣ*) |
| iii. 5, 6 | *taš-ku-un* (*iškun*) |

*lu-* instead of *li-* in precatives

| | |
|---|---|
| iii. 19 | *lu-ḫar-ri-šá* |
| iv. 30 | *lu-šá-bu-u* (*lišebbû*) |
| iv. 48 | *lu-li-id* |
| vi. 27 | *lu-ri-id* |

Vowel harmony, etc.

| | |
|---|---|
| v. 33 | *šu-ḫu-rat* (*šaḫurrat*) |
| vi. 17 | *e-tar-bu-ma* |

[1] In his *Chaldean Account of Genesis* ([1] 153–6; 1880, 155–8) he refers to the epic as known from one copy only, and confuses obverse and reverse of the tablet. He translates the bottom half of column iv of K 3399+3934 and then from K 8562 as the last preserved portion.

[2] dub.1.kám.ma *e-n*[*u-ma* . . .

Short form of verbal suffixes

iii. 12 *ú-ka-la-la-ši-na*

Assyrian II/1

iv. 32 *ka-i-la*

Late Assyrian preference for *a* (cf. *RA* 53. 125)

iv. 35 *kat-ra-ba-ma*

These forms certainly result from Assyrianization of an underlying Babylonian text, since often the Babylonian form occurs more frequently. For example, as against the one example of the short form of the verbal suffix there are three examples of the longer *-šināti* (iv. 11, 15, 38). Assyrian influence also occurs in orthography, and some of these features are very curious. Single consonants are often written where most scribes would write double, and the tablet is not self-consistent. It contains some glosses, which, however, are of significance for the study of Late Assyrian rather than for *Atra-ḫasīs*. A few examples only are given:

Unusual writings: *ti-ta* iv. 42, 52
*ni-še-e* iv. 42, 52

Single consonants: *a-li-te* (*ālitte*), *li-na-di* (*linnadi*) iii. 15

Inconsistencies: *i-im-ru/i'-ru* iv. 49, 59
*it-ta-*⸢'⸣*-*[*dar*]*/at-ta-a-*$^{di\text{-}ir}$*dar* iv. 2, 7

Three reasons support the assignment of U to the Assyrian Recension. First, U obv. 5–8 is a pair of repeated couplets like S iv. 23–6 (both are restored a little). They are of a kind not found in any other text of the epic. Secondly, U rev. 20 and S iv. 30 both use KA (gù) for *rigmu* (as proved by the main recension's parallel lines), something very unusual in Akkadian texts generally. Thirdly, U shows the same kinds of divergence from the main recension as S. For orthography note ⸢*i*⸣*-ta-ṣa-a* (*ittaṣâ*: rev. 18), and for grammar *si-qu-šú siq-si-qu* (rev. 7), which shows *s* for *z*, as is characteristic for many Middle Assyrian literary texts and copies.

From internal evidence it may be suspected that the Assyrian Recension goes back to a Middle Assyrian original. Such Akkadian literary texts as do survive in Middle Assyrian copies (e.g. *AS* 16. 283–8) show the same mixture of Assyrian and Babylonian forms (see also *BWL* 334 on b) and the same orthographic features. Whether this recension had a longer history in Assyria cannot be ascertained. The use of *GI* for *kí* in iii. 5 is an Old Assyrian custom, but it is possible that the correct explanation is grammatical rather than orthographic, that the Geers Law did not fully operate and the word should be read *girṣu* or *qirṣu*. Since it is known that Tukulti-Ninurta I used his sack of Babylon to acquire literary and other texts (*AfO* 18. 44. 2–11), and that Tiglath-pileser I had a library of such material (*AfO* 16. 197 ff.), it is perhaps more probable that this recension was Assyrianized in the middle period.

So far as can be told from its incomplete state, the Assyrian Recension follows the order of events in the main recension. There is nothing to suggest that it differed in more than detail. For example, its Tablet I, column ii, offers a fragment of narrative sharing some wording with the main recension, but it is different in details of the events. These do not, however, affect the general run of the story. In the description of the averting of the first plague the editor has avoided the repetition of the main recension (his iv. 29–36 covers I. 372–415!), but conversely his account seems to conflate at each occurrence the events of the second, third, and fourth attempts of the gods to quieten the human race, which both obscures the plot and pads out the narrative. The biggest difference between the two recensions is in wording. While there is some phraseology in common, there is much more of the epic where the wording has been changed quite deliberately on one side or the other. Generally it seems a reasonable conclusion that the main recension is primary and the Assyrian Recension secondary. This is particularly clear where obscure words and phrases of the Old Babylonian text have been altered:

II. i. 11 (*zunnīšu*) *li-ša-aq-qí-il* = *zu-un-na-šu lu-šá-qir* (iv. 44)

II. iv. 14 *i-na ši-it-ku-ki na-pí-i*[*š-ti*] = *i-na šu-par-ke-e napišti* (v. 26 = vi. 15)

The same kind of corrections can be observed between Tablet III of the main recension and *Gilgameš* XI. Metrically too the Assyrian Recension is far less consistent than the main recension. Its lines more commonly diverge from the accepted patterns, and some parts are not written in couplets even though the corresponding Old Babylonian lines are, e.g. S v. 12–26 = vi. 1–15 compared with II. iv. 7–18.

In short, the Assyrian Recension is a reworking of Ku-Aya's text (or a similar one) and it is scarcely an improvement. Whether the editorial work was done in Babylonia before the text was taken to Assyria, where local dialectal forms were inserted, or whether both sets of changes were Assyrian is at present an unanswerable question. There is one passage which shows that the other Late Assyrian copies could have connections with the Assyrian Recension: for II. i. 5–6, Q has substituted a couplet of roughly the same content but differently worded. This is also found in S iv. 4–5.

The two Late Babylonian fragments, x and y, are hardly big enough for their recensional characteristics to be drawn out. But clearly they do differ from the Old Babylonian edition in some places quite substantially, and they too may not always keep the Old Babylonian couplet form. However, they do not agree among themselves on who guarded the 'middle earth'.

Our reconstructed text is based on Ku-Aya's tablets where they are preserved, but the text is arranged metrically. Lines of poetry spread over two lines of script due to the narrowness of the Old Babylonian columns have been joined and spacing is used to indicate couplets. Tablet I is cited by line only (e.g. I. 241) since, with the help of the ten-marks (those for 220 and 320 are omitted in *CT* 46. 1) and the total number of lines given in the colophon it is possible to give a consecutive numbering throughout. In Tablets II and III the gaps between the preserved portions of the columns cannot be estimated accurately, so these tablets have to be cited by tablet, column, and line number, e.g. III. iv. 17. Where the ten-marks enable it, the ancient line numbers are used; otherwise the preserved lines are numbered from 1. So far as possible, all other tablets, both Old Babylonian and later, are cited in the apparatus. However, where Ku-Aya's edition is deficient, it has been restored from other Old Babylonian texts without any special indication of this fact when it is reasonably certain that they can properly be so used. This applies almost exclusively to **E** in Tablet I and **D** in Tablet II. Where the Late Assyrian fragments that are descended from Ku-Aya's text, or something similar, alone are preserved, they are used to restore the Old Babylonian text, but distinguished by smaller type. This occurs only in Tablet I, 171 ff. and 251 ff. With the divergent texts, the smaller pieces have been inserted, where possible, in opportune gaps in the main recension. Thus of the first tablet of the Assyrian Recension, the small surviving portions of the obverse are inserted in the course of Tablet I, but the larger portions of the columns on the reverse are given on their own after the end of Tablet III. And so with the other divergent pieces. The location of each can be found from the following list of manuscripts.

# LIST OF MANUSCRIPTS

| Symbol | Museum number | Copy | Lines preserved[1] |
|---|---|---|---|
| OLD BABYLONIAN | | | |
| **A** = | BM 78941+78943 (Bu 89–4–26, 234+236) | *CT* 46. 1[2] | I. 1–50, 52; 57–114; 115–30, 139–70; 209–27; 228–51; 281–308, 319–20, 322, 324–5, 327–33; 334–89; 390–416 |
| **B** = | MLC 1889 | *RT* xx. 56–8 *YOR* v/3, pls. I, II *BRM* IV. 1 | II. i. 1–20; ii. 8–9, 13–24; vii. 37–54; viii. 33–7 |
| **C** = **$C_1$** = | BM 78942+78971+80385 (Bu 89–4–26, 235+266+ Bu 91–5–9, 524) | *CT* 46. 3[2] | III. i. 28–50; ii. 28–55; iii. 3–54; iv. 3–28, 39–48; v. 8–14, 28–52; vi. 1–27, 38–51; vii. 1–27; viii. 3–19 |
| and **$C_2$** = | MAH 16064 (see *JCS* 5. 18) | *RA* 28. 92, 94 Pls. 7–8 | III. i. 11–26; ii. 9–21; vii. 36–41 |
| **D** = | Ni 2552+2560+2564 | Pls. 1–6 | II. i. 2–23; ii. 8–36; iii. 1–35; iv. 1–25; v. 1–33; vi. 1–32; vii. 30–53; viii. 31–7 |
| **E** = | BM 92608 (Bu 91–5–9, 269) | *CT* 6. 5 *PBS* x/1, pls. III, IV = *Le Poème* pl. x *CT* 46. 4 | I. 123–46; 188–220; 271–300; traces *c.* 340 |
| **F** = | BM 17596*a* (94–1–15, 310*a*) | *CT* 46. 2 | I. unidentified; 103–24 |
| **G** = | BM 78257 (Bu 88–5–12, 113) | *CT* 44. 20[2] | I. 158–66; (182–97); unidentified |
| MIDDLE BABYLONIAN | | | |
| 𝕳 = | RS 22. 421 | *Ugaritica* v. 167 | (II–III). P. 132 |
| 𝕴 = | CBS 13532 | *BE* Ser. D v/1 | unidentified; (III. i). P. 126 |
| LATE ASSYRIAN (all from Ashurbanipal's library) | | | |
| J = | K 10082 | *CT* 46. 7 | (I. 49–52); 109–11? |

[1] The semicolons separate the material of the preserved columns in sequence of each tablet or fragment. Where a recension widely differing from Ku-Aya's is offered, the corresponding line- and column-numbers of his recension are given in brackets. Where the lines concerned have not been used for our main text and are not given adjacent to the corresponding passage, they can be located from the page references given in the above list.

[2] Collations are given on pl. 11.

| *Symbol* | *Museum number* | *Copy* | *Lines preserved* |
|---|---|---|---|
| K = | K 6235 | *CT* 46. 10[1] | I. 68–80; 168–77; unidentified |
| | (J and K are probably parts of the same tablet) | | |
| L = | K 6831 | *CT* 46. 12[1] | I. 106–22; 169–75 |
| M = | K 7109+9979 | *CT* 46. 11 | I. 163–81 |
| N = | Bu 89–4–26, 97 | *CT* 46. 8 | I. 172–9 |
| O = | K 14697 | Pl. 5 | I. 226–33 |
| P = | K 7816+13863 | *BA* v. 688 (7816 only) *CT* 46. 13 (complete) | I. 237–60; 288–306 |
| | (O and P are probably parts of the same tablet) | | |
| Q = | Sm 292 | *JSS* v. 123 *CT* 46. 14[1] | (I. 410–II. i. 13); (II. i–ii) |
| R = | K 4539 | *BWL* pl. 65 | III. vii. 10–18? |
| S = | K 3399+3934+8562 | *CT* 15. 49 (3399+3934), *CT* 46. 6 (8562) | (I. 18–40); (I. 170 ff.); (I. 253 ff.); (I. 352–II. i); (II. ii–iii); (II. iv). Pp. 106–14 |
| T = | K 12000*c* | *CT* 13. 31 | (II. iv). P. 114 |
| | (T is probably the end of the same tablet as S) | | |
| U = | BM 98977+99231 (Ki 1904–10–9, 6+263) | *JSS* v. 116 | (III. i); (III. iii). Pp. 122–4 |
| V = | K 6634 | *CT* 46. 9 | (I. 189–91); (I. 360 ff.) |
| W = | DT 42 | Delitzsch, $AL^3$ 101, IV. $R^1$ 50, IV. $R^2$ Additions p. 9, Haupt, *Nimrodepos* p. 131, *CT* 46. 15[1] | (III. i). P. 128 |
| NEO-LATE BABYLONIAN | | | |
| x = | BE 39099 (Photo Babylon 1804) | Pls. 4, 9–10 | Unidentified; (II. ii–iii) (II. v–vi). Pp. 116–20 |
| y = | BE 36669/24a (Photo Babylon 1601) | Pl. 5 | (II. ii–iii). P. 116 |

PHOTOGRAPHS

**B**: *RT* xx, pl. with 55–9; Johns, *Cuneiform Inscriptions*, Frontispiece and p. 11; *YOR* v/3 pls. v–VI; *BRM* IV, pl. II; Clay, *Origin of the Biblical Traditions* 223 (enlargements of some signs)

**$C_2$**: *RA* 28, pl. with pp. 91–7

**𝕵**: *BE* Ser. D v/1

S: Bezold, *Catalogue* v, pl. VIII (part only)

W: E. Sollberger, *The Babylonian Legend of the Flood*, p. 37

[1] Collations are given on pl. 11.

# TABLET I

**A**

1 *i-nu-ma i-lu a-wi-lum*
2 *ub-lu du-ul-la* *iz-bi-lu šu-up-ši-[i]k-ka*

3 *šu-up-ši-ik i-li ra-bi-[m]a*
4 *du-ul-lu-um ka-bi-it* *ma-a-ad ša-ap-ša-qum*

5 *ra-bu-tum* $^{d}$*a-nun-na-ku si-bi-it-tam*
6 *du-ul-lam ú-ša-az-ba-lu* $^{d}$*i-⌜gi-gi⌝*

7 *a-nu a-bu-šu-nu ša[r-r]u*
8 *[m]a-li-ik-šu-nu qú-ra-d[u]* $^{d}$*en-líl*

9 *[*$gu_5$*-u]z-za-lu-šu-n[u]* $^{d}$*[ni]n-urta*
10 *[ù] gal-lu-šu-nu* $^{d}$*[en]-nu-gi*

11 *[q]a-tam i-ḫu-zu qa-ti-ša*
12 *is-qá-am id-du-ú* *i-lu iz-zu-zu*

13 *⌜a-nu⌝ i-te-li š[a-me]-⌜e⌝-ša*
14 [× ×] × × × *⌜er⌝-ṣe-tam ba-ú-la-⌜tu⌝-uš-šu*

15 *[ši-ga-ra n]a-aḫ-ba-lu ti-a-am-tim*
16 *[it-ta-a]d-nu a-na* $^{d}$*en-ki na-aš-ši-⌜ki⌝*

17 *[iš-tu a-nu-u]m i-lu-⌜ú ša⌝-me-e-ša*
18 *[ù* $^{d}$*en-ki a-na a]p-si-⌜i⌝ [i]-ta-ar-du*

| | | |
|---|---|---|
| 19 | . . .] ú × *[š]a-ma-i* | . . .] . . the heavens |
| 20 | . . .] × *[e]-lu* $^{d}$*i-gi-gi* | . . .] . upon the Igigi |
| 21 | . . .] *i-ḫe-er-ru-nim* | . . .] they were digging |
| 22 | . . . *n]a-pí-iš-ti ma-tim* | . . .] the life of the land |
| 23 | . . . *i]-ḫe-er-ru-nim* | . . .] they were digging |
| 24 | . . . *na-p]í-iš-ti ma-tim* | . . .] the life of the land |
| 25 | . . . $^{id}$*idi]glat na-ra-am* | . . .] the Tigris river |
| 26 | . . .] ×*-di/ki-tam* | . . .] . . . |

**1** Quoted as title in the colophons of **ABC** (with a gloss in **C**: *a-wi-⌜lu⌝*); as *e-n[u-* in the colophon of T; and as *e-nu-ma i-*$lu_4$ *a-[* in K 4175+ (see p. 35). **7–10** cf. *Gilg.* XI. 15–18.

# TABLET I

i 1 When the gods like men
2 Bore the work and suffered the toil—

3 The toil of the gods was great,
4 The work was heavy, the distress was much—

5 The Seven great Anunnaki
6 Were making the Igigi suffer the work.

7 Anu, their father, was the king;
8 Their counsellor was the warrior Enlil;

9 Their chamberlain was Ninurta;
10 And their sheriff Ennugi.

11 The gods had clasped hands together,
12 Had cast lots and had divided.

13 Anu had gone up to heaven,
14 [. .] . . . the earth to his subjects.

15 [The bolt], the bar of the sea,
16 [They had given] to Enki, the prince.

17 [After Anu] had gone up to heaven
18 [And Enki] had gone down to the Apsû,

* * * * *

The Assyrian Recension of lines 19 ff. is offered by K 8562 (S), column i:

| | | |
|---|---|---|
| 1 | . . .] ⌜*e*⌝-*tar-du* | ] went down |
| 2 | . . . *ma-li-k*]*u-ut ap-se-e* | ruler]ship of the Apsû |
| 3 | . . . -*r*]*i-du-ma* | went] down |
| 4 | . . .] × ud $^{d}$*ea*(idim) | ] . . Ea |
| 5 | . . . *i-ḫer*]-*ru-ú nāra* | ] were digging the river |
| 6 | . . . *n*]*a-púl-ti māti* | ] the life of the land |
| 7 | . . .] × *pu-ra-na-ta ar-ki-šá* | ] . the Euphrates after it |
| 8 | . . .] *i-na naq-bi* | ] from the deep |
| 9 | . . .]-*šu-nu il-ták-nu* | ] their [. . .] they set up |

A

| | | |
|---|---|---|
| 27 | . . . *i-na n*]*a-aq-bi* | . . . from] the deep |
| 28 | . . . *iš-t*]*a-ak-nu* | . . .] they set up |
| 29 | . . . *a*]*p-*⸢*sa*⸣*-a* | . . .] the Apsû |
| 30 | . . .] ×*-at ma-tim* | . . .] . . of the land |
| 31 | . . .]*-a qí-ri-ib-šu* | . . .] . within it |
| 32 | . . . *ul-l*]*u-ú re-ši-šu* | . . .] they raised its head |

33 . . . *k*]*a*?*-la ša-di-i*
34 [*šanātim im-nu-ú*] *ša šu-up-ši-ik-ki*

35 . . .] × *ṣú-ṣi-a ra-bi-a*
36 [*šanātim im*]*-nu-ú ša šu-up-ši-ik-ki*

37 . . .] × 40 *šanātim*(mu.ḫi.a) *at-ra-am*
38 [× × *du*]*-ul-lam iz-bi-lu mu-ši ù ur-ri*

39 [*i-da-bu*]*-bu-ma i-ik-ka-lu ka-ar-ṣi*
40 [*ut-ta-az*]*-za-mu i-na ka-la-ak-ki*

41 [× ×] ×*-ni guzzalâ i ni-im-ḫu-ur-ma*
42 [*ka-a*]*b-tam du-ul-la-ni li-ša-sí-ik el-ni*

43 [× × *m*]*a-li-ik i-li qú-ra-dam*
44 [*al-k*]*a-nim i ni-iš-ši-a i-na šu-ub-ti-šu*

45 [$^{d}$*en-líl m*]*a-li-ik i-li qú-ra-dam*
46 [*al-k*]*a-nim i ni-iš-ši-a i-na šu-ub-ti-šu*

47 [$^{d}$×] × *pí-a-šu i-pu-ša-am-ma*
48 [*is-sà-qa*]*r a-na i-li aḫ-ḫi-šu*

49 . . .] × ⸢GU.ZA.LÁ *la-bi*⸣*-ru-tim*
50 . . .] ×

51 [. . . . . . . . . . . . . . .]
52 . . .] ×*-ni*

* * * * *

The last four lines of Column i, 53–6, are broken away, but K 10082 (J) probably belongs at this point:

1 . . .]*-a i ni-*⸢*na-ra*⸣*-a*[*š-šu*]
2 . . .] × *i ni-iš-bi-ir ni-ra*
3 [$^{d}$. . . *pâ-šu*] *i-pu-ša-am-ma*
4 [*is-sa-aq-qa-r*]*a ana i-lu aḫ-ḫe-e-šu*
5 . . .] × *guzalê*$^{e}$ *la-bi-ru-tim*

| | | |
|---|---|---|
| 10 | ${}^{\text{meš}}$]-*ma i-za-bi-lu tup-ši-ka* | [For 10 years (?)] they suffered the toil, |
| 11 | ${}^{\text{m}}$]${}^{\text{eš}}$-*ma i-za-bi-lu tup-ši-ka* | [For 20 years (?)] they suffered the toil, |
| 12 | ${}^{\text{m}}$]${}^{\text{eš}}$-*ma i-za-bi-lu tup-ši-ka* | [For 30 years (?)] they suffered the toil, |
| 13 | ${}^{\text{m}}$]${}^{\text{eš}}$-*ma i-za-bi-lu tup-ši-ka* | [For 40 years (?)] they suffered the toil. |
| 14 | . .] ⌜šum⌝ *il-mu-ú* kak bu? la | ] . they surrounded . . . |
| 15 | traces | |

* * * * *

33 . . .] all the mountains,
34 [They counted the years] of the toil.

35 . . .] . the great marsh,
36 [They] counted [the years] of the toil.

37 Excessive [. . . . . .] for 40 years
38 [. .] they suffered the work night and day.

39 They [were complaining], backbiting,
40 Grumbling in the excavation:

41 'Let us confront our [. .] ., the chamberlain,
42 That he may relieve us of our heavy work.

43 [. .] the counsellor of the gods, the hero,
44 Come, let us unnerve him in his dwelling!

45 [Enlil], counsellor of the gods, the hero,
46 Come, let us unnerve him in his dwelling!'

47 [. .] . opened his mouth
48 [And addressed] the gods, his brothers,

49 '. . . .] . the chamberlain of old time

* * * * *

## K 10082 (J)

1 . . .] . let us kill [him]
2 . . .] . let us break the yoke!'
3 [. . .] opened [his mouth]
4 [And addressed] the gods his brothers,
5 '. . .] . the chamberlain of old time

6 . . .] *i-ša-ak-ka-na* $^{d}$*en-líl*
7 . . . *ša*]-*né-e i-ša-ka-an*
8 . . .] × × *iq-qú-ú* × × × ×

* * * * *

A

57 *ma-li-*[*ik*] *i-*[*li*] *qú-ra-dam*
58 *al-k*[*a*]-⟨*nim*⟩ ⸢*i*⸣ *ni-iš-ši-a i-na šu-ub-ti-šu*

59 $^{d}$*en-líl* [*ma-li-i*]*k i-li qú-ra-dam*
60 *al-*[*ka*]-⟨*nim*⟩ *i ni-iš-ši-a i-na šu-ub-ti-šu*

61 *a-nu-um-ma ti-si-a tu-*⸢*qú*⸣*-um-tam*
62 *ta-ḫa-za i ni-ib-lu-la qá-ab-la-am*

63 *i-lu iš-mu-ú sí-qí-ir-šu*
64 *i-ša-tam ne-pí-ši-šu-nu id-du-ú-ma*

65 *ma-ar-ri-šu-nu i-ša-ta-am*
66 *šu-up-ši-ik-ki-šu-nu* $^{d}$*girra* 67 *it-ta-ak-šu*

K

68 *i-ta-aḫ-zu-nim i-il-la-ku-nim*
69 *ba-bi-ša-at-ma-ni qú-ra-di* $^{d}$*en-líl*

70 *mi-ši-il ma-aṣ-ṣa-ar-ti mu-šum i-ba-aš-ši*
71 *bītu la-wi i-lu ú-ul i-di*

72 *mi-ši-il ma-aṣ-ṣa-ar-ti mu-šum i-ba-aš-ši*
73 *é-kur la-wi* $^{d}$*en-líl ú-ul i-di*

74 *ú-te-eq-qí* $^{d}$*kal-kal ú-te-*[*ši*]
75 *il-pu-ut si-ik-ku-ra i-ḫi-iṭ* [× ×]

76 $^{d}$*kal-kal id-de-ki* $^{d}$[*nusku*]
77 *ri-ig-ma i-še-em-mu-ú š*[*a* . . .]

78 $^{d}$*nusku id-de-ki be-*[*el-šu*]
79 *i-na ma-ia-li ú-še-et-*[*bi-šu*]

80 *be-lí la-wi bi-*[*it-ka*]
81 *qá-ab-lum i-ru-ṣa* ⸢*a*⸣-[*na ba-bi-ka*]

82 $^{d}$*en-líl la-w*[*i bi-i*]*t-ka*
83 *qá-ab-l*[*um i-ru*]-⸢*ṣa*⸣ *a-na* [*b*]*a-bi-ka*

84 $^{d}$*en-líl* × × × *ú-ša-ar-di a-na šu-ub-ti-šu*

**68** K: [*i-taḫ-z*]*u-ni* **71** K: [*bi-t*]*i, u*[*l* **73** K: [*bi*]-*ti* **74** K: ⸢*ú*⸣-*ta-qi-im*
**75** K: [*š*]*i-ik-ku-r*[*a* **79** K: *m*]*a-a-a-al* [

6 . . .] Enlil will appoint
7 . . .] will appoint another
8 . . .] . . . . . . . . .

⋆ ⋆ ⋆ ⋆ ⋆

ii 57 The counsellor of the gods, the hero,
58 Come, let us unnerve him in his dwelling!

59 Enlil, counsellor of the gods, the hero,
60 Come, let us unnerve him in his dwelling!

61 Now, proclaim war,
62 Let us mingle hostilities and battle.'

63 The gods heeded his words:
64 They set fire to their tools,

65 Fire to their spades they put
66 And flame to their hods.

68 They held them as they went
69 To the gate of the shrine of the hero Enlil.

70 It was night, half-way through the watch,
71 The temple was surrounded, but the god did not know.

72 It was night, half-way through the watch,
73 Ekur was surrounded, but Enlil did not know.

74 Kalkal observed it and was disturbed.
75 He slid the bolt and watched [. .]

76 Kalkal roused [Nusku],
77 And they listened to the noise of [. . .]

78 Nusku roused [his] lord,
79 He got [him] out of his bed,

80 'My lord, [your] temple is surrounded,
81 Battle has come right up [to your gate].

82 Enlil, your temple is surrounded,
83 Battle has come right up to your gate.'

84 Enlil . . . . . . . to his dwelling.

A

85 [$^{d}$]*en-líl pa-a-šu i-pu-ša-am-ma*
86 *a-na šukkalli* $^{d}$*nusku is-sà-qar*

87 $^{d}$*nusku e-di-il ba-ab-ka*
88 *ka-ak-ki-ka li-qí i-zi-iz ma-aḫ-ri-ia*

89 $^{d}$*nusku i-di-il ba-ab-šu*
90 *ka-ak-ki-šu il-qí it-ta-zi-iz ma-ḫar* $^{d}$*en-líl*

91 $^{d}$*nusku pí-a-šu i-pu-ša-am-ma*
92 *is-sà-qar a-na qú-ra-di* $^{d}$*en-líl*

93 *be-lí bi-nu bu-nu-ka*
94 *ma-ru ra-ma-ni-ka mi-in-šu ta-du-ur*

95 $^{d}$*en-líl bi-nu bu-nu-ka*
96 *ma-ru ra-ma-ni-ka mi-in-šu ta-du-ur*

97 *šu-pu-ur a-na*[*m*] *li-še-ri-du-*[*nim-m*]*a*
98 $^{d}$*en-ki*! *li-ib-bi-ku-nim a-na m*[*a-aḫ-ri-k*]*a*

99 *iš-pu-ur a-nam ú-še-ri-*[*du-ni-i*]*š-šu*
100 $^{d}$*en-ki ib-bi-ku-nim a-na ma-a*[*ḫ-ri*]*-šu*

101 *wa-ši-ib a-nu šar-ri* [*ša*]*-me-e*
102 *šar-ri ap-si-i* $^{d}$*en-*⌜*ki i*⌝*-*[*me-re-e*]*k-*⌜*ki*⌝

F

103 *ra-bu-tum* $^{d}$*a-nun-*[*na*(*-ku*) *w*]*a-aš-bu*
104 $^{d}$*en-líl it-bi-ma ša* [. . .]*-di/ki-nu*

L

105 $^{d}$*en-líl pí-a-šu i-*[*pu-ša-a*]*m-ma*
106 *is-sà-qar a-n*[*a i-li ra-b*]*u-tim*

F

107 *ia-a-ši-im-ma-a it-te-né-e*[*p-pu-uš*]
108 *ta-ḫa-za e-ep-pu-uš ša* × × × [(×)]

109 *i-ni mi-na-a a-mu-ur a-*[*n*]*a-ku*
110 *qá-ab-lum i-ru-ṣa a-na ba-bi-ia*

111 *a-nu pí-a-šu i-pu-ša-am-ma*
112 *is-sà-qar a-na qú-ra-di* $^{d}$*en-líl*

113 *sí-iq-ra ša* $^{d}$*i-gi-gu* 114 ⌜*il*⌝*-mu-ú ba-bi-iš-ka*
115 *li-ṣi-ma* $^{d}$*nusku* × [. . .

116 *te-er-ta* × [. . .
117 *a-na ma-*[*ri-ka* . . .

**98** Tablet (**A**): $^{d}$*en-líl* **105–6** om. **F**? **106** L: *ana i*[*lí*$^{me}$]$^{š}$ *aḫ-*[*ḫe-e-šu*] **107** **F**: *ia-ši-im-ma*[ **108** L: ] × × × ú ti [ **109** **F**: *mi-na* **111** L:

85 Enlil opened his mouth
86 And addressed the vizier Nusku,

87 'Nusku, bar your gate,
88 Take your weapons and stand before me.'

89 Nusku barred his gate,
90 Took his weapons and stood before Enlil.

91 Nusku opened his mouth
92 And addressed the hero Enlil,

93 'My lord, sons are your . . .
94 Why do you fear your own sons?

95 Enlil, sons are your . . .
96 Why do you fear your own sons?

97 Send that Anu be fetched down
98 And that Enki be brought to your presence.'

99 He sent and Anu was fetched down,
100 Enki was brought also to his presence.

101 Anu, king of heaven, was present,
102 King of the Apsû, Enki, was in attendance.

103 With the great Anunnaki present
104 Enlil arose . [. . .] . .

105 Enlil opened his mouth
106 And addressed the great [gods],

107 'Is it against me that it is being done?
108 Must I engage in hostilities . . . . .?

109 What did my very own eyes see?
110 That battle has come right up to my gate!'

111 Anu opened his mouth
112 And addressed the hero Enlil,

113 'The reason why the Igigi have surrounded your gate
iii 115 Let Nusku go out and [ascertain (?)].

116 A command . [. . .
117 To [your] sons [. . .'

---

$^{d}$*a-nu-um pa-a-*[ **F**: AN$^{nu}$ *pa-a-*⌜*šu*⌝ **112** L: *-a*]*q-qar ana a-ḫi-šu* [ **113** L: $^{d}$*i-g*[*i*$_4$- **116–17** om. L

A FL

118 *$^{d}$en-líl pí-a-šu i-[pu-ša-am-ma]*
119 *is-sà-qar a-na [šukkalli $^{d}$nusku]*

120 *$^{d}$nusku pí-te [ba-ab-ka]*
121 *ka-ak-ki-ka l[i-qí . . .*

E

122 *i-na pu-úḫ-ri [ka-la i-li-ma]*
123 *ki-mi-is i-zi-i[z . . . . . . . .]-ni*

124 *iš-pu-ra-an-ni [a-bu-ku-nu] a-nu*
125 *ma-li-ik-ku-nu [qú-ra-du $^{d}$en-l]íl*

126 *gu$_5$-uz-za-lu-ku-[nu $^{d}$nin]-urta*
127 *ù gal-lu-ku-n[u $^{d}$en]-nu-gi*

128 *ma-an-nu-um-mi [. . . . qá]-ab-lim*
129 *ma-an-nu-um-[mi . . . . . ta-ḫ]a-zi*

130 *ma-an-nu-u[m-mi ig-ra-am t]u-qú-um-tam*
131 *[qá-ab-lam . . . . . . . .]* × × ×

132 *[i-na . . . . . . . . . . . . .]* × ×
133 *[ib-ba- . . . . . . . . . . . .]* × × × × *$^{d}$en-líl*

134 *[il-li-ik $^{d}$nusku a-na pu-úḫ-ri k]a-la i-li-ma*
135 *. . .]* × × × *ip-šu-ur*

136 *[iš-pu-ra-an-ni a]-bu-ku-nu a-nu*
137 *[ma-li-ik-ku-nu qú-ra]-du $^{d}$en-[lí]l*

A

138 *[gu$_5$-uz-za-lu-ku-nu $^{d}$n]in-urta*
139 *⌜ù⌝ [gal-lu-ku-nu $^{d}$e]n-nu-gi*

140 *ma-[an-nu-um-mi . . . . . . . . .qá]-ab-lim*
141 *ma-[an-nu-um-mi . . . . . . . . .ta-ḫa]-zi*

142 *ma-[an-nu-um-mi ig-ra-am tu-qú-u]m-tam*
143 *qá-a[b-lam . . . . . . . . . . . . . . . . . .]* × ×

144 *i-na [. . . . . . . . . . . . . . . . . . . . . . . .]*×
145 *ib-ba-[. . . . . . . . . . . . . $^{d}$en-l]íl*

146 *ku-ul-la-a[t ka-la i-li-ma ni-ig-ra-am tu-qú-um-ta]m*
147 *ni-iš-ku-u[n* × ×*-ni]* 148 *i-na k[a-la-ak-ki]*

149 *šu-up-ši-ik-[ku at-ru id-du-uk-ni-a-ti]*
150 *ka-bi-it du-[ul-la-ni-ma ma-a-ad ša-ap-ša-qum]*

**118** FL: *pa-a-šu* **119** L: *-a]q-qar ana i-*× [ **120** L: *pi-te* **122** F: *pu-ḫu-ur* L: ]*-ru* **146** E: *ì-l]í?*

118 Enlil opened his mouth
119 And addressed [vizier Nusku],

120 'Nusku, open [your gate],
121 Take your weapons [. . .

122 In the assembly of [all the gods]
123 Bow down, stand up, [and repeat to them] our [words]:

124 "Anu, [your father],
125 Your counsellor, [the warrior] Enlil,

126 Your chamberlain Ninurta,
127 And your sheriff Ennugi, have sent me (to say),

128 'Who is [the instigator of] battle?
129 Who is [the provoker of] hostilities?

130 Who [declared] war
131 [And . . . . . . . . battle]?'

132 [In . . . . . . . .] . .
133 [Bring . . . . . . .] . . . . Enlil."'

134 [Nusku went to the assembly of] all the gods,
135 . . .] . . . he explained,

136 'Anu, your father,
137 [Your counsellor, the] warrior Enlil,

138 [Your chamberlain] Ninurta,
139 And [your sheriff] Ennugi, [have sent me (to say)],

140 "Who is [the instigator of] battle?
141 Who is [the provoker of] hostilities?

142 Who [declared] war
143 [And . . . . . . . .] battle?"

144 In [. . . . . . . . . . . . .] .
145 Bring [. . . . . . . . . . . . .] Enlil.'

146 'Every single [one of us gods has declared] war;
147 We have . . . our [.] . in the [excavation].

149 [Excessive] toil [has killed us],
150 [Our] work was heavy, [the distress much].

A

151 *ù ku-ul-l[a-at ka-la i-li-ma]*
152 *ub-la pí-i-ni* [*na-×-×-am it-ti* $^{d}$*en-líl*]

153 $^{d}$⌜*nusku*⌝ *il-q[í ka-ak-ki-šu* (. . .)]
154 *il-li-ik ú-×* [. . .

155 *be-lí a-n[a . . . . . ta-aš-pu-ra]-*⌜*an-ni*⌝
156 *al-l[i-ik . . . . . . . . . . . . .]* × × *ti*

G

157 *ap-šu-u[r . . . . . . . . . . .]* × *ra-bi-tam*
158 *na-ab-*[. . . . . . . . . . .] × × zi

159 *k[u-ul-la-at ka-la i-l]i-ma-mi* 160 *ni-ig-ra-am* ⌜*tu-qú-um*⌝*-ta-am*
161 *n[i-iš-ku-un* ×] ×*-ni i-na ka-la-ak-ki*

M

162 *š[u-up-ši-ik-ku]* ⌜*at-ru id*⌝*-du-uk-ni-a-ti*
163 [*ka-bi-it du-u*]*l-la-ni-ma* *ma-a-ad ša-ap-ša-qum*

164 [*ù ku-ul-l*]*a-at ka-la i-li-ma*
165 *u[b-la]* ⌜*pí-i-ni*⌝ *na-×-×-am it-ti* $^{d}$*en-líl*

166 *iš-[me] a-wa-tam šu-a-ti*
167 $^{d}$*en-líl* [*i*]*l-la-ka di-ma-šu*

K L

168 $^{d}$*en-líl i-×-ar a-wa-as-su*
169 *is-sà-q[ar a-na q]ú-ra-di a-nim*

170 *e-te-el-li iš-ti-ka a-na ša-ma-i*
171 *par-ṣa-am ta-ba-al-ma* *li-qí id-ka*

N

172 *aš-bu* $^{d}$*a-nun-na-ki ma-ḫar-ka*
173 *i-lu iš-te-en ši-si-m[a l]i-id-du-šú tam-ta*

174 $^{d}$*a-nu pa-a-šu i-pu-šá-[am-ma]*
175 [*is-sà*]*-aq-qar ana i-li aḫ-ḫi-šú*

176 *mi-nam kar-ṣi-šú-nu n[i-ik]-ka-al*
177 ⌜*ka-bit*⌝ *dul-la-šú-un* *m[a-a-a]d ša-ap-šaq-šu-un*

178 [$u_4$*-mi-šam-m*]*a ir-*[*ṣi*-× (. . .)]×*-na-a-ṭu*
179 [*tuk-ku ka-b*]*i-i[t* *ni?-še-e*]*m-me ri-ig-ma*

180 . . .] × *e-pe-ši*
181 . . . *iš-k*]*a-ra-a-tu*

* * * * *

**160** **G**: × *ig-ra-am tu-qum-tam* **162** **G**: *-d*]*u-uk an-ni-a-am* **163** M: *ša-ap-ša-a*]*q?-ni* **164** **G**: *ili*]$^{\text{meš}}$*-ma* **165** M: *n*]*a?-bi-?/ḫu?-za* KI **166** M: *šu-a-tu* **G** (end): ]× **167** M: *di-ma-a-šu* **168** K: [ × ] × ka [ M: ] × : *is-sà-aq-*

151 Now, every single [one of us gods]
152 Has spoken in favour of . . . with Enlil.'

153 Nusku took [his weapons . . .
154 He went, he . [. . .

155 'My lord to the [. . . . . you sent] me
156 I went [. . . . . . . . . . . . .] . . .

157 I explained [. . . .] great [. . . . .] .
158 . . [. . . . . . . . . . . .] . . .

159 ["Every single one of us] gods has declared war;
161 We [have . . . . .] our [. .] . in the excavation.

162 Excessive [toil] has killed us;
163 Our work [was heavy], the distress much.

164 [Now, every] single one of us gods
165 Has spoken in favour of . . . . with Enlil."'

166 When Enlil heard that speech
167 His tears flowed.

168 Enlil . . . his words
169 And addressed the warrior Anu,

170 'Noble one, with you to heaven
iv 171 Carry your authority, take your power,

172 While the Anunnaki are present before you
173 Summon one god and have him done to death.'

174 Anu opened his mouth
175 And addressed the gods his brothers,

176 'What are we accusing them of?
177 Their work was heavy, their distress was much!

178 [Every day] . [. . . . . . . . . .] . . .
179 [The lamentation was] heavy, [we could] hear the noise.

180 . . .] . to do
181 . . . assigned] tasks

* * * * *

---

*qar ana a-ḫi-šu* $^{d}$*a-nu* **169** K: $^{d}$*en-líl i-ta-*× [ L: ] × × × mu × × [ M: *i*]*s-*⌜*sà*⌝*-aq-qar ana a-ḫi-šu* $^{d}$*a-nu* **170** K: *e-tel-li* M: *-m*]*a-mi* **177** K: ⌜*du*⌝*-ul-*[

The last eleven lines, obtained from the Late Assyrian fragments, have been numbered and organized as continuing the Old Babylonian **A**, since they overlap it where it is preserved at the bottom of column iii. Column ii of the Old Babylonian **G** has a speech assigned to Ea which begins like 176 ff., but then diverges. The differences are recensional, but it is quite possible that in the main recension Ea spoke after Anu and repeated some of his words before making the suggestion about the creation of man.

## K 8562 (S), Column ii

1 trace
2 *lu-*× [. . .
3 *at-t*[*a* . . .
4 *li-q*[*í* . . .
5 *áš-bu-ma* [$^{d}$*a-nun-na-ki ma-ḫar-ka*]
6 *áš-bat* $^{d}$*be-let-i*[*lī*$^{meš}$ *šà-as-su-ru*]
7 *ištēn ši-si-ma* *i-d*[*i-šu tam-ta*]

---

8 $^{d}$*a-nu pâ-šú īpuša*$^{ša}$ *i-qab-bi izzakar* (MU) [*ana* . . .
9 $^{d}$*nusku pi-te bāb-ka*: $^{giš}$*kakkī*$^{meš}$*-ka* [*li-qí* . . .
10 *i-na puḫri šá ilāni*$^{meš}$ *rabûti*$^{meš}$: *ki-m*[*is* . . .
11 *qí-ba-šu-nu-ti* [. . .
12 *iš-pu-ra-an-ni* $^{d}$*a-*[*num abī-ku-nu*]
13 *ma-lik-ku-nu q*[*u-ra-du* $^{d}$*en-líl*]
14 traces

* * * * *

## BM 78257 (G), Column ii

1 $^{d}$*é-a pa-a-šu* ⌜*i*⌝-[*pu-ša-am-ma*]
2 *is-sà-qar a-na ilī*$^{meš}$ *a*[*ḫ-ḫi-šu*]

3 *mi-nam kar-ṣí-šu-nu ni-i*[*k-ka-al*]
4 *ka-bi-it du-ul-la-šu-u*[*n* *ma-a-ad ša-ap-ša-qum*]

5 *u*$_4$*-mi-ša-am-ma ir-ṣi-*× [. . .
6 *tu-uk-kum ka-b*[*i-it* . . .

7 *i-ba-aš-ši* × [. . .
8 *wa-aš-ba-at* $^{d}$[*be-le-et-ì-lí šà-as-su-ru*]

9 *li-ib-ni-ma lu-u*[*l-la-a a-wi-lam*]
10 *ab-ša-nam li-bi-i*[*l* . . .

If this is correct, Ea will be the speaker where the main recension sets in again. The obverse of the Late Assyrian V substantially duplicates the latter part of Ea's speech on the Old Babylonian **G**, so these two portions are given here. First, however, column ii of the Assyrian Recension S is interposed, since this offers a third recension, by which the proposal to slaughter a god is followed by a further trip of Nusku to the rebels.

## K 8562 (S), Column ii

3 You [. . .
4 Take [. . .
5 [While the Anunnaki] are present [before you],
6 And while Bēlet-ilī, [the birth-goddess], is present,
7 Summon one and do [him to death].

---

8 Anu opened his mouth to speak, addressing [. . .
9 'Nusku, open your gate, [take] your weapons [. . .
10 In the assembly of the great gods bow down [. . .
11 Speak to them [. . .
12 "Anu [your father] has sent me,
13 Also your counsellor, [the warrior Enlil],

* * * * *

## BM 78257 (**G**), Column ii

1 Ea [opened] his mouth
2 And addressed the gods [his brothers],

3 'What are we [accusing] them of?
4 Their work was heavy, [the distress was much]!

5 Every day . . . [. . .
6 The lamentation was heavy [. . .

7 There is/was . [. . .
8 While [Bēlet-ilī, the birth-goddess, is present],

9 Let her create *Lullû*-[man] .
10 Let him bear the yoke [. . .

11 [*ab-š*]*a-n*[*am l*]*i-bi-i*[*l* . . .
12 [*šu-up-ši*]*-ku ili* [*a-wi-lum li-iš-ši*]

13 [× ×] × × × [ 14 broken away. 15 trace.
16 *a*]*b-ša-n*[*am* 17–18 traces.

* * * * *

## K 6634 (V), Obverse

1 *áš-bat* $^{d}$*be-le-et-ì-lí sa-as-*[*su-ru*]
2 *sa-as-su-ru* lú.u$_x$.l[u-*a li-ib-ni-ma*]
3 *tu-up-ši-ik-ku i-li* ⸢*a*⸣-[*me-lu liš-ši*]
4 *li-ib-ni-ma* lú.⸢u$_x$⸣.[lu-*a a-me-lu*]
5 ⸢*ab-šá-a*⸣*-nam li-bi-i*[*l* . . .
6 [*ab-šá-a-n*]*am li-bi-i*[*l* . . .
7 trace

* * * * *

E

188 . . .] × ×
189 *wa-aš-*⸢*ba-at*⸣ $^{d}$*b*[*e-le-et-ì-lí šà-as-s*]*ú-ru*

190 [*š*]*à-as-sú-ru li-gim?-ma?-a* ⸢*li*⸣*-ib-ni-ma*
191 *šu-up-ši-ik ilim a-wi-lum li-iš-ši*

192 *il-ta-am is-sú-ú i-ša-lu*
193 *tab-sú-ut ilī*$^{meš}$ *e-ri-iš-tam* $^{d}$*ma-mi*

194 *at-ti-i-ma šà-as-sú-ru ba-ni-a-*⸢*at*⸣ *a-wi-lu-ti*
195 *bi-ni-ma lu-ul-la-a li-bi-il*$_5$ *ab-ša-nam*

196 *ab-ša-nam li-bi-il ši-pí-ir* $^{d}$*en-líl*
197 *šu-up-ši-ik ilim a-wi-lum li-iš-ši*

198 $^{d}$*nin-tu pí-a-ša te-pu-*[*š*]*a-am-ma*
199 *is-sà-qar a-na ilī*$^{meš}$ *ra-bu-ti*

200 *it-ti-ia-ma la na-ṭú a-na e-pé-ši*
201 *it-ti* $^{d}$*en-ki-ma i-ba-aš-ši ši-ip-ru*

202 *šu-ú-ma* ⸢*ú-ul*⸣*-la-*[*a*]*l ka-la-ma*
203 *ṭi-iṭ-ṭa-am li-id-di-nam-ma a-na-ku lu-pu-uš*

204 $^{d}$*en-ki pí-a-šu i-pu-ša-am-ma*
205 *is-sà-qar a-na ilī*$^{meš}$ *ra-bu-ti*

206 *i-na ar-ḫi se-bu-ti ù ša-pa-at-ti*
207 *te-li-il-tam lu-ša-aš-ki-in ri-im-ka*

11 Let him bear the yoke [. . .
12 [Let man carry the] toil of the gods.

*    *    *    *    *

## K 6634 (V), Obverse

1 While Bēlet-ilī, the birth-goddess, is present,
2 Let the birth-goddess [create] *Lullû*.
3 [Let man carry] the toil of the gods,
4 Let her create *Lullû*-[man].
5 Let him bear the yoke [. . .
6 Let him bear the yoke [. . .

*    *    *    *    *

189 While [Bēlet-ilī, the birth-goddess], is present,

190 Let the birth-goddess create offspring (?),
191 And let man bear the toil of the gods.'

192 They summoned and asked the goddess,
193 The midwife of the gods, wise Mami,

194 'You are the birth-goddess, creatress of mankind,
195 Create *Lullû* that he may bear the yoke,

196 Let him bear the yoke assigned by Enlil,
197 Let man carry the toil of the gods.'

198 Nintu opened her mouth
199 And addressed the great gods,

200 'It is not possible for me to make things,
201 Skill lies with Enki.

202 Since he can cleanse everything
203 Let him give me the clay so that I can make it.'

204 Enki opened his mouth
205 And addressed the great gods,

206 'On the first, seventh, and fifteenth day of the month
207 I will make a purifying bath.

E

A 208 *ilam iš-te-en li-iṭ-bu-ḫu-ma*
209 *li-te-el-li-lu ilū*$^{meš}$ *i-na ṭi-⌜i⌝-bi*

210 *i-na ši-ri-šu ù da-mi-šu*
211 $^{d}$*nin-tu li-ba-al-li-il ṭi-iṭ-ṭa*

212 *i-lu-um-ma ù a-wi-lum*
*li-ib-ta-al-li-lu* 213 *pu-ḫu-ur i-na ṭi-iṭ-ṭi*

214 *aḫ-ri-a-ti-iš u*$_4$*-mi up-pa i ni-iš-me*
215 *i-na ši-i-ir i-li e-ṭe-em-mu li-ib-ši*

216 *ba-al-ṭa it-ta-šu li-še-di-⌜šu⌝-ma*
217 *aš-šu la mu-uš-ši-i e-ṭe-em-mu li-ib-ši*

218 *i-na pu-úḫ-ri i-pu-lu a-an-na*
219 *ra-bu-tum* $^{d}$*a-nun-na* 220 *pa-qí-du ši-ma-ti*

221 *i-na ar-ḫi se-bu-ti ù ša-pa-at-ti*
222 *te-li-il-tam ú-ša-aš-⌜ki⌝-in ri-im-ka*

223 $^{d}$*we-e-i-la ša i-šu-⌜ú⌝ ṭe*$_4$*-e-ma*
224 *i-na pu-úḫ-ri-šu-nu iṭ-ṭa-ab-ḫu*

O 225 *i-na ši-ri-šu ù da-mi-šu*
226 $^{d}$*nin-tu ú-⌜ba⌝-li-il ṭi-iṭ-ṭa*

227 *aḫ-ri-a-t[i-iš u*$_4$*-mi up-pa iš-mu]-⌜ú⌝*
228 *i-na ši-i-ir i-li e-ṭe-[em-mu ib-ši]*

229 *ba-al-ṭa it-ta-šu ú-še-di-š[u-ma]*
230 *aš-šu la mu-uš-ši-i e-ṭe-em-mu [ib-ši]*

231 *iš-tu-ma ib-lu-la ṭi-ṭa ša-⌜ti⌝*
232 *is-si* $^{d}$*a-nun-na i-li ra-bu-⌜ti⌝*

233 $^{d}$*i-gi-gu i-lu ra-bu-tum*
234 *ru-u'-tam id-du-ú e-lu ṭi-iṭ-ṭi*

235 *[*$^{d}$*m]a-mi pí-a-ša te-pu-ša-am-ma*
236 *[is-s]à-qar a-na i-li ra-bu-tim*

P

237 *[ši-i]p-ra ta-aq-bi-a-ni-im-ma* 238 *ú-ša-ak-li-il*
239 *i-lam ta-aṭ-bu-ḫa qá-du ṭe*$_4$*-mi-šu*

240 *ka-ab-tam du-ul-la-ku-nu ⌜ú-ša-as⌝-sí-ik*
241 *šu-up-ši-ik-ka-ku-nu a-wi-[l]am e-mi-id*

**209** A: *i-l]u* **211** E: *li-ba-li-il* **212** E: *ilum-ma* **215** E: *⌜ši-ir⌝ ilim* PI-*ṭe-em-mu lib-ši* **217** E: PI-*ṭe-em-mu l[ib-* **226** O: + ] *à-wi-l[um]*; ] *ṭi-iṭ-ṭ[i]* (cf. 212–13) **227** O: *ú-še-eš-m[e]* **228** O: om. **229** O: *ú-še-di-š[u]*

208 Let one god be slaughtered
209 So that all the gods may be cleansed in a dipping.

210 From his flesh and blood
211 Let Nintu mix clay,

212 That god and man
213 May be thoroughly mixed in the clay,

214 So that we may hear the drum for the rest of time
215 Let there be a spirit from the god's flesh.

216 Let it proclaim living (man) as its sign,
217 So that this be not forgotten let there be a spirit.'

218 In the assembly answered 'Yes'
219 The great Anunnaki, who administer destinies.

221 On the first, seventh, and fifteenth day of the month
222 He made a purifying bath.

223 Wê-ila, who had personality,
224 They slaughtered in their assembly.

225 From his flesh and blood
226 Nintu mixed clay.

227 For the rest [of time they heard the drum],
v 228 From the flesh of the god [there was] a spirit.

229 It proclaimed living (man) as its sign,
230 And so that this was not forgotten [there was] a spirit.

231 After she had mixed that clay
232 She summoned the Anunnaki, the great gods.

233 The Igigi, the great gods,
234 Spat upon the clay.

235 Mami opened her mouth
236 And addressed the great gods,

237 'You commanded me a task, I have completed it;
239 You have slaughtered a god together with his personality.

240 I have removed your heavy work,
241 I have imposed your toil on man.

---

**230** O: *e-ṭem-m*[*u*] **231–3** O: *ṭ*]*i-ṭa-a-š̌*[*a*]; [d]]⌜*i*⌝-*gi*$_4$-*g*[*i*$_4$]; *ra-b*]*u-t*[*um*] **237–40** P: ] × × [×]; ] ⌜*ú*⌝-*ul-la-d*[*u*]; ] *a-me-lu-tim*

AP

242 *ta-aš-ta-'i-ṭa ri-ig-ma a-na ⌜a-wi-lu⌝-ti*
243 *ap-ṭú-ur ul-la an-du-ra-[ra aš-ku-u]n*

244 *iš-mu-ma an-ni-a-am qá-ba-ša*
245 *id-da-ar-ru-ma ú-na-aš-ši-qú še-pi-ša*

246 *pa-na-mi* $^{d}$*ma-mi ni-ša-si-ki*
247 *i-na-an-na be-le-[et] ka-la i-li* 248 *lu-ú š[u-um]-ki*

249 *i-te-er-bu a-na bīt ši-im-ti*
250 *ni-iš-š[i-ku]* $^{d}$*é-a e-riš-tu* $^{d}$*ma-ma*

251 *š[à-a]s-su-ra-a-tum pu-úḫ-ḫu-ra-ma*
252 *[ṭi-i]ṭ-ṭa i-kab-ba-sa-am ma-aḫ-ri-ša*

253 *[ši]-⌜i⌝ ši-ip-ta it-ta-na-an-di*
254 *⌜ú⌝-šam-na-ši* $^{d}$*é-a a-ši-ib ma-aḫ-ri-ša*

255 *iš-tu-ma ig-mu-ru ši-pa-as-s*[$a_6$]
256 *[k]i-ir-ṣi* 14 *uk-ta-ar-ri-i[ṣ]*

257 ⌜7⌝ *ki-ir-ṣi a-na i-mi-it-t[i]*
258 ⌜7⌝ *ki-ir-ṣi a-na šu-me-li iš-k[un]*

259 *[i-na b]i-⌜ri-šu⌝-nu it-ta-di li-bit-t[i]*
260 . . .] × × *a-bu-un-na-ti* u[š] ×(×)

* * * * *

There is a gap in the main recension and the related late copies, but the Assyrian Recension fills this gap and overlaps a little at beginning and end.

## K 3399+3934 (S), Obverse iii

1 [$^{d}$*nin-ši-kù* $^{d}$]*é-a is-sà-qar*
2 . . .] × *ú-šám*$^{šá-am}$*-na-ši*
3 . . . *tam]-nu ši-ip-ta*
*iš-tu-ma tam-nu-ú ši-pa-sa*
4 *[qá-sa ta-at]-ta-di eli ṭí-iṭ-ṭí-šá*
5 [14 *kí-ir]-ṣi tàk-ri-iṣ*
7 *kí-ir-ṣi ana imitti*(zag) *taš-ku-un*
6 [7 *kí*]*-ir-ṣi ana šumēli*(gùb) *taš-ku-un*
*i-na be-ru-šu-nu i-ta-di libitta*
7 [. . . . *-d]a-a ap-pa-ri ba-ti*!*-iq a-bu-un-na-te tep-te-ši*

**242** P: *a-me-lu-tim* **243** P: *qá-d]u-um ṭè-mi-šu* **244** P: *qa-ba-ša* **246** P: $^{d}$*ma-m]a* **247, 248** P: *-l]et, lu šum-ki* **250** P: [$^{d}$*nin*]*-ši-kù* **7** Tablet: *ba-*RI*-iq*

242 You raised a cry for mankind,
243 I have loosed the yoke, I have established freedom.'

244 They heard this speech of hers,
245 They ran together and kissed her feet, (saying,)

246 'Formerly we used to call you Mami,
247 Now let your name be Mistress-of-All-the-Gods (Bēlet-kāla-ilī).'

249 They entered the house of destiny
250 Did prince Ea and the wise Mami.

251 With the birth-goddesses assembled
252 He trod the clay in her presence.

253 She kept reciting the incantation,
254 Ea, seated before her, was prompting her.

255 After she had finished her incantation
256 She nipped off fourteen pieces of clay.

257 Seven she put on the right,
258 Seven on the left.

259 Between them she placed the brick
260 . . .] . . the umbilical cord . . .

* * * * *

## K 3399+3934 (S), Obverse iii

1 [Prince] Ea spoke
2 . . .] . he was prompting her
3 . . . she] recited the incantation
After she had recited her incantation
4 [She] put [her hand out] to her clay.
5 She nipped off [fourteen] pieces of clay,
Seven she put on the right,
6 [Seven] she put on the left,
Between them she placed the brick.
7 [. .] . . hair (?), she . . . the cutter of the umbilical cord.

8 *[paḫ-r]a-ma er-še-te mu-te-ti*
9 [7] ⌜*ù*⌝ 7 *šà-su-ra-ti*
7 *ú-ba-na-a zikarī*(nitá$^{meš}$)
10 [7] *ú-ba-na-a sinnišāti*$^{meš}$
11 *[š]à-su-ru ba-na-at ši-im-tu*
12 *ši-na-šàm*$^{šá-na}$ *ú-ka-la-la-ši-na*
13 *ši-na-šàm*$^{šá-na}$ *ú-ka-la-la maḫ-ru-šá*
14 *ú-ṣu-ra-te šá niši*$^{meš}$*-ma* *ú-ṣa-ar* $^{d}$*ma-mi*

---

15 *i-na bīt a-li-te ḫa-riš-ti*
7 *ūmī*$^{meš}$ *li-na-di libittu*
16 *i tùk-ta-bit bēlet-ilī*(dingir.maḫ) *e-riš-ta* $^{d}$*ma-mi*
17 *šab-su-tu-um-ma ina bīt ḫa-riš-ti li-iḫ-du*
18 *ak-ki a-li-it-tu ú-la-du-ma*
19 *ummi šèr-ri* *lu-ḫar-ri-šá ra-ma-an-[šá]*
20 *[z]i-ka-ru* ⌜*a-na*⌝ *[ardate]*
21 [×] × el li × [. . .

* * * * *

E
271 . . .] × × [× ×]
272 . . .] *i-ir-ti-ša*
273 . . .]-*ti*? *zi-iq-nu*
274 . . .] × *li-it eṭ-li*
275 . . . *ib]-ra-ti ù šu-li-i*
276 . . .]-*ti*-ši *aš-ša-tum ù mu-us-sà*
277 *[šà-as-s]ú-ra-tum pu-uḫ-ḫu-ra-ma*
278 *[wa-aš-ba]-at* $^{d}$*nin-tu* 279 *[i-ma]-an-nu ar-ḫi*
A 280 *[si-ma-nu] ši-ma-ti* *is-sú-ú eš-ra arḫa*
281 *eš-ru arḫu il-li-ka-am-ma*
282 *[ḫ]a-lu-up pa-le-e* *si-li-tam ip-te*
283 *[n]a-am-ru-ma ḫa-du-ú pa-nu-ša*
284 *u'-pu-ur ka-aq-qá-as-sà* 285 *ša-ab-su-ta-am i-pu-uš*
P 286 *[q]á-ab-li-ša i-te-zi-iḫ* 287 *i-ka-ar-ra-ab*
288 *i-ṣi-ir qé-ma* *ù li-bi-it-ta id-di*
289 *a-na-ku-mi ab-ni* *i-pu-ša qá-ta-ia*
290 *ša-[ab]-sú-tum i-na bi-it qá-di-iš-ti li-iḫ-du*
291 *a-li a-li-it-tum ú-ul-la-du-ma*
292 *um-mi še-er-ri* 293 *ú-ḫ[a-ar]-ru-ú ra-ma-an-ša*

**14** cf. R 5 **285** E: RU(error for *šà*)-*ab*-⌜*su*⌝-*ta*!-*am* **289** P: *qá-ta-a*-⌜*a*⌝
**290** E: *tab-sú-tum* **291** P: ]-*la-du-ú-m[a]* **293** E: *ú-ḫa[r]-ru-ú* P: *ra-ma-an-šá*

8 The wise and learned
9 Twice seven birth-goddesses had assembled,
Seven produced males,
10 [Seven] produced females.
11 The birth-goddess, creatress of destiny—
12 They completed them in pairs,
13 They completed them in pairs in her presence,
14 Since Mami conceived the regulations for the human race.

---

15 In the house of the pregnant woman in confinement
Let the brick be in place for seven days,
16 That Bēlet-ilī, the wise Mami, may be honoured.
17 Let the midwife rejoice in the house of the woman in confinement,
18 And when the pregnant woman gives birth
19 Let the mother of the babe sever herself.
20 The man to [the young lady]
21 [.] . . . . [. . .

* * * * *

272 . . .] her breasts
273 . . .] . beard
274 . . .] . the cheek of the young man
275 . . .] open air shrine and street
276 . . .] . . wife and her husband.

277 The birth-goddesses were assembled
278 And Nintu [sat] counting the months.

280 [At the] destined [moment] the tenth month was summoned.
vi 281 The tenth month arrived
282 And the elapse of the period opened the womb.

283 With a beaming, joyful face
284 And covered head she performed the midwifery.

286 She girded her loins as she pronounced the blessing,
288 She drew a pattern in meal and placed the brick,

289 'I have created, my hands have made it.
290 Let the midwife rejoice in the prostitute's house.

291 Where the pregnant woman gives birth
292 And the mother of the babe severs herself,

AE P

294 9 $u_4$-[mi l]i-in-na-di li-bi-it-tum
295 i tu-uk-t[a]-bi-it $^{d}$nin-tu sa-as-sú-ru

296 $^{d}$ma-m[i ×] ×-sú-nu i-ta-ab-bi
297 i-t[a-ad s]a-as-sú-ra 298 i-ta-ad ke-ša

299 i-na [. . . .] × na-de-e e-er-ši
300 li-⸢i'⸣-ti-[lu aš-ša]-tum ù mu-sà

301 i-nu-ma! ⟨a-na⟩ aš-š[u-ti] ù mu-tu-ti
302 i-na bi-it [e-mi ra-bé]-⸢e⸣ i-ta-'i-du iš-tar

303 9 $u_4$-mi [li-iš-š]a-ki-in ḫi-du-tum
304 iš-tar [li-it-ta-a]b-bu-ú $^{d}$iš-ḫa-ra

305 i-na [. . . . . .]×-ti si-ma-nu ši-im-ti
306 . . . -t]a-ab-bi-×

307 . . .] × ir × × [. . .
308 trace

* * * * *

319 × [. . .
320 r[i- . . .
321 [. . .
322 $^{d}$[. . .
323 [. . .
324 ú-× [. . .
325 × [. . .
326 [. . .
327 ⸢i⸣-[. . .
328 a-wi-lum [. . .
329 zu-uk-ki mu-ša-[ab . . .
330 ma-ru a-na a-bi-[šu . . .
331 × gi iš × [. . .
332 ⸢it-ta⸣-aš-bu-ma n[i . . .
333 šu-ú na-ši × [. . .
334 i-mu-ur-ma [. . .
335 $^{d}$en-líl × [× ×]-ar i-[. . .
336 i-ta-aṣ-ṣú-la qá-ti × × [(×)] ×
337 al-li ma-ar-ri ib-nu-ú eš-[re]-ti
338 i-ki ib-nu-ú ra-bu-t[im]

**294** P: li-bit-tum **295** E: -t]ab-bi-it $^{d}$be-le-et-ì-lí P: ]-as-su-ru
**296** E: i-tab-bi **298** P: ke-e-šá **A**: ke-T[A]-am-DIŠ **299** EP: giš.ná
**300** E: mu-⸢us-sà⸣ **301** Tablet (**A**): i-nu-ZU

294 Let the brick be in place for nine days,
295 That Nintu, the birth-goddess, may be honoured.'

296 Without ceasing proclaim Mami their [.] .
297 Without ceasing praise the birth-goddess, praise Kesh!

299 When [. . . .] . the bed is laid
300 Let the wife and her husband lie together.

301 When, to institute marriage,
302 They heed Ištar in the house of [the father-in-law],

303 Let there be rejoicing for nine days,
304 Let them call Ištar Išḫara.

305 . . [. . . .] . . at the destined moment

* * * * *

328 A man [. . .
329 Cleanse the dwelling (?) [. . .
330 The son to [his] father [. . .
331 . . . [. . .
332 They sat and . [. . .
333 He was carrying . [. . .
vii 334 He saw and [. . .
335 Enlil . [. .] . . [. . .
336 Were becoming stiff . . . .[.] .
337 With picks and spades they built the shrines,
338 They built the big canal banks.

---

**301–2** P: (-*t*]*u-ú-tim*, -*d*]*u* dingir.maḫ) places between 295 and 296 **303** P: *liš-*⸢*šá*⸣-[
**304** P: *l*]*i-ib-bu-*[*ú* **306** P: ] × tu × [

**A**

339 *bu-bu-ti-iš ni-ši* *ti-i-ti-iš* [*i-li*]
340 . . .] × li [. . . . .]
341 a-[. . .
342 . . .] × × [. . . . . . .] pa ×
343 . . .] *šu*-×-[*t*]*im*
344 . . .] *šu*-[(×)]-*nu*
345 . . .] li × ×
346 . . .] × × ši
347 . . . *d*]*i*/*k*]*i-il*
348 . . .] li × × [× (×)] ×-*am-na*
349 . . .] × *ka-an* [× (×)] ×-*ša*
350 . . .]-*na-an-na*
350*a*[1] . . .] × la ×
351 . . . *š*]*e-er-ra*

352 [*ú-ul il-li-ik-ma* 600].600 mu.ḫi.a
353 [*ma-tum ir-ta-pí-iš*] *ni-šu im-ti-da*

354 *m*[*a-tum ki-ma li*]-⸢*i i-ša*⸣-*ab-bu*
355 *i-na* [*ḫu-bu-ri-ši-na*] *i-lu* ⸢*it*⸣-*ta*-⸢*a*'-*da*⸣-*ar*

356 [$^{d}$*en-líl iš-te-me*] *ri*-⸢*gi-im*⸣-*ši-in*
357 [*is-sà-qar a*]-*na i-li* ⸢*ra*⸣-*bu-tim*

358 [*ik-ta-ab-ta*] ⸢*ri-gi-im*⸣ *a-wi-lu-ti*
359 [*i-na ḫu-bu-ri-ši*]-*na ú-za*-⸢*am*⸣-*ma ši-it-ta*

360 . . . *šu-r*]*u-up-pu-ú li-ib*-⸢*ši*⸣
361 . . .] × × *ši-n*[*a*] × × ×

362 × [. . . . . . .] × × × [. . .]
363 *li*-× [. . .

364 *ù šu*-[*ú* $^{I}$*at-ra-am-ḫa-si-is*]
365 *il-šu* $^{d}$*en-ki ú-ba*-[*as-sa-ar*]

366 *i-ta-mu i*[*t-ti i-li-šu*]
367 *ù šu-ú il-šu it-t*[*i-šu i-ta-mu*]

368 $^{I}$*at-ra-am-ḫa-si-is* ⸢*pí-a*⸣-[*šu i-pu-ša-am-ma*]
369 *is-sà-qar a-na be*-[*lí-šu*]

[1] Note: the remains at the right of the column between lines 340 and 350 show one more line than the ten-marks at the left of the column permit, so that one of these 'lines' must be an overrun. Since the overrun cannot be identified, the numbering is consecutive' and 350*a* accounts for the extra 'line'.

339 For food for the peoples, for the sustenance of [the gods]

*    *    *    *    *

352 Twelve hundred years [had not yet passed]
353 [When the land extended] and the peoples multiplied.

354 The [land] was bellowing [like a bull],
355 The god got disturbed with [their uproar].

356 [Enlil heard] their noise
357 [And addressed] the great gods,

358 'The noise of mankind [has become too intense for me],
359 [With their uproar] I am deprived of sleep.

360 . . .] let there be plague
361 . . .] . . . . . . .

362 . [. . . . .] . . . [. . .]
363 . . [. . .'

364 Now [Atra-ḫasīs]
365 Was informing his god Enki.

366 He spoke [with his god]
367 And his god [spoke] with him.

368 Atra-ḫasīs [opened] his mouth
369 And addressed [his] lord,

---

**352–9**: restored from II. i. 1–8. A differing recension from this point onwards is offered by S, see pp. 106–14. **360** ff. cf. V rev.: *šu-ru*]*-up-pu-u* [; ] *li-ik-* × [; *ri-g*]*im-ši-na ki-m*[*a*; *š*]*u-ru-up-pu-u* [

A

370 *a-di-ma-mi ib-*[. . .
371 *mu-ur-ṣa i-im-mi-du-ni-a-ti a-*[*na da-ri*]

372 $^{d}$*en-ki pí-a-šu i-pu-ša-a*[*m-ma*]
373 *is-sà-qar a-na ar-di-*[*šu*]

374 *š*[*i*]*-bu-ti si-*[*m*]*a-ni-*⸢*i*⸣
375 ⸢*ú*⸣?-[*r*]*a*? *ni-a qí-ri-*⸢*ib*⸣ *bi-ti mil-k*[*a*]

376 [*qí-b*]*a-ma-mi li-i*[*s-s*]*u-ú na-gi-ru*
377 *ri-*[*ig*]*-ma li-*[*še*]*-eb-bu-*⸢*ú i-na ma-tim*⸣

378 *e t*[*a*]*-ap-la-ḫa* ⸢*i*⸣*-li-ku-un*
379 *e tu-*[*sa*]*-al-li-a* [*i*]*š-ta-ar-ku-un*

380 ⸢*nam-ta*⸣*-r*[*a*] *ši-a ba-ab-šu*
381 *bi-*⸢*la e-pí-ta a-na*⸣ *qú-ud-mi-šu*

382 *li-il-li-ik-šu ma-as-ḫa-tum ni-q*[*ú-ú*]
383 *li-ba-aš-ma i-na* ⸢*ka-at*⸣*-*[*re-e*] 384 *li-ša-*⸢*aq-qí-il qá-as*⸣*-sú*

385 $^{I}$*at-ra-am-ḫa-si-is il-*⸢*qí-a*⸣ *te-er-tam*
386 *ši-bu-ti ú-pa-aḫ-ḫi-ir a-*⸢*na*⸣ *ba-bi-šu*

387 $^{I}$*at-ra-am-ḫa-si-is pí-a-šu* [*i*]*-p*[*u-ša-am-ma*]
388 [*is*]*-sà-*⸢*qar*⸣ *a-na ši-bu-*[*ti*]

389 *ši-bu-ti si-*[*m*]*a-ni-*⸢*i*⸣
390 [*ú*?*-ra*? *a-ni-a qí-ri-ib bi*]*-ti* ⸢*mil-ka*⸣

391 [*qí-ba-ma li-is*]*-*⸢*su*⸣*-ú na-gi-ru*
392 [*ri-ig-ma li-še-e*]*b-bu-ú i-na ma-tim*

393 [*e ta-ap-la-ḫa*] ⸢*i-li-ku*⸣*-un*
394 [*e tu-sa-al-l*]*i-a i*[*š-tar-k*]*u-un*

395 [*nam-ta-ra ši-a*] *ba-*⸢*ab*⸣*-šu*
396 [*bi-la e-pí-ta a-na q*]*ú-ud-mi-ša*

397 [*li-i*]*l-li-ik-šu ma-as-ḫa-tum n*[*i-qú-ú*]
398 [*li*]*-ba-aš-ma i-na ka-at-re-e* 399 [*li-š*]*a-aq-qí-il qá-*⸢*as-sú*⸣

400 [*ši-b*]*u-tum iš-mu-ú sí-q*[*í-ir-šu*]
401 [*n*]*am-ta-ra i-na a-*[*li* 402 *i*]*b-nu-ú bi-*[*is-sú*]

403 [*iq*]*-bu-ma is-su-ú* [*na-gi-ru*]
404 [*ri-i*]*g-ma ú-še-eb-b*[*u-ú i-na ma-tim*]

405 [*ú-ul*] *ip-la-ḫu i-*[*li-šu-un*]
406 [*ú-ul*] *ú-se-el-lu-ú* [*iš-tar-šu-un*]

370 'So long as . [. . .
371 Will they impose disease on us [for ever]?'

372 Enki opened his mouth
373 And addressed his slave,

374 'The elders . . . .
375 . . . . counsel in the house,

376 "[Command] that heralds proclaim,
377 And make a loud noise in the land,

378 'Do not reverence your gods,
379 Do not pray to your goddesses,

380 But seek the door of Namtara
381 And bring a baked (loaf) in front of it.

382 The offering of sesame-meal may be pleasing to him,
383 Then he will be put to shame by the gift and will lift his hand.'"'

385 Atra-ḫasīs received the command
386 And gathered the elders to his gate.

387 Atra-ḫasīs opened his mouth
388 And addressed the elders,

389 'Elders . . . .
viii 390 [. . . .] counsel [in] the house,

391 [Command] that heralds proclaim,
392 And make a loud [noise] in the land,

393 "[Do not reverence] your gods,
394 [Do not] pray to your [goddesses],

395 [But seek] the door of [Namtara],
396 [And bring a baked (loaf)] in front of it.

397 The offering of sesame-meal may be pleasing to him,
398 Then he will be put to shame by the gift and will lift his hand."'

400 The elders hearkened to [his] words,
401 They built a temple for Namtara in the city.

403 They commanded and [heralds] proclaimed,
404 They made a loud noise [in the land],

405 They did [not] reverence their gods,
406 They did [not] pray to [their goddesses],

A

407 [*nam-ta*]-*ra* ⌜*i*⌝-*ši*-⌜*ú*⌝ [*ba-ab-šu*]
408 [*ub-lu*] ⌜*e*⌝-*pí-tam a-na qú-ud-m*[*i-šu*]

Q

409 [*i-il-li-i*]*k-šu ma-as-ḫa-tum ni*-[*qú-ú*]
410 [*i-ba-aš-m*]*a i-na ka-at-r*[*e-e* 411 *ú-ša-aq-q*]*í-il qá-as-su*

412 [*šu-ru-up-pu-ú i-te-z*]*i-ib-ši-na-ti*
413 . . .]-*na it*-⌜*tu-ru*⌝

414 . . .] × ru ×
415 × am ku × [. . .] × [. . .]

416 [*ú*]-*ul il*-⟨*li*⟩-*ik*-[*ma*] 600.600 m[u.ḫi.a]

**411** Q: ]-*qil qa-as-su* **412** Q: -*z*]*i-ib-ši-na-a-ti* **413–15** Q: ] *it*-UD-*ru*; ] × *ri-gim-ši-na*; ] *it-tu-ru*; ] *u ne-e-ši*; ] ×-*ni sar-ru* **416** Q: ] × *šá-na-a-tim*

407 But they sought [the door] of Namtara
408 And [brought] a baked (loaf) in front of [it].

409 The offering of sesame-meal was pleasing to him,
410 [He was put to shame] by the gift and lifted his hand.

412 [Plague] left them
413 . . .] . they returned.

414 . . .] . . .
415. . . . [. . .] . [. . .]

416 Twelve hundred years had not yet passed

# TABLET II

## Column i: **B** 1–20, **D** 2–23, Q 1–13

i 1 *ú-ul il-⸢li⸣-ik-m[a]* ⸢600.600⸣ mu.ḫi.a
2 *ma-tum ir-ta-pí-iš* *ni-š[u im]-ti-da*

3 *[m]a-tum ki-ma li-i i-ša-ab-bu*
4 *[i-n]a ḫu-bu-ri-ši-na i-lu it-ta-aʾ-da-ar*

5 *[$^{d}$en-l]íl iš-te-me ri-gi-im-ši-in*
6 *is-sà-qar a-na i-li ra-bu-tim*

7 *ik-ta-ab-ta ri-gi-im a-wi-lu-ti*
8 *i-na ḫu-bu-ri-ši-na ú-za-am-ma ši-it-ta*

9 *[p]u-ur-sa a-na ni-ši te-i-ta*
10 *[a-n]a ⸢bu⸣-bu-ti-ši-na li-wi-ṣú ša-am-mu*

11 *zu-un-ni-šu $^{d}$adad li-ša-aq-qí-il*
12 *ša!-ap!-li!-iš a-ii-il-li-ka* [13] *mi-lu i-na na-aq-bi*

14 *li-il-li-ik ša-ru* [15] *ka-aq-qá-ra li-e-er-ri*
16 *er-pé-e-tum li-iḫ-ta-an-ni-ba* [17] *ti-ku a-ii-it-tu-uk*

18 *⸢li⸣-iš-šu-ur eqlu iš-pí-ki-šu*
19 *⸢li-te-ed-di⸣-li-ir-ta-ša $^{d}$nisaba*

20 *a-ii-ib-ši-ši-na-ši ri-iš-t[um]*
21 *lu-ú qú-ut-⸢tu⸣-ur ma-[. . . .]*

22 *a-ii-*[. . .] × [. . .
23 × × [. . .

Rest of column missing

*   *   *   *   *

The first seven lines of Column ii are also missing from the OB tablets, but the reverse of Sm 292 (Q) offers a late recension of the end of Column i and the beginning of Column ii, overlapping a little where the OB evidence sets in again.

**1** Q: ] × *šá-na-a-tim* **2** Q: $^{me}$]$^{š}$ *im-te-da* **4** Q: *il]āni*$^{meš}$ *it-tar-du*
**5–6** Q: *-a]n pu-ḫur-šú, il]āni ma-re-e-šú* (cf. S iv. 4–5) **7–12** cf. S iv. 40–5
**7** Q: ]*-ig-me a-me-lu-tim* **8** Q: *šit-tú* **9** **B**: *te-i-tam* Q: *ti-wi-tú*

# TABLET II

## Column i

1 Twelve hundred years had not yet passed
2 When the land extended and the peoples multiplied.

3 The land was bellowing like a bull,
4 The god got disturbed with their uproar.

5 Enlil heard their noise
6 And addressed the great gods,

7 'The noise of mankind has become too intense for me,
8 With their uproar I am deprived of sleep.

9 Cut off supplies for the peoples,
10 Let there be a scarcity of plant-life to satisfy their hunger.

11 Adad should withhold his rain,
12 And below, the flood should not come up from the abyss.

14 Let the wind blow and parch the ground,
16 Let the clouds thicken but not release a downpour,

18 Let the fields diminish their yields,
19 Let Nisaba stop up her breast.

20 There must be no rejoicing among them,
21 [. . . .] must be suppressed.

22 May there not [. . .

* * * * *

---

**10** **D**: *li*-ŠE-*ṣú* Q: *šam-ma* **11** Q: ]-*ni* **12** Tablets (**BD**): *ḫ*$^{i\text{-}pí}$*iš*
**13** Q: *na-aq-b*]*e* **18–19** cf. S iv. 46–7

## Column ii: **B** 8–9, 13–24, **D** 8–36, Q 1′–12

1′ . . .] ×
2′ . . .] × ⸢*i*⸣*-zi-ib*
3′ . . .] *ina a-la-ki*
4′ . . .] *be-lí-šú*
5′ . . .] *ana ḫa-la-qí*
6′ . . .] × *šip-ra-ši-na*
7′ . . .] ×*-ri-im-ma*
8′ . . . *a*]*l-ta-si*
9′ . . .] ×*-ú-ma*
10′ . . . *-b*]*a-šu*
11′ . . . *p*]*u-uḫ-ru*
12′ . . .] *ma-mi-tú*

13′ [*ši-bu-ti si-ma*]*-né-e*
14′ [*ú?-ra? a?-né?-'?* *qí-rib bi-tu*]*m mil-ki*

15′ [*qí-ba-ma li-is-su-ú*] *na-gi-ru*
8 *ri-*[*ig-ma li-še-eb-bu-ú*] *in ma-ti*

9 *e ta-ap-l*[*a-ḫa*] ⸢*e*⸣*-li-ku-un*
10 *e* ⸢*tu-sa*⸣*-al-li-*[*a iš-ta*]*r-ku-un*

11 $^{d}$*adad š*[*i-a ba-ab*]*-šú*
12 *bi-la e-pí-ta* [*a-na qú-ud-mi-š*]*ú*

13 *li-il-li-ik-šu* [*ma-as-ḫa-tum ni-qú-ú*]
14 *li-ba-aš-ma* [*i-na ka-a*]*t-re-*⸢*e*⸣ 15 *li-ša-aq-qí-*[*il*] *qá-as-su*

16 *i-na še-re-ti ib-ba-ra li-ša-az-ni-in*
17 *li-iš-ta-ar-ri-iq i-na mu-ši-im-ma* 18 *li-ša-az-ni-in na-al-ša*
19 *eqlu ki-ma ša-ar-ra-qí-tu* *šu-a li-iš-ši*

20 *ša* $^{d}$*adad i-na a-li* *ib-nu-ú bi-is-su*

21 *iq-bu-ma is-su-ú na-gi-ru*
22 *ri-ig-ma ú-še-eb-bu-ú i-na ma-tim*

23 *ú-ul ip-la-ḫu i-li-šu!-un*
24 [*ú-ul*] ⸢*ú-se-el*⸣*-lu-ú iš-tar-šu!-un*

25 [$^{d}$*adad i-š*]*i-ú ba-ab-šu*
26 [*ub-lu*] ⸢*e*⸣*-pí-ta a-na qú-ud-mi-šu*

**18 B**: *na-aš-*[*ša*] **23, 24** Tablet (**D**): -KU-*un*

## Column ii

2′ . . .] . left
3′ . . .] to go
4′ . . .] his lord
5′ . . .] to disappear
6′ . . .] . their work
7′ . . .] . . . .
8′ . . .] I shouted
9′ . . .] . . .
10′ . . .] . .
11′ . . .] assembly
12′ . . .] oath

13′ [. .] . . [elders]
14′ [. . . . .] counsel [in the house].

15′ '[Command that] heralds [proclaim],
8 [And make a loud] noise in the land,

9 "Do not reverence your gods,
10 Do not pray to your [goddesses],

11 But seek [the door of] Adad
12 And bring a baked (loaf) [in front of it].

13 [The offering of sesame-meal] may be pleasing to him,
14 Then he will be put to shame [by the] gift and will lift his hand.

16 He may rain down a mist in the morning
17 And may furtively rain down a dew in the night,
19 So that the fields will furtively bear grain."'

20 They built a temple for Adad in the city.

21 They commanded, and the heralds proclaimed
22 And made a loud noise in the land.

23 They did not reverence their gods,
24 They did [not] pray to their goddesses,

25 But they [sought] the door [of Adad],
26 [And brought] a baked (loaf) in front of it.

27 [i-il-li-i]k-šu ma-as-ḫa-tum ni-qú-ú
28 [i-ba]-aš-⸢ma⸣ i-na ka-at-re-e 29 [ú-š]a-aq-qí-il qá-as-su

30 [i-n]a ⸢še⸣-re-ti ib-ba-ra ú-ša-az-ni-in
31 ⸢iš-ta-ar-ri-iq⸣ i-na mu-ši-im-ma 32 [ú-š]a-a[z-ni-i]n na-al-ša

33 [eqlu ki-ma ša-ar-r]a-qí-tu šu-a iš-ši
34 . . . i-t]e-zi-ib-ši-na-ti
35 . . .]-ši-na it-tu-ru
36 . . .] × ú ri × × ×

Remainder of column lost

★ ★ ★ ★ ★

## Column iii (**D**)

1 . . .] × i ki/di
2 . . .] i-li-šu
3 [i-na] ×-li še-ep-šu iš-ku-un

4 [$u_4$]-mi-ša-am-ma ib-ta-na-ak-ki
5 [m]u-uš-ša-ak-ki i-za-ab-bi-il 6 [i-n]a še-re-ti

7 [×] ×-a i-li ta-mi-ma
8 [uz-na] i-ša-ak-ka-na i-na šu-na-a-ti

9 [× ×-a] $^{d}$en-ki ta-mi-ma
10 [uz-na i-š]a-ak-ka-na i-na šu-na-a-ti

11 . . .] bi-it i-li-šu
12 . . . u]š-⸢ša⸣-ab ib-ta-ak-ki

13 . . .] × × ⸢id-di⸣
14 . . . uš-š]a-ab ib-⸢ta⸣-ak-⸢ki⸣

15 i-[. . . . . . . . . . . . .] × ša-ḫu-ur-ra-at
16 i-na [. . . . . . . . . .] ×-a-šu iq-te

17 ši-i[d?- . . . . . . . . . .] × a-am-ru
18 is-sà-q[ar a-na . . . . . . . .] na-ri

19 li-il-q[í? . . . . . . . li-b]i-il na-ru
20 li-il-l[i?- . . . . . . . . . . . .]-ul-ti

21 a-na ma-aḫ-[. . . . . . . . . .]×-ia
22 li-mu-u[r . . . . . . . . . . . . .] ×

**4–5** cf. x rev. i. 13–14, y 11–12 **15** cf. S v. 33, x rev. i. 15, y 13 **17–33** cf. x rev. i. 17–31

27 The offering of sesame-meal was pleasing to him,
28 He was put to shame by the gift and lifted his hand.

30 In the morning he rained down a mist,
31 And furtively rained down a dew in the night.

33 [The fields] furtively bore grain,
34 . . . the famine (?)] left them.
35 . . .] their [. .] they returned.

* * * * *

## Column iii

2 . . .] of his god
3 [. .] . . he set his foot.

4 Every day he wept,
5 Bringing oblations in the morning.

7 He swore by [.] . . of the god,
8 Giving [attention] to dreams.

9 He swore by [. . .] of Enki,
10 Giving [attention] to dreams.

11 . . .] the temple of his god
12 . . .] seated, he wept.

13 . . .] . . put
14 . . .] seated, he wept.

15 . [. . . . . . . .] . was still
16 In [. . . . . .] . . . finished

17 . . [. . . . . .] . seen
18 Addressed [. . . .] of the river,

19 'Let the river take (?) [. . .] and bear away,
20 Let it . [. . . . . .] . .

21 To . . [. . . .] my [. . . .]
22 May he see [. . . . . . . . . .] .

23 li-iḫ-[. . . . . . . . . . . . .] ×
24 a-na-ku i-na mu-š[i . . .

25 iš-tu-ma i[š- . . .
26 pu-ti-iš na-ri [. . .

27 i-na ki!-ib-ri × [. . .
28 a-na ap-si-i ú-[. . .

29 iš-me-e-ma ᵈen-k[i a-wa-as-su]
30 a-na la-aḫ-mi ú-[. . .

31 a-wi-lum ša × [. . .
32 an-nu-ú-ma li-id-[. . .

33 al-ka-ma te-er-t[a . . .
34 ša-la × [. . .

35 × × [. . .

Remainder of column missing

*  *  *  *  *

## Column iv (**D**)

1 e-le-nu-um mi-[. . .
2 ša-ap-li-iš ú-ul i[l-li-ka]  3 mi-lu i-na na-aq-b[i]

4 ú-ul ul-da er-ṣe-tum re-e[m-ša]
5 ša-am-mu ú-ul ú-ṣi-a [. .]

6 ni-šu ú-ul am-ra-[(a)-ma]

7 ṣa-al-mu-tum ip-ṣú-ú ú-g[a-ru]
8 ṣe-ru pa-ar-ku  ma-li id-r[a-na]

9 iš-ti-ta ša-at-tam  i-ku-la la-a[r?-da?]
10 ša-ni-ta ša-at-tam  ú-na-ak-ki-ma! na-ak-ka-am-t[a]

11 ša-lu-uš-tum ša-at-tum il-li-k[a-am-ma]
12 i-na bu-bu-tim zi-mu-ši-na [it-ta-ak-ru]

13 ki-ma bu-uq-li ⸢ka⸣-at-[mu pa-nu-ši-in]
14 i-na ši-it-ku-ki na-pí-i[š-ti ba-al-ṭa]

15 ar-qú-tum am-ru pa-n[u-ši-in]
16 ⸢qá⸣-ad-di-iš i-il-la-ka ⸢i⸣-[na sú-qí]

**26** cf. S v. 32  **27** Tablet (**D**): DI-ib-ri  **4–5** cf. S iv. 58b–59 = v. 7b–8
**7–8** cf. S iv. 57b–58a = v. 6b–7a  **10** Tablet (**D**): ú-na-ak-ki-× [  **10–12** cf. S

23 May he [. . .
24 In the night I [. . .'

25 After he [. . .
26 Facing the river [. . .

27 On the bank [. . .
28 To the Apsû he [. . .

29 Enki heard [his words]
30 And [instructed] the water-monsters [as follows],

31 'The man who . [. . .
32 Let this being . [. . .

33 Go, the order [. . .
34 Ask . [. . .

* * * * *

## Column iv

1 Above . [. . .
2 Below, the flood did not [rise] from the abyss.

4 The womb of earth did not bear,
5 Vegetation did not sprout [. .]

6 People were not seen [. .]

7 The black fields became white,
8 The broad plain was choked with salt.

9 For one year they ate couch-grass (?);
10 For the second year they suffered the itch.

11 The third year came
12 [And] their features [were altered] by hunger.

13 [Their faces] were encrusted, like malt,
14 [And they were living] on the verge of death.

15 [Their] faces appeared green,
16 They walked hunched [in the street].

---

v. 12–14 = vi. 1–3 = vi. 4b–6 **13–14** cf. S v. 25–6 = vi. 14–15 **16–18** cf. S v. 15b–17

17 *ra-ap-šu-tum bu-da-ši-na* [*is-si-qá*]
18 *ar-*⌜*ku*⌝*-tum ma-az-za-zu-ši-na* [*ik-ru-ni*]

19 *ši-ip-ru* ⌜*il-qú-ú*⌝ [(×)] × × [. . .
20 *qú-ud-mi-iš* ta × [×] i × [. . .
21 *iz-za-az-zu-ma* pa/ú [×] an [. . .
22 *te-re-et* × × [. . .
23 [*q*]*ú-ud-mi-i*[*š* . . .
24 × at? × [. . .
25 [×] × × [. . .

Remainder of column missing

* * * * *

## Column v (**D**)

About the first 25 lines of the column missing

1 × za? × [. . .
2 *iq-bu-ú* × [. . .
3 *ed-lu-tum ú-ša*?-[. . .
4 *ú-*× [×] × × × [. . .
5 *i-na* 5 [×] × × × [. . .
6 × × [×] × × [. . .
7 *ed-lu-*[*t*]*i*[*m*] *i-za-*× [. . .
8 *sa-a*[*b-* . .] × [. . .
9 *ed-l*[*u-* . . .
10 *i-ba-a-ar* × [. . .
11 ×*-la-te ú-*[. . .
12 *ar-ma-na i-te-*× [. . .
13 *li-ib-ba-ti ma-l*[*i ša* $^{d}$*i-gi-gi*]

14 *ra-bu-tum-mi* $^{d}$*a-n*[*un-na ka-lu-ni*]
15 *ub-la pí-i-ni iš-ti-*[*ni-iš ur-tam*]

16 *iṣ-ṣú-ur a-nu* $^{d}$[*adad e-le-e-nu*]
17 ⌜*a-na-ku*⌝ *aṣ-ṣú-ur* *er-ṣ*[*e-tam ša-ap-li-tam*]

18 *a-ša-ar* $^{d}$*en-ki* [*il-li-ku-ma*]
19 *ip-ṭú-ur ul-l*[*a* *an-du-ra-ra iš-ku-un*]

20 *ú-*[*m*]*a-aš-š*[*e-er a-na ni-ši mi-še-er-tam*]
21 *iš-*[*k*]*u-un* × [×*-tam* *i-na aš-qú-la-lu ša-am-ši*]

iv **19–22** cf. S vi. 16–18

17 Their broad shoulders [became narrow],
18 Their long legs [became short].

19 The command which they received [.] . . [. . .
20 Before . . [.] . . [. . .
21 They were present and . . . [. . .
22 The decree [. . .
23 Before [. . .

* * * * *

## Column v

2 They commanded . [. . .
3 Barred . . [. . .
4 . . [.] . . . [. . .
5 In the fifth/five [.] . . . [. . .
6 . . [.] . . [. . .
7 Barred . . . [. . .
8 . . [. .] . [. . .
9 Barred [. . .
10 Was firm/Rebelled . [. . .
11 . . . . [. . .
12 A pomegranate (?) . . . [. . .
13 He was filled with anger [at the Igigi].

14 '[All we] great Anunnaki
15 Decided together [on a rule].

16 Anu and [Adad] guarded [the upper regions],
17 I guarded the [lower] earth.

18 Where Enki [went]
19 He loosed the yoke [and established freedom].

20 He let loose [abundance for the peoples],
21 He established . [. . in/from the . . . . of the sun].'

22 $^{d}$*en-líl pí-a-*⸢*šu i*⸣-[*pu-ša-am-ma*]
23 *a-na šukkalli* $^{d}$*nusku* [*is-sà-qar*]

24 še? na × [*ma-r*]*i li-ib-*[*bi-ku-nim*]
25 *li-*[*še-ri-b*]*u-ni a-na ma-aḫ-r*[*i-ia*]

26 še? na × *ma-ri ib-bi-ku-n*[*i-iš-šu*]
27 *is-sà-qar-šu-nu-ši qú-ra-du* $^{d}$[*en-líl*]

28 *ra-bu-tum-mi* $^{d}$*a-nun-na k*[*a-lu-ni*]
29 *ub-la pí-i-ni iš-ti-ni-iš ur-*[*ta-am*]

30 *iṣ-ṣú-ur a-nu* $^{d}$*adad e-le-*[*e-nu*]
31 *a-na-*⸢*ku*⸣ *aṣ-ṣú-ur* *er-ṣe-tam* ⸢*ša*⸣*-a*[*p-li-tam*]

32 *a-ša-ar a*[*t*]*-ta ta-a*[*l-li-ku-ma*]
1′ [*ta-ap-ṭú-ur ul-la* *an-du-ra-ra ta-aš-ku-un*]

2′ [*tu-ma-aš-še-er a-na ni-ši mi-še-er-tam*]
3′ [*ta-aš-ku-un* × ×*-tam* *i-na aš-qú-la-lu ša-am-ši*]

* * * * *

## Column vi (**D**)

About the first 25 lines of the column missing

1 . . .] *ti-a-am-tim*
2 . . .] × ši *a-na un-*[×]
3 . . .] × *šu-nu-ti*
4 . . .] × ir × × ×
5 . . .] *ur-ri* × × × ⸢*šu*⸣*-nu-ti*
6 . . .] × mu × × × *ur-tu*
7 . . .] × pa ⸢ru⸣ × × × r[i]
8 . . .] uš × × × *am-ma*
9 . . .] × i × [× ×(×)] ra
10 [*ú-ša-az-ni-i*]*n* $^{d}$*adad* ⸢*zu*⸣*-un-ni-šu*
11 . . .] *im-*⸢*lu*⸣*-ú ú-ga-ra*
12 [*ù*? *er*?*-p*]*é*?*-tum ú-ka-la-la* × × ×

13 [*la tu-ša*]*-ka-la-*⸢*nim*⸣ *te-ni-še-šu*
14 [*ù la t*]*e-ep-pí-ra-nim nu-ḫu-uš ni-ši* $^{d}$*nisaba*

15 [*i-lu*]*-ma i-ta-šu-uš a-ša-ba-am*
16 [*i-n*]*a pu-úḫ-ri ša i-li* *ṣi-iḫ-tum i-ku-ul-šu*

17 [$^{d}$*en-ki*] *i-ta-šu-uš a-ša-ba-am*
18 [*i-na pu-ú*]*ḫ-ri ša i-li* *ṣi-iḫ-tum i-ku-ul-šu*

22 Enlil [opened] his mouth
23 [And addressed] the vizier Nusku,

24 'Let them bring [to me] . . . [.] .
25 Let them [send] them into [my] presence.'

26 They brought [to him] . . . . .
27 And the warrior [Enlil] addressed them,

28 '[All we] great Anunnaki
29 Decided together on a rule.

30 Anu and Adad guarded the upper [regions],
31 I guarded the lower earth.

32 Where you [went]
1′ [You loosed the yoke and established freedom].

2′ [You let loose abundance for the peoples],
3′ [You established . . . in/from the . . . . of the sun].'

* * * * *

## Column vi

1 . . .] sea
2 . . .] . . to . [.]
3 . . .] . them
4 . . .] . . . . .
5 . . .] . . . . . them
6 . . .] . . . . . rule
7 . . .] . . . . . . .
8 . . .] . . . . . .
9 . . .] . . . [. . .] .
10 Adad [sent down] his rain
11 . . .] filled the fields
12 [And] the clouds (?) covered . . .

13 [Do not] feed his peoples,
14 [And do not] supply corn rations, on which the peoples thrive.'

15 [The god] got fed up with sitting,
16 [In] the assembly of the gods laughter overcame him.

17 [Enki] got fed up with sitting,
18 [In] the assembly of the gods laughter overcame him.

19 . . .] *te-*⌜*qí*⌝*-ta i-na qá-ti-šu*
20 . . .] ×*-mi-a* ×*-ti-šu*
21 . . .] *ša* ⌜*i-li*⌝ × × ud
22 . . .] × ⌜$^{d}$*en-ki ù* $^{d}$*en-líl*⌝

23 [*ra-bu-tum* $^{d}$*a-nun-n*]*a* [*ka-lu-ni*]
24 [*ub-la*] ⌜*pí-i-ni iš-ti*⌝*-*[*ni-iš ur-ta-am*]

25 [*iṣ-ṣ*]*ú-ur a-nu* $^{d}$*adad e-le-e-nu*
26 [*a-n*]*a-*⌜*ku aṣ-ṣú*⌝*-ur* *er-ṣe-tam ša-ap-*⌜*li*⌝*-tam*

27 [*a-ša*]*r at-ta ta-al-li-ku-ma*
28 [*ta-a*]*p-ṭú-ur ul-la* *an-du-ra-ra ta-aš-ku-un*

29 [*tu-m*]*a-aš-še-er a-na ni-ši mi-še-er-tam*
30 [*ta-aš-ku-un*] × ×*-tam* *i-na aš-qú-la-lu* ⌜*ša-am*⌝*-ši*

31 . . .] i še × × ×
32 . . . *q*]*ú-ra-*[*du*] $^{d}$*en-*⌜*líl*⌝

* * * * *

## Column vii: **B**: 37–54, **D**: 30–53

The first 29 lines of the column are missing

30 . . .] × × [. . .
31 [*šu-up-ši-i*]*k-ka-ku-nu* [*a-wi-lam e-mi-id*]
32 [*ta-aš-t*]*a-'i-ṭa ri-ig-m*[*a a-na a-wi-lu-ti*]
33 [*ilam t*]*a-aṭ-bu-ḫa qá-d*[*u ṭe*$_{4}$*-mi-šu*]
34 [*ta-at-t*]*a-aš-ba-ma ta-ar-*× [. . .
35 [×] × *ši-i-ma ú-ub-ba-a*[*l* . . .
36 [*ub-l*]*a-ma li-ib-ba-ku-nu u*[*r-ta* . . .
37 *ši-*[*i*] *li-tu-ur a-na up-*[. . .
38 *i n*[*u-t*]*a-am-*MU-NI (sic) *ma-áš-*× [. .] 39 $^{d}$*en-ki ni-iš-š*[*i-ka*]

40 $^{d}$*en-ki pí-a-šu i-pu-*[*ša-am-ma*]
41 *is-sà-qar a-na i-*[*li aḫ-ḫi-šu*]

42 *a-na mi-nim tu-ta-am-ma-n*[*i* . . .]
43 *ú-ub-ba-al qá-ti a-na n*[*i-ši-ia-ma*]

44 *a-bu-bu ša ta-qá-ab-b*[*a-ni-in-ni*]
45 *ma-an-nu šu-ú* *a-na-ku* [*ú-ul i-di*]

46 *a-na-ku-ma ú-ul-la-da* [*a-bu-ba*]
47 *ši-pí-ir-šu i-ba-aš-ši it-*[*ti* $^{d}$*en-líl*]

19 . . .] slander in his hand
20 . . .] . . . . . .
21 . . .] of the gods . . .
22 . . .] . Enki and Enlil,

23 '[All we great Anunnaki]
24 [Decided] together [on a rule].

25 Anu and Adad guarded the upper regions,
26 I guarded the lower earth.

27 Where you went
28 [You] loosed the yoke and established freedom.

29 [You] let loose abundance for the peoples
30 [You established] . . . in/from the . . . . of the sun.'

31 . . .] . . . . .
32 . . .] the warrior Enlil

* * * * *

## Column vii

31 [She(?) imposed] your toil [on man],
32 [You] raised a cry [for mankind],
33 You slaughtered [a god] together with [his personality],
34 [You] sat and . . . [. . .
35 [.] . . . . bring [. . .
36 You determined on a [rule . . .
37 Let it turn to . [. . .
38 Let us bind prince Enki . . [. .] by an oath.'

40 Enki opened his mouth
41 And addressed the gods [his brothers],

42 'Why will you bind me with an oath [. . .]?
43 Am I to lay my hands on [my own peoples]?

44 The flood that you are commanding [me],
45 Who is it? I [do not know].

46 Am I to give birth to [a flood]?
47 That is the task of [Enlil].

48 *li-ib-te-ru šu-ú* [. . .
49 $^{\mathrm{d}}$*šu-ul-la-at ù* $^{\mathrm{d}}$[*ḫa-ni-iš*] 50 *li-il-li-ku i-na* [*ma-aḫ-ri*]

51 *ta-ar-ku-ul-li* $^{\mathrm{d}}$*er-*[*ra-kal li-na-si-iḫ*]
52 *li-il-li-i*[*k* $^{\mathrm{d}}$*nin-urta*] 53 *li-ir-*[*di mi-iḫ-ra*]

54 × [. . .

One or two lines missing to the end of the column

⋆ ⋆ ⋆ ⋆ ⋆

## Column viii: **B**: 33–7, **D**: 31–7

The first 30 lines of the column missing

31 × × × [. . .
32 *pu-úḫ-ra* × × [. . .
33 *e ta-aš-mi-a a-na ši-*KU-× [. . .

34 *i-lu iq-bu-ú ga-me-er-t*[*am*]
35 *ši-ip-ra le-em-na a-na ni-ši i-pu-uš* $^{\mathrm{d}}$*e*[*n-líl*]

36 $^{\mathrm{I}}$*at-ra-am-ḫa-si-is pí-a-šu i-pu-ša-ma*
37 *is-sà-qar a-na be-lí-šu*

**48 D**: *li-ib-te-e-r*[*u* **49–53** cf. U rev. 14–15, *Gilg.* XI. 99–102 **36 B**: *i-pu-ša-a*[*m*?*-ma*]

48 Let him [and . . . . .] choose,
49 Let Šullat and [Ḫaniš] go [in front],

51 Let Errakal [tear up] the mooring poles,
52 Let [Ninurta] go and make [the dykes] overflow.

* * * * *

## Column viii

32 The Assembly . . [. . .
33 Do not obey . . . [. . .'

34 The gods commanded total destruction,
35 Enlil did an evil deed on the peoples.

36 Atra-ḫasīs opened his mouth
37 And addressed his lord,

# TABLET III

## **C** throughout unless otherwise stated; i 1–2 from **BD**

i 1 *$^{I}$at-ra-am-ḫa-si-is pí-a-šu i-pu-ša-ma*
2 *is-sà-qar a-na be-lí-šu*

*　　*　　*　　*　　*

10 . . .] × ×

11 [*$^{I}$at-ra-am-ḫa-si-is*] *pí-a-šu i-*⌜*pu-ša*⌝*-am-ma*
12 [*is-sà-qar*] *a-na be-lí-šu*

13 [*ša šu-ut-ti w*]*u-ud-di-a qí-ri-ib-ša*
14 [× × ×] ×*-di lu-uš-te-e si-ib-ba-as-sà*

15 [*$^{d}$en-ki p*]*í-a-šu i-pu-ša-am-ma*
16 [*is*]*-sà-qar a-na ar-di-šu*

17 [*m*]*a-šu-um-ma lu-uš-te-i ta-qá-ab-bi*
18 *ši-ip-ra ša a-qá-ab-bu-ku* 19 *šu-uṣ-ṣi-ir at-ta*

20 *i-ga-ru ši-ta-am-mi-a-an-ni*
21 *ki-ki-šu šu-uṣ-ṣi-ri ka-la sí-iq-ri*!*-ia*

22 *ú-bu-ut bi-ta* *bi-ni e-le-ep-pa*
23 *ma-ak-ku-ra zé-e-er-ma* 24 *na-pí-iš-ta bu-ul-li-iṭ*

25 [*e*]*-le-ep-pu ša ta-ba-an-nu-*⌜*ú*⌝*-*[*ši*]
26 . . .] *mi-it-ḫ*[*u-ra-at* (. .)]

*　　*　　*　　*　　*

28 . . .] × ur pa? ti × × [. . .
29 [*k*]*i-ma ap-si-i šu-a-ti ṣú-ul-li-il-ši*

30 *a-ú-i-mu-ur $^{d}$šamaš qí-ri-ib-ša*
31 *lu-ú ṣú-ul-lu-la-at e-li-iš ù ša-ap-li-iš*

32 *lu-ú du-un-nu-na ú-ni-a-tum*
33 *ku-up-ru lu-ú da-a-an* *e-mu-qá šu-ur-ši*

34 *a-na-ku ul-li-iš ú-ša-az-na-na-ak-ku*
35 *ḫi-iṣ-bi iṣ-ṣú-ri* *bu-du-ri nu-ni*

**20–9** cf. *Gilg.* XI. 21–31 **21** Tablet (**C**): *sí-iq*-ZI-*ia* **33** cf. W 3 **34–5** cf. *Gilg.* XI. 43–4

# TABLET III

i 1 Atra-ḫasīs opened his mouth
2 And addressed his lord,

*    *    *    *    *

11 Atra-ḫasīs opened his mouth
12 And addressed his lord,

13 'Teach me the meaning [of the dream],
14 [. . .] . . that I may seek its outcome.'

15 [Enki] opened his mouth
16 And addressed his slave,

17 'You say, "What am I to seek?"
18 Observe the message that I will speak to you:

20 Wall, listen to me!
21 Reed wall, observe all my words!

22 Destroy your house, build a boat,
23 Spurn property and save life.

25 The boat which you build
26 . . .] be equal [(. .)]

*    *    *    *    *

29 Roof it over like the Apsû.

30 So that the sun shall not see inside it
31 Let it be roofed over above and below.

32 The tackle should be very strong,
33 Let the pitch be tough, and so give (the boat) strength.

34 I will rain down upon you here
35 An abundance of birds, a profusion of fishes.'

36 *ip-te ma-al-ta-ak-ta* *šu-a-ti ú-ma-al-li*
37 *ba-a-a' a-bu-bi* 7 *mu-ši-šu iq-bi-šu*

38 $^{\mathrm{I}}$*at-ra-am-ḫa-si-is il-qí-a te-er-tam*
39 *ši-bu-ti ú-pa-aḫ-ḫi-ir a-na ba-bi-šu*

40 $^{\mathrm{I}}$*at-ra-am-ḫa-si-is pí-a-šu i-pu-ša-⸢am-ma⸣*
41 [*i*]*s-sà-qar a-na ši-bu-*[*ti*]

42 [*i*]*t-ti i-li-ku-nu i-li* ⸢*ú*⸣-[*ul ma-gi-ir*]
43 [*i*]*-te-te-zi-zu* $^{\mathrm{d}}$*en-ki* ⸢*ù*⸣ [$^{\mathrm{d}}$*en-líl*]
44 [*iṭ*]-*ṭa-ar-du-ni-in-ni i-na* [× × ×]

45 [*iš*]-*tu-ma ap-ta-na-a*[*l-la-ḫu* $^{\mathrm{d}}$*en-ki*]
46 [*a-w*]*a-tam an-ni-*[*tam iq-bi*]

47 [*ú-ul*] *ú-uš-ša-ab i-na š*[*a-* . . .
48 [*i-na*] *er-ṣe-et* $^{\mathrm{d}}$*en-líl ú-ul a-*[*ša-ak-ka-an še-pí-ia*]

49 [*it*]-*ti i-li ú-*× [. . .
50 [*an-ni-ta*]*m* ⸢*iq-bi-a*⸣-*a*[*m* . . .

Four or five lines missing to end of column

* * * * *

ii 9 *i*[*k-*. . .
10 *ši-bu-*[*tum* . . .

11 *na-ga-*[*ru na-ši pa-as-su*]
12 *at-ku-up-*[*pu na-ši a-ba-an-šu*]

13 *ku-up-ra* [*it-ta-ši še-er-ru*]
14 *la-ap-nu* [*ḫi-šiḫ-ta ub-la*]

15 *ú-*× [. . .
16 *ut-ta-a*[*k-* . . .

17 *bu-*[. . .
18 $^{\mathrm{I}}$*at-r*[*a-am-ḫa-si-is* . . .
19 *ú-li-*× [. . .

20 *i-*[. . .
21 *ru-*[. . .

* * * * *

28 me? [. . .
29 ⸢*ú*⸣-*ub-b*[*a-al* . . .

**47–8** cf. *Gilg.* XI. 40–1 **11–12** cf. *Gilg.* XI. 50–1 **13–14** cf. *Gilg.* XI. 54–5

36 He opened the water-clock and filled it;
37 He announced to him the coming of the flood for the seventh night.

38 Atra-ḫasīs received the command,
39 He assembled the elders to his gate.

40 Atra-ḫasīs opened his mouth
41 And addressed the elders,

42 'My god [does not agree] with your god,
43 Enki and [Enlil] are angry with one another.
44 They have expelled me from [my house (?)],

45 Since I reverence [Enki],
46 [He told me] of this matter.

47 I can[not] live in [your . . .],
48 I cannot [set my feet on] the earth of Enlil.

49 With the gods . . [. . .
50 [This] is what he told me [. . .'

Four or five lines missing to end of column

* * * * *

ii 10 The elders [. . .

11 The carpenter [carried his axe],
12 The reed-worker [carried his stone].

13 [The child carried] the pitch,
14 The poor man [brought what was needed].

15 . [. . .
16 He/They . . [. . .

17 . [. . .
18 Atra-ḫasīs [. . .

* * * * *

29 Bringing [. . .

30 *mi-im-ma* ⌜*i*⌝-[*šu-ú* . . .
31 *mi-im-ma i-š*[*u-ú* . . .

32 *el-lu-ti it-*[. . . . . . . . . . . . . .] ×
33 *ka-ab-ru-ti* [. . . . . . . . . . .]-*ri*

34 *i-bi-ir-*[*ma uš-te-r*]*i-ib*
35 *mu-up-pa-a*[*r-ša iṣ-ṣú-ur*] *ša-ma-ií*

36 *bu-*⌜*ú*⌝-[*ul*? . . . . . . . . . . . . . . . . . .] ×-*ka-an*
37 *na-*[*ma-aš-še-e* (?) . . . . . . . . . . . .] × *ṣe-ri*

38 × [. . . . . . . . . . . . . . . *uš*]-*te-ri-ib*
39 . . . *ib-ba-b*]*i-il ar-ḫu*

40 . . .] *ni-ši-šu iq-ri*
41 . . .] ⌜*a*⌝-*na qé-re-ti*

42 . . .] × ⌜*ki*⌝-*im-ta-šu uš-te-ri-ib*
43 [*a-ki-l*]*u i-ik-ka-al* 44 [*ša*]-*tu-ú i-ša-at-ti*

45 *i-ir-ru-ub ù ú-uṣ-ṣí* 46 *ú-ul ú-uš-ša-ab ú-ul i-ka-am-mi-is*
47 *ḫe-pí-i-ma li-ib-ba-šu* *i-ma-a' ma-ar-ta-am*

48 $u_4$-*mu iš-nu-ú pa-nu-ú-šu*
49 *iš-ta-ag-na* $^{d}$*adad i-na er-pé-ti*

50 *i-la iš-mu-ú ri-gi-im-šu*
51 [*k*]*u-up-ru ba-bi-il* *i-pé-eḫ-ḫi ba-ab-šu*

52 *iš-tu-ma i-di-lu ba-ab-šu*
53 $^{d}$*adad i-ša-ag-gu-um i-na er-pé-ti*

54 *ša-ru uz-zu-zu i-na te-bi-šu*
55 *ip-ru-u' ma-ar-ka-sa* *e-le-ep-pa ip-ṭú-ur*

* * * * *

Two lines missing

3 . . .] × × × [. . .
4 . . .] *pu-ra-i*
5 . . .] ×-*en me-ḫu-ú*
6 . . . *i*]*ṣ-ṣa-am-du*
7 [$^{d}$*zu-ú i-na ṣ*]*ú-up-ri-šu* 8 [*ú-ša-ar-ri-iṭ*] *ša-ma-i*

9 [. . . . . . . . . . . *m*]*a-ta-am*
10 [*ki-ma ka-ar-pa-ti r*]*i-gi-im-ša iḫ-pí*

**30–1** cf. *Gilg.* XI. 81–3 **7–12** cf. U rev. 16–19 **9–10** cf. *Gilg.* XI. 107

30 Whatever he [had . . .
31 Whatever he had [. . .

32 Clean (animals) . [. . . . . . . . . . . .] .
33 Fat (animals) [. . . . . . . . . . .] .

34 He caught [and put on board]
35 The winged [birds of] the heavens.

36 The cattle (?) [. . . . . . . . . . . .] . . .
37 The wild [creatures (?) . . . . . . . . . .] .

38 . [. . . . . . . . . .] he put on board
39 . . .] the moon disappeared.

40 . . .] he invited his people
41 . . .] to a banquet.

42 . . .] . he sent his family on board,
43 They ate and they drank.

45 But he was in and out: he could not sit, could not crouch,
47 For his heart was broken and he was vomiting gall.

48 The appearance of the weather changed,
49 Adad roared in the clouds.

50 As soon as he heard Adad's voice
51 Pitch was brought for him to close his door.

52 After he had bolted his door
53 Adad was roaring in the clouds,

54 The winds became savage as he arose,
55 He severed the hawser and set the boat adrift.

* * * * *

Three lines missing

iii 4 . . .] . . .
5 . . .] . . the storm
6 . . .] were yoked
7 [Zû with] his talons [rent] the heavens.

9 [He . . . .] the land
10 And shattered its noise [like a pot].

11 [. . . . . . . it-ta-ṣa-a] a-bu-bu
12 [ki-ma qá-ab-l]i ⌜e⌝-li ni-ši    i-ba-a' ka-šu-šu

13 [ú-ul] ⌜i⌝-mu-ur a-ḫu a-ḫa-šu
14 [ú-ul] ú-te-ed-du-ú i-na ka-ra-ši

15 [a-bu-b]u ki-ma li-i i-ša-ab-bu
16 [ki-ma p]a-ri-i na-e-ri    17 [× × (×)-ni]m ša-ru

18 [ša-pa-at e]-ṭú-tu    $^{d}$šamaš la-aš-šu
19 . . .] ×-šu ki-ma su-ub-bi
20 . . . -i]m? a-bu-bi
21 . . .] × [(×)]-ḫu-zu
22 . . .]-bu
23 . . .] ri-gi-im a-[bu-b]i
24 . . .]-bi i-li uš-ta-⌜ka-an⌝

25 [$^{d}$en-ki i]š-ta-ni ṭe$_4$-⌜e⌝-em-šu
26 [×] ma-ru-šu ub-⌜bu⌝-ku 27 [a-n]a ma-aḫ-ri-šu

28 [$^{d}$ni]n-tu be-el-tum ra-bi-tum
29 [bu-u]l-ḫi-ta ú-ka-la-la ša-ap-ta-ša

30 [$^{d}$]a-nun-na i-lu ra-bu-tum
31 [wa-aš]-b[u] i-na ṣú-mi ù bu-bu-ti

32 ⌜i⌝-mu-ur-ma il-tum i-ba-ak-k[i]
33 ta-ab-su-ut i-li e-ri-iš-ta $^{d}$ma-m[i]

34 u$_4$-mu-um li-id-da-⌜i⌝-[im]
35 li-tu-ur li-ki-[il]

36 a-na-ku i-na pu-úḫ-ri ša ⌜i⌝-[li]
37 ki-i aq-[bi] 38 it-ti-šu-nu ga-me-er-ta-a[m]

39 $^{d}$en-líl id-pí-ra    ú-ša-aq-bi bi-i-[ša]
40 ki-ma ti-ru-ru šu-a-t[i]    41 ú-ša-as-ḫi bi-i-š[a]

42 a-na ra-ma-ni-ia ù pa-ag-ri-i[a]
43 i-na ṣe-ri-ia-ma ri-gi-im-ši-na eš-me

44 e-le-nu-ia ki-ma zu-ub-bi    45 i-wu-ú li-il-li-du
46 ù a-na-ku ki-i a-ša-bi    47 i-na bi-it di-im-ma-ti
ša-ḫu-ur-ru ri-ig-mi

48 e-te-el-li-i-ma a-na ša-ma-i
49 tu-ša wa-aš-ba-a-ku 50 i-na bi-it na-ak-⌜ma⌝-ti

**11–14** cf. *Gilg.* XI. 109–12    **23–7** cf. U rev. 20–2    **36–7** cf. *Gilg.* XI. 119–20

11 [. . . .] the flood [set out],
12 Its might came upon the peoples [like a battle array].

13 One person did [not] see another,
14 They were [not] recognizable in the destruction.

15 [The flood] bellowed like a bull,
16 [Like] a whinnying wild ass the winds [howled].

18 The darkness [was dense], there was no sun
19 . . .] . . like . . .
20 . . .] . of the flood
21 . . .] . [.] . .
22 . . .] .
23 . . .] the noise of the [flood]
24 It was trying [. . . .] . of the gods.

25 [Enki] was beside himself,
26 [Seeing that] his sons were thrown down before him.

28 Nintu, the great lady,
29 Her lips were covered with feverishness.

30 The Anunnaki, the great gods,
31 Were sitting in thirst and hunger.

32 The goddess saw it as she wept,
33 The midwife of the gods, the wise Mami.

34 (She spoke,) 'Let the day become dark,
35 Let it become gloom again.

36 In the assembly of the gods
37 How did I, with them, command total destruction?

39 Enlil has had enough of bringing about an evil command,
40 Like that Tiruru, he uttered abominable evil.

42 As a result of my own choice
43 And to my own hurt I have listened to their noise.

44 My offspring—cut off from me—have become like flies!
46 And as for me, like the occupant of a house of lamentation
My cry has died away.

48 Shall I go up to heaven
49 As if I were to live in a treasure house?

51 *e-ša-a a-nu il-li-kam be-el ṭe*$_4$*-mi*
52 *i-lu ma-ru-šu iš-mu-ú sí-qí-ir-šu*

53 *ša la im-ta-al-ku-ma iš-ku-*⌜*nu a*⌝*-*[*bu-ba*]
54 *ni-ši* ⌜*ik-mi-su*⌝ *a-na ka-*[*ra-ši*]

One line missing to end of column

* * * * *

First two lines of column missing

iv 3 . . .] × × [. . .
4 *ú-na-ab-ba* $^{d}$*n*[*in-tu* . . .

5 *a-bu-ma-an ul-*⌜*da*⌝ *g*[*al-la-ta* (?)] 6 *ti-a-am-ta*
*ki-ma ku-li-li* 7 *im-la-a-nim na-ra-am*

8 *ki-ma a-mi-im i-mi-da a-na s*[*a-pa*]*n-*[*ni*]
9 *ki-ma a-mi-im i-na ṣe-ri i-mi-da a-na ki-ib-ri*

10 *a-mu-ur-ma e-li-ši-na ab-ki*
11 *ú-qá-at-ti di-im-ma-ti i-na ṣe-ri-ši-in*

12 *ib-ki-i-ma li-ib-ba-ša ú-na-ap-pí-iš*
13 *ú-na-ab-ba* $^{d}$*nin-tu* 14 *la-la-ša iṣ-ru-up*

15 *i-lu it-ti-ša ib-ku-ú a-na ma-tim*
16 *iš-bi ni-is-sà-tam* 17 *ṣa-mi-a-at ši-ik-ri-iš*

18 *ši-i a-šar uš-bu i-na bi-ki-ti* 19 *uš-bu-ma*
*ki-ma im-me-ri* 20 *im-lu-nim ra-ṭa-am*

21 *ṣa-mi-a ša-ap-ta-šu-nu bu-ul-ḫi-ta*
22 ⌜*i-na*⌝ *bu-bu-ti* 23 *i-ta-na-ar-ra-ar-ru*

24 7 *u*$_4$*-mi* 7 *mu-š*[*i-a-tim*]
25 *il-li-ik ra-*⌜*du*⌝ *me-ḫu-*⌜*ú*⌝ [*a-bu-bu*]

26 *a-šar is-r*[*i-* . . .
27 *sa-ki-i*[*p* . . .
28 *ṣa-*× [. . .

* * * * *

39 *i*[*b-* . . .
40 *is-*× [. . .
41 *bi-*× [. . .
42 *a*[*b*? . . .

**53–4** cf. *Gilg.* XI. 168–9 **14** cf. U rev. 23 **15** cf. *Gilg.* XI. 124 **18** cf. *Gil* . XI. 125 **21** cf. *Gilg.* XI. 126 **24–5** cf. *Gilg.* XI. 127–8

51 Where has Anu the president gone,
52 Whose divine sons obeyed his command?

53 He who did not consider but brought about a flood
54 And consigned the peoples to destruction?'

One line missing to end of column

★ ★ ★ ★ ★

First three lines of column missing

iv 4 Nintu was wailing [. . .

5 'What? Have they given birth to the [rolling (?)] sea?
6 They have filled the river like dragon flies!

8 Like a raft they have put in to the edge,
9 Like a raft . . . . they have put in to the bank!

10 I have seen and wept over them;
11 I have ended my lamentation for them.'

12 She wept and eased her feelings;
13 Nintu wailed and spent her emotion.

15 The gods wept with her for the land,
16 She was surfeited with grief and thirsted for beer.

18 Where she sat, they sat weeping,
20 Like sheep, they filled the trough.

21 Their lips were feverishly athirst,
22 They were suffering cramp from hunger.

24 For seven days and seven nights
25 Came the deluge, the storm, [the flood].

26 Where it . [. . .
27 Was thrown down [. . .

Twenty-five or twenty-six lines missing to end of column

★ ★ ★ ★ ★

43 × [. . .
44 *ú*-[. . .
45 *i-n*[*a* . . .
46 *id*-× [. . .
47 *iš*/*il*-[. . .
48 × [. . .

Five or six lines missing to end of column

★ ★ ★ ★ ★

First seven lines of column missing

v 8 × [. . .
9 × [. . .
10 *ú*?-[. . .
11 *i*-[. . .
12–14 traces

★ ★ ★ ★ ★

28 × [. . .
29 *i-ra*/*si*-[. . .
30 *a-na ša-a-r*[*i* . . .
31 [*i*]*t-ta-di* [. . .
32 *i-za-an-nu-un* [. . .
33 . . .] × ×

34 [*i-ṣi-nu i-l*]*u e-re-ša*
35 [*ki-ma zu-ub-b*]*i e-lu ni-qí-i pa-aḫ-ru*

36 [*iš-tu-m*]*a i-ku-lu ni-qí-a-am*
37 [$^{d}$*nin*]-*tu it-bé-e-ma* 38 ⌜*na-ap*⌝-*ḫa-ar-šu-nu ut-ta-az-za-am*

39 *e-ša-a a-nu il-li-ka-am* 40 *be-el ṭe*$_4$-*e-mi*
41 $^{d}$*en-líl iṭ-ḫi-a a-na qú-ut-ri-ni*

42 *ša la im-ta-al-ku-ú-ma iš-ku-nu a-bu-ba*
43 *ni-ši ik-mi-su a-na ka-ra-ši*

44 *ub-la pí-i-ku-nu ga-me-er-tam*
45 *el-lu-tu*[*m*] *z*[*i*]-*mu-ši-na i'-a-ad-ru*

46 *ù ši-i iṭ-ḫe-e-ma a-na su-bé-e ra-bu-ti*
47 *ša a-nu i*-⟨*pu*⟩-*šu-ma i-pa-an-qá-l*[*u*]/*a*[*l*]

48 *ia-a-at-tum ni-is-sà-s*[*ú*] 49 *lu-ú ši-im-ti i-ba*-[*a*]
50 *li-še-ṣa-an-ni-ma i-na né-el-m*[*e-ni*] 51 *pa-ni-ia li-ip-t*[*e*]

**30** cf. *Gilg*. XI. 155 **34–5** cf. *Gilg*. XI. 159–61 **42–3** cf. *Gilg*. XI. 168–9
**46–7** cf. *Gilg*. XI. 163

First twenty-nine lines of column missing

v 30 To the [four] winds [. . .
31 He put [. . .
32 Providing food [. . .
33 . . .] . .

34 [The gods sniffed] the smell,
35 They gathered [like flies] over the offering.

36 [After] they had eaten the offering
37 Nintu arose to complain against all of them,

39 'Where has Anu the president gone?
41 Has Enlil come to the incense?

42 They, who did not consider but brought about a flood
43 And consigned the peoples to destruction?

44 You decided on total destruction,
45 Now their clean faces have become dark.'

46 Then she approached the big flies
47 Which Anu had made (?) and was carrying,

48 (She said), 'His grief is mine! Now determine my destiny!
50 Let him get me out of this distress and relieve (?) me.

52 *lu-ú* zi ši a MAL × [×] mu? × × × × [× ×]

(Probably no line missing)

vi 1 *i-na ma-*× [. . .

2 *zu-ub-bu-ú a*[*n-nu-tum*] 3 *lu-ú uq-ni ki-ša-di-i*[*a-a-ma*]

4 *lu-uḫ-sú-ús-sú* $u_4$*-mi* [. . .] zi [. . .]

5 *ma-qú-ra i-ta-ma-ar q*[*ú-ra-du* $^{d}$*en-líl*]

6 *li-ib-ba-ti ma-li ša* $^{d}$⸢*i*⸣*-g*[*i-gi*]

7 *ra-bu-tum* $^{d}$*a-*⸢*nun*⸣*-na* ⸢*ka*⸣*-lu-n*[*i*]

8 *ub-la pí-i-ni iš-ti-ni-iš ma-mi-tam*

9 *a-ia-a-nu ú-ṣi na!-pí!-iš-tum*

10 *ki-i ib-lu-uṭ* ⸢*a-wi*⸣*-lum i-na* ⸢*ka*⸣*-*[*r*]*a-ši*

11 *a-nu pí-a-šu i-pu-ša-am-ma*

12 *is-sà-qar a-na qú-ra-*⸢*di*⸣ $^{d}$*en-líl*

13 *ma-an-nu an-ni-tam* 14 ⸢*ša la*⸣ $^{d}$*en-ki i-ip-pu-uš*

15 [× (×)] ul? *ú-ša-ap-ta sí-iq-r*[*a*]

16 [$^{d}$*en-ki*] *pí-a-šu i-*⸢*pu*⸣*-ša-am-*[*ma*]

17 [*is-sà-qar*] *a-na i-li ra-bu-ti*

18 [*lu-ú e*]*-pu-uš i-na pa-ni-*⸢*ku*⸣*-u*[*n*]

19 [*ú-uš-t*]*a-ṣi-ra na-pí-i*[*š-tam* [(. .)] × × × [× ×]

20 . . .] × *i-l*[*i*? . . .] × bi?

21 . . . *a-b*]*u-ba*

22 . . .] ×*-ku-un*

23 . . . *l*]*i-ib-ba-ka*

24 . . .] *ù ru-um-mi*

25 [*be-el ar-n*]*im šu-ku-un še-re-et-ka*

26 [*ù*] ⸢*a*⸣*-iu-ú ša ú-ša-a*[*s*]*-sà-ku a-wa-at-ka*

27 . . .]*-nu pu-úḫ-ra* [. . .

About ten lines missing

38 . . .] ×*ši-a-ti*

39 . . .] *iš-ku-nu*

40 [*ú-na-ap-p*]*i-iš li-ib-bi*

41 [$^{d}$*en-líl p*]*í-a-šu i-pu-ša-am-ma*

42 [*is-sà*]*-qar a-na* $^{d}$*en-ki ni-iš-ši-ki*

**2–4** cf. *Gilg.* XI. 164–5 **5–6** cf. *Gilg.* XI. 171–2 **9** Tablet (**C**): *pí-ti-iš-tum* **9–10** cf. *Gilg.* XI. 173 **13** cf. *Gilg.* XI. 175 **24** cf. *Gilg.* XI. 181 **25** cf. *Gilg.* XI. 180

52 Verily . . . . . [.] . . . . . [. .]

(Probably no line missing)

vi 1 In . . [. . .
2 Let [these] flies be the lapis around my neck
4 That I may remember it [every (?)] day [and for ever (?)].'

5 [The warrior Enlil] saw the vessel,
6 And was filled with anger at the Igigi,

7 'All we great Anunnaki
8 Decided together on an oath.

9 Where did life escape?
10 How did man survive in the destruction?'

11 Anu opened his mouth
12 And addressed the warrior Enlil,

13 'Who but Enki could do this?
15 [. . .] I did not (?) reveal the command.'

16 [Enki] opened his mouth
17 [And addressed] the great gods,

18 'I did it [indeed] in front of you!
19 [I am responsible] for saving life [.] . . . [. .]

20 . . .] . gods [. . .] . .
21 . . .] the flood
22 . . .] . . .
23 . . .] your heart
24 . . .] and relax
25 Impose your penalty [on the criminal]
26 [And] whoever disregards your command
27 . . .] . the assembly [. . .

About ten lines missing

38 . . .] her/it
39 . . .] he/she/they put
40 [I have] eased my feelings.'

41 [Enlil] opened his mouth
42 And addressed Enki the prince,

43 *[ga-na sa-a]s-sú-ra* $^{d}$*nin-tu ši-si-ma*
44 *[at-t]a ù ši-i* *mi-it-li-ka i-na pu-uḫ-ri*

45 *[*$^{d}$*en-ki pí]-a-šu i-pu-ša-am-ma*
46 *[is-sà-qar] a-na* $^{d}$*nin-tu sa-as-sú-ri*

47 *[at-ti sa-a]s-sú-ru* *ba-ni-a-at ši-ma-ti*
48 . . .] *a-na ni-ši*
49 . . . *-l]i-li*
50 . . . *l]i-ib-ši*
51 . . .] ×

Probably one line missing to end of column

* * * * *

vii 1 *[a]p-pu-na ša-lu-uš-tum li-i[b]-ši i-na ni-ši*
2 *i-na ni-ši a-li-it-tum-ma la a-li-it-tum*

3 *li-ib-ši-ma i-na ni-ši pa-ši-it-tu*
4 *li-iṣ-ba-at še-er-ra* 5 *i-na bi-ir-ku a-li-it-ti*

6 *šu-uk-ni ú-uk-ba-ak-ka-ti* *e-ne-ti* 7 *ù e-gi-ṣi· a-ti*
8 *lu-ú ik-ki-bu ši-na-ma* 9 ⌜*a*⌝*-la-da-*⌜*am*⌝ *pu-ur-*⌜*si*⌝

10 [× (×)] ni ṣ[i?] × × × × ×*-tam*
11 [. . . . . . . .] *ù [na-pí]-iš-tam*
12 . . .] ra ma [× ×] × na
13 . . .] bi li? [. .]*-ši-in*
14 . . .] × [. . . . .] ×*-mi-šu*
15 . . .]*-tum* [. . .] ×
16 × [. . . . . . . . . . . . . . . .] ×
17 *eṭ-*[. . .
18 *li-*[. . .
19 × × [. . .
20 *a-š[i-* . . .
21 ⌜$^{d}$*en*⌝*-lí[l* . . .
22 × × [. . .
23 × [. . .
24 *ma-*× [. . .
25 *me-ḫu-*× [. . .
26 *ma-ta* [. . .
27 × [. . .
28–35 missing

43 '[Come], summon Nintu, the birth-goddess,
44 [You] and she, confer in the assembly.'

45 [Enki] opened his mouth
46 And [addressed] Nintu, the birth-goddess,

47 '[You], birth-goddess, creatress of destinies,
48 . . .] for the peoples
49 . . .] . .
50 . . .] let there be

Probably one line missing to end of column

* * * * *

vii 1 In addition let there be a third category among the peoples,
2 (Let there be) among the peoples women who bear and women who do not bear.

3 Let there be among the peoples the *Pāšittu*-demon
4 To snatch the baby from the lap of her who bore it.

6 Establish *Ugbabtu*-women, *Entu*-women, and *Igiṣītu*-women,
8 And let them be taboo and so stop childbirth.

10 [. .] . . . . . . . .
11 [. . . .] and life (?)

* * * * *

36 × [. . .
37 *ḫu*-× [. . .
38 *ma*-[. . .
39 *i*-[. . .
40 *ur/lu*-[. . .
41 *š*[*a* . . .

* * * * *

A late recension of the above damaged section is probably contained in K 4539 (R), cf. its 9–10 with 17–18 above:

1 . . .] × × [. . .
2 . . .] × ra a × [. . .
3 [(×)] × i ba li a × [. . .
4 ⌜*ša*⌝-*am-ni* [. . .
5 *ú-ṣú-ra-at ni-ši* × [. . .
6 *zi-ka-ru* [. . .
7 *a-na ar-da-ti* [. . .
8 *ar-da-tum* [. . .
9 *eṭ-lu a-na ar-d*[*a-ti* . . .
10 ⌜*li*⌝-*il-qí a*[*r-da-tum* . . .

* * * * *

viii 3 . . .] ×
4 . . .] ×
5 . . .] ×
6 [×] × [. . . . . . .]-*da*
7 [×] ma? ši × [. . . . . .] ×
8 [*i*]*b-ba-š*[*u*?-*ú*? . . . . . . .] ×

9 *ki-ma ni-iš-ku-*[*nu a-bu-b*]*a*
10 *a-wi-lum ib-lu-ṭ*[*ú i-na ka-ra-ši*]

11 *at-ta ma-li-ik i-*[*li ra-bu-ti*]
12 *te-re-ti-iš-*[*ka*] 13 *ú-ša-ab-ši qá-a*[*b-la*]

14 *ša-ni-it-ti-iš-*[*ka*] 15 *an-ni-a-am za-ma-*[*ra*]
16 *li-iš-mu-ma* $^{d}$*i-gi-g*[*u*] 17 *li-iṣ-ṣí-ru na-ar-bi-ka*

18 *a-bu-ba a-na ku-ul-la-at ni-ši* 19 *ú-za-am-me-er*
*ši-me-a*

A late recension of the above damaged and untranslated section may be contained in K 4539 (R):

4 Oil [. . .
5 Regulations for the human race [. . .
6 The male [. . .
7 To the young lady [. . .
8 The young lady [. . .
9 The young man to the young [lady . . .
10 Let the young [lady] take [. . .

* * * * *

viii 9 That we brought about [the flood],
10 But man survived [the destruction].

11 You, the counsellor of the [great] gods,
12 At [your] decree I set battle in motion.

14 For your praise let the Igigi hear
16 This song and extol your greatness to one another.

18 I have sung of the flood to all the peoples.
Hear it!

# THE ASSYRIAN RECENSION

## K 3399+3934 (S), Reverse iv

1 [*ul il-li-ka* 1200 *šanātu*]$^{\text{meš}}$
⌜*mātu*⌝ *ir-ta-pi*[*š*  *ni-šu im-ti-da*]

2 [*i-na*] *ríg*$^{\text{ri-gi}}$*-me-ši-na it-ta-*⌜'⌝-[*dar*]
3 [*i-na*] *ḫu-bu-ri-ši-na la i-ṣa-ba-su* [*ši-tu*]

4 [$^{\text{d}}$*e*]*n-líl il-ta-kan pu-ḫur-š*[*u*]
5 [*iz-z*]*a-ka-ra a-na ilāni*$^{\text{meš}}$ *mārē*$^{\text{meš}}$*-šu*

6 [*ik*]*-tab-ta-m*[*a r*]*i-gi-im a-me-lu-te*

7 [*i-na r*]*íg*$^{\text{ri-g}}$[$^{\text{i}}$]*-me-*[*ši-n*]*a at-ta-a-*$^{\text{di-ir}}$*dar*
8 [*i-na ḫ*]*u-*[*bu*]*-ri-ši-na la i-ṣa-ba-ta-ni ši-tu*

9 [*qi-b*]*a-ma šu-ru-pu-u lib-ši*
10 [*li-š*]*ak-li-ṣi ri-gim-ši-na nam-tar*

11 [*ki-m*]*a me-ḫe-e li-zi-qa-ši-na-ti-ma*
12 [*mur*]*-ṣu di-'u šu-ru-pu-u a-sa-ku*

---

13 [*iq-b*]*u-ma šu-ru-pu-u ib-ši*
14 [*ú*]*-riš*$^{\text{ri-iš}}$ *i-ṣi ri-gim-ši-na nam-tar*

15 [*ki-m*]*a me-ḫe-e i-zi-qa-ši-na-ti-ma*
16 [*mur*]*-ṣu di-'u šu-ru-pu-u a-sa-ku*

---

17 [*bēl t*]*a-ši-im-ti* $^{\text{m}}$*a-tar-ḫasīs*(geštu) *amēlu*
18 [*a-na bēli*]*-šu* $^{\text{d}}$*é-a*  *uzun-šú pi-ta-at*

19 [*i-t*]*a-mu it-ti ili-šu*
20 [*ù š*]*u* $^{\text{d}}$*é-a*  *it-ti-šú i-ta-mu*

---

21 [$^{\text{m}}$]*a-tar-ḫasīs*(geštu) *pâ-šú īpuša*$^{\text{šá}}$ *i-qab-bi*
22 [*izzakar*] *a-na* $^{\text{d}}$*é-a bēli-šu*

23 [*ma*] *bēl*  *ut-ta-za-ma ta-ni-še-ti*
24 [*mur-ṣ*]*i-ku-nu-ma e-kal mātu*$^{\text{tu}}$

25 [$^{\text{d}}$*é*]*-a bēl*  *ut-ta-za-ma ta-ni-še-ti*
26 [*mur-ṣu*] *šá ilāni*$^{\text{meš}}$*-ma e-kal mātu*$^{\text{tu}}$

# THE ASSYRIAN RECENSION

## Reverse iv

1 [Twelve hundred years had not yet passed]
When the land extended [and the peoples multiplied].

2 He got disturbed [with] their noise,
3 [With] their uproar [sleep] did not overcome him.

4 Enlil convened his assembly
5 And addressed the gods his sons,

6 'The noise of mankind has become too intense for me,

7 I have got disturbed [with] their noise,
8 [With] their uproar sleep does not overcome me.

9 Command that there be plague,
10 Let Namtar diminish their noise.

11 Let disease, sickness, plague and pestilence
12 Blow upon them like a tornado.'

---

13 They commanded and there was plague,
14 Namtar diminished their noise.

15 Disease, sickness, plague and pestilence
16 Blew upon them like a tornado.

---

17 The discerning one, the man Atra-ḫasīs,
18 Kept an open ear [to his lord], Ea.

19 [He] spoke with his god,
20 [And] Ea spoke with him.

---

21 Atra-ḫasīs opened his mouth to speak
22 [And addressed] Ea his lord,

23 'Lord, the human race is groaning,
24 Your [disease] is consuming the land.

25 Ea, lord, the human race is groaning,
26 [The disease] from the gods is consuming the land.

27 [*iš-t*]*u-ma te-eb-nu-na-ši-ma*
28 [*ta-pa-ra*]*-sa mur-ṣa di-'a šu-ru-pu-u a-sa-ku*

---

29 [$^{d}$*é-a pâ-šú īpuša*$^{šá}$ *i*]*-qab-bi*
*a-na* $^{m}$*a-tar-ḫasīs*(geštu)*-me izzakar*(mu)*-šu*

30 [*qi-ba-ma li-is-su-ú nāg*]*iru*
*rigma*(KA) *lu-šá-bu-ú i-na māti*$^{ti}$

31 [*e ta-ap-la-ḫa ilāni*$^{meš}$*-ku-un*] ⸢*e*⸣ *tu-sa-pa-a* $^{d}$*ištar*(u.dar)*-ku-un*
32 . . .] × × *ka-i-la pár-ṣi-šu*
33 . . . *mas-ḫ*]*a-tu niqû*(siskur)
34 . . . *a-n*]*a qud-me-šá*
35 . . .] × *kat-ra-ba-ma*
36 . . .] ×*-nu ka-at-r*[*e-e il?-t*]*a?-kán*$^{ka\text{-}an}$ *qat-su*

---

37 [$^{d}$*en-líl*] *il-ta-kán pu-ḫur-šu*
*izzakar*(mu) *a-na ilāni*$^{meš}$ *mārē*$^{meš}$*-šu*

38 ×*-ra-me e ta-áš-ku-na-ši-na-ti*
39 [*ni-š*]*u la im-ṭa-a* *a-na šá pa-na i-ta-at-ra*

40 [*i-na*] *ríg-me-ši-na at-ta-a-dar*
41 [*i-na ḫ*]*u-bu-ri-ši-na la i-ṣa-ba-ta-ni ši-tu*

42 *p*[*ur*]*-sa-ma a-na ni-še-e ti-ta*
43 ⸢*i-na*⸣ *kar-ši-ši-na li-me-ṣu šam-mu*

44 ⸢*e*⸣*-liš* $^{d}$*adad* *zu-un-na-šu lu-šá-qir*
45 ⸢*li*⸣*-sa-kír šap-liš ia iš-šá-a me-lu i-na na-aq-bi*

46 ⸢*li*⸣*-šur eqlu iš-pi-ke-e-šu*
47 ⸢*li*⸣*-né-' irta-šá* $^{d}$*nisaba*

*ṣalmūti*$^{meš}$ *lip-ṣu-ú ugāru*
48 *ṣēru pal-ku-ú* *lu-li-id id-ra-nu*

49 ⸢*li*⸣*-bal-kat erṣetu re-em-šá*
*šam-mu ia ú-ṣa-a* *šu-ú ia i-im-ru*

50 *l*[*iš*]*-šá-kín-ma a-na nišē*$^{meš}$ *a-sa-ku*
51 ⸢*rēmu*⸣(arḫuš) *lu ku-ṣur-ma* *ia ú-še-šèr šèr-ra*

---

52 *ip-t*[*ar-s*]*u a-na ni-še-e ti-ta*
53 *i-na kar-ši-ši-na e-me-ṣu šam-mu*

27 Since you created us
28 [Will you] remove the disease, sickness, plague and pestilence?'

---

29 [Ea opened his mouth to] speak
And addressed Atra-ḫasīs,

30 '[Command that] heralds [proclaim]
And make a loud noise in the land,

31 "[Do not reverence your gods], do not pray to your goddesses,
32 . . .] . . observe his rites
33 . . .] the offering of sesame-meal
34 . . .] in front of it
35 . . .] . speak a benediction
36 . . .] . . gift [. .] . his hand."'

---

37 [Enlil] convened his assembly
And addressed the gods his sons,

38 'Do not . . . . . . them,
39 The peoples are not diminished, but have become more numerous than before!

40 I have got disturbed [with] their noise,
41 [With] their uproar sleep does not overcome me.

42 Cut off food supplies from the peoples,
43 Let plant life be in short supply in their stomachs,

44 Let Adad above make his rain scarce,
45 Below, let (the river) be blocked up and let it not raise the flood from the Abyss.

46 Let the fields diminish their yields,
47 Let Nisaba turn aside her breast,

Let the black fields become white,
48 Let the broad plain produce salt,

49 Let the earth's womb rebel,
Let no vegetables shoot up, no cereals grow,

50 Let pestilence be laid on the peoples,
51 That the womb may be constricted and give birth to no child.'

---

52 They cut off food supplies from the peoples,
53 Vegetables were in short supply in their stomachs,

54 *e-liš $^{d}$adad zu-un-na-šu ú-šá-qir*
55 *is-sa-kír šap-liš ul iš-šá-a mi-lu ina na-aq-bi*

56 *iš-šur eqlu iš-pi-ke-šú*
57 *i-né-' irta-šá $^{d}$nisaba*
*ṣalmūti$^{meš}$ ip-ṣu-u ugāru*
58 *ṣēru pal-ku-ú ú-li-id id-ra-na*
*ib-bal-kat erṣetu re-em-šá*
59 *šam-mu ul ú-ṣa-a šu-ú ul i'-ru*
60 *iš-šá-kín-ma a-na nišē$^{meš}$ a-sa-ku*
61 *rēmu ku-ṣur-ma ul ú-še-šèr šèr-ra*

---

* * * * *

## Reverse v

1 *ši-g[a-ra na-aḫ̮-bal tam-tim]*
2 *iṣ-ṣur [$^{d}$é-a qa-du šam-me-šu]*
3 *e-liš $^{d}$[adad zu-un-na-šu ú-šá-qir]*
4 *is-sa-kír šap-[liš ul iš-šá-a mi-lu i-na na-aq-bi]*

5 ⸢*iš-šur*⸣ *eql[u iš-pi-ke-šú]*
6 *[i-né-' irta-šá] $^{d}$nisaba*
*[ṣalmūti$^{meš}$ ip-ṣu-u ugāru]*
7 *[ṣēru pal-ku-ú ú]-li-id id-[ra-na]*
*[ib-bal-kat erṣetu re-em-šá]*
8 *[šam-mu ul ú-ṣa]-*⸢*a*⸣ *šu-*⸢*ú*⸣ *[ul i'-ru]*
9 *[iš-šá-kín-ma a-na nišē$^{meš}$ a-sa-ku]*
*[rēmu ku-ṣur-ma ul ú-š]e-[šèr šèr-ra]*
10 [. . . . . . . . . . . . . . . .]
11 [. . . . . . . . . . t]u? × [(×)]
12 [2 *šattu*(mu) *i-na ka-šá-di*]
[*ú-na-ak-ki-ma*] *na-kám-t[a]*
13 [3 *šattu*(mu.an.na) *i-na*] *ka-šá-di*
14 [*ni-šu i-na bu-bu-te zi-mu-ši-na*] *it-tak-ru*
15 [4 *šattu*(mu) *i-na ka-šá-di*]
[*ar-ku-tu ma-za-z*]*i-šu-nu ik-ru-ni*
16 [*rap-šá-tu bu-da-ši-na*] *is-si-qa*

54 Adad above made his rain scarce,
55 Below, (the river) was blocked up and did not raise the flood from the Abyss.

56 The fields diminished their yields,
57 Nisaba turned aside her breast,

The black fields became white,
58 The broad plain produced salt,

Earth's womb rebelled,
59 No vegetables shot up, no cereals grew,

60 Pestilence was laid upon the peoples,
61 So that the womb was constricted and gave birth to no child.

* * * * *

## Reverse v

1 The bolt, [the bar of the sea],
2 [Ea] guarded [together with his plants],

3 [Adad] above [made his rain scarce],
4 Below, (the river) was blocked up [and did not raise the flood from the Abyss],

5 The fields diminished [their yields],
6 Nisaba [turned aside her breast],

[The black fields became white],
7 [The broad plain] produced salt,

[Earth's womb rebelled],
8 [No vegetables] shot up, no cereals [grew],

9 [Pestilence was laid on the peoples],
[So that the womb was constricted and gave] birth [to no child],

10 [. . . . . . . . . . . . . . . .]
11 [. . . . . . . . . .] . . [.]
12 [When the second year arrived]
[They suffered] the itch.
13 [When the third year] arrived
14 [The peoples's features] were distorted [by hunger].
15 [When the fourth year arrived]
Their [long] legs became short,
16 [Their broad shoulders] became narrow.

17 [*qa-da-níš it-ta-na-la-ka* *ni-š*]*u i-na su-qi*
18 [5 *šattu*(mu) *i-na ka-šá-di*]
[*e-reb*] *ummi mārtu i-da-gal*
19 [*ummu a-na mārte* *ul i-p*]*a-te bāb-šá*
20 [*zi-ba-ni-it ummi mārt*]*u i-na-ṭal*
21 [*zi-ba-ni-it mārte*] ⸢*i*⸣*-na-ṭal ummu*
22 [6 *šattu*(mu) *i-na ka-šá-di*]
[*il-tàk-nu*] *a-na nap-ta-ni mārta*
23 [*a-na kurummate*(ŠUK)$^{te}$ *bu-na*] *il-tàk-nu*
24 [*im-la-ni ma-*× . . . . . . .]
[*bītu i*]*l-ta-nu* *šanû*$^{ú}$ *i-re-ḫa-ma*
25 [*ki-i buqli*(še.DIM$_4$) *me-te* *pa-nu-š*]*i-na kat-mu*
26 [*ni-šu i-na šu-par-k*]*e-e napišti bal-ṭa-at*

---

27 [*bēl ta-ši-im-t*]*i* $^{m}$*a-tar-ḫasīs*(geštu) *amēlu*
28 [*a-na bēli-šú* $^{d}$*é*]*-a* *uzun-šu pi-ta-at*

29 [*i-ta-m*]*u it-ti ili-šu*
30 [*ù šu* $^{d}$*é*]*-a* *it-ti-šú i-ta-mu*

31 [*i-še*] *bāb ili-šu*
32 [*i-n*]*a pu-ut nāri il-ta-kán ma-a-a-al-šu*
33 ⸢*ù*⸣ *me-ed-ra-tu šu-ḫu-rat*

* * * * *

## Reverse vi

1 [2] *šattu*(mu].an.n[a) [*i-na ka-šá-di ú-na-ak-ki-ma na-kám-ta*]
2 ⸢3⸣ *šattu*(mu.an.na) [*i-na ka-šá-di*]
3 *ni-šu i-na* [*bu-bu-te* *zi-m*]*u-ši-na it-tak-ru*
4 4 *šattu*(mu) *i-na k*[*a-šá-di*]
[*ar-ku-t*]*u ma-za-zi-šu-nu ik-ru-ni*
5 *rap-šá-tu* [*bu-da*]*-ši-na is-si-qa*
6 *qa-da-níš i*[*t-ta-n*]*a-la-ka* *ni-šu i-na su-qí*
7 5 *šattu*(mu) *i-na ka-šá-*[*di*]
*e-reb ummi mārtu i-da-gal*
8 *ummu a-na mārte* *ul i-pa-te bāb-š*[*á*]
9 *zi-ba-ni-it ummi mārtu i-n*[*a-ṭal*]
10 *zi-ba-ni-it mārte i-na-ṭal* [*ummu*]
11 6 *šattu*(mu) *i-na ka-šá-di*
*il-tàk-nu ana nap-t*[*a-ni mārta*]

17 [They walked hunched] in the street.
18 [When the fifth year arrived]
Daughter watched the mother's [going in],
19 [But the mother would not] open her door [to the daughter].
20 [The daughter] watched [the scales (at the sale) of the mother],
21 The mother watched [the scales (at the sale) of the daughter].
22 [When the sixth year arrived]
[They served up] the daughter for dinner,
23 They served up [the son for food].
24 [. . . were filled . . . . . . .]
One [house] consumed another,
25 Their [faces] were overlaid [like dead malt].
26 [The peoples] were living [on the edge] of death.

---

27 [The discerning one], the man Atra-ḫasīs,
28 Kept an open ear [to his lord], Ea.

29 [He spoke] with his god,
30 [And] Ea spoke with him.

31 [He sought] the gate of his god,
32 He placed his bed facing the river.
33 The stream was quiet

* * * * *

## Reverse vi

1 [When the second] year [arrived they suffered the itch].
2 [When] the third year [arrived]
3 The peoples' [features] were distorted by [hunger].
4 When the fourth year [arrived]
Their [long] legs became short,
5 Their broad [shoulders] became narrow,
6 They walked hunched in the street.
7 When the fifth year arrived
Daughter watched the mother's going in,
8 But the mother would not open her door to the daughter.
9 The daughter watched the scales (at the sale) of the mother,
10 [The mother] watched the scales (at the sale) of the daughter.
11 When the sixth year arrived
They served up [the daughter] for dinner,

12 *a-na kurummate*(ŠUK)$^{te}$ *bu-na il-tàk-nu*
*im-la-ni ma-×* [. . .
13 *bītu il-ta-nu šanû*$^{ú}$ *i-*[*re-ḫa-ma*]
14 *ki-i buqli*(še.DIM$_4$) *me-te* *pa-nu-ši-n*[*a kat-mu*]
15 *ni-šu i-na šu-par-ke-e* [*napišti bal-ṭa-at*]

---

16 *šipru*(kin) *il-qu-*[*ú* . . .
17 *e-tar-bu-ma* [. . .
18 *te-er-ti* $^{m}$⌜*a-tar*⌝*-ḫ*[*a-si-is* . . .
19 *ma bēl mātu*[$^{tu}$ . . .
20 [*it*]*-ta ia-a* [. . .
21 × ma × [. . .
22 [(×)] × ma [. . .
23 [(×)] × [. . .

(Probable continuation, on K 12000*c*)

24 × *ki?-ma?* × [. . .
25 *ia-e šá bi-la* × [. . .
26 *iš-tu-ma* × [. . .
27 *lu-ri-id a*[*p-* . . .

---

28 1 *šattu*(mu.an.na) [. . .

* * * * *

12 They served up the son for food.
. . [.] were filled [. . .
13 One house consumed another,
14 Their faces [were overlaid] like dead malt.
15 The peoples [were living] on the edge of [death].

---

16 The command which they received [. . .
17 They entered and [. . .
18 The message of Atra-[ḫasīs . . .
19 'Lord, the land [. . .
20 A sign . . [. . .
21 . . . [. . .
22 [.] . . [. . .
23 [.] . [. . .

(Probable continuation, on K 12000*c* (T))

24 . . . . [. . .
25 . . . . . . [. . .
26 After . [. . .
27 Let me go down [to the Apsû . . .

---

28 One/The first year [. . .

* * * * *

# BE 39099 FROM PHOTO BABYLON 1804 (x)

## Reverse i

[$^{d}$en-líl pa-a-šú i-pu-uš-ma i-qab-bi]
1 iz-z[a-kar a-na . . .
2 ik-t[ab-ta ri-gim a-me-lu-ti]
3 ina ḫu-bu-[r]i-šin? ⌜ú⌝-[za-am-ma šit-tú]
4 qí-ba?-ma? ⌜li-iṣ-ṣu-ru⌝ [$^{d}$a-num u $^{d}$adad e-le-nu]
5 $^{d}$sin(30) u $^{d}$nergal(u.gur) li-iṣ-[ṣu-ru er-ṣe-tim qab-li-tim]
6 ši-ga-ru na-aḫ-⌜ba⌝-l[u ta-am-ti]
7 $^{d}$é-a li-iṣ-ṣur qá-d[u šam-mi-šu]

---

8 iq-bi-ma iṣ-ṣu-ru $^{d}$a-⌜num⌝ u $^{d}$[adad e-le-nu]
9 $^{d}$sin(30) u $^{d}$nergal(u.gur) iṣ-ṣu-ru er-ṣe-tim q[ab-li-tim]
10 ši-ga-ru na-aḫ-ba-lu ta-am-[ti]
11 $^{d}$é-a iṣ-ṣur qá-da šam-m[i-šu]
12 ù šu-ú at-ra-ḫa-si-i[s . . .
13 $u_4$-mi-šam-ma ib-ta-a[k-ki . . .
14 maš-šak-ka ⌜i-zab⌝-bi-× × [. . .
15 e-nu-ma mid-ra-tum? × [. . .
16 mu-šu i-zu-uz-ma [. . .
17 š[i] × × × [. . .
18 iz-zak-kar a-na [. . .
19 lil-qé-e-ma × [. . .
20 liš-šá-kin šu-pu-ul [. . .
21 li-mur $^{d}$é-a × [. . .
22 a-na-ku ina mu-ši × [. . .
23 iš-tu-m[a . . .

---

24 i-na pu-ut n[āri . . .
25 i-na pu-ut [. . .
26 a-na apsî [. . .
27 iš-[m]é-e-ma $^{d}$[é-a . . .
28 ⌜i⌝-bi-ik l[àḫ-mi (?) . . .
29 amēlu šá na × × [. . .
30 an-nu-ú [. . .
31 ga-na ḫu × [. . .
32 ši × ab [. . .

BE 36669/24a, Photo Bab. 1601 (y)

1 ⌜ši-ga-ru na-aḫ-ba-lu⌝ [. . .
2 $^{d}$⌜é⌝-a ⌜li⌝-iṣ-⌜ṣú⌝-ru [. . .
3 iq-b[i-m]a [. . .
4 ù $^{d}$adad [. . .
5 $^{d}$en-líl [. . .
6 iṣ-ṣú-ru [. . .
7 ši-ga-ru na-aḫ-[b]a-l[u . . .
8 $^{d}$é-a iṣ-ṣú-ru [. . .
9 ù šu-ú at-ra-ḫ[a-si-is . . .
10 ìl-šu $^{d}$é-a-ma [. . .
11 [$u_4$-m]i-šam-ma [. . .
12 [maš-š]ak-ka i-za-ab-[. . .
13 ⌜e⌝-nu-ma mi-id-r[a- . . .

# BE 39099 (x)

## Reverse i

[Enlil opened his mouth to speak],
1 And addressed [. . .
2 '[The noise of mankind] has become [too intense for me],
3 With their uproar I [am deprived of sleep].
4 Command that [Anu and Adad] guard [the upper regions],
5 That Sin and Nergal guard [the middle earth],
6 That the bolt, the bar [of the sea],
7 Ea may guard together with [his plants].'

---

8 He commanded, and Anu and [Adad] guarded [the upper regions],
9 Sin and Nergal guarded the [middle] earth,
10 The bolt, the bar of the sea,
11 Ea guarded together with [his] plants.
12 Now Atra-ḫasīs, [whose god was Ea],
13 Every day he wept [. . .
14 He used to bring offerings . [. . .
15 When the river [(. .) was quiet],
16 The night was still [. . .
17 . . . . [. . .
18 He spoke to [. . .
19 May [. . .] take [. . .
20 May it be established under [. . .
21 Let Ea see . [. . .
22 In the night I . [. . .
23 After [. . .

---

24 Facing the [river . . .
25 Facing [. . .
26 To the Apsû [. . .
27 [Ea] heard [. . .
28 And brought the [water monsters (?) . . .
29 The man who . . . [. . .
30 [Let] this being [. . .
31 Come . . [. . .
32 . . . [. . .

33 *i*-× [. . .
34 *i*-× [. . .
35 × [. . .
36 *li*-× [. . .
37 *at-ta* × × [. . .
38 *a-na apsî* × [. . .
39 *iš-mé-ma* $^{d}$[*é-a* . . .
40 *ù an-na-a* × [. . .
41 × × × AN × [. . .
42 *mi-nam i-na* × [. . .
43 *ul* × × × [. . .
44 *a-na* × × [. . .

## Reverse ii

1 . . .] × AN × × × × [. . .]

---

2 [(. .) *aq-bi-ma* $^{d}$]⌜*a*⌝*-nu u* $^{d}$*adad i-na-aṣ-ṣa-ru* ⌜*e*⌝-[*le-nu*]
3 [$^{d}$*sin*(30) *u* $^{d}$*nergal*(u.gur) *i-n*]*a-aṣ-ṣa-ru erṣetim*$^{tim}$ *qab-*⌜*li*⌝*-tú*
4 [*ši-ga-ru na-aḫ*]*-ba-lu tam-ti*
5 [*at-ta ta-na-a*]*ṣ-ṣa-ra qá-du šam-mi-ka*
6 [*tu-ma-áš-šè*]*r a-na nišī*$^{meš}$ *mi-šèr-tú*
7 . . .] *ta-ma-tú ra-pa-áš-tú*
8 [*ter-ti* $^{d}$*en*]*-líl a-na* $^{d}$*é-a ú-šá-an-nu-ú*
9 [. . *aq-bi-m*]*a* $^{d}$*a-nu u* $^{d}$*adad i!-na!-aṣ!-ṣa!-ru e-le-nu*
10 [$^{d}$*sin*(30) *u* $^{d}$*nergal*(u.gur)] ⌜*i*⌝*-na-ṣa-ru er-ṣe-tim qa-ab-li-tim*
11 [*ši-ga-ru na*]*-aḫ-ba-lu ta-am-ta*
12 [*at-ta ta*]*-na-aṣ-ṣa-ru qá-du šam-mi-ka*
13 [*tu-ma-áš*]*-šèr ana nišī*$^{meš}$ *me-šèr-tú*
14 [$^{d}$*é-a pa-a*]*-šú īpuš-ma i-qab-bi*
15 [*iz-za-kar*] *ana mār šip-ri*
16 [. .] × *taq-bi-ma* ⟨$^{d}$*a-nu u*⟩ $^{d}$*adad iṣ-ṣur e-le-nu*
17 [$^{d}$*sin*(30) *u* $^{d}$*nerga*]*l*(u.gu]r) *iṣ-ṣur erṣetu*$^{tú}$ *qab-li-tum*
18 [*ši-ga-ru n*]*a-aḫ-ba-lu tam-tú*
19 [*a-na-ku aṣ*]*-ṣur qá-du šam-me-iá*
20 [. . .] *ki-i ú-ṣa-an-ni*
21 [. . K]U$_{6}^{meš}$ I *šár nūnī*$^{meš}$ I *šár*$^{ta.àm}$ id ḫu ×
22 [. . K]U$_{6}^{meš}$ *ú-gap-pi-šam-ma iḫ-liq-ma*
23 [*šá ši-ga-r*]*u iš-bi-ru mi-šil-šu*

---

24 [. . . *a*]*d-du-*⌜*ku*⌝ *ma-aṣ-ṣa-ru tam-ti*

**9** Tablet: *iṣ-ṣú-ru*

33 . . [. . .
34 . . [. . .
35 . [. . .
36 Let . [. . .
37 You . . [. . .
38 To the Apsû . [. . .'
39 [Ea] heard [. . .
40 And this being . [. . .
41 . . . . . [. . .
42 What in . [. . .
43 . . . . [. . .
44 To . . [. . .

## Reverse ii

2 '[(. .) I commanded that] Anu and Adad should guard [the upper regions],
3 [That Sin and Nergal] should guard the middle earth,
4 [That the bolt], the bar of the sea,
5 [You should] guard together with your plants.
6 [But you let loose] abundance for the peoples!'
7 . . .] the wide sea
8 Repeated [the message of] Enlil to Ea,
9 '[. . I commanded] that Anu and Adad should guard the upper regions,
10 [That Sin and Nergal] should guard the middle earth,
11 [That the bolt], the bar of the sea,
12 [You should] guard together with your plants.
13 [But you let] loose abundance for the peoples!'
14 [Ea] opened his [mouth] to speak
15 And [addressed] the messenger,
16 '[. .] . you commanded and ⟨Anu and⟩ Adad did guard the upper regions
17 [Sin and Nergal] did guard the middle earth,
18 [The bolt], the bar of the sea,
19 [I did] guard together with my plants.
20 When [. . .] escaped from me
21 [. .] . . a myriad of fish, one myriad . . .
22 [. .] . . I got together and it disappeared,
23 And they broke half of [the bolt].

---

24 [After (?)] I had killed the guards of the sea

25 [× × × *áš*]*-kun-šu-nu-ti-ma e-*⟨*te*⟩*-nin-šu-nu-ti*
26 [*iš-tu-ma*] *e-ni-nu-šu-nu-ti*
27 [*ú-tir-ram*]*-ma šèr-ta e-mi-id*
28 [× × ×] *il-qu-ú ter-ta*

---

29 [. . .] *ta-ma-tú ra-pa-áš-tú*
30 [*il-li-k*]*u-ma ú-šá-an-nu-ú*
31 [*ter-ti* $^{d}$*é*]-⌜*a a*⌝*-na qu-ra-di* $^{d}$*en-líl*
32 [. . .] × *taq-bi-ma* $^{d}$*a-nu u* $^{d}$*adad iṣ-ṣu-ru e-le-nu*
33 [$^{d}$*sin*(30) *u* $^{d}$*n*]*ergal*(u].gur) *iṣ-ṣu-ru er-ṣe-tú qab-*[*l*]*i-tú*
34 [*ši-ga-ru n*]*a-aḫ-ba-lu ti-am-ti*
35 [*a-na*]-⌜*a*⌝?*-ku aṣ-ṣu-ra qá-du šam-mi-ia*
36 [. . .] *ki-i ú-ṣa-an-ni*
37 [. .] KU$_{6}^{meš}$ I *šár nūnī*$^{meš}$ I *šár*$^{ta.àm}$ id? pi ×
38 [. .] KU$_{6}^{meš}$ *ú-gap-pi-šam-ma iḫ-liq-ma*
39 [*šá ši-ga*]*-ru iš-bi-ru mi-šil-šu*
40 [. . .] *ad-du-ka ma-aṣ-ṣa-ru tam-ti*
41 [× ×] × *áš-kun-šu-nu-ti-*[*m*]*a e-te-nin-šú-nu-ti*
42 [*iš*]*-tu-ma e-ni-nu-šu-*⟨*nu*⟩*-ti*
43 [*ú*]*-tir-ram-ma šèr-ta e-mi-id*

---

44 [$^{d}$*en*]*-líl pa-a-šú i-pu-uš-ma i-qab-bi*
45 [*a*]*-na pu-ḫur ka-la ilī*$^{meš}$ *iz-za-kár*
46 [*a*]*l-ka-ni ka-la-ni a-na ma-mi-tú a-bu-bi*
47 $^{d}$*a-nam i-na pa-ni* ⌜*ta*⌝*-mu-ni*
48 $^{d}$*en-líl it-ta-mi mārē*$^{meš}$*-šú it-ti-šú ta-mu-ni*

25 I laid [. . .] on them and punished them.
26 [After] I had punished them
27 [I repeated it] and imposed a penalty.'
28 [. . .] took the message

---

29 [. . .] the wide sea
30 [Went] and repeated
31 [The message of] Ea to Enlil,
32 '[. . .] . you commanded and Anu and Adad did guard the upper regions,
33 [Sin and] Nergal did guard the middle earth,
34 [The bolt], the bar of the sea,
35 [I] did guard together with my plants.
36 When [. . .] escaped from me
37 [. .] . . a myriad of fish, one myriad . . .
38 [. .] . . I got together and it disappeared
39 And they broke half of [the bolt].
40 [After (?)] I had killed the guards of the sea
41 I laid [. .] . on them and punished them.
42 After I had punished them
43 [I] repeated it and imposed a penalty.'

---

44 Enlil opened his mouth to speak
45 And addressed the assembly of all the gods,
46 'Come, all of us, and take an oath to bring a flood.'
47 Anu swore first;
48 Enlil swore, his sons swore with him.

# THE ASSYRIAN RECENSION

## BM 98977+99231 (U), Obverse

1 [$^{d}$*é*]-⸢*a*⸣ *bēl e-re-ba-ka* [*áš-me-ma*]
2 [*ú-t*]*e-qí-ma šikna ki-ma šikin šēp*[*ē*$^{\text{II.meš}}$*-ka*]

3 [$^{m}$*a-tar-ḫasīs*] *ik-mis uš-kín i-ta-zi-iz* × [× (×)]
4 [*pâ-šú*] *īpuša*$^{ša}$*-ma izzakar*(mu)$^{ár}$

5 [*ma bēl*] *e-re-ba-ka áš-me-ma*
6 [*ú-te-qí*]*-ma šikna ki-ma šikin šēpē*$^{\text{II.meš}}$*-k*[*a*]

7 [$^{d}$*é-a bē*]*l e-re-ba-ka áš-me-m*[*a*]
8 [*ú-te-q*]*í-ma šikna ki-ma šikin šēpē*$^{\text{II.meš}}$-[*ka*]

9 [× ×] × *ki-i* 7 *šanāti*(mu)$^{m}$[$^{\text{eš}}$]
10 . . .] ×*-ma-ka ú-ṣé-mi ḫaš-ḫa-*[*šá*]

11 . . .] ×$^{ḫi\text{-}pí\ eš\text{-}šú}$*-ka a-ta-mar pa-ni-k*[*a*]
12 . . .] ×*-ru-ku-nu qí-ba-a ia-a-š*[*i*]

13 [$^{d}$*é-a p*]*â-šu īpuša*$^{ša}$ *i-qab-bi*
14 [*iz-za-ka*]*r a-na ki-ki-ši*

15 . . .] *ki-kiš ki-k*[*iš*]
16 . . . *ši*]*-ta-ma-ni*

17 . . .] × biš × [. .]
18 . . .] × ia [. .]
19 . . .] × i ta [. .]
20 . . .] × × × [. .]

*    *    *    *    *

## Reverse

1 traces

2 [. . . *it*]*-ta-di ri-*× [× (×)]
3 [*i-ru-u*]*m-ma ip-ḫa-a* $^{gi}$[$^{š}$*eleppa*]
4 [*š*]*a-ru*$^{ḫi\text{-}pí\ eš\text{-}šú}$*-il-ma ib-bak me-ḫ*[*u-ú*]
5 $^{d}$*adad i-na šār erbetti*(im.limmu.ba) *ir-ta-kab pa-re-*⸢*e*⸣-[*šu*]
6 *šu-ú-tu il-ta-nu šadû*$^{ú}$ *a-mur-*[*ru*]

# THE ASSYRIAN RECENSION

## BM 98977+99231 (U), Obverse

---

1 Ea, lord, [I heard] your entry,
2 [I] noticed steps like [your] footsteps.'

---

3 [Atra-ḫasīs] bowed down, he prostrated himself, he stood up . [. .]
4 He opened [his mouth] and said,

5 '[Lord], I heard your entry,
6 [I noticed] steps like your footsteps.

7 [Ea, lord], I heard your entry,
8 [I noticed] steps like your footsteps.

---

9 [. .] . like seven years
10 . . .] your . . has made the feeble thirsty

11 . . .] . (new break) . I have seen your face
12 . . .] tell me your (pl.) . . [. .]'

---

13 [Ea] opened his mouth to speak
14 [And addressed] the reed-hut,

15 '. . .] Reed-hut! Reed-hut!
16 . . .] pay attention to me!

* * * * *

## Reverse

---

2 [. . . he] put . . [. .]
3 [He] entered and shut up the [boat].
4 The wind (new break) . and brought the [storm].
5 Adad rode on the four winds, [his] asses,
6 The south wind, the north wind, the east wind, the west wind.

7 *si-qu-šú siq-si-qu me-ḫu-ú rādu*(aga[r$_x$])
8 *im-ḫul-lu* ad ma ḫu lu *te-bu-ú šārū*$^{\text{m}}$[$^{\text{eš}}$]
9 *ur*$^{\textit{hi-pí}}$*-qù-da it-ba-a id-šú šu-tu*
10 [*i*]*-zi-qù a-na idi-šú a-mur-ru*
11 [×] × [×] × *i-ba-'* ki ši ×

---

12 [× ×]ŠE*-ri ru-ku-ub ilāni*$^{\text{meš}}$ *muš-šu-*× [× ×]
13 [*i-r*]*a-ḫi-iṣ i-da-ak i-da-áš* [× × ×]

14 [*il*]*-lak* $^{\text{d}}$*nin-urta mi-iḫ-ra* [*ú-šar-di*]
15 $^{\text{d}}$*èr-ra-kal ú-na-sa-ḫa t*[*ar-kul-li*]

16 [$^{\text{d}}$*z*]*u i-na ṣu-up-ri-šu šamê*$^{e}$ ⌜*ú*⌝-[*šar-riṭ*]
17 [× × *m*]*āta ki-ma karpati mi-lik-šá is-p*[*u-uḫ*]

18 [× × ×] ⌜*i*⌝*-ta-ṣa-a a-bu-bu*
19 [*ki-ma qab-li el*]*i ni-še i-ba-a ka-šu-šu*

---

20 . . . $^{\text{d}}$]*a*?*-nu rigim*(KA) *a-bu-bi*
21 . . . *ilāni*]$^{\text{meš}}$ *ul-ta-dar*

22 . . .] × *mārū*$^{\text{meš}}$*-šá ub-bu-ku a-na pi-šá*

---

23 . . .] × *la-lu-šá i*[*ṣ-ru-u*]*p*
24 . . .] ⌜ma li⌝ [. . .
25 . . .]$^{\text{meš}}$ × [. . .

7 The storm, the gale, the tempest blew for him,
8 The Evil Wind . . . . the winds arose.
9 The south wind . (break) . . arose at his side,
10 The west wind blew at his side,
11 [.] . [.] . reached . . .

---

12 [. .] . . the chariot of the gods . . . [. .]
13 [It] sweeps forward, it kills, it threshes [. . .]

14 Ninurta went on and [made] the dykes [overflow],
15 Errakal tore up [the mooring poles].

16 [Zû] with his talons [rent] the heavens,
17 [He . .] the land like a pot, he scattered its counsel.

18 [. . .] the flood set out,
19 Its might came [upon] the peoples [like a battle array].

---

20 . . .] Anu (?) [. . .] the noise of the flood,
21 . . .] set the [gods] atremble.

22 . . .] . her sons were thrown down at her own command.

---

23 . . .] . spent her emotion

* * * * *

# CBS 13532 (𝕵)[1]

## Obverse

1. ]×-*bi* 3. ]× *i-ba-aš-šu-ú* 5. *i-b*]*a-aš-šu-ú*

## Reverse

1 . . .] × a? ši × i? [× ×] ×-*ka*
2 . . .] *a-pa-aš-šar*
3 . . .] *ka-la ni-ši iš-te-niš i-ṣa-bat*
4 . . .]-*ti la-am a-bu-bi wa-ṣe-e*
5 . . .] ×-*a-ni ma-la i-ba-aš-šu-ú lu kin ub-bu-ku lu pu-ut-tu ḫu-ru-šu*
6 . . .] $^{giš}$*eleppa ra-bí-tam bi-ni-ma*
7 . . .] *qá-ne-e gáb-bi lu bi-nu-us-sà*
8 . . .] *ši-i lu* $^{giš}$*maqurqurrum*(má.gur.gur)-*ma šum-ša lu na-ṣi-rat na-piš-tim*
9 . . .] × *ṣú-lu-la dan-na ṣú-ul-lil*
10 . . .] *te-ep-pu-šu*
11 . . .] × *ú-ma-am ṣe-rim iṣ-ṣur ša-me-e*
12 . . .] *ku-um-mi-ir*(! tablet -*ni*)
13 . . .] × u kin? ta ×
14 (trace)

[1] The Middle, not Old, Babylonian date of this fragment has been argued by G. A. Barton, *JAOS* 31. 37–46, and E. I. Gordon, *Journal of Biblical Literature* 75. 336.

# CBS 13532 (J)

2 . . .] I will explain
3 . . . a flood] will seize all the peoples together
4 . . .] . before the flood sets out
5 . . .] . . . all that there are . . . . . . . . . . . .
6 . . .] build a big boat.
7 Let its structure be [. . . . .] entirely of reeds.
8 . . .] let it be a *maqurqurrum*-boat with the name, The Life Saver.

9 . . .] roof it over with a strong covering.
10 [Into the boat which] you will make
11 [Send . . .] . wild creatures of the steppe, birds of the heavens
12 . . .] heap up

# DT 42 (W)

1 [× × ×] × *lu-u* × [. . .
2 [× × ×] × *ki-ma kip-pa-ti* [. . .
3 [*ku-up-ru*] *lu da-an e-liš u š*[*ap-liš*]
4 [× (×)] × e *pi-ḫi* $^{\text{giš}}$[*eleppa*]
5 [*ú-ṣur*] *a-dan-na šá a-šap-pa-rak-*[*ka*]
6 [$^{\text{giš}}$*eleppa*] *e-ru-um-ma bāb* $^{\text{giš}}$*eleppi tir-*[*ra*]
7 [*šu-li ana*] *lìb-bi-šá uṭṭat*(še.bar)-*ka bušâ*(níg.šu)-*ka u makkūr*(níg.ga)-[*ka*]
8 [*aššat-k*]*a ki-mat-ka sa-lat-ka u mārī*$^{\text{meš}}$ *um-m*[*a-ni*]
9 [*bu-ul*] *ṣēri ú-ma-am ṣēri ma-la urqētu*(ú.šim) *me-er-*[*'i-sun*]

10 [*a-šap*]*-pa-rak-kúm-ma i-na-aṣ-ṣa-ru bāb-k*[*a*]

---

11 [$^{\text{m}}$*at-r*]*a-ḫa-sis pa-a-šú īpuš*(dù)-*ma iqabbi*(dug$_4$.g[a])
12 [*i-zak*]*-kar ana* $^{\text{d}}$*é-a be-lí-*[*šú*]
13 [*ma-t*]*i-ma-a* $^{\text{giš}}$*eleppa ul e-pu-uš* × [×]
14 [*ina qaq*]*-qa-ri e-ṣir ú-*[*ṣur-tú*]
15 [*ú-ṣur*]*-tu lu-mur-ma* $^{\text{giš}}$*eleppa* [*lu-pu-uš*]
16 [$^{\text{d}}$*é*]-⌈*a*⌉ *ina qaq-qa-ri e-*[*ṣir ú-ṣur-tu*]
17 [× × (×) *b*]*e-lí šá taq-ba-*⌈*a*⌉ [. . .

* * * * *

# DT 42 (W)

1 [. . .] . let it . [. . .
2 [. . .] . like a circle [. . .
3 Let [the pitch] be strong above and below,
4 [. .] . . caulk the [boat].
5 [Observe] the appointed time of which I will inform you,
6 Enter [the boat] and close the boat's door.
7 [Send up into] it your barley, your goods, your property,
8 [Your wife], your kith, your kin, and the skilled workers.
9 [Creatures] of the steppe, all the wild creatures of the steppe that eat grass,
10 [I] will send to you and they will wait at your door.'

---

11 Atra-ḫasīs opened his mouth to speak
12 And addressed Ea, [his] lord,
13 'I have never built a boat . [.]
14 Draw the design on the ground
15 That I may see [the design] and [build] the boat.'
16 Ea drew [the design] on the ground.
17 '[. .] my lord, what you commanded [. . .

* * * * *

# THE FLOOD STORY FROM RAS SHAMRA

## *Ugaritica* v. 167 = RS 22. 421 (𝕳)

THIS small fragment, that was announced by J. Nougayrol in *Académie des Inscriptions et Belles-Lettres, Comptes Rendus*, 1960. 170, and published by him in *Ugaritica* v, represents the only version of the Babylonian flood story found outside Mesopotamia so far. Unlike *Atra-ḫasīs*, it covered only the flood itself, not the creation of man and Enlil's attempts to diminish their numbers. It was written on a single tablet, of which the beginning and end only survive, and it dates from about the fourteenth century B.C.

Atra-ḫasīs himself begins to speak in obverse 6, and it sounds as though he is going to tell the story, as happens in *Gilgameš* XI, where the immortal flood hero explains to Gilgameš how he escaped death. The first five lines contain no similar explanation for use of the first person here. The orthography and grammar of the tablet mark it out as having been written in the West, but what little of the text remains suggests a good Babylonian work of literature, not a Syrian composition.

## Obverse

1 ⌜*e*⌝*-nu-ma ilānu*$^{\text{meš}}$ *im-taš-ku mil-ká* $^{2}$ *i-na mātāti*$^{\text{meš}.ti}$
*a-bu-ba iš-ku-nu* $^{3}$ *i-na kí-ib-ra-ti*

---

4 × × × × *i-še*[*m*]*-me* [(. .)]
5 *i-*× × × [. . . . . .]*-bit-ti* $^{\text{d}}$*é-a ina libbi-š*[*u*]

---

6 $^{\text{m}}$*at-ra-am-ḫa-sí-sum-me a-na-ku-*[*ma*]
7 *i-na bīt* $^{\text{d}}$*é-a bēli-ia aš-ba-*[*ku*]
8 *ú-*×*-*×*-ma i-*× [×]

---

9 *i-de*$_{4}$ *mil-ká* *ša ilāni*$^{\text{meš}}$ *ra-ab-bu-ti*
10 *i-de*$_{4}$ *ma-me-et-šu-nu* *ù ú-ul* $^{11}$*i-pa-at-tu-ú a-na ia-a-ši*

---

12 *a-ma-te-šu-nu a-na ki-ik-ki-*[*ši*] $^{13}$ *i-ša-an-*[*ni*]

---

14 [*i*]*-ga-ru-ma ši-m*[*e-* . . .
15 [×] ki ? ma *i-*[. . .

* * * * *

## Reverse

1 [. . . .] × *ilāni*$^{\text{m}}$[$^{\text{eš}}$] *ba-l*[*a-ṭá* . . .
2 [× ×(×)] ×*-ta aššat-ka* × [. . .
3 [×] ×*-a tuk-la-at ù* × [. . .
4 *ki-i ilāni*$^{\text{meš}}$ *ba-la-ṭá lu-ú* [. . .

---

5 šu $^{\text{m}}$sig$_{5}$.$^{\text{d}}$nè.iri$_{\text{x}}$.gal
6 × (×) an.šu.šá.ku ?.na

---

## Obverse

1 When the gods took counsel in the lands
3 And brought about a flood in the regions of the world,

---

4 . . . . hears [. .]
5 . . . . [. . . .] . . Ea in his heart.

---

6 'I am Atra-ḫasīs,
7 I lived in the temple of Ea, my lord,
8 . . . . . . [.]

---

9 I knew the counsel of the great gods,
10 I knew of their oath, though they did not reveal it to me.

---

12 He repeated their words to the wall,

---

14 "Wall, hear [. . .

* * * * *

## Reverse

1 [. . . .] . the gods life [. . .
2 [. . .] . . your wife . [. . .
3 [. .] . help and . [. . .
4 Life like the gods [you will] indeed [possess].'

---

5 Written by Mudammiq-Nergal
6 Property (?) of . . . . .

# BEROSSUS

BEROSSUS was a priest of Babylon, who, at some time in his life, settled on the island of Cos and opened a school. He calls himself a contemporary of Alexander the Great, but since the latter died young Berossus outlived him and his work in Greek, *Babyloniaka*, was dedicated to Antiochus I, who reigned either as co-regent or as sole monarch from 292 to 261 B.C. The purpose of this book was to present Babylonian history, with its vast antiquity, to the Greeks. Despite the considerable interest in that kind of material in the Hellenistic world, incredibly few people read the book, and it is now lost. For the flood (and most other things) we have to depend on Alexander Polyhistor, a Greek of the first century B.C., who quoted Berossus extensively. This work too is lost, but it was in turn quoted by Eusebius, especially in his *Chronicles*, which survives in an Armenian translation. However, the passage relating to the flood is quoted from Eusebius in Greek by the Byzantine chronicler Syncellus. Another writer who gives a briefer account of the flood ultimately derived from Berossus is Abydenus. His date is uncertain, but since he seems to depend on Polyhistor and is quoted in turn by Eusebius (his work is no longer extant) the limits between which he must be put are fixed. The relevant section is quoted by Eusebius twice, in his *Chronicles* and in his *Praeparatio Evangelica*. With such a devious tradition one must ask how reliable it is. There are differences between Polyhistor and Abydenus. According to the former the second group of birds returned to the ark in a muddy condition, but the third group according to the latter. The former states that pitch from the remains of the ark in Armenia was used for amulets, but the latter asserts that wood served this purpose. If it is accepted that Abydenus depended on Polyhistor (the evidence is plausible), then obviously the excerpts from Polyhistor are to be preferred. However, Abydenus records that the first group of birds were let out three days after the rain stopped. No similar time period is given by Polyhistor as we know his version. This raises the question of whether Eusebius quotes Polyhistor in full, or is using a digest. Josephus, *Antiquities of the Jews*, I. iii. 6, also quotes the sentence about use of the pitch (not wood!) as amulets, and there is a considerable amount of verbal agreement between his and Eusebius' version, especially if one allows that Josephus' literary helpers may have touched up Berossus' style. However, a more serious problem is raised in the account of creation where Eusebius, professing to quote Polyhistor, gives a conflated version made up of two separate accounts, the one undoubtedly Berossus, the other a combination of Babylonian and Hebrew elements. Details will be given in the first-named author's forthcoming *Babylonian Creation Myths*. At whatever stage in the line of transmission this conflation took place, it throws doubt on the integrity of the whole tradition. Fortunately there is no similar objection to any major part of the story of the flood.

The Greek text of Berossus, with a German version of excerpts from the Armenian, can be read both in P. Schnabel, *Berossus und die babylonisch-hellenistische Literatur*, and in F. Jacoby, *Die Fragmente der griechischen Historiker* (*FGH*) III C, pp. 364 ff. The only English translation of at least the major fragments is that of I. P. Cory, *Ancient Fragments* (best edition, 1832).

The flood came in the second book of Berossus' *Babyloniaka*, after the ten kings and the related sages. The last two of the kings are given as Otiartes (or Ardates), a corruption of Ubār-Tutu, and Xisuthros, i.e. Ziusudra. They are said to have reigned in Larak.

## BEROSSUS, ACCORDING TO POLYHISTOR

The same Alexander, going still further down from the ninth king Ardates as far as the tenth, called by them Xisuthros, reports on the authority of the Chaldean writings as follows: After the death of Ardates his son Xisuthros ruled for eighteen sars and in his time a great flood occurred, of which this account is on record:

> Kronos appeared to him in the course of a dream and said that on the fifteenth day of the month Daisios mankind would be destroyed by a flood. So he ordered him to dig a hole and to bury the beginnings, middles, and ends of all writings in Sippar, the city of the Sun(-god); and after building a boat, to embark with his kinsfolk and close friends. He was to stow food and drink and put both birds and animals on board and then sail away when he had got everything ready. If asked where he was sailing, he was to reply, 'To the gods, to pray for blessings on men.'
>
> He did not disobey, but got a boat built, five stades long and two stades wide, and when everything was properly arranged he sent his wife and children and closest friends on board. When the flood had occurred and as soon as it had subsided, Xisuthros let out some of the birds, which, finding no food or place to rest, came back to the vessel. After a few days Xisuthros again let out the birds, and they again returned to the ship, this time with their feet covered in mud. When

they were let out for the third time they failed to return to the boat, and Xisuthros inferred that land had appeared. Thereupon he prized open a portion of the seams of the boat, and seeing that it had run aground on some mountain, he disembarked with his wife, his daughter, and his pilot, prostrated himself to the ground, set up an altar and sacrificed to the gods, and then disappeared along with those who had disembarked with him. When Xisuthros and his party did not come back, those who had stayed in the boat disembarked and looked for him, calling him by name. Xisuthros himself did not appear to them any more, but there was a voice out of the air instructing them on the need to worship the gods, seeing that he was going to dwell with the gods because of his piety, and that his wife, daughter, and pilot shared in the same honour. He told them to return to Babylon, and, as was destined for them, to rescue the writings from Sippar and disseminate them to mankind. Also he told them that they were in the country of Armenia. They heard this, sacrificed to the gods, and journeyed on foot to Babylon. A part of the boat, which came to rest in the Gordyaean mountains of Armenia, still remains, and some people scrape pitch off the boat and use it as charms. So when they came to Babylon they dug up the writings from Sippar, and, after founding many cities and setting up shrines, they once more established Babylon.

Jacoby, *FHG* III C, pp. 378–82

### BEROSSUS, ACCORDING TO ABYDENUS

After whom others ruled, and Sisithros, to whom Kronos revealed that there would be a deluge on the fifteenth day of Daisios, and ordered him to conceal in Sippar, the city of the Sun(-god), every available writing. Sisithros accomplished all these things, immediately sailed to Armenia, and thereupon what the god had announced happened. On the third day, after the rain abated, he let loose birds in the attempt to ascertain if they would see land not covered with water. Not knowing where to alight, being confronted with a boundless sea, they returned to Sisithros. And similarly with others. When he succeeded with a third group—they returned with muddy feathers—the gods took him away from mankind. However, the boat in Armenia supplied the local inhabitants with wooden amulets as charms.

Jacoby, *FHG* III C, pp. 401–2

Berossus departs from all known cuneiform sources in only two respects. First, he gives a particular month and day for the beginning of the flood.

Daisios is a Macedonian month corresponding with the Babylonian Iyyar, the second month of the year. It is not clear if this datum is part of a precise chronology of the flood, like that in Genesis, or if it was a solitary item with some other, perhaps cultic, significance. Secondly, the burying of all writings in Sippar is known from Berossus alone. The phrase 'beginnings, middles and ends', meaning simply 'all', can be paralleled from a Babylonian text which prescribes the recitation of prayers twice by saying 'the beginning of the inscription and the end of the inscription shall be recited twice' (*JAOS* 87, Kh 1932.26), meaning 'from beginning to end'. The mention of Sippar in this connection surely implies a local tradition of Sippar, which is interesting because Berossus' list of the ten kings is plainly altered, as compared with second millennium examples, in favour of Babylon. The ten kings are spread over three cities, the first Babylon, replacing the earlier Eridu, the second and third being Badtibira and Larak, both completely unimportant places in the first millennium. Evidently there was no version of the flood which set the scene in Babylon, so a Sipparian version was employed, though this is not used either in *Atra-ḫasīs* or *Gilgameš* XI. The apotheosis of the flood hero could have been contained in the damaged ending of *Atra-ḫasīs*. In addition to Berossus and *Gilgameš* XI, another attestation of this item occurs on the Babylonian Mappa Mundi, where under the name Ut-napištim the flood hero is described as living in a remote corner of the universe (*CT* 22. 48 obv. 10).

# THE SUMERIAN FLOOD STORY

by M. CIVIL

THE Sumerian flood story is preserved in CBS 10673, the bottom third, approximately, of the complete tablet, apparently from Nippur. It was published by Arno Poebel in 1914 (*PBS* V, no. 1, and pls. LXXXVI–LXXXVII [photos]).[1] Poebel himself gave a complete study of the text in *PBS* IV/1. 7–70. The text aroused considerable interest and a certain number of studies, most of which by now offer little except historical interest, followed Poebel's publication.[2] The only serious attempt to bring Poebel's work up to date can be found in S. N. Kramer's translation in *ANET* 42 ff. In the philological notes, references to Poebel and Kramer without further specification are to *PBS* IV/1.7 ff. and *ANET* 42 ff. respectively.

So far no duplicates of CBS 10673 have turned up. A few isolated fragments might belong to the same text: the bilingual *CT* 46. 5 (see pp. 14 and 17) could belong to the missing part of column iii; *STVC* 87 B (see pp. 16 and 26) also could well belong to this story. However, nothing more positive than a similarity of content recommends their attribution to this text.

The present edition follows Kramer's line numbering, which gives a good idea of the extent of the gaps, though it does not take indented lines into account.

In the absence of a colophon, a tablet can be dated only by palaeographic, orthographic, linguistic, and other internal criteria. Cuneiform palaeography, it is sad to say, has hardly made any progress in the last forty years, and little could be added to Poebel's conclusions (*PBS* IV/1. 69), which are still valid. It must be stressed, however, that generally a literary tablet cannot be dated by a simple comparison of its sign forms with those of the administrative texts. Different calligraphic styles coexisted, and served for different genres of tablets. In any case CBS 10673 is not earlier than Late Old Babylonian.

[1] Poebel's hand-copy is reproduced in S. N. Kramer, *Sumerian Mythology*, fig. 2, and *From the Tablets of Sumer* 178, fig. 60.

[2] A. T. Clay, *YOR* V/3 (1922); C. J. Gadd, *Sumerian Reading Book* 130 ff. (1924), reproduces lines 145–211 of the text; H. Gressmann (ed.), *Altorientalische Texte zum alten Testament*[2] 198 ff. (1926); L. W. King, *Legends of Babylon and Egypt* (*Schweich Lectures* 1916) 41 ff.; A. Heidel, *The Gilgamesh Epic and Old Testament Parallels* 102 ff. (1949); S. N. Kramer, *Sumerian Mythology* 97 ff. (1944), *From the Tablets of Sumer* 176 ff. (1956). Remarks on parts of the text are given by T. Jacobsen, *AS* 11. 58 f., 64 f.; and by J. Laessøe, *BiOr* 13. 90 ff.

Since Poebel's initial publication knowledge of the standard Sumerian literary corpus, mainly from the Nippur school, secondarily from that of Ur, has increased so much that the grammatical and lexical irregularities of this text, some of which were already pointed out by Poebel in *PBS* IV/1. 68, are much more obvious. Most of the verbal forms, for example, do not fit into the paradigms of standard Sumerian. Unless one can trace a Sumerian model (see, e.g., the note on 100) or an Akkadian construction (e.g. in 202 ùr with ugu renders the phrase *bâ'u eli*), then a translation cannot be offered with much assurance. Some of the more doubtful passages have been italicized in the translation. However, it would be unwise to start building conclusions on the precise wording of still others. For example, the text begins with allusions to the destruction of man, although he is at this point newly created. Lines 38 and 39 are not quite complete, and the preceding lines are missing. With what is preserved the translation given seems the only one possible. Was there, then, a first destruction of the human race prior to the one recorded in *Atra-ḫasīs*? In the present state of knowledge it would be incautious positively to affirm it.

The theme of a flood which destroys mankind does not seem to belong to the main body of Sumerian traditions. Allusions to it are lacking in the texts which are presumed to go back to older originals, and so best represent Sumerian literary themes. When a primeval cosmic storm seems to be referred to (see Van Dijk, *Acta Orientalia* 28. 37), it has quite different implications and the destruction of the human race is not associated with it.[1] The original short form of the *Sumerian King List* may or may not have contained an opening reference to the flood, but it certainly included no antediluvian kings. The oldest datable occurrences of the standard phrase egir a-ma-ru ba-ùr-ra-ta 'after the storm had swept . . .' (line 40 of the longer form of the *Sumerian King List*) and its variants are in a hymn of Išme-Dagan (1953–1935 B.C.) and in a text which mentions Ur-Ninurta (1923–1896 B.C.), see pp. 16 and 26.[2] Judging from the information available at present, the theme of the flood which wiped out all but a handful of the human race became popular during the Isin dynasty. In view of the large number of artificial grammatical forms and lexical peculiarities in CBS 10673, it was very likely composed at a later date.

[1] Nor the storm associated with Inanna (*Enmerkar and the Lord of Aratta* 572 ff.; *Enmešarra* 10 ff.) or Enlil (*Hoe and Plow Contest* 168 ff.); the storm as a metaphor in the lamentations is also a case apart.

[2] Duplicates: S. N. Kramer, *Sumerian Literary Texts from Nippur* 137; *VAS* 10. 204. iii; and unpublished texts.

(i)

37 [. . . . . . . . . . . . .] im-gá-g[á . . .]
38 nam-⌜lú-u$_x$⌝(GIŠGAL)-mu ḫa-lam-ma-bi a ga-ba-n[i- . . .]
39 $^{d}$nin-tu-ra níg-dím-dím-ma-mu sì-[. . . . . . .] ga-ba-ni-ib-gi$_4$-g[i$_4$]
40 un ki-ùr-bi-ta ga-ba-ni-ib-gur-ru-ne
41 uru$^{ki}$-me-a-bi ḫé-im-mi-in-dù gissu-bi ní ga-ba-ab-dúb-bu
42 uru?-me-a sig$_4$-bi ki-kù-ga ḫé-im-mi-in-šub
43 ki?-eš-me-a ki-kù-ga ḫé-im-mi-ni-ib-ri
44 kù?-a níg-izi-te-na si mi-ni-in-si-sá
45 garza me-maḫ šu mi-ni-ib-šu-du$_7$
46 ki a im-ma-ab-dug$_4$ silim ga-mu-ni-in-gar
47 an $^{d}$en-líl $^{d}$en-ki $^{d}$nin-ḫur-sag-gá-ke$_4$
48 sag-gi$_6$-ga mu-un-dím-eš-a-ba
49 níg-ge$_{16}$ ki-ta ki-ta mu-lu-lu
50 máš-anše níg-úr-4 edin-na me-te-a-aš bí-íb-gál

(gap)

(ii)

84 [. . . . . . . . . . . . . .] àm [. . . . . . . . . .]
85 [× ×]⌜×⌝ ri-g[a] ga-ba-ni-in-[. . . . . .]
86 [du-l]um-bi igi ga-ba-ni-ib-du$_8$-d[u$_8$-×]
87 ⌜×⌝ šidim-kalam-ma-ke$_4$ uš-gi ⌜ḫa⌝-ba-ab-ba-[al]
88 [u$_4$ (×)]⌜×⌝-nam-lugal-la an-ta e$_{11}$-d[è]-a-ba
89 ⌜men⌝-maḫ $^{giš}$g[u-z]a-nam-lugal-la an-ta e$_{11}$-a-ba
90 [. . . . . . . . . . . . .š]u mi-ni-ib-šu-du$_7$
91 [× × ×]-ga u[ru . . . . . .b]a-an-da-šub
92 ⌜mu-bi ba-an-sa$_4$ KAB⌝-dug$_4$-g[a ba-ḫal-ḫ]al-la
93 (ni)sag$_x$-uru-bi-e-ne eridu$^{ki}$ máš-sag $^{d}$nu-dím-mud mi-ni-in-sum
94 2-kam-ma-šè nu-gig-ra bad-tibira$^{ki}$ mi-ni-in-sum
95 3-kam-ma la-ra-ag $^{d}$pa-bíl-⟨⟨ḫur⟩⟩-sag mi-ni-in-sum
96 4-kam-ma zimbir$^{ki}$ šul-$^{d}$utu mi-ni-in-sum
97 5-kam-ma šuruppak $^{d}$sùd$^{ki}$-ra mi-ni-in-sum
98 uru-bi-e-ne mu-bi ba-an-sa$_4$ -a KAB-dug$_4$-ga ba-ḫal-ḫal-la
99 a-gi$_4$ la-ba-an-šú-àm im ba-al-la a im-ma-an-túm
100 íd-tur-tur-re šu-luḫ-bi gar ḫur-ḫur mi-ni-íb-gar-gar

(gap)

(i)

38 'I want to [. . .] the destruction of my human race,
39 For Nintu, I want to *stop* the annih[ilation of] my creatures,
40 I want the people to come back to their dwelling grounds.
41 Let all their cities be built, I want their shade to be restful.
42 Let the bricks of all cities be laid on holy places,
43 Let all . . . rest on holy places,
44 The *pure water which quenches the fire* I will put conveniently there.
45 I perfected the divine rules and the lofty *me*,
46 The land will be irrigated, I want there to be peace.'
47 After An, Enlil, (and) Ninḫursag
48 Had created the black-headed people,
49 Animals multiplied everywhere,
50 Animals of all sizes, the quadrupeds, were placed as a fitting ornament of the plains

(gap)

(ii)

86 I want to consider their p[ainstaking efforts].
87 [. . .] *bricklayer* of the country, let him d[ig] a solid foundation.
88 [When the . . .] of kingship had come down from heaven,
89 After the lofty crown and the throne of kingship had come down from heaven,
90 [. . .] perfected [. . .],
91 Founded [. . .] cities in [. . .],
92 Gave them their names, apportioned the capitals;
93 The first of these cities, Eridu, he gave to the leader Nudimmud,
94 The second, Badtibira, he gave to the 'nugig',
95 The third, Larag, he gave to Pabilsag,
96 The fourth, Sippar, he gave to the hero Utu,
97 The fifth, Šuruppak, he gave to Sud.
98 He gave the names to these cities, apportioned the capitals.
99 He did not stop the (yearly) flood, (but) dug the ground (and) brought the water,
100 He established the cleaning of the small canals and the irrigation ditches.

(gap)

(iii)

135 ki-tuš? an-na ⌜×⌝[. . . . . . . . .]
136 e [. . . . . . . . . . . . . . . . . . . . .]
137 a-ma-ru [. . . . . . . . . . . . . . .]
138 (traces)
139 ⌜ur$_5$-gin$_x$⌝ bí-in-ak [. . . . . . . . . .]
140 u$_4$-bi-a $^{d}$nin-t[u × ×] DÍM a [. . .]
141 kù-$^{d}$inanna-ke$_4$ un-bi-šè a-nir mu-[un-gá-gá]
142 $^{d}$en-ki šà-ní-te-na-ke$_4$ ad i-ni-i[n-gi$_4$-gi$_4$]
143 an $^{d}$en-líl $^{d}$en-ki $^{d}$nin-ḫur-sag-gá-[ke$_4$]
144 dingir-an-ki-ke$_4$ mu-an-$^{d}$en-líl mu-⌜×⌝-[pà]
145 u$_4$-ba zi-u$_4$-sud-rá lugal-àm gudu$_4$ ⌜×⌝[.]
146 an-sag-NIGIN mu-un-dím-dím en [. . . . .]
147 nam-du$_9$-na inim-sì-sì-ge ní-te-gá [. . . . .]
148 u$_4$-šú-uš-e sag-ús gub-ba [. . . . . . . . . . .]
149 ma-mú nu-me-a è-dè inim-ba[l . . . . . . .]
150 mu-an-ki-bi-ta pà-pà-dè [. . . . . . . .]

(iv)

151 ⌜ki?⌝-ùr-šè dingir-re-e-ne e-ga[r$_8$ . . . .]
152 zi-u$_4$-sud-ra da-bé gub-ba giš mu-[un-tuk]
153 iz-zi-da á-gùb-bu mu-gub ba-[. . . . .]
154 iz-zi-da inim ga-ra-ab-dug$_4$ inim-[mu ḫé-dab]
155 na-de$_5$-ga-mu gizz[al ḫé-im-ši-ak]
156 DAG?-me-a a-ma-ru ugu-KAB-d[ug$_4$-ga . .] ba-ù[r . . .]
157 numun-nam-lú-u$_x$ ḫa-lam-e ⌜×⌝[. . . . . . . .]
158 di-til-la inim pu-úḫ-ru-[um . . . . . . . .]
159 inim-dug$_4$-ga an $^{d}$en-[líl $^{d}$nin-ḫur-sag-gá-ke$_4$]
160 nam-lugal-bi bal-bi ⌜×⌝ [. . . . . . . . . . . . . .]
161 ⌜e-ne⌝-šè [. . . . . . . . . . . . . . . . . . . . .]
162 ⌜×⌝-na mu ⌜×⌝ [. . . . . . . . . . . . . . . . .]

(gap)

(v)

201 im-ḫul-im-ḫul im-si-si-ig dù-a-bi téš.bi ì-su$_8$-ge-eš
202 a-ma-ru ugu-KAB-dug$_4$-ga ba-an-da-ab-ùr-e
203 u$_4$-7-àm gi$_6$-7-àm
204 a-ma-ru kalam-ma ba-ùr-ra-ta

(iii)

140 Then Nin[tu . . . her] crea[tures? . . .]
141 Holy Inanna we[pt] because of the people,
142 Enki bethought himself (of the situation even though)
143 An, Enlil, Enki (and) Ninḫursag,
144 The gods of the universe, had [taken an oath by] the names of An and Enlil.
145 At that time, the king Ziusudra, the anointed [. . .],
146 He made . . . [. . .]
147 With humility (and) well chosen words, in reverence [. . .]
148 Every day he stood constantly present at [. . .].
149 It was not a dream, coming out and spea[king . . .]
150 Conjured by heaven and underworld [. . .]

(iv)

151 In the ki-ur (?), the gods, a wall [. . .]
152 Ziusudra hea[rd], standing by its side,
153 He stood at the left of the side-wall[. . .]
154 'Side-wall, I want to talk to you, [hold on] to my word,
155 [Pay atten]tion to my instructions:
156 On all dwellings (?), over the capitals the storm will [sweep].
157 The destruction of the descent of mankind [. . .],
158 The final sentence, the word of the assembly [. . .]
159 The word spoken by An and En[lil and Ninḫursag],
160 The overthrowing of the kingship [. . .].
Now [. . .]

(gap)

(v)

201 All the destructive winds (and) gales were present,
202 The storm swept over the capitals.
203 After the storm had swept the country for seven days and seven nights

205 $^{\text{giš}}$má-gur$_4$-gur$_4$ a-gal-la im-ḫul tuk$_4$-tuk$_4$-a-ta
206 $^{d}$utu i-im-ma-ra-è an-ki-a u$_4$ gá-gá
207 zi-u$_4$-sud-rá $^{\text{giš}}$má-gur$_4$-gur$_4$ ⌜ab⌝-BÚR mu-un-da-buru$_3$
208 ù? $^{d}$utu giš-nu$_x$(ŠIR)-ni-da $^{\text{giš}}$má-gur$_4$-gur$_4$-šè ba-an-ku$_4$-re-en
209 zi-u$_4$-sud-rá lugal-àm
210 igi-$^{d}$utu-šè KA ki-su-ub ba-gub
211 lugal-e gud im-ma-ab-gaz-e udu im-ma-ab-šár-re
212 [× ×]⌜×⌝ si-gal [. . . . . .si]kil-la-da
213 [. . . . . . . . . . . . . . .]⌜×⌝ mu-un-na-⌜× - ×⌝-ba
214 [. . . . . . . . . . . . . . . . . . . . . . . . . . . . . . . . . . . .]
215 [. . . . . . . . . . . . . . . . . . . . . .] bí-in-si
216 [. . . . . . . . . . . . . . . . . . . . .]⌜×⌝ tab-ba
217 [. . . . . . . . . . . . . . . . . . . . . . . . . . . . . .] a ⌜×⌝

(gap)

(vi)

251 zi-an-na zi-ki-a ì-pà-dè-en-zé-en za-zu-da ḫé-im-da-lá
252 an $^{d}$en-líl zi-an-na zi-ki-a ì-pà-dè-zé-en za-da-ne-ne im-da-lá
253 níg-ge$_{16}$ ki-⌜ta⌝ e$_{11}$-dè im-ma-ra-e$_{11}$-dè
254 zi-u$_4$-sud-rá lugal-àm
255 igi-an-$^{d}$en-líl-lá-šè KA ki-su-ub ba-gub
255*a* an $^{d}$en-líl zi-u$_4$-sud-rá SAL-e ⌜×⌝ [. . . .]
256 ti dingir-gin$_x$ mu-un-na-sum-mu
257 zi-da-rí dingir-gin$_x$ mu-un-ab-e$_{11}$-dè
258 u$_4$-ba zi-u$_4$-sud-rá lugal-àm
259 mu-níg-ge$_{16}$-ma numun-nam-lú-u$_x$ uri$_3$-ak
260 kur-bal kur-dilmun-na ki-$^{d}$utu-è-šè mu-un-tìl-eš
261 za-e ⌜×⌝ [. . . . . . . . . . . .]

(rest broken)

205 And the destructive wind had rocked the huge boat in the high water,
206 The Sun came out, illuminating the earth and the sky.
207 Ziusudra made an opening in the huge boat,
208 And the Sun with its rays entered the huge boat.
209 The king Ziusudra
210 Prostrated himself before the Sun-god,
211 The king slaughtered a large number of bulls and sheep.

(gap)

(vi)

251 Be conjured by heaven and underworld, let . . .
252 An (and) Enlil, be conjured by heaven and underworld, . . .
253 He/they made *come up* the animals which emerge from the earth.
254 The king Ziusudra
255 Prostrated himself before An (and) Enlil
255*a* (see note)
256 (Who) gave him life, like a god,
257 Elevated him to eternal life, like a god.
258 At that time, the king Ziusudra
259 Who protected the seed of mankind at the time (?) of destruction,
260 They settled in an overseas country, in the orient, in Dilmun.

(end broken)

# PHILOLOGICAL NOTES

## TABLET I

1 *a-wi-lum* has the locative *-um* with the meaning of the comparative *-iš*, as in *k -ma ša-ar-ra-qí-tu* (II. ii. 19, 33, see note), where *kīma* is used pleonastically like *ina* in *ina balûm* in the *Code of Hammurabi*. These are the first examples to be noted of comparative *-um*, but they need cause no difficulty as *-um* and *-iš* interchange freely before suffixes, so it is fully conceivable that they might do the same without suffixes also. The occurrence of comparative *-iš* as early as the Old Babylonian period has been denied by von Soden (*ZA* 41. 128–9), but it is not clear why *ewû* was disregarded, since it can be construed with either *kīma* or *-iš* already in the Old Babylonian period.

5 Recent literature on the Anunnaki and Igigi is plentiful: von Soden, *Compte rendu de l'onzième rencontre assyriologique internationale* 102 ff.; A. Falkenstein and B. Kienast in *AS* 16. 127 ff. and 141 ff. respectively; von Soden, *Iraq* 28. 140 ff. The opinion of Kienast, that the two terms are mostly synonymous, we accept for the Old Babylonian period generally (though not nearly so much as he for the later periods). Twice in *Atra-ḫasīs* (I. 232–3, III. vi. 6–7) the author has juxtaposed the two terms, as in *Enūma Eliš* VI. 20–7, so as to identify them. This line under discussion, however, contains the only example in the Old Babylonian copies of $^{d}$*a-nun-na-ku*. Elsewhere (I. 219, 232; II. v. 28; III. iii. 30, vi. 7) $^{d}$*a-nun-na*, the traditional orthography, is written. A similarly 'modern' orthography in the opening lines is the sign *qa* in 11 below. (Elsewhere the Old Babylonian copies write this syllable with the GA sign.) The Seven great Anunnaki are certainly those referred to as gods of the destinies in the following three passages:

dingir.nam.tar.ra imin.na.ne.ne
*Enlil and Ninlil*, Barton, *MBI* 4. ii. 14 = *SEM* 77. ii. 6
dìm.me.er.nam.tar.ra imin.ne.ne
*ilāni*$^{meš}$ *ši-ma-a-ti si-bit-ti-šú-nu*
*SBH* p. 135. iii. 27–8 = p. 92. 23, cf. p. 87. 34; *SBP* 164. 34
*ilāni*$^{meš}$ *šīmāti*$^{meš}$ *sibitti-šú-nu*
*Enūma Eliš* VI. 81

The gods of the destinies are those who fixed, and who alone could change, the *status quo*, cf. 219, below; thus if the gods had to toil it was certainly this group that had so ordained, even though the text only alludes to their number rather than their full title. The accusative *sibittam* is unexpected but perhaps explicable. The function of this case in Akkadian is always limiting. If one says *imḫaṣ* 'he struck', the meaning is so general as to be incomprehensible, but *imḫaṣ awīlam* 'he struck the man' so limits the action of the verb by the addition of the accusative that meaning results. This can occur with a stative verb too, as shown in the example *igpuš libba* 'he became great as to his heart' (quoted in a very fine section of the 2nd and 3rd editions of A. Ungnad's *Babylonisch-Assyrische Grammatik*, § 19, unfortunately dropped from the 4th edition). The term 'adverbial accusative' has been used to describe other kinds of limiting achieved by use of this case. All these, however, limit verbs, but here *sibittam* limits the noun *anunnakku*. Without *sibittam* it would mean all the great gods generally. The accusative limits the group down to seven particular ones. Von Soden in *JNES* 19. 163 ff. has collected the examples of such phrases as *damqam īni*, seen also in the name *watram-ḫasīs*, which are remarkable both for the ending on what would normally be in the construct state and for the regularity with which the ending seems to be an accusative. All the occurrences are descriptive phrases, since with the name one must understand '(the man) abounding in wisdom'. Perhaps here too we are to understand the accusatives as limiting a noun, whether expressed or not.

9 Neither *CAD* nor *AHw* attempts to define the meaning of *guzalû* precisely. There is certainly no proof that the official who no doubt originally carried his lord's chair still performed this menial duty in the Old Babylonian period, any more than the Lord Chamberlain in twentieth-century Britain supervises the monarch's bedroom. From line 49 below and the related J it may be suspected that as conceived by the author of *Atra-ḫasīs* the *guzalû* supervised the forced labour.

10 Cf. 127. *gallû* here is certainly not 'demon', but is explained in *Erimḫuš* VI in a group with two other civic officials:

| | | | |
|---|---|---|---|
| 18 | li.bi.ir | = | *gal-lu-u* |
| 19 | dub.si | = | *gu-za-lu-u* |
| 20 | ab.ba.uru | = | *ši-i-ib a-li* |

A semantic parallel is offered by maškim = *rābiṣu*, which also means both 'a demon' and 'an official'. While these two examples of this meaning of *gallû* seem to be the only ones, it may be noted that the demons called gal$_5$.lá act as the constabulary of Ereškigal in the Sumerian *Descent of Innin*. Ennugi is first mentioned, it seems, in the Ur III offering list *TCL* 5. 6053 ii (1 udu $^{d}$en.nu.gi$_4$) in a section dealing with the minor gods of Enlil's court. He appears again in the same context in the Old Babylonian forerunner to *AN* = *Anum* (*TCL* 15, pl. XXIX. 324), and this is taken over and elaborated in *AN* = *Anum* I as follows:

| | |
|---|---|
| $^{d}$en.nu.gi | gu.za.lá $^{d}$en.líl.lá.ke$_4$ |
| $^{d}$ŠEŠú.ru.ma.ášMAŠ | $^{d}$en.nu.gi |
| $^{d}$nisaba | dam.bi gu.za.lá $^{d}$nin.líl.lá.ke$_4$ |
| | *CT* 24. 10. 7–9 and dup. |

His connection with Enlil is further confirmed by the litany that names $^{d}$en.nu.gi dumu.$^{d}$en.líl.lá.ra (*SBH* p. 137. 36, dup. K 5148: 'to Ennugi, son of Enlil'), and by the exorcistic text *ABRT* I. 57 rev. 2–5 that names him among *ilāni*$^{meš}$ *šá é-*[*kur*] *ilāni*$^{meš}$ *šá é-šu-me-ša*$_4$ ('gods of Ekur, gods of Ešumeša', cf. Zimmern, *ZA* 32. 66[2]). He is no doubt meant in *Šurpu* VIII. 14: $^{d}$*en-nu-gi* gu.za.lá $^{d}$DI.KUD, *UET* VI/2. 408. 4, but the context is unhelpful, and it is not clear to which of these two the title belongs, since both can bear it. A completely different god appears in *AN* = *Anum* V. 223–5, $^{d}$⌜en⌝.[nu].⌜gi$_4$⌝.gi$_4$, one of the two doorkeepers of Ereškigal (*CT* 25. 5. 37, restored). In *KAR* 142. iv. 12–15 $^{d}$*en-nu-gi*$_4$*-gi*$_4$ is given as the last of the seven doorkeepers of Ereškigal, and in the myth *Nergal and Ereškigal* he appears in charge of the seventh gate leading to the shades ($^{d}$*en-nu-g*[*i*$_4$*-gi*$_4$]: *STT* 28. iii. 47′ = *AnSt* X. 116). There is a mass of evidence showing that single and reduplicated roots freely interchange in Sumerian, so that by name alone one cannot distinguish between the 'chamberlain of Enlil' and the keeper of the seventh gate in the underworld. Indeed, an etymological god list, *CT* 25. 49 rev. 3 explains $^{d}$*en-nu-gi* as *bēl erṣetim*$^{tim}$ *bēl la ta-*[*a-ri*]. (The similarity of $^{d}$en.nu.gi and kur.nu.gi could hardly be missed!) Yet a third Ennugi figure can be identified. The third of seven gods listed in Thureau-Dangin, *Rit. acc.* 5. 3 ff. is:

$^{d}$šeg$_9$.bar.ra.gim$_4$.gim$_4$.me a.šà.mar.ra.ke$_4$
$^{d}$*en-nu-gi šá-kin eq-li*

This list occurs also in *RA* 16. 145 obv. 11–12, and in unilingual form only in *AN* = *Anum* I. 139 ff. (*CT* 24. 4. 29 ff.), where they are expressly called the seven sons of Enmešarra. Ennugi is not one of them, but is identified with one, and must therefore have had some at least of the same characteristics. He is also named as one of the 'Enlils' on a brick inscription from Ur: [é.(×)].gú.kù.ga [ki.tuš/gub] $^{d}$en.nu.gi.ke$_4$ (*UET* I. 182, cf. 173–81), and he appears in a similar context in *RA* 41. 32. 23. These groups of seven are all somewhat demonic in character and are usually represented as divine malefactors. It is certain therefore that the chamberlain of Enlil must be distinguished from the other two Ennugis, and doubtful if these two can be identified. *Gilg.* XI. 18 instead of *gallû*, which fits the context very well, offers *gú-gal-la-šú-nu*, which is quite inappropriate for an officer in a divine assembly. Most likely it is a scribal error influenced by the preceding line. However, it is curious that *Šurpu* IV. 103 names $^{d}$*en-nu-gi bēl iki*(e) *u palgi* (pa$_5$). Perhaps that line or something similar elsewhere contributed to the corruption in *Gilg.* It is uncertain which Ennugi is meant in the temple list that calls both é.rab.ri.ri and é.rab.AG.AG the temple of Ennugi (é $^{d}$*en-nu-gi*: *PSBA* 22. 362, K 4374+8377. i. 9–10). A mere curiosity is that in *AN* = *Anum* III. 86, where $^{d}$*ga-a-a-ú* sipa $^{d}$en.zu.na.ke$_4$ is mentioned, a variant gives sipa $^{d}$en.nu.gi.ke$_4$ (*CT* 24. 48. 19), though Sin is equated with Ennugi in *RA* 16. 145 obv. 12 in a late syncretistic text.

11 Literally: 'they took hand in its hand', *qa-ti-ša* = *qātišša*, cf. *Gilg.* III. i. 19: *iṣ-ṣab-tu-ma qa-tu qa-tu-us-su-un.*

13, 17 With *ša-me-e-ša* cf. *im-ta-qut ap-si-ša* (*MIO* XII. 54. 4). These are the only two cases known to the writers, so one cannot tell if the ending is -*ša*(*m*) or -*iša*(*m*), but it is certainly equivalent to *ana.*

15 The restoration is from x rev. i. 6, etc., where the mythology is also discussed in the note.

16 *naššīku*, if correctly restored here, seems to be a *hapax legomenon*, but it can hardly be separated from the well-known title of Ea, *niššīku*. This occurs most commonly in Agušaya (*VAS* X. 214 = Zimmern, *BSGW* 68/1, iv. 12, v. 16 and 28; *RA* 15. 159 ff. viii. 17) written *ni-*(*iš*)*-ši-i-ku/ki*. In *Atra-ḫasīs* it occurs (in addition to II. vii. 39 and III. vi. 42) below line 250, where the Old Babylonian copy offers *ni-iš-š*[*i-* and the Late Assyrian ]-ŠI-*kù*. This proves that the title of Ea commonly read $^{d}$*nin-igi-kù* should in fact be read $^{d}$*nin-ši-kù*, and is another writing of *niššīku*. Confirmation and explanation of this fact becomes apparent when it is noted that $^{d}$*nin-ši-kù* has not yet been found in any Sumerian or Akkadian text from the Old Babylonian period. It only occurs in later sources and in later Akkadian copies. *niššīku*, on the other hand, occurs in Old Babylonian Akkadian literary texts, with one exception, $^{d}$*niš-ši-ku* in *KAR* 38 (dup. K 8863) rev. 21. Thus it appears that $^{d}$*nin-ši-kù* is a spurious Sumerianization of a probably Semitic *niššīku* invented in the Cassite period. The Cassite-period god lists *CT* 24. 42. 113 (and dup.) and *CT* 25. 48. 6 both explain it as $^{d}$*é-a ša né-me-qí*, no doubt basing

themselves on kù in nam.kù.zu = *nēmequ*. The meaning and etymology of *niššīku* are not definitely known. The proposal to connect it with ensi = *iššakku* (Zimmern, *BSGW* 68/1, p. 33) and with nu.èš = *nešakkum* (see von Soden, *ZA* 41. 166[6]; Edzard, *ZA* 55. 93–5; Jacobsen, *AnBib* XII/. 138–9) can be discounted on formal and semantic grounds. A possibility is that *niššīku* is another form of *nasīku* 'chieftain' in Late Assyrian, also found in Biblical and later Hebrew and in the Aramaic *Aḥiqar* 119 (see the lexica) as *nāsîk*. This is plausible since in Sumerian religious texts nun is a common epithet of Enki, and in some Akkadian texts Ea is referred to as *ea šarru*.

22, 24 The Euphrates is referred to as *na-piš-ti ma-a-ti* in *JNES* 15. 134. 49.

25 Cf. *i-di-ig-lat nāra* in *JRAS* 1927. 536. 7. The placing of a kind of determinative as description after a name is not usual.

S i 7 Cf. $^{\text{íd}}$*pu-ra-na-ti* (*KAR* 360. 7) and *purantum* in the Mari letters (*ARM* XV. 131). Since the Sumerian is buranun, and in view of this evidence, Borger's correction of *KAR* 360 to $^{\text{íd}}$*pu-ra-át*(?)-*ti* (*Asarhaddon*, p. 91) is unnecessary.

42 *li-ša-si-ik* (cf. 240 below) is taken for *lišassik*, from *nasāku*, with von Soden, *ArOr* 17/2. 366–7.

44, 46, 58, 60 The most obvious derivation of *i ni-iš-ši-a*, from *našû*, 'let us carry', gives so poor a sense that it can hardly be right. The view provisionally adopted here is that the verb is *šašû*, the same as appears in *Gilg.* v. iii. 11 and 14, where *šá-šá-ku* is used by Gilgameš to describe himself on awaking from a frightening dream, and *šá-šá-át* to describe the dream. These forms could be either from *šâšu* or from *šašû*. Campbell Thompson's citation of the Syriac *šawweš* 'turbavit' (ad loc.) is quite inconclusive, and the evidence from *Atra-ḫasīs* can be used in favour of the other alternative. An objection could be raised from the statement in S. Moscati, *An Introduction to the Comparative Grammar of the Semitic Languages*, p. 74: 'In no Semitic language can two identical consonants . . . appear next to each other in first and second position; and it is rare for such consonants to be found as first and third radicals.' In Akkadian there is *ḫaḫû*, a verb, and *dadânu*, a noun, to quote two obvious exceptions, and the scribes who wrote derivatives of the root *wbl* with the radicals *bbl* obviously did not know this rule. There is, therefore, every possibility of a verb *šašû* meaning 'to disturb'.

61 *ti-si-a* is taken for *šisiā*, with von Soden, *BiOr* XXIII. 52, who quotes *ti-si*, *ti-si-ma*, and *ti-si-i-ma* from Old Babylonian letters, where the contexts clearly compel a derivation from *šasû*.

63 In Old Babylonian literature generally the root is *saqāru*, not *zakāru*. In addition to passages cited by von Soden, *ZA* 41. 168[1] note *i-sa-qa-ra-am* (*BWL* 156. 2; *JNES* 16. 256 obv. 13 (*i-sa*!-*qa*!-*ra*!-*am*! collated) and rev. 22); *is-sà-qá-ra-am-ma* (*AfO* 13. 47. 13); also passages quoted by Sonnek, *ZA* 46. 226–31. This does not of course prove that *sqr* is right for the reign of Ammi-ṣaduqa and Sippar, where Ku-Aya probably worked, but a better case cannot be made for *zkr*.

64–6 In *MSL* II. 127. 28–9 the same Sumerian word (restored as ku-ú KU) is explained by *na-du-u*$_4$ and *na-ka-a-šum*. Landsberger translates both '(Eier) legen', but in the note ad loc. cites only *na-du-u* [*šá*] *iṣṣūri* (without Sumerian equivalent) and the pair *na-du-u na-ka-šu* (with equivalent, apparently restored, gá) in *CT* 12. 21, BM 37485. While the existence of *nadû* 'lay eggs' is not in question (the Latin *pono* could be compared), the evidence cited does not prove this meaning for *nadû* associated with *nakāšu*, and in the context of *Atra-ḫasīs* we have *nadû* followed by *ittakšu*, which must have roughly the same meaning. The obvious conclusion is that *nakāšu* means 'put', the common meaning of *nadû*.

69 *ba-bi-ša-at-ma-ni* is a sandhi-writing for *bābiš atmāni*.

70–2 i.e. 'midnight'; the watch referred to must be the *maṣṣartum qablītum*.

74 Kalkal is the door-keeper of Ekur, see the literature cited by A. Sjöberg, *Nanna-Suen* 156, and in addition Ebeling, *Stiftungen* 26. 1. Kol. 3 with note, and K 5148 obv. 13–14, a bilingual duplicate of Langdon, *SBP* 154. 34, which, with the other duplicates given by Langdon in *Babylonian Liturgies*, p. 138, *sub voce* kalkalag, now reads:

$^{d}$kal.kal ša$_{6}$.ga ni.du$_{8}$.gal.é.kur.ra
$^{d}$MIN *da-an-qu ni-*[*du*$_{8}$]*-ga*[*l*] *é-kur*
Comely Kalkal, chief door-keeper of Ekur

Another example is *CT* 46. 51 rev. 24: $^{d}$*kal-kal dan-dan-nu áš-ṭu ta-me-eḫ* $^{giš}$*ḫaṭṭi ni-rib* × [, where the etymology implied in *dandannu* need not be taken too seriously.

78 In the tablets of Ku-Aya, and also in the two other Old Babylonian tablets of *Atra-ḫasīs* in which the name Nusku occurs, **D** and **F**, it is written $^{d}$PA+LU, not $^{d}$PA+TÚG as most commonly. However, $^{d}$PA+LU is found elsewhere in Old Babylonian tablets: *STVC* 37 (see Van Dijk, *SGL* II. 149) and *UET* VIII. 85. 17. Also the unpublished Old Babylonian god list from Nippur (*Diri* VII?) offers both $^{d}$PA+TÚG and $^{d}$PA+LU with the gloss *nu-ús-ka* (courtesy T. Jacobsen). The etymological god list *CT* 25. 49 rev. 4 also shows knowledge of this writing, since it explains $^{d}$PA+TÚG: *re-'-ú* (PA+LU), *a-kil ṭè-e-mi* (ugula umuš), *mu-šá-pu-ú* [. . .] (pa [KU/LU]).

81, 83, etc. For *râṣu* as a verb of motion, like the Hebrew *rûṣ* 'run', see *BWL* 310 note on 288, and *STC* II, pl. LXXIV. v. 13 (restored) *ú-ra-ṣu di-ma-ta* 'they made tears flow'.

85–6 The grammar of . . . *pâšu īpušamma* . . . *is-sà-qar* is not clear. In this and similar cases in this epic one might easily explain *issaqar* as I/1 perfect following upon the preterite with *-ma* as in normal Old Babylonian sequence of tenses. This, however, is not possible without further explanation in the Pennsylvania and Yale tablets of *Gilg.*, which use *is-sà-qar-am*. If this is a I/1 perfect, why does it not become *issaqram*? This question is reinforced by those texts, including Old Babylonian ones, which write a doubled middle radical, e.g. *CT* 15. 3. 7: . . . *i-pu-ša-am-ma* . . . *is-sà-aq-qá-ar*. Kienast accordingly in *ZA* 54. 92[5] construes the form as a IV/1 present in an ingressive sense. This may suffice for the last and similar examples, but in the *Gilg.* tablets quoted the same form *is-sà-qar-am* occurs without any preceding verb in the sentence (e.g. Penn. i. 16), where it must be either a preterite or perfect. By the normal forms of verbs there is no solution to this problem.

93, 95 *binū būnūka* has the ring of a proverbial saying, and *binu* is certainly 'son' in view of *mārū* in the parallel line. The real problem is the meaning of *būnu*. In the Assyrian recension, S v. 23 = vi. 12, *bunu* occurs also with the meaning 'son' (see the note ad loc.), but this line is lacking from the Old Babylonian text, and here a rendering 'your sons are sons' hardly gives sense. No other known meaning of *būnu* or *bunnu* is more certain for this passage, but if the phrase is proverbial one need not be over concerned: proverbs often depend on catching a sense not fully expressed in the words but suggested by the context in which it is used. Here Enlil is probably being encouraged to trust that his sons will not be altogether pitiless to their father.

98, 100 Elsewhere *abāku* is an a/u class verb, though in *CT* 15. 3. 10 and 11 a preterite *ibbuk* occurs, which shares the peculiarity of the doubled *b* found here and in the same form in II. v. 24 and 26. Cf. also the preterite *i-bi-ik* in x rev. i. 28 (Late Babylonian) and the present *ibbak* in U rev. 4 (Late Assyrian).

102 The tentative restoration from *nemerkû* is based on the view that many of the passages are as well suited with 'be present' as with the usual 'remain behind'. For example, the earliest example: *ša* [giš]*ma-gar-ra-šu bīt i-mit-ti šarri bēli-šú la im-mer-ku-ma ma-gar-ra-šú uk-til-la* (*BBSt* p. 32. 26 f. and 36 f.) 'whose chariot was not present at the right hand of the king, his lord, but his chariot was held back'. The translation of Heidel (*AS* 13. 77), 'whose chariot did not remain behind the right of the king', is just playing with words, since 'remain behind' (when others have passed on) is something quite different from 'remain behind' in the sense of following closely.

104 One might restore *ša-*[*šum uš*]*-ki-nu* 'they bowed down to him', but there seems not enough room for *ša-*[*pa-al-šu uš*]*-ki-nu* 'they bowed beneath him'.

108 The remains of L are consistent with a restoration *ša ni-su-ú-ti-ia*: '(Am I to make war) out of my own kith and kin?'

109 Note how, with the first person verb, a part of the person is expressed as the subject. The same occurs in *Ludlul* III m: *mut-tu-tu am-ma-šid ab-bu-ut-tum ap-pa-šir* (*BWL* 54). This is the 'whole and part' construction.

113–15 Since *siqru* is often an explanatory speech, the liberty has been taken of translating it 'reason', and the verb of which it is the object is presumably lost at the end of 115.

149, 162 Other examples of a metaphorical use of *dâku* are quoted under *CAD dâku* 1 c.

173 This *tam-ta* is the same as that in *YBT* IX. 35. iii. 1: DAM-*tam e-li-šu iš-pu-uk*, discussed by Goetze in *AnOr* XII. 185 ff. A further example is *KAR* 88 fragment 5 rev. 7 (and dups.) = *ArOr* 21. 422: *bēl qabli u ta-ma-tú/ta-amtu*. Further evidence comes from the commentary on *Enūma Eliš* VII. 116, 128, 132, where erím is equated with *tâmtim* (Tiāmat), though this involves a play on words.

178–9 The reconstruction of the text is in some doubt, as one cannot formally prove that N, which supplies the middles of the lines in our text, really belongs to this recension rather than to, say, that known from **G**. With 179 the restoration based on N and **G** ii. 6 produces a very plausible line, and since 176–7 do correspond with **G** ii. 3–4, it has been assumed that 178 must be the same as **G** ii. 5, though a complete restoration has not been achieved. At the end one might restore something either from *naṭû* 'be suitable' or the homophone 'strike'. If 180 agreed with **G** ii. 7 one might restore it: *i-ba-aš-ši š*[*i-ip-ru a-n*]*a e-pe-ši* 'there is work to be done', but since 181 does not correspond with **G** ii. 8 this must remain doubtful. *tukku* here, as in the lexical texts (see Kupper, *RA* 45. 120 ff.), is clearly 'lamentation'. Other examples occur in incantations: *mar-ṣa tuk-ka-ka ta-at-ta-di el*[*ī-ia*] (K 7641. 9); *ina šamê$^{e}$ id-du-ú tuk-ku* (BM 45637+ rev. 18–19); also in a myth: *a-na* $^{d}$nà *tup-šar é-sag-íl šu-kun tuk-ka* (A 7882. 13).

**G** ii. 9, cf. V obv. 2 While it is now certain that *lullû* is a loan from the Sumerian lú.u$_{x}$.lu and means 'man', some still cling to overtones such as 'savage' or 'primitive', but *Atra-ḫasīs* offers no support to such a view, which is a false generalization based on Enkidu. See *JSS* 12. 105.

V obv. 1 A full discussion of *sassuru*, *šassuru*, etc. will appear in the first-named author's forthcoming *Babylonian Creation Myths*.

190 The reading *li-gim-ma-a*, suggested by J. J. Finkelstein, does not appear to be quite certain, and the parallel lines in **G** ii. 9 and V obv. 2 would suggest *lullâ*, which, however, is impossible with the clear initial *li-*. A reading *li-il-la-a* is epigraphically improbable, though there is a little late evidence for *lillû* as well as *lullû* (*KAR* 162 rev. 4).

193 For *šabsūtu*, *tabsūtu*, see von Soden, *AfO* 18. 119–21, and note *mu-šá-lit-*[*tu*] = *šab-su-tum* (*Malku* I. 127, *JAOS* 83. 427).

213 The adverbial *puḫur* occurs again in *CT* 15. 2. viii. 4: *it-mu-ú-šu* $^{d}$*ištar*(mùš) *ù šu-ú pu-ḫu-ur ur-du-ni-i-im* 'Ištar and he were going (*it-mu-šu* = *a-la-a-ku*: *CT* 18. 6 obv. 52), together they went down.' It also occurs in the Mari letters (see *ARM* xv. 239).

214 Although the precise allusion to the drum *uppu* is obscure, there is no better alternative. The drum called *uppu* had a cultic use, and was 'heard', whereas no other object called *uppu* could be so described. Perhaps at the time of the composition of this epic the daily meals of the gods were introduced in the sanctum to a beating of the drum.

215 Since the first vowel of *eṭemmu* is always *e* or *i*, the writing of **E**, PI-*ṭe-em-mu*, requires a new value, $e_{x}$ = PI. Since this sign occurs *passim* for *wa*/*wi*/*we*/*wu* in Old Babylonian texts generally, and for *à* in Old Babylonian literary texts (see von Soden, *Akkadische Syllabar*[2]), there is nothing improbable in its occurring for vowels other than *a*, though it could be argued, with E. Reiner, *Studies Presented to A. Leo Oppenheim* 167–80, that phonemically the PI stands for '*e*.

216, 229 These are extraordinarily important but very perplexing lines. While there is no problem in an adjective coming before its noun in poetry, it is very doubtful indeed if *balṭa ittašu* can be taken together, since the adjective is masc. while the noun is fem. Thus *balṭa* can only be in apposition to the suffix *-šu-* on the verb. The subject of the verb is naturally *eṭemmu* after 215b and 228b. The identification of the verb's object is not so simple. In the immediate context *šīr* and *ili* seem unlikely, since they are other aspects of the *eṭemmu*. Since the fundamental contrast in this section is that stated in 212, god and man, it is assumed here that since the subject of the verb is *eṭemmu*, the object is man. See further p. 22.

219 The Anunnaki who determine the destinies are the Seven mentioned in line 5 above. Only they had the power to authorize so great a change in the constitution of the universe. See the note to that line.

223 One may read either $^{\mathrm{d}}$PI-*e i-la* or $^{\mathrm{d}}$PI-*e-i-la*. Stylistically the former is unlikely. 'So-and-so, the god who . . .' reads peculiarly for an Akkadian text, and especially here since so far gods are the only beings in existence. The strongest argument in favour of this first alternative is that one could expect the god named in 47 above, who persuaded the others to take direct action against Enlil instead of approaching the vizier, to be the one here who was made to pay the penalty. And in 47 there is room for a two-sign name, and the trace that remains, while it is too small to commend a restoration [$^{\mathrm{d}}$PI]-⌜*e*⌝, at least permits it. For the second alternative one may quote the divine name $^{\mathrm{d}}$*sa-al-i-la*, which occurs among Marduk names in a late list which seems to concentrate on the rare and unusual (*CT* 25. 35 obv. 4 = 36 obv. 3, see *RLA* art. *Götterlisten*, § 9). If one does read $^{\mathrm{d}}$PI-*e-i-la*, it is presumably a West Semitic name, and the first element will be *we-e*. The *-e* will mark vowel length and in principle could be omitted. The sign PI has exactly the same number of wedges as SAL, and in some scripts very little displacement of wedges converts the one to the other. It is, therefore, quite possible that an original $^{\mathrm{d}}$PI-*i-la*, because it was unknown to the scribes, got corrupted to $^{\mathrm{d}}$SAL-*i-la*, and this was then written out as $^{\mathrm{d}}$*sa-al-i-la*. That it occurs among Marduk names is no problem, since in the lists Qingu, the counterpart of $^{\mathrm{d}}$PI-*e*(-)*i-la* in *Enūma Eliš*, is also a name of Marduk. A further consideration against reading *i-la* as the common noun is the difficulty of finding an acceptable reading for $^{\mathrm{d}}$PI-*e*. A Semitic name Wê (or Pê?) and indeclinable seems improbable, and while one might think of $^{\mathrm{d}}$geštug.e as Sumerian, the .e is inexplicable and geštu(g) is not usually written with the PI-sign alone. An etymological play on geštu and *ṭēmu* is not impossible, but the normal equivalent of geštu is *ḫasīsu*. A further objection is the meaning of *ṭēmu* in this portion of the epic.

The importance of *ṭēmu* is shown not only by its mention here, but also in 239 (cf. 243 P and II. vii. 33) the god is said to have been killed 'with his *ṭēmu*'. It is difficult to believe that 'with his intelligence' is right, and here the general drift of the narrative is that something special was passed on to man from the slain god. As preserved the epic says nothing about man's intelligence. What is passed on is the *eṭemmu*, and one must therefore adopt the sense of *ṭēmu* when it parallels *rāmānu* (see the passages cited in *BWL* 293 on 83), namely 'self' or 'personality'. Quite possibly the term was suggested by a play of words on *eṭemmu* and *ṭēmu*. See further p. 22.

233–4 There has been widespread belief in a supernatural power in spittle, see Hastings, *Encyclopaedia of Religion and Ethics*, art. 'Saliva', and it is probably this that was foremost in the author's mind, though the consideration that clay needs to be moistened for a potter's use may also have been present.

246–7 *Enūma Eliš* V. 109–10 seem to have been modelled after this couplet or something similar.

259 The 'brick' is the brick structure on which a woman lay for her labour. See further the first named author's forthcoming *Babylonian Creation Myths*.

S iii. 4 Restored after *Enki and Ninmaḫ*: $^{\mathrm{d}}$nin.maḫ.e im.ugu.abzu.a šu.ni mu.ni.in.ti 'Ninmaḫ laid her hand on the clay above the Apsû' (*TCL* 16, pl. CXXXVII. 60′).

S iii. 7 *ba*-RI-*iq* is corrected after *Gilg*. Penn. iv. 36–7 : *i-na bi-ti-iq a-bu-un-na-ti-šu ši-ma-as-súm*, and BM 34208 rev. 11 : $^{\text{uzu}}$LI].dur.kud.da = *ba-ti-iq a-bu-un-na-tú*.

S iii. 8 *mu-te-ti* is taken as queer orthography for *mūdâti*.

S iii. 11 The title of the mother goddess *bānât šīmti* also occurs in III. vi. 47 and *Gilg*. X. vi. 37.

S iii. 12, 13 Von Soden (*ZA* 41. 113[5]) took the gloss seriously and treated *šinašan* as a reduplicated form. We are not inclined to attach too much importance to these glosses (cf. ṢU$^{ri\text{-}gi}$*-me-ši-na*, iv. 2) and regard the *-šam* as the same ending seen in *ūmišam*, etc. The value *šan* for *šàm* needs better support. *kullulu* in the context of these lines must be taken as having the meaning of *šuklulu*, apparently a unique phenomenon, but it is not known if it also occurred in this form in the Old Babylonian text. Elsewhere in the Old Babylonian copies *kullulu* occurs twice (II. vi. 12 and III. iii. 29), and in the latter instance it has the sense 'be covered', and probably either 'cover' or 'be covered' in the former case. Outside the epic 'cover' is well attested, since the verb serves as a denominative of both *kallatu* '(veiled) bride' and *kilīlu*/*kulūlu* 'crown', but there seems to be no other example of the II/1 having a passive meaning.

S iii. 16 This line and 295 below reveal a previously unsuspected item of grammar. The third person precative is normally *liprus* for both genders in Babylonian, and the same for masc. in Assyrian, but *lū taprus* for the fem. Since the fem. with *t-* in Babylonian occurs only rarely in literary texts (apart from late examples in letters under the influence of Aramaic) hitherto no attention has been devoted to what its precative would be. This line and its parallel in the main recension show that the *i* normally found with the first person plural is also used for the third person fem. with *t-*. Other examples occur in the *ikribs*:

35 $^{\text{d}}$*nisaba elleti*$^{ti}$ *šá-ru-uḫ-tú ṣir-tú mārat* $^{\text{d}}$*a-nim*
36 *šá-sa-at ilāni*$^{\text{meš}}$ *rabûti*$^{\text{meš}}$ *šá-sa-at ilāni*$^{\text{meš}}$ *daiāni*$^{\text{meš}}$
37 *mu-paḫ-ḫi-rat ilāni*$^{\text{meš}}$ *rabûti*$^{\text{meš}}$ *mu-paḫ-ḫi-rat ilāni*$^{\text{meš}}$ *daiāni*$^{\text{meš}}$
38 *i tu-pa-ḫi-ra-ma ilāni*$^{\text{meš}}$ *rabûti*[$^{\text{meš}}$]
39 *i tu-pa-ḫi-ra-ma ilāni*$^{\text{meš}}$ *daiāni*[$^{\text{meš}}$]
40 *ti-iš-ba-nim-ma ina niqî* (siskur$_{\text{x}}$) *i ta-pul d*[*i*?-*na*?]

Zimmern, *BBR* 89–90, now joined to K 3654+ as rev. iii

35 Nisaba the pure, exalted, lofty, daughter of Anu,
36 Who summons the great gods, who summons the divine judges,
37 Who convenes the great gods, who convenes the divine judges,
38 May she convene the great gods,
39 May she convene the divine judges,
40 Sit (Šamaš and Adad) in the offering, may she answer the [case (?)].

S iii. 19 A comparison with 293 below suggests that *ḫurrušu* here (see *CAD ḫarāšu* A; *AHw ḫarāšu* I) may be originally a mistake derived from *ḫurrû*, perhaps occasioned by the rarity of the latter.

282 [*ḫ*]*a-lu-up* seems the only possible restoration, but so far no other occurrence of a noun *ḫalūpu* is known. However, *ḫalāpu* 'to slip in', with the cognates in Hebrew 'pass on' and Arabic 'succeed', supplies a very suitable meaning, and the rarity of other words in this epic cautions us against dismissing the possibility of a *hapax legomenon*.

285 As suggested by J. J. Finkelstein, *šabsūtam* is abstract, for *šabsūtūtam*, to avoid the ugly succession of the full form.

293 No other examples of this *ḫurrû* have been noted, but the meaning can be guessed.

301–4 This brings to mind the passage in *Gilg.* Penn. iv–v, where, in the *bīt emūtim*, the bed is laid for Išḫara, thus confirming what is presumed here, that Ištar during the marriage rites was called Išḫara. It also suggests the restoration of 302, since *emu rabû* occurs in lists (see *CAD sub vocibus*), while the trace cannot be restored to *bīt emūtim*.

336 *i-ta-aṣ-ṣú-la* is read because the I/3 of *eṣēlu* is well documented, but until the rest of the line can be completed it must remain a little uncertain. There are other ways of reading the signs.

370 The parallel line in S, iv. 27, suggests that a part of *banû* must be restored.

374–5 = 389–90 = II. ii. 13′–14′ This couplet is perplexing. The first time it is an instruction from Enki to Atra-ḫasīs, apparently telling him to advise the elders. The second time it follows a formula which normally introduces direct speech so that it appears to be addressed to the elders by Atra-ḫasīs. The last time the preceding lines are too broken for the context to be clear. *ni-a . . . mil-k*[*a*] is a conceivable phrase meaning 'dispense advice', but the uncertainty about the meaning of *simānî* (the reading seems sure) and the reading of *ú*?-[*r*]*a*? obscures the rest of the couplet.

377 For this *šubbû* (or *šuppû*) see *BWL* 285 on 71–2.

381 While a fem. noun *epītu* from *epû* 'bake' is not otherwise attested, it is a very plausible derivative.

382 *alāku eli* = 'be pleasant to' (*CAD alāku*, p. 321. 10′), and a dative suffix on a verb can take the place of *eli* with suffix.

384 The II stem of *šaqālu* occurs here (and in the parallel lines 399, 410, II. ii. 15, 29) with *qātu* as object, and in II. i. 11 with *zunnu* as object. While the latter with *šaqālu* is well known in omens (see *CAD sub voce zunnu*), there has been some doubt as to whether the meaning is 'scarce' or 'moderate' (*MSL* I. 228; Oppenheim, *Interpretation of Dreams* 282[105]), but now the context of II. i. 11 establishes the former. This is confirmed by the parallel line in the Assyrian recension (S iv. 44) which replaces *zunnīšu . . . lišaqqil* with *zunnašu lišāqir*. It is, however, quite another question whether a 'hand' can be 'scarce'. The background of this use of 'hand' is that when men are afflicted the gods' 'hand' is heavy on them, cf. *Ludlul* III. 1 *kab-ta-at qāt-su* (*BWL* 48), and the divine name dšu.ni.dugud (*CT* 25. 1. 1). Thus *šuqqulu* must in some way indicate the lifting of Namtara's hand. The primary meaning of *šaqālu* is 'suspend' and so 'weigh', and 'suspend' is found in Akkadian (*BWL* 319 on 22) as well as in the cognate languages. By a semantic development what is weighed is limited and so scanty. In Hebrew *mᵉṯê mispār* 'men of number' are men who can be counted, and so few. Thus *zunnu šaqlu* 'weighed rain' and so 'scanty'. In this way the active 'weigh' developed a stative meaning 'be scanty' and

so a II stem 'make scarce'. Only in *Atra-ḫasīs*, apparently, is there a II stem meaning 'make to suspend', as in the line under discussion.

396 The fem. suffix here, contrasting with the masc. in 381, suggests that the door and not Namtara is meant, since *bābu* is of common gender.

## TABLET II

i. 11 See the note on I. 384.

i. 14–17 This couplet, which is lacking from between S iv. 45–6, is related to šà.zi.ga incantations:

> én *lil-lik šāru* *li-nu-uš kirû*
> *liš-tak-ṣir er-pe-tum₄-ma* *ti-ku lit-tuk*
> R. D. Biggs, *Šà.zi.ga* 35. 12–13
> én *li-lik šāru* *šadêe l[i-nu-š]u*
> *lik-ta-ṣir ur-pa-tum₄-ma* *ti-ku lit-tuk*
> R. D. Biggs, op. cit. 32–3. 1–2
> [én *l*]*il-lik šāru* *a-a i-nu-u*[*š kirû*]
> *erpētu* ([IM].DIRImeš) *lik-ta-aṣ-ṣi-r*[*a* *t*]*i-ik-ki a-a i*[*t-tuk*]
> R. D. Biggs, op. cit. 37. no. 17. 6′–8′

Most probably the epic has borrowed a magic formula. *li'erri* is the same as in *BAM* 240. 14: *gul-gul* nam.lú.ux.lu *ina išāti li-er-ri-ma* 'let him parch a human skull with fire', and there is no need to emend both passages to *li'errir* so as to assign them to the root *urruru* 'dry', on which see Köcher, *AS* 16. 323–5. There is also, in these two passages, an *urrû* 'dry'. *ḫanābu* 'grow luxuriantly' in the I/3 (cf. *Ḫarra* II. 286: gú.me.er.me.er = *ḫi-tan-nu-bu*) has the sense of getting matted together and thick, like *kiṣṣuru*/*kutaṣṣuru* in the incantations. *tīku* is no doubt derived from *natāku*.

i. 19 The first two words, *līteddil irtaša*, are coupled by a sandhi-writing.

i. 21 A verb *qutturu* connected with smoke exists, but here and in other passages (see E. Ebeling, *Die Welt des Orients* I. 479) the meaning is 'destroy' or 'put an end to' with no smoky associations.

ii. 17–19 The root *šrq* 'steal' shows the same semantic development as in the Latin *fur—furtive* 'thief—stealthily'. For example *KAR* 92 rev. 29 = *LKA* 144 obv. 14–15: *šu-nu šar-qiš e-pu-šu-ni a-na-ku šu-piš* [*e*]*-pu-us-su-nu-ti* 'they secretly bewitched me, I have publicly bewitched them'. Thus *lištarriq . . . lišaznin* is a hendiadys, as translated. Enki wants the rain to fall without Enlil's noticing it. *kīma šarrāqītu* is an adverbial phrase, *šarrāqu*+*i'u*, and fem. to agree with *eqlu*: 'like a thieving one'. The *-u* ending is locative, see the note on I. 1.

iii. 5 The suggestion of A. L. Oppenheim (*Interpretation of Dreams* 222), that *muššakku* is a kind of incense from the smoke of which omens were derived, is neither proved nor disproved by this line and those related to it in x and y, but the use of *zbl* does perhaps favour some kind of present being brought along for the god.

iii. 30 The fifty la.ḫa.ma engur.ra act as the constabulary of Enki in Sumerian epic, etc., see Falkenstein's note on line 184 of *Enki und die Weltordnung*: *ZA* 56. 71.

iv. 4 This line confirms Landsberger's construction of S iv. 49, 58, in *WZKM* 56. 113[16].

iv. 9 A boundary stone curse included: [*ki*]-*mu-ú uṭṭati*(še.bar) *la-ar-da ki-mu-ú mê*$^{\text{meš}}$ *id-ra-na* 'couch-grass (?) instead of barley, salt instead of water' (*BBSt* p. 62, ii. 11–13). Clearly *lardu* was coarse grass that would grow even in times of drought, so that it fits the context here very well, though its restoration is not quite sure.

iv. 10 For the root *nkm* referring to a disease see *BWL* 54 f and the passages quoted in the comments on pp. 299–300. The meaning, or meanings if there is more than one root, is still uncertain.

iv. 13 The parallel line in S, v. 25 = vi. 14, has *buqli me-te*, and the two versions are explained from: [*k*]*i-i* še.DIM$_4$ *er-ri e-ša-aṭ-ṭu-u šá-lam-tu* (Bauer, *Das Inschriftenwerk Assurbanipals* 1. 39, K 4443. 8), 'they scattered the corpses like dried malt'. The simile arises from the brewing process in which barley was first encouraged to sprout but was then prevented from growing by spreading and drying. 'Dead' and 'dried' malt are clearly the same, and the appearance of humans in an advanced state of starvation might well be compared to grain in that state.

iv. 14 There seem to be no other examples of *šitkuku*/*šitququ*, and S turned it into *šuparkê* 'lack of' (v. 26 = vi. 15). However, the context suggests the meaning, and a metaphorical development from *šakāku* 'harrow' is quite possible.

iv. 17 Parts of the body, including *būdu*, are so regularly fem. that one may suspect that *rapšūtum* is an error. S v. 16 = vi. 5 has *rapšātu*.

iv. 18 *mazzāzu* as a part of the body seems to occur only here and in the parallel lines of S, but since it is a *nomen loci* in form, and in view of the context, it must mean 'leg'.

v. 17, 31 and vi. 26 'Lower earth' here presumably means 'lower' in relation to the regions named in the previous line, rather than 'lower' of two earths. Enlil lived on the earth proper and would guard that, just as Anu was appointed to guard heaven, his dwelling. See the note on x rev. i. 4–7.

v. 20 This line, restored from vi. 29 below, cf. x rev. ii. 6 and 13, reopens the question of *miḫirtu*/*mišertu* discussed by Landsberger in *JNES* 8. 259[54]. Due to the use of the EZEN-sign many of the examples are ambiguous, and individual writings of *mi-ḫi-ir-*, *mi-še-er-* and *me-še-er-* prove that both words do exist. Landsberger is now of a different opinion, which he expounds in an excursus to *MSL* IX, 222. (His help in this note is gratefully acknowledged, though he is not responsible for the opinions.) The important question here concerns the many passages put by von Soden in *AHw* under *meḫertu* d). They use the word of fishes, the sea and the (cosmic) river. IV *R*$^2$ 20. 21–2 and *Erra* II. c. 26 are particularly important, since the concept in them is clearly that of a marine cornucopia. All these passages are written ambiguously, but they cannot be separated from *mišertu* in *Atra-ḫasīs*, since here it is clearly some kind of cornucopia, and in x especially its marine connection is transparent. Thus the ambiguous writings referred to must be taken as *mišertu*, and it may be noted that *me-še-er-tum* in *KAR*

300, obv. 6, occurs in the apodosis of one of a group of omens concerning fish. The etymology of the word is unknown. In the phrase *muššuru mišerta* it may have been employed as a cognate accusative, but if so this is probably only folk-etymology, since a I stem of the root is unknown. The Sumerian equivalent in IV $R^2$ 20. 21 (za.ba.lam) is irrelevant, since the Sumerian of that text is late and, so far as the sense is concerned, secondary. This is hardly the same word as giš.sa.tur = *mēšer/štum*, since that is 'small net' and to be derived from *ešēšu* 'catch in a net'. The root *mšr* 'sweep along' seems unlikely, as does *mīšertu* 'regular measure' from *yšr*.

v. 24, 26 See note on I. 98.

vi. 12 For *kullulu* see the note on I S iii. 12, 13.

vi. 13 This line seems to attest a masc. pl. *tēnišū* 'men'; cf. *MSL* III. 60. 19–20 [LU] = *ni-i-šu, te-ni-šu*.

vi. 19 *tēqītu* is apparently derived from *eqû* 'paint' and means 'slander'. For passages in context see *ARM* I. 130 rev. 5–6 and *AbB* II. 117. 13–14. Its use here with 'hand' is not easy, but until the whole of the line is known it cannot be properly considered. The sense 'complaint' is suggested in *JCS* 12. 23[13].

vii. 45 It is not clear why the personal interrogative is used, unless perhaps Enki is represented as pretending to take *abūbu* as a personal name.

vii. 49 The occurrences of Šullat and Ḫaniš, with discussion of some of the problems, are collected by Gelb in *ArOr* XVIII/1–2. 189–98. The only additions are a few more examples of Ḫaniš in Akkadian personal names from the Ur III period (*MAD* III *sub voce*). The identity and characteristics of this divine duo are still not really clear. From the line under discussion and the related *Gilg.* XI. 99 they seem gods of the storm, but there is no certainty that *Gilg.* XI. 100 further alludes to them as *guzalû*. The omen passages (*CT* 31. 9. 1–2, 4, 6) speak of them as accompanying an army to grant its victory. Their identification with Šamaš and Adad is only attested after the Old Babylonian period, in *AN* = *Anum*, *mulAPIN* and other texts of no earlier date, but Gelb is incorrect to speak of them as 'belonging to the circle' of Šamaš and Adad (p. 192). The lists say, not that they belong to the circle of, but that they are Šamaš and Adad. A certain absurdity results, it is true. Adad is clearly a separate deity in the flood story, and Šamaš is altogether inappropriate in that context. The problem is explained by the techniques of identification. Even a single common noun is rarely equateable with another in all its shades and areas of meaning. With divine duos there were so few available that congruence cannot be expected. Šamaš and Adad normally occur together in the giving of oracles, see *La Divination en Mésopotamie ancienne, XIVe Rencontre Assyriologique Internationale* 119–23, and Adad in other respects was roughly equivalent with Šullat and Ḫaniš so that he with Šamaš was the best duo the ancient scholars could find.

viii. 34 *gamertu* in the sense 'total destruction' seems to occur only here and in III. iii. 38 and v. 44 below. But the I, II, and IV stems of the verb are well attested in the sense 'annihilate'. As a little-known word *Gilg.* XI. 119–20 replaces the occurrence in III. iii. 37 with *lemuttu*.

## TABLET III

i. 13 See *BWL* 291 on 48 for šà.zu = *qirba lamādu*, of which *qirba idû* is a variant. Gudea, *Cylinder A* (*TCL* 8) i. 28 and iv. 21 use šà.zu of understanding the meaning of dreams, and this, with the fem. suffix on *qiribša* here, suggests the restoration.

i. 14 *zibbatu* 'tail' has figurative meanings and an Old Babylonian form *sibbatum* (see *CAD sub voce*). However, there is so far no exact parallel for the meaning guessed here from the context.

i. 17 [*m*]*a-šu-um-ma* seems quite certain, but it is unexplained from other passages. It is assumed to be an interrogative **manšum-ma*, cf. *miššum* 'why?'.

i. 31 It is not clear how the boat could be roofed over both 'above' and 'below'.

i. 34 One may suspect a word-play in *ušaznanakku*: *zanānu* 'rain' and *zanānu* 'provision'. While Enlil does the former, Enki will do the latter.

i. 35 This line, and the corresponding *Gilg.* XI. 44, is paralleled in an Ur-Nammu text, *JCS* 20. 139. 25–6 with a variant form in *UET* VI. 76 rev. 10–12 and 77. 4–6:

uru.mà a.rá.a.bi ku$_6$.àm diri.bi mušen.àm (*JCS*)
uru$^{ki}$.mà a.rá.bi ku$_6$.um ḫi!.li.bi mu.še.na (*UET*)
urím$^{ki}$.ma a.rá.a.bi ku$_6$.àm diri.bi mušen.àm (*JCS*)
. . . a.rá.bi ku$_6$.um ḫi!.li.bi mu.še.na/mu.sig$_5$ (*UET*)
The increase of my city is fish, its surplus fowl,
The increase of Ur is fish, its surplus fowl.

We take a.rá here in the mathematical sense of multiplication, with Hallo, *JCS* 20. 134[13]. Clearly we are dealing with a literary cliché, and it is possible that x rev. ii. 21–2 = 37–8 also reflect it, but they are too damaged for certainty. The word with 'birds', diri, ḫi.li, *ḫiṣbu*, is clear in every case, but not the word with 'fishes'. The Sumerian a.rá can be explained, but it is not a usual usage. Both form and meaning (except in a general way) of the Akkadian are in doubt. For *bu-du-ri* here *Gilg.* XI. 44 offers *bu-zu-ur*. *CAD* identifies the word with *budduru* (q.v.)/*bunduru*/*buṭṭuru*, which is only lexically attested, and is explained in *Ḫargud*: [gi].LAGAB × Ú+AŠ = *bu-un-du-ru* = *bil-ti šá* GI$^{meš}$ (v *R* 32 no. 4. 52 = *MSL* VII. 68. 18b). If it is correctly rendered as 'a load of reeds' one may doubt its relevance. It is also uncertain if it is the same word in *A* I/2. 87 (*CT* 12. 25. i, eighth from bottom): la-gab LAGAB = *bu-ut-tu-rum*. The Sumerian lagab commonly indicates stoutness or solidity. A further problem of using the lexical item for *Atra-ḫasīs* is that in the literary tradition it changed from *bud*(*d*)*uru* (or perhaps *buṭ*(*ṭ*)*uru*) to *buz*(*z*)*uru*, while in the lexical tradition the dental was preserved to the end. Assuming the epic word to be unrelated to this other one, one might compare the Arabic *bad̠ara* 'scatter' and assume a *qutūl* form, noting that in Ugaritic the proto-Semitic *d̠* remains *d*, though in Akkadian it normally becomes *z*.

i. 37 A reading *ba-a-aṣ* 'sand' is also possible, but does not give so good a sense. The couplet corresponds roughly to *Gilg.* XI. 86 and W 5. -*šu* on *mūšišu* is for -*šum* = *ana*.

i. 48 Collation of *Gilg.* XI. 41 shows traces of gìr$^{II}$ on K 8517, and while on Sm 2131+ the remaining sign could be i]gi (= *pānu*) or -p]i, the spacing on this tablet requires a restoration *a-šak-ka-na* [*še-p*]*i-ia-a-ma*. In any case *pāna šakānu* 'determine' is no suitable sense.

ii. 11–12 Restored from *Gilg.* XI. 50–1:

. . . *n*]*a-ši pa-as-*[ × ]
. . . *n*]*a-ši a-b*[*a*/*z*[*u-* × × ] (collated)

Elsewhere the *naggāru* and *atkuppu* are associated as shipbuilders: Salonen, *Wasserfahrzeuge* 134–7; *AHw atkuppu*. The *pāšu* is also given as the basic tool of the *naggāru* in *Erra* I. 155–6. The tool of the reed-worker is given in *Ḫargud* (*LTBA* I. 86. vi. 21):

na₄.*šak?-ka-ru-u* = (*vacat*) = *abnu šá* lú*atkuppi*

R. D. Biggs writes on this point (privately), 'Judging from modern practices, the *atkuppu* needs only two basic implements: a knife to cut the reeds and something to flatten them'. The latter was his 'stone'.

ii. 13–14 Restored from *Gilg.* XI. 54–5. Apparently 55 had an extra word, but of the traces on K 2252+ only the first horizontal is really sure.

ii. 34 The preterite of *bâru* 'catch birds' is elsewhere *ibār*, but there are parallels to a verb belonging to more than one class, see the note on I. 98. Equally possible is a derivation from *ebēlu* 'snare birds', since *l* and *r* can interchange, cf. II. iv. 8 (*ṣe-ru pa-ar-ku*) and S iv. 58 (*ṣēru pal-ku-ú*).

ii. 36 A restoration *bu-*⌜*ú*⌝*-u*[*l ša-a*]*k?-ka-an* deserves mention.

ii. 39 Since the noun *bibbulu*/*bubbulu* means the day of the moon's disappearance at the end of the month, this time is probably meant here.

ii. 49 A I/1 perfect or I/2 preterite of *šakānu*—*ištakna*—gives no sense here, and, with an eye on 53 below, a derivation from *šagāmu* seems inescapable. The change of *m* to *n* after *g* does not seem to occur elsewhere in Akkadian, though after a sibilant it is well attested: *lismu*/*lisnu* (*AHw*); *išmē-karāb*/*išnī-karāb* (E. Ebeling, *Tod und Leben*, p. 21 II); *šašmû*/*šašnû* (*ZA* 41. 169).

ii. 50 That *ila* is a conjunction (otherwise unattested) meaning 'as soon as' is mere conjecture. But no better alternative has occurred to the present writers. One could emend the text to *i-lu*! 'the gods (heard etc.)', but that creates a needless intrusion in the context, which states how *Atra-ḫasīs* acted as the flood began.

iii. 5 One might restore $u_4$*-ma iš-t*]*e-en* from *Gilg.* XI. 108, or *i-ṭ*]$e_4$*-en* 'it grinds' in the spirit of U rev. 13.

iii. 9–10 Cf. *Gilg.* XI. 107 (collated): [×] giš *māta kīma karp*[*ati* . . .] × *iḫ-p*[*u-u*]/*-p*[*i*]. The incomplete sign in the middle is not *š*]*á* or *š*]*a*, but, e.g., *t*]*i*; thus *rigimša* cannot be restored. The restoration *iḫ-p*[*u-u*] was already suggested by Haupt, *Das bab. Nimrodepos* 139[5] as 'nicht unwahrscheinlich'. U rev. 17 is also based on this Old Babylonian couplet, and a comparison of all three forms suggests that the later editors could not stomach the metaphor 'shattered the noise of the land', and so they modified it.

iii. 18 Restored from *Gilg.* IX. v. 36.

iii. 19 See note on v. 46–vi. 6 below.

iii. 26 Restore [*ù*] or [*ša*]?

iii. 29 For *kullulu* see the note on I S iii. 12. *bulḫītu* is restored here from iv. 21 below: both lines concern lips. Other occurrences are lexical:

[× ×].te.KA.KA = *šap-tan šá bul-ḫe-e-ti le-qa-a*
[×] ×.te.gar.gar = MIN *le-qa-a*
*Nabnītu* (*CT* 19. 37, Rm II. 40 rev. 14–15)
. . . ].gi$_4$ = *bu-ul-ḫi-tu*
. . . ].šà = KI.MIN
*List of Diseases* (*CT* 19. 45, K 264 obv. 23–4 = *MSL* IX. 96. 165–6)
KA × [X.m]ud = *bu-ul-ḫe-e-tum*
*Erimḫuš* VI. 233 (preceded by *laqlaqqu*, as in the *List of Diseases*)
[KA . . . ] = *bu-ul-ḫi-tum*
[KA . . ] × = *šu-ur-pí-tum* ('burning')
*Kagal* D Frag. 8. 4 (OB, *SLT* 248. i)
*šà-kúm-mu-u* = *bu-ul-ḫi-tú*
*Malku* IV. 81 (*LTBA* II. I. xii. 110 = *CT* 18. 20, K 8312. 11)

The explicit connection with lips in *Nabnītu* shows that this is the word, and its occurrence in the *List of Diseases* indicates that it is something physiological. As to meaning, 'heat' is indicated by the evidence already quoted. *šakummû* is a loan from the Sumerian šà 'stomach' and kúm 'hot' (for which see Landsberger, *JNES* 8. 248. 14; ibid. 286[121]; E. I. Gordon, *Sumerian Proverbs*, p. 116). This meaning is confirmed in that it can be established that *bulḫītu* is a phonetic variant of *buḫrītu*, from *buḫḫuru* 'to heat'. The clearest evidence on this point comes from *Gilg.* XI. 126, which is the equivalent of *Atra-ḫasīs* III. iv. 21:

*šab-ba/kàt-ma šap-ta-šú-nu le-qa-a bu-uḫ-re-e-ti*

The reading *leqâ* needs explanation (its connection with the line of *Nabnītu* does not). Campbell Thompson gave only × [(.)]-*a*, with a note that it was not sure that the trace belonged to the word ending -*a*. But a glance at any photograph of K 3375 shows room for only ×-×-*a*, and traces of the first two signs are still on the tablet, though Campbell Thompson did not copy them. In the nineteenth century the tablet was better preserved, as shown on the older photographs, e.g. R. W. Rogers, *Cuneiform Parallels*[2], pl. 12, and the first sign ends in two uprights and the middle one is -*qa*-. Already in 1885 Delitzsch had read ⌜*le-é*⌝?-*a* (*AL*[3] 104. 120), and Haupt in 1891 (*Das bab. Nimrodepos* 139[28]) read it ×-*qa-a* and had correctly identified the form as third person fem. pl. of a third weak verb (*BA* I. 133). In Pinches's copy of Haupt's *Nimrodepos* (now in the possession of the first-named author), Pinches has copied in the margin the latter half of a LI and has written:

*sabba/katma šapta-šunu i*(?)-*li*(?)-*qa-a puḫrēti*

The only real error here is the *i*(?), for the traces (on K 7752+) are, on collation, *t*[*u* or *l*[*i*. Campbell Thompson's copy is badly proportioned. Thus the combination of the *l*[*e*- of K 7752+ with the [*l*]*e-qa-a* on K 3375 gives the complete word.

The word also occurs in *AMT* 49. 6 rev. 5: *bu-uḫ-ri-ta* KÚ$^{\text{meš}}$, where the context proves that it means 'he will eat hot food'. Another occurrence in a medical text, but in a broken context, is *BE* 31. 26. 12: [*b*]*u-uḫ-ri-ta* [ (courtesy F. Köcher).

A medical problem remains. What is the complaint *bulḫītu/buḫrītu*? That *šakummû* involves šà/*libbu* is no difficulty, since the *List of Diseases* has two Sumerian equivalents for *bulḫītu*, the second of which ends ].šà. The first, then, presumably refers to lips. In the line under discussion it is not clear if Nintu's lips are suffering due to general agitation or from lack of drink, but in iv. 21 the latter is explicitly the cause. In the modern Western world we would not describe a thirsty person as having hot lips, but clearly the Babylonians did. *šabba* in *Gilg.* XI means 'burn' (not 'dry', as von Soden, *Or* N.S. 25. 242[1]), see the lexica; and note te.te = *ṣur-ru-pu* ('burn'), *bul-lu-ḫu* (*CT* 19. 3. iii. 12–13 = *MSL* IX. 95. 132–3).

iii. 33 One expects *erištu(m)*, not the accusative here, and curiously the Assyrian Recension (I. S iii. 16) has an exactly similar case with *erišta* $^{d}$*mami*. However, this is a late copy, and the Old Babylonian text in this case (I. 295) has a nominative (*sassuru*), so probably one must take *erišta* here as no more than an error.

iii. 34–5 The day becomes dark when one experiences calamity. See also the Sumerian 'Poem of the Righteous Sufferer' (*Vetus Testamentum*, Supplements III. 170 ff. 68): dingir.mu kalam.e ud ba.zalag mà.ar ud ma.$ku_{10}$.$ku_{10}$ 'My god, the day shines bright over the land, for me the day is dark'.

iii. 39–40 *bīšu* is used specifically of speech, but this seems to be the first example in an Old Babylonian text. In lists Tiruru is a name of Ištar: $^{d}$*ti-ru-ru* = $^{d}$*iš-tar šá* BI-ŠUL-*ti* (*CT* 24. 41. 78), and in three other lists of Ištar names it occurs immediately before S/Šiduri: *CT* 25. 30 rev. i. 18; *KAV* 48. 11; *KAV* 173. 15. Her form is described in the Göttertypentext (*MIO* I. 80–2), but this is all that is known of her. Perhaps Tiruru had a reputation like that of Lamaštu, who, 'for her distasteful ideas and her abominable counsel' (*a-na ṭé-mì-ša lá dam-qí-im ma-al-ki-ša pá-ru-im/sà-aḫ-i-im*) was kicked by Anu from heaven to earth (*BIN* IV. 126, *Or* N.S. 25. 142–3).

iii. 42 *ù pa-ag-ri-ia* merely emphasizes *ra-ma-ni-ia*, see other examples *apud* F. R. Kraus, *Edikt* 169, and Finkelstein, *JCS* 11. 84. iii. 15. *ana* is taken as 'at the discretion of', cf. *Code of Hammurabi*, § 132: *a-na mu-ti-ša* $^{d}$*nāram i-ša-al-li* 'at her husband's discretion she must undergo the river-ordeal'.

iii. 49 For *tūša* cf. *Malku* VIII (*STT* 394) 114: *tu-u-šá* = *ki-i šá*; Held, *JCS* 15. 22; von Soden, *ZA* 49. 187–90. While potentiality is certainly one nuance of *tūša*, there is no need to exclude others, and the equations in the lists with *appūna*, *minde*, *pīqa*, *pīqat*, and *uqa* need not be discounted. As a whole, the couplet seems to presume that Anu had gone up to heaven and was staying there as though he were in a state of prosperity, when in fact the source of supplies had been cut off with the loss of the human race. Yet he as president (*bēl ṭēmi*—only occurring here and v. 40 below in OB) was in part responsible. So Bēlet-ilī sarcastically suggests that she might do the same.

iv. 5–9 Cf. *a-ba/a-bu* in *Gilg.* VI. 89 and *CAD aba*. The two lines of this couplet express in different and somewhat clashing figures that the waters were covered with floating bodies. If *ul-*⌜*da*⌝ is correctly read and understood, Nintu, seeing only bodies where the sea should be, declares that the human race has begotten it. The figure of (dead) dragon-flies floating on the surface of a river occurs also in *Gilg.* X. vi. 30: *ku-li-li* ⟨*iq*⟩-*qé-lep-pa-a ina nāri* 'dragon-flies drift on the river', and here lines 8–9 develop this figure: the dead, like insects, have matted together on the surface of the water and then get pushed to the side by the current. We do not venture to guess what *ina ṣēri* means in this context. The second of these two figures is suppressed altogether in *Gilg.* XI, and the first is modified to: 'like young fish they fill the sea' (*kī mārī nūnī umallâ tâmtamma*) in line 123. This is certainly easier wording, but it misses the point that the bodies were floating, whence the horror of the scene. See also the note on v. 46–7 below.

iv. 14 In *CAD* the occurrences of *ṣarāpu* I/1 are so arranged that it appears that it is transitive in the meanings 'refine (metals)' and 'fire (bricks)', but intransitive in figurative uses. However, of the five examples cited for the latter, one is indecisive, being a stative, a second—if correctly restored—is also stative and so indecisive; a third is an infinitive in a list, and so no more helpful; a fourth occurs in a phrase grammatically peculiar in both words (*iṣ-rip ka-bat-su*: should be *iṣrup kabtatsu*); this leaves one example only, *Tukulti-Ninurta Epic* iii. 28. But among the bilingual passages there is one active example: *eṭ-lu šá ni-is-sa-tú zu-mur-šú iṣ-ru-pu* (*JTVI* 26. 153. i. 10) 'a man whose body grief burned'. *lalâša iṣrup* is another active example.

iv. 18–19*a* This clumsy line is corrupted in *Gilg.* XI. 125. K 3375 offers *ilāni*$^{meš}$ *aš-ru áš-bi i-na bi-ki-ti* 'the gods humbly sat weeping', and K 7752+ has: AŠ *nu-ru-ub ni-is-sa-ti* S[I? 'in the moistness of grief.' (??). Probably this latter results from editorial work on a corruption of *aš-ru áš-bu ina nissati*. Von Soden's emendation of *aš-ru* to *ina libbi* (*ZA* 53. 232) cannot be sustained.

iv. 19*b* The picture is of sheep standing crowded together in a dry trough waiting for water.

iv. 24 In *Gilg.* XI. 127 collation of K 2252+ reveals that 7 is as possible as 6, at the beginning of the line.

iv. 25 This agrees better with the reading of K 7752+ in *Gilg.* XI. 128 (*šá-a-ru ra-a-du mi-ḫu-ú a-b*[*u-bu*]), than with that of K 3375 (*šá-a-ru a-bu-bu me-ḫu-ú*).

v. 39–43 *Gilg.* XI. 167–9 puts the blame on Enlil alone.

v. 46–vi. 6 The episode of the flies corresponds to *Gilg.* XI. 162–5, and *su-bé-e ra-bu-ti* here to nim$^{meš}$ gal$^{meš}$ there. Essentially the episode is aetiological, explaining manufactured flies in the jewellery of the goddess Bēlet-ilī and no doubt other deities. A gold fly is specifically mentioned in a necklace in the Qatna inventories, as well as part of a breast ornament (*RA* 43. 168. 315 and 170. 337: 1 nim guškin). The gold fly also appears in *Ḫarra* XII. 349: nim guškin = *zu-um-bu* (*MSL* VII. 169). Flies of lapis appear in *Ḫarra* XVI: in the Alalaḫ forerunner, Wiseman no. 447. II. 15 (na$_4$.nim.za.gìn), of which the bilingual version is: [na$_4$.nim.za].gìn = *zu-um-bu* (*TCL* 6. 36, rev. 43). *Ḫargud* on Tablet XIV of *Ḫarra* also lists: nim.za.gìn.na = (blank) = nim [ (*CT* 14. 8 rev. 17 = *MSL* VIII/2. 47), but the corresponding line of *Ḫarra* is not known. Actual lapis beads in fly-shape are known (E. D. Van Buren, *Fauna* 108), and their triangular shape made them particularly suitable for necklaces, if indeed their functional shape did not suggest the fly in the first place. The idea that *Gilg.* XI refers to flies in amber is clearly untenable. Granting that the author is explaining an item of cultic jewellery, the next question is how the flies come into the story of the flood. In *Gilg.* XI the only other occurrence of the word is in 161, only two lines above, where the gods gather 'like flies', as in *Atra-ḫasīs* III. v. 35 (restored). But psychologically it is quite unsatisfying to have Bēlet-ilī seize upon some jewellery flies as a reminder of the disaster, when they only speak of the hungry gods' first meal. The truncation of the story in *Gilg.* XI has removed the earlier passages about flies in *Atra-ḫasīs*, see the note on iv. 5–9 above, and in addition iii. 44: *ki-ma zu-ub-bi*. The orthography is bewildering: *zu-ub-bi, su-bé-e, zu-ub-bu-ú*. The Semitic root is *ḏbb*, and *zubbu* is therefore the primary form in Akkadian, but in view of the variants *zakāru/saqāru* and *zibbatu/sibbatu*, etc., it is quite possible that iii. 19 above, *ki-ma su-ub-bi*, is the same simile, and that all the other passages should be corrected from that to *sú-*. Since the context of iii. 19 is not complete we have left the various writings in their simplest form. Thus the flies in the story are a memorial of the drowned offspring of Bēlet-ilī, and the idea may have been suggested to its originator by a proverb or cliché about dragon-flies drifting down the river.

Line 47 is crowded, and under these circumstances one cannot be sure if the sign is *i*-ŠU-*ma* or *i*-KU-*ma*. The latter suggests no meaning at all, and the former could be taken from *ešû*: 'which Anu in his confusion . . .', but we prefer to think that *Gilg.* XI. 163 is in this case correct: *šá* $^{d}$*a-nu-um i-pu-šú*, and that the one sign is omitted from *Atra-ḫasīs* by a scribal error. The immediately following *ipangal*(*u*) can be explained from *Erimḫuš* V. 195–7:

ir = *ba-ba-lum*
DU$^{tu.um.}$ma = *a-ru-ú*
DU$^{di.di.}$DU = *ba-qa-a-lu*
*TCL* 6. 35, rev. ii. 1–3

This is marked off as a section, and since elsewhere DU.DU equates *abālu* and *arû* (*ŠL* 206. 66–7) one is at a loss to understand how *CAD* and *AHw* connect this *baqālu* with *buqlu* 'malt' and render it 'to sprout' and 'mältzen' respectively. Such a verb may exist, but this one means 'bring' or 'carry'. Since *b* and *p* may interchange one must certainly connect this verb with *ipangal*(*u*), but it must remain an open question if *iš-ši* in *Gilg.* XI. 163 is a reflection of *ipangal*(*u*). It is also possible that *ki-i ṣu-ḫi-šú* was used to replace it in quite another sense. (This phrase involves a sense not yet understood, cf. *BAM* 310. 8–9: *e-gír-tú* 37 *abnī*$^{meš}$ *ṣu-ḫi* $^{na_4}$*uqnî*.) Certainly v. 48–vi. 1 are omitted in *Gilg.* XI, and to us their incompleteness obscures them, but it appears that Bēlet-ilī, exploiting her grief as some women would, uses the occasion to get some special dispensation out of Anu. Whether this was only the rights to the flies is not now clear. The close parallelism of vi. 2–4 with *Gilg.* XI. 163–5 has suggested the restoration *a*[*n-nu-tum*]. The peculiarity of *ilāni*$^{meš}$ *an-nu-ti* in *Gilg.* as a vocative, and the repetition of *ayamši* at the ends of both 164 and 165 suggest that our restoration of *Atra-ḫasīs* vi. 2–3 lies behind *Gilg.* XI. 164. But the suffix on *luḫsussu* in vi. 4 precludes $u_4$*-mi* being its object, as in *Gilg.* XI. 165. One might restore $u_4$*-mi-*[*ša-am-ma ù*] *ṣí-*[*a-ti-iš*], 'every day and for ever'.

vi. 9 The *textus receptus* of *Gilg.* XI. 173a is curious in the lack of gender concord between *ayyumma* and *napišti*, but a new duplicate, VAT 11087, has ]*-nu-um-ma ú-ṣu n*[*a-*, which suggests that a *-nu-* has dropped out of the received text due to a scribal omission. This confirmation of the identity of the line under discussion with *Gilg.* XI. 173a encourages the view that BI*-ti-iš-tum* in *Atra-ḫasīs* is an error.

vi. 19 Restoration conjectural.

vi. 25 The reading of K 2252+ in *Gilg.* XI. 180 (*be-el ár-ni*), rather than that of K 3375 (*be-el ḫi-ṭi*), supplies the restoration here.

vi. 40 *unappiš* is restored after iv. 12, but if correct it is the only example in the tablets of Ku-Aya of the sign PI with the same value.

vii. 3 For the *pāšittu* demon see von Soden, *BiOr* XVIII. 72.

vii. 6–7 *ukbakkāti* has been identified by J. J. Finkelstein as a plural of *ugbabtu*. This is most probably a Sumerian loan-word, and the change from *g* to *b* is well known, especially in Emesal. Cf. gig = *kibtu*, and the examples *apud* A. Falkenstein, *Das Sumerische*, p. 30. In lists *entu* and *ugbabtu* both equate nin.dingir.ra (K 10194 (*CT* 18. 47) + K 4328 (*CT* 19. 41) i. 2–3; *MAOG* XIII/2. 38. 6–7), and they equate each other in *Malku* I. 134 (*JAOS* 83. 427). Apart from the line under discussion *i/egiṣītu* only occurs lexically: *MAOG* XIII/2. 38. 18, also the forerunner to this entry *apud CAD sub voce igiṣītu*. She was some kind of high-ranking lady in a religious order.

vii. 8–9 The last sign can be either ⌜*ra*⌝ or ⌜*si*⌝, and the reading *pu-ur-si* has been suggested by B. Landsberger. It is known that these women did not marry or bear children. This helps to explain the birth legend of Sargon of Akkad (*CT* 13. 42). His mother was an *ēntu* (*e-né-tum*), who, on his birth, put him on the river like Moses. In view of the rules of her order she had to conceal his birth. Literature on this subject is cited in footnote 1 on page 13. If the last sign is read ⌜*ra*⌝ the line must be taken as: *lū ikkibušināma alādam burra* 'let it be taboo for them to bear a son'. The difficulties here are (i) that the acc. *alādam* cannot be explained, though other difficult uses of this case occur here, see p. 29, and (ii) *burra* for *bukra* is without parallel.

viii. 9–19 The damaged state of the epilogue is most unfortunate since apparently it contained an ascription of authorship. Note the first person pl. in 9, and while *ušabši* and *uzammer* (12, 19) could be first or third person in isolation, in the context only the first fits. Thus a deity who confesses to participating in the bringing of the flood at Enlil's command claims to have sung this 'song', which is equivalent to authorship. The Mother Goddess is a possible candidate.

viii. 14 The question with ŠA-*ni-ti-iš*-[*ka*] is whether it is a scribal error for *ta*-, or a phonetic variant of *tanīttu*. Some of the other examples of a similar interchange are foreign words, e.g. *šupšikku*, *tupšikku* and *šabsūtu*, *tabsūtu*; but there are purely Akkadian examples. Von Soden in *BiOr* XXIII. 52 quotes *taḫ-lu-uq-ti* (instead of *šaḫluqti*, from Boghazköy) and *ti-si-a* (for *šisia*) from *Atra-ḫasīs* I. 61 (see above and *JNES* 27. 218–19). Thus the phonetic explanation seems preferable.

viii. 17 *li-iṣ-ṣí-ru* is from *ṣurru*, a reflexive II/2: 'make famous to one another'.

## K 3399+3934 (S), Reverse iv

S iv. 10, 14 The gloss in the second of these lines shows that the copyist or editor wanted us to read [*li-r*]*iš li-ṣi* in the first. However, while the context demands a meaning 'diminish', no interpretation of these two forms will provide this. The first could be 'ask' or 'plant' (*erēšu*), or 'rejoice' (*râšu*). The second, if from *mêṣu*, would mean 'be little', and a II or III stem would be needed to give 'diminish'. Furthermore, in 43 and 53 below where this verb certainly occurs, it is written *mêṣu*, not *êṣu*. Thus the most satisfactory explanation is that *li-šak-li-ṣi* is correct in 10, and in 14 the text has been altered to fit a misconception about 10. *kalāṣu* is 'contract' and a metaphorical sense must be assumed.

S iv. 45 Since *našû* means 'raise' not 'rise' an ellipsis of *nāru* has been assumed.

S v. 1–2 See the note on x rev. i. 4–7.

S v. 18–24 (= vi. 7–13) With these signs of famine see generally A. L. Oppenheim, '"Siege Documents" from Nippur', *Iraq* XVII. 69–89. In 18–19 the mother has driven the daughter out of the house to reduce the number of mouths, as in a prophecy: *ummu eli mārti bāb-šá id-dil* (*JCS* 18. 20. 15). In 20–1 the picture is of wives and children being sold so that the father can buy food at famine-inflated prices. In 22–4 the horrors of cannibalism are reached. Note *Explicit Malku* I. 174h: *bu-ú-nu* = *ma-a-ru* (*JAOS* 83. 436).

S v. 33 Cf. *Malku* II. 41: *mid-ra-tum* = *na-a-ru* (*ZA* 43. 235). In view of II. iii. 15 and x rev. i. 15 *šu-ḫu-rat* is clearly an Assyrian form of *šaḫurrat*.

## BE 39099 (x)

x rev. i. 4–7 This oft-repeated section may have occurred in some form at this point in the main recension since the context—the command to reinforce the drought—is lost between II. ii and iii. It is referred back to in II. v. 16–21 and 30–3′, according to which the upper level was guarded by Anu and Adad, and the 'lower' by Enlil himself. Presumably Enki guarded the bottom level, though in the end he failed to co-operate. S also preserves the end of a statement that this arrangement was put into effect, v. 1–2. The Babylonian exercise tablet y probably preserves what the main recension had, orthography apart. But x has put Sin and Nergal in place of Enlil. These gods occur again as a pair on a Middle Assyrian tablet of incantations: $^{d}$30 *u* $^{d}$u.gur *e-ṭí-ru-tu* (*AS* 16. 286 rev. 21, 27). If more were known of these two as a pair it might be possible to determine the location of 'the middle earth' more certainly. By *elênu* one suspects that all the cosmos above the earth is meant, and the god of heaven and the storm god are appropriate as guardians of this area. 'Middle earth' seems to occur elsewhere only in *KAR* 307 obv. 34–7, where there is a full sequence: *erṣetum elītum*, *qablītum*, and *šaplītum*. The first of these is the abode of men, the second Enki's realm, and the third the underworld proper. However, *Atra-ḫasīs* gives no sign of subscribing to so complex a scheme. At the very beginning, I. 11–18, a three-decker universe is explained, one level each for Anu, Enlil, and Enki in descending order. There too *šigaru naḫbalu ti'āmtim* is used for Enki's realm. By this one is forced to take *erṣetum qablītum* not as 'the middle earth' (of other earths), but as 'the earth which is central' (in the cosmos). The phrase 'the bolt, the bar of the sea' has not yet been found outside this epic, but the idea it enshrines is well known in Babylonian and other mythologies. The primeval sea, usually after a battle, was thrust down below at the time of creation and a cosmic bar was laid upon it to keep it down there out of the way. If x rev. ii. 23 and 39 have been correctly restored, when the drought was broken through Enki's machinations he somehow got half of this bar broken so that water reached parched mankind. The phrase *qá-du ú/šam-mi-šu* is ambiguous. Were these things being guarded along with *šigaru naḫbalu tâmtim*, or were they helping Enki to guard the latter? If the second alternative is taken one must read *ú-mi-šu*, and assume that *ūmū* can refer to the Seven Apkallus or some other group in Enki's court. Certainly *ūmu* would bear this meaning, but there is the difficulty that x, which alone has the word, despite an extraordinarily inconsistent orthography, writes this word always *ú-/šam-*, not $u_4$- as would be expected if the word were *ūmu*. Of course, it could have been handed down without change from an earlier period when *ú-* in *ūmu* was normal, but this remains an objection none the less. The reading *šammu* can be justified on the ancient view that plants had their origin in the underworld, from which they shoot up, and an incantation states Enki's connection with plants:

én *šu-un-du* $^{d}$*a-num ir-ḫu-u šamû*$^{ú}$
$^{d}$*é-a ina erṣetim*$^{tim}$ *ú-kin-nu šam-mu*
*AMT* 42. 4 rev. restored from BM 98584+
After Anu had begotten the heavens
And Ea had established plants in the underworld

Thus Enki was required to stop plants from growing at this time.

## BM 98977+99231 (U)

U obv. 2, 6, 8 For *šikin šēpē* 'placing of the feet' see S. Langdon, *SBP* $92^{5}$; F. R. Kraus, *Or*. N.S. 16. $199^{2}$; and R. Borger *BiOr* 14. 191.

U rev. 7 *si-qu-šú siq-si-qu* = *zīqūšu ziqziqqu*. For agar$_{x}$ see *Diri* IV. 117: a-gar = $^{\text{IM}}_{\text{IM}}\times$ = [im.min.na.bi *gi*]*-li-mu-ú* = *ra-a-du* (*MSL* III. 98. 40 and V. 192. 40). *rādu* occurs in *Gilg*. XI. 128 in K 7752+, but not in K 3375.

U rev. 9 One might restore *ur-taq-qù-da* 'danced'.

U rev. 15 In *Gilg*. XI. 101 K 2252+ reads $^{d}$*èr-ra-kal ú-n*[*a-*, but K 3375 has ]*-gal i-na-as-saḫ*.

U rev. 16 *ú-*[*šar-riṭ*] is restored by conjecture alone, as is [$^{d}$*z*]*u*. The latter is of course normally written AN.*zu-ú*, but U has other unusual orthographies (see p. 37). As a flying creature Zû (for this reading see *Or* N.S. 36 130) is very suitable for rending the heavens. Note also *AfO* 13. 46 rev. ii. 3: $^{d}$im.dugud *ṣu-up-ra-ka*, and the drug name *ṣu-pur* $^{d}$*zi-i* (*BAM* 307. 25).

# THE SUMERIAN FLOOD STORY

## (by M. Civil)

38 The a can be taken as a locative suffix to be joined to the preceding -bi, and this interpretation is supported by the presence of the infix -ni- in the verbal chain, but due to the inconsistency of the grammar in the present text, the possibility of a compound verb a—[×] cannot be dismissed completely.

39 sì-[sì-ga-bi], with sì in the sense of *sapānu*, would be a likely parallel to ḫa-lam-ma-bi.

40 ki-ùr means, in addition to other, probably secondary, meanings such as cultic spaces in Nippur and Ereš, the land assigned to someone to live there, but still as an 'undeveloped plot' (for references, see Van Dijk, *Acta Orientalia* 28. 488 ff.); a close parallel to our line can be found in Letter 7 of collection B, line 24 (quoted

from Fadhil A. Ali's unpublished edition [Philadelphia, 1964]): the sender finds himself in a foreign city and concludes his petition to the king by saying: lugal-mu èn-mu ḫé-en-tar-re ki-ùr-mu-šè ḫé-im-mi-ib-$gi_4$-$gi_4$-in '(I wish) that my King could investigate my case, (and) that I could go back to my land.' The fact that in late Sumerian the contrast between -ta, -šè, and -a is often lost, makes the interpretation of this line somewhat doubtful. If the original sense of -ta is to be retained, the line implies that mankind will leave the grounds where they live now, and where there are no buildings (i.e. nomadic life?), to move to the cities; if -ta is for -šè, it means that people will go back to their territories, which they left after a destruction, and where cities will now be (re)built.[1] Without the missing part preceding line 37, it is not possible to reach a conclusion. The incorrect use of the suffix -e-ne, which can be only an object suffix referring to un 'people', is a Semitism.

41 In lines 41–4 the suffix -me-a-(bi) is hardly the first person plural possessive (Kramer), because the juxtaposition of the first person possessive and the third person collective -bi (referring to un) is impossible. It is preferable to take -me-a as a plural mark used in late texts to remedy the lack of plural morphemes in standard Sumerian, a lack which seems to have run against the linguistic feelings of the authors of such late texts. An example of this use of -me-a is: [IM].dal-ḫa-mun edin ḫuš an-ta ⟨⟨×⟩⟩ na-ba-$gi_4$-$gi_4$-dè[2] udug(!)-ḫul-a-me-àm ì-gál, *UET* VI. 184. 3 ff. in a hemerological text (probably of Cassite origin); -me-àm obviously takes here the place of -meš. The plural function of me-a is derived from me-a 'how many' in standard Sumerian. The meaning 'how many' is particularly clear when me-a goes with the verb lu 'to be numerous' as in: me-a lu áb me-a lu-lu Sjöberg, *Nanna-Suen* I. 13. 1 (modified reading) or e $^d$nanna áb-zu me-a mu-$u_8$-lu 'oh, Nanna, how great have you made the number of your cows!' (*PBS* x/4. 7. 17). A typical passage for me-a 'how many' is *Laḫar-Ašnan* 130 ff.:

> $u_4$-šú-uš-e níg-$kas_x$(ŠID)-zu ì-ak-e
> giš-šid-ma-zu ki ì-tag-tag-ge
> na-gada-zu $u_8$-me-a $sila_4$-tur-tur-me-a
> ùz-me-a máš-tur-tur-me-a lú-ù mu-un-na-ab-bé
> Every day an account of you is made,
> the tally sticks are planted in the ground,
> your shepherd tells the owner, how many ewes and how many little lambs,
> how many goats and how many little kids (there are).

The same me-a is found in a-na-me-a-bi (cf. Poebel, *GSG* § 264 ff.) 'as many of them as there are.'

42 The first sign is not clear, it can be uru or é.

43 I am unable to offer any suggestion for translating ki(DI is also possible)-eš, except that perhaps we must read ki-eš-⟨bar⟩.

44 One has the impression that Poebel thought that he was copying ×-me-a at the beginning of the line, although he transliterates kù-a. My translation, which follows Kramer, is perfectly admissible in itself (only the place of kù before a is abnormal), but it is somewhat startling in this context. Perhaps we must consider as one of the sub-themes of the tale a contrast between the orderly use of water (cf. i. 46 and ii. 99 f.) against the destructive flood of the storm.

[1] The verb dù in some instances may be translated by 'rebuild'.

[2] Corresponds to the Akk. *ašamšūtu ina ṣēri la ušamḫar* (*KAR* 177 rev. iii. 8; ii. 48; 178 rev. iv. 34).

46 The usual meaning of a-dug$_4$ is 'to irrigate' (see H. Sauren *Topographie der Provinz Umma* I. 74 f., 197 ff.) and 'to flood' and hence 'to destroy' (IV. *R* 28*. 4. 33 f. and duplicates). If one takes the last meaning, the first clause must be considered relative: 'In the place which had been destroyed, I want there to be peace (or: well-being)'; even if the nominalizing -a is missing, the infix -ni- in the second clause authorizes the translation of the first one as relative. The translation given in the text is a perfectly acceptable alternative; the choice between the two depends once again on the missing links in the plot.

48 The line shows that sag-gi$_6$ is a designation of human beings in contrast with animals (see commentary to the following line), as in the parallels mentioned by W. Leslau, *Lexique Soqotri* 193, and W. Vycichl, *AfO* 20. 96, and not an ethnic designation.

49 The translation 'animals' for níg-GILIM (the sign which appeared doubtful to Poebel is reasonably certain according to my own collation) is based on one hand on the assumption that GILIM stands for gilim$_x$ (PÉŠ) for which the meaning 'animals' is given in *Ea* I. 199 ff.:

| | | |
|---|---|---|
| PÉŠ kilim | = | *nammaštu* |
| gilim$_x$ | = | ,, |
| gilili | = | *nammašû* |
| ge$_{16}$ | = | ,, |

and on the other hand on the word níg-ki equated in *Ḫarra* XIV. 401a, 402 with *nammaštu* and *zērmandu*.[1] In the meaning 'destruction' (Akk. *šaḫluqtu*) the word is normally written with a final -ma; cf. line 259 and *JCS* 19. 6. 73 f.[2] ki-ta ki-ta does not mean 'from the earth', but is rather an adverbial 'everywhere' (for ki-a ki-a).

86 There seems to be enough space at the beginning of the line for [du-lu]m-bi 'their painstaking efforts'; [si]g$_4$-bi 'their/its brickwork' is palaeographically more difficult.

87 A single unidentifiable half-broken sign is preserved before DÍM. For uš 'foundation' see A. Falkenstein, *Or* N.S. 35. 229 ff. Neither the verb ba-al nor its Akkadian counterpart *ḫerû* is used elsewhere for 'to dig a foundation'. uš bal seems to have something to do with modifying the location of the long side of a field, see Deimel, *ŠL* 211. 45. The meaning of the line remains highly doubtful.

88 The words gidru 'sceptre' and aga 'crown' are possible restorations for the gap before nam-lugal-la.

89 The reading ⸢men⸣-maḫ follows Kramer; the traces do not point to gidru (see preceding line); $^{giš}$šibir (Jacobsen, *AS* 11. 56) is palaeographically unlikely; furthermore, this word does not mean sceptre.

[1] níg.ki is found in context in: níg-zi-gál níg-ki u$_5$-a zi-dùg-ga ši-im-da-pa-an-pa-an 'the living beings, the animals in heat, they breathe with pleasure' (*Enlil Hymn* 150, Falkenstein, *SGL* I. 18, restored by unpublished duplicates).

[2] Cf. also péš-níg-gilim-ma = *aštikissu* (a small rodent), *Ḫarra* XIV. 196 and XI. 65. There is a possibility that some connection exists between níg-gilim/kilim$_x$ and $^{d}$nin-kilim/gilim$_x$ (written $^{d}$nin-PÉŠ$^{gi_4\text{-lí-na}}$ in Urukagina, Cone C v. 1; cf. Sollberger, *ZA* 54. 13, no. 43). The níg-gilim-ma which appears as a descriptive element in a certain number of expressions, mostly designating manufactured objects (*Ḫarra* V. 243; VIII. 350; Forerunner VIII–IX. 178; X. 208; cf. II. 289) seems to mean some kind of lattice-work, and does not help in translating níg-gilim in our context.

91 The sign after -ga is u[ru] according to Poebel. In any case, the word uru must be restored somewhere in this line because of the -bi of line 92.

92 Restored from line 98. The term KAB-dug$_4$-ga has been the object of the most diverse interpretations: 'Kultort' Deimel, *Orientalia* 17 (1925) 35, followed by Jacobsen, *AS* 11. 59[111] and Kramer; an epithet of the 'deluge-demon' and the 'gods', Poebel; 'divine rulers' King, *Legends of Babylon and Egypt* 58 ff.; 'surface of the earth' Kramer, *Sumerian Mythology* 97; etc. The term KAB-dug$_4$-ga appears in *YBT* 4. 1. 1 f., a legal record dating from the 44th year of Šulgi: someone had indulged in the illegal use of irrigation waters and ensi$_2$-ke$_4$ é-gal-la di-da KAB in-na-an-dug$_4$ 'the governor presided over the trial in the palace'. If 'presided', which seems the most logical translation, is correct, the term refers in our context to the rights of the cities to the successive hegemony of the country, a meaning which would suit perfectly the fact that the cities listed here are the dynastic cities of the ante-diluvian period according to the King List and the fragment *CT* 46. 5. The only other occurrence of KAB-dug$_4$-ga known to the present writer is CBS 14233: kaš KAB-dug$_4$-ga ⌜íb⌝-nag, $^{d}$sùd um-ta-è, é-$^{d}$sùd-ka izi ba-ra-íl 'he drank the beer of the "president" (or "presidency"), Sud came out, and then the house of Sud burned down'; the passage, which could belong to the Enlil-Ninlil-Sud tale discussed in *JNES* 26. 200 ff., is too badly broken to enable one to draw any useful conclusions.

93 The reading sag$_x$ or nisag$_x$ of the first sign is correctly given by Van Dijk in *JCS* 19. 20; cf., earlier, C. J. Gadd in *Studies G. R. Driver* 68, commentary to line 30.

94 It is better to consider the sign following -ma as a superfluous -šè (as read by Poebel), than to read túg (Kramer) which hopelessly complicates the line. The nu-gig must be here Inanna, entitled to Bad-Tibira because of her relationship with Dumuzi.

95 Since Pabilsag is well attested as the god of Larag: $^{d}$pa-bíl-sag ù-mu-un la-ra-ag$^{ki}$ (*CT* 42, no. 3. v. 20 and duplicates, see E. Bergmann, *ZA* 56. 33), there is no need to introduce a hypothetical deity Ḫendurbilḫursag, and the insertion of the ḫur before sag has to be considered as a scribal mistake, perhaps due to a partial confusion with the name of Ḫendursaga.

99 The translation given is inspired by the fact that the following line has to do with irrigation waters. a-gi$_4$ is considered here as an irregular writing for a-gi$_6$ (cf. *CAD* I/1. 157 f. *agû* B). The meaning 'to stop the flow of water' of the verb šú is clearly needed in kù-gál íd-da šú-šú-gin$_x$ 'like an irrigation chief stopping the flow of the water' (*UET* VI/2. 144. 26), and is confirmed by the fragmentary lexical entry šú/šú-šú = *edēl*[*u ša mê* (?)] (*Antagal* 5. iv. 8′) to which we must probably relate [. . .] = [(*edēlu*) *š*]*a* A (*Nabnītu* G 11).

100 This line goes back to:

> [íd-tu]r-tur-ra šu-luḫ ba-an-ak sùr-sùr (var. sur-sur) mi-ni-íb-gar-gar
> The smallest canals were cleaned by him, he put there irrigation ditches

*Bird-Fish Contest* 8. The comparison with the text of *PBS* V. 1 shows perfectly the problems the philologist faces in the interpretation of the Flood tale: ba-an-ak has been changed to gar, and ḪAR-ḪAR replaces sùr-sùr (*ḫarru*). The usual interpretation (Falkenstein, *ZA* 57. 121) reads šu-luḫ-bi níg-ḪAR-ḪAR . . . and has the inconvenience of giving an unlikely níg-ḪAR-ḪAR for which one could suggest 'digging' (in the restricted sense of dredging and widening the canal), but ḪAR = *ḫarāru*, the only basis for it, is a problematical entry (*CAD* VI. 92a *ḫarāru* C). Although the correct technical term for 'to clean a canal' is šu-luḫ—ak, šu-luḫ—gar is also attested (but not for a canal) in standard Sumerian: ki-uz-ga šu-luḫ-e gar-ra-zu, *Curse of Agade* 258 (cf. Falkenstein, *ZA* 57. 63).

146 an-sag NIGIN remains unexplained; is it sag for zag = *tamītu*?

147 Cf. inim-sì-sì-ga kiri$_3$ šu mar-r[a-ta] bar-zu ḫé-en-šed$_8$-e-[dè]: *ina te-me-eq u la-ban ap-pi* [*ka-bit-t*]*a l*[*i-pa-aš-ši*]*-iḫ*, *Rit. Acc.* 109 (AO 6461 rev. 11 f.), but *tēmequ* elsewhere translates inim-šag$_5$-šag$_5$ (*ASKT* 14. 115. 5 f.); the sense '(prayer with) well chosen words' is confirmed by the occurrences of the verb inim—sì-(g) (Falkenstein, *ZA* 49. 138; Jacobsen, *ZA* 52. 127[80]; Van Dijk, *JCS* 19. 12).

149 The form nu-me-a means 'it is not, without being' everywhere except in a very localized scribal peculiarity of the Larsa texts (*TCL* 10. 5. 10, 18. 12, 26. 15, etc.) where, as pointed out by Poebel (*GSG* § 265 f.), -nu-me stands for -na-me. The normal meaning 'it was not a dream' suits the context better.

151 ⌜ki⌝-ùr-šè was already suggested by Poebel, but must be considered doubtful.

153 One can cut á-gùb-bu-mu (for -gá) gub-ba (participle or imperative), or as in the text. The passage, describing how the divine secrets about the incoming flood are transmitted to Ziusudra through a wall, is an obvious parallel to the reed hut episode in *Gilgameš* XI. 20 ff. and *Atra-ḫasīs* III. Since one expects a vocative before inim ga-ra-ab-dug$_4$, and Ziusudra is not a vocative in line 152 (because of the verbal form giš mu-[un-tuk] which is not an imperative) the vocative must be iz-zi-da and the conclusion that, starting in line 154, the words are directed by Enki first to the wall seems most likely in the present state of preservation of the text.

201 The reduplicated plural of im-ḫul is found also in *CT* 16. 19. 38 f. The im before si-si-ig is in all probability a determinative. The word si-si-ig (with variants si-si-ga, sig-sig, sìg-sìg, and sìg-si-ga) is translated by *šāru*, *meḫû*, and *zaqīqu* (most of the lexical references can be found in *CAD* XXI. 58), but in Sumerian the meaning 'ghost' seems restricted to líl (cf., however, E. I. Gordon, *BiOr* 17. 129[57]). su$_8$-g is the plural *marû*-form of gub 'to stand up, to be present at work', not of gin/du 'to come', so that one can translate 'arose' or 'were present (at the destructive task)', but not 'came'.

202 The ugu, superfluous from the Sumerian point of view, is due to the underlying Akkadian model which had *bâ'u* (translated by ùr, cf. *Angim* II. 13 and *SBH* p. 38. 8; 73. 19 f. for ùr with a-ma-ru) with *eli* as in *Gilg.* XI. 110 or *KAH* I. 30. 10.

205 The boat's name is written $^{giš}$má-gur-gur = *(*ma*)*qurqurru* in *Ḫarra* IV. 291, and as a logogram in 𝕵 rev. 8. The only thing we know about this type of boat is its large size, according to the latter reference. For etymological parallels see A. Salonen, *Wasserfahrzeuge* 51; the suggestion there that the word comes from gur-gur 'to impregnate with bitumen' cannot be taken seriously.

207 As seen already by C. J. Gadd, *Sumerian Reading Book* 133, and partly suggested by Poebel, 'to open a window' is to be taken in the sense of 'making the opening' (bùr = *palāšu*), not of 'opening a closed window', which would be bad = *petû* or the like. The ⌜ab⌝-búr window is otherwise unknown; for a list of types of window see *CAD* I/2 *aptu*. For the -en of the third person, see J. Krecher, *ZA* 56. 29 ff.

208 ⌈ù⌉ is doubtful; Poebel and Kramer prefer šul.

211 A stock phrase often found in Sumerian literature: *ZA* 50. 68. 52; 52. 18. 39; *PBS* v. iv. 45; *KAR* 16. rev. 24 f.; etc.; literally 'slaughtered bulls, made sheep numerous' (hendiadys).

255 Kramer's suggestion to insert here the line from the left edge of the tablet is in all probability correct, but the reconstruction of the verb as a form of mí-dug$_4$ is open to doubt; a translation '[provided] Ziusudra with a wife' is also possible.

256 The translation assumes that the verbal form stands for mu-un-na-sum-mu-uš.

259 While the second part of the line is reasonably clear (cf. already Poebel's remarks on this line as well as [*z*]*e-ru na-aṣ-ru á la-šam a-bu-bi*, *JCS* 21, "Enmeduranki" i. 8), the first part of the line remains uncertain. The translation assumes that mu means here 'year', 'time', rather than 'since'.

# ADDENDA

I J 1 B. Landsberger would like to read *ni-⌈ba-ra⌉-a*[*š-šu*] 'let us rebel against him'. By OB standards this is better grammar than *nināraššu* 'let us kill him', but the traces can only be read *ba* by emendation. As to sense, if the rebels are threatening to kill Enlil, this is something remarkable, if not downright improbable. However, they may be threatening to kill the task master. What remains of lines 5–7 can be interpreted to agree with this latter sense. The proposal to kill the task master is met with the answer that Enlil would simply appoint another.

I 63 An unambiguous writing of the root *sqr*/*zkr* occurs in an OB text probably from Sippar and the reign of Ammi-ṣaduqa: *ša pa-qí-dam ù sa-ḫi-ra-am la i-šu-ú* (cultic text, *JCS* 20. 96. 38). This implies a form *skr*, since *ḫ* and *k* interchange in OB, as is well known. However, this hardly settles the form in Atra-ḫasīs.

I 242 The form *ta-aš-ta*-AḪ-*ṭa* has been taken as a I/3 since in the context there is no reason for its being a I/1 perfect or I/2. This involves accepting the value *'i*, which is not otherwise attested so early. However, in I 302 the verb can only be a I/2 present, so that one must read *i-ta-'i-du* with this value.

II i. 16 W. von Soden reads *li-iḫ-ta-an-ni-ma* (*AHw ḫanānum*).

II vii. 38 In view of line 42 one suspects that the text must have a part of *tummû*, but if *i nutammi* as translated is correct, the text as it stands must be corrupt.

II vii 49 Šullat and Ḫaniš further occur in an OB seal inscription somewhat misread by M. Lambert in *Cahiers de Byrsa* VII. 69. 107. It reads: *ḫu-na-ba-tum*, dam ᵈen.zu-*ḫa-zi-ir*, gemé ᵈPA ᵈLUGAL. Another occurrence of Ḫaniš alone, and one which confirms his character as a god of devastation, is found in Erra IV. 145: *ki-i aḫ-ra* ᵈLUGAL *i-ti-qu e-me qí-i-šum-ma* 'the reed beds became as after Ḫaniš has passed by' (beginning of line from IB 212, collated, and end from K 2619).

S rev. iv. 10, 14 The reading of Jensen in *KB* VI, [*sur-r*]*iš li*/*i-ṣe* from the Assyrian *ṣê'u* (*OLZ* 1964 35) is perhaps preferable, as suggested by W. von Soden.

# BIBLIOGRAPHY

## (i) EDITIONS OF WHOLE OR PART


1874 G. Smith, *Transactions of the Society of Biblical Archaeology* III. 540–2 (W).
1880 F. Lenormant, *Les Origines de l'histoire* 604–5 (W).
1883 P. Haupt, *apud* E. Schrader, *Die Keilinschriften und das Alte Testament*[2] 58, 61 (W).
1890 P. Jensen, *Die Kosmologie der Babylonier* 370–3 (W).
1892 H. Winckler, *Keilinschriftliches Textbuch zum Alten Testament*[1] 84–5 (W).
1898 V. Scheil, *RT* xx. 55–9 (**B**).
1898 V. Scheil, *Revue biblique* 7. 5–9 (**B**: text in cuneiform type).
1900 H. Zimmern, *ZA* 14. 277–92 (**E**, K 3399+3934).
1900 P. Jensen, *Assyrisch-babylonische Mythen und Epen* (*Keilinschriftliche Bibliothek* VI/1) 274–91 and 539–48 (K 3399+3934, **B**, **E**).
1903 H. Winckler, *Keilinschriftliches Textbuch zum Alten Testament*[2] 94–5 (W).
1907 É. Dhorme, *Choix de textes religieux Assyro-babyloniens* 128–39 (K 3399+3934).
1909 H. Winckler, *Keilinschriftliches Textbuch zum Alten Testament*[3] 88 (W).
1910 H. V. Hilprecht, *BE* ser. D v/1 (**𝕵**).
1910 H. V. Hilprecht, *Der neue Fund zur Sintflutgeschichte aus der Tempelbibliothek von Nippur* (**𝕵**).
1910 T. G. Pinches, *Expository Times* 21. 364–9 (**𝕵**: added comments by F. Hommel).
1910 J. D. Prince and F. A. Vandenburgh, *AJSL* 26. 303–8 (**𝕵**).
1911 G. A. Barton, *JAOS* 31. 30–48 (**𝕵**).
1912 R. W. Rogers, *Cuneiform parallels to the Old Testament*[1] 103–9, 113–21 (W, **B**, **𝕵**, K 3399+3934).
1915 S. H. Langdon, *PBS* x/1. 24–6 (**E**).
1919 S. H. Langdon, *Le Poème Sumérien du Paradis* 34–9 (**E**).
1922 A. T. Clay, *A Hebrew deluge story in Cuneiform* (*YOR* v/3) 58–69, 81–2 (**B**, K 3399+3934, W, **𝕵**).
1926 R. W. Rogers, *Cuneiform parallels to the Old Testament*[2] 103–9, 113–21 (W, **B**, **𝕵**, K 3399+3934).
1931 A. Boissier, *RA* 28. 91–7 ($\mathbf{C}_2$).
1931 E. Ebeling, *Tod und Leben* 172–7 (**E**, K 7816 with S iii).
1956 J. Laessøe, *BiOr* XIII. 90–102 (excerpts and discussion).
1957 W. von Soden, *Or* N.S. 26. 306–15 (**E**).
1960 W. G. Lambert, *JSS* 5. 113–23 (U, Q).


## (ii) TRANSLATIONS WITHOUT TEXT (MOSTLY PARTIAL)


1875 G. Smith, *Assyrian discoveries* 186 (W).
1876, 1880 G. Smith, *The Chaldean account of Genesis*[1] 153–6, 265–6; [2]155–8, 281 (S, W).
1876 G. Smith, *Chaldäische Genesis* 127–30, 224–5 (S, W).
1879 J. Oppert, *apud* E. Ledrain, *Histoire d'Israel, première partie* 426 (W).
1901 W. Muss-Arnolt, *apud* R. F. Harper, *Assyrian and Babylonian literature* 369–71 (**B**).

1902, 1903, 1908 T. G. Pinches, *The Old Testament in the light of the historical records and legends of Assyria and Babylonia*[1, 2, 3] 117 (W).

1904, 1906, 1918, 1930 A. Jeremias, *Das Alte Testament im Lichte des alten Orients*[1] 130, [2]233, [3]125 (W), 120 (𝕵), [4]136 (W).

1909 A. Ungnad, *apud* H. Gressmann, *Altorientalische Texte und Bilder zum Alten Testamente*[1] 57–8 (W, **B**).

1911 A. Ungnad, *Das Gilgamesch-Epos* 69–70 (W, **B**).

1921 A. Ungnad, *Die Religion der Babylonier und Assyrer* 122–7 (W, S).

1923 A. T. Clay, *The origin of Biblical traditions* 173–86 (**B**).

1923 C.-F. Jean, *Le Milieu biblique* II. 33–5 (𝕵).

1924 C.-F. Jean, *La Littérature des Babyloniens et Assyriens* 24–5 (𝕵).

1925 G. Hilion, *Le Déluge dans la Bible et les inscriptions akkadiennes et sumériennes* 34–5 (W, 𝕵: thesis done under J. Plessis).

1926 E. Ebeling, *apud* H. Gressmann, *Altorientalische Texte zum Alten Testament*[2] 199–206 (𝕵, W, **B**, S).

1942, 1951 (1954, 1963) A. Heidel, *The Babylonian Genesis*[1] 54–6, [2]66–7 (**E**).

1946, 1949 (1963) A. Heidel, *The Gilgamesh Epic*[1, 2] 106–16 (**B**, $\mathbf{C}_2$, W, S, P).

1950, 1955 E. A. Speiser, *apud* J. B. Pritchard, *Ancient Near Eastern texts*[1, 2] 99–100, 104–6 (**E**, S, P, **B**, $\mathbf{C}_2$, 𝕵, W, S).

1952 G. Contenau, *Le Déluge babylonien*[2] 97–9 (**B**, $\mathbf{C}_2$ W, K 3399+3934).

### (iii) GENERAL DISCUSSIONS, PARTICULAR NOTES, ETC.

1875 G. Smith, *Assyrian discoveries* 97 (finding of W).

1889 P. Haupt, *BA* I. 122, 151 (W not part of *Gilgameš* XI).

1903 H. Zimmern, *apud* E. Schrader, *Die Keilinschriften und das Alte Testament*[3] 551–4.

1906 P. Jensen, *Das Gilgamesch-Epos in der Weltliteratur* 55–6 (argues that there must have been seven plagues!).

1906 B. Meissner, *OLZ* 9. 549 (identification of K 7816).

1907 O. Weber, *Die Literatur der Babylonier und Assyrer* 94–6.

1908 A. Ungnad, *OLZ* 11. 536–7 (*qa-da-niš* in S vi 6 haplography for *qa-da-da-niš*).

1914 M. Jastrow, *Hebrew and Babylonian traditions* 340–4 (**B**, 𝕵, W).

1922 C. Fossey, *Journal Asiatique, Onzième serie* XIX. 18–23 (S viii. 12; iv. 47b, 49b; I. 191).

1922 R. Campbell Thompson, *The Times Literary Supplement*, Oct. 12. 646 (review of Clay, *YOR* v/3).

1923 D. D. Luckenbill, *AJSL* 39. 153–60 (critical review of Clay, *YOR* v/3).

1925 S. Smith, *RA* 22. 63–4 (S iv. 47b–48 = 57b–58) and 67–8 (II. i. 8 and S iv. 8).

1931 S. H. Langdon, *apud* J. A. MacCulloch (ed.), *Mythology of all races* v, *Semitic* 270–6.

1933 B. Landsberger, *ZA* 41. 315–16 (translation of S iv. 42–51).

1947 F. R. Kraus, *JCS* I. 115 (identification of **D**).

1956 R. Borger, *AfO* 17. 293 (identification of T).

1959 P. Garelli and M. Leibovici, *apud Sources orientales, La Naissance du monde* 129–30.

1961 S. N. Kramer, *Mythologies of the ancient world* 126–7.

1967 J. Aro, *Teologinen Aikakauskirja* 72. 70–83.

1967 H. Hirsch, *ZA* 58. 333–4 (review of *CT* 46).

1967 L. Matouš, *ArOr* 35. 1–16 (review article on *CT* 46).

1967 A. R. Millard, *Tyndale bulletin* 18. 1–18.

1967 J. J. Finkelstein, *RA* 61. 133 (note on I 299–304).

# GLOSSARY

THE glossary contains all words found in *Atra-ḫasīs* arranged by consonants, and by root consonants for Semitic words. Where the script writes an initial vowel, the glottal stop has been posited. Similarly with the so-called hollow roots, an *āleph*-sign is used to indicate the middle consonant. Since the purpose is nearer that of a concordance than a dictionary, only a brief, and often incomplete, attempt at meaning is given. The glossary is intended not only to help the finding of words and passages, but also to indicate the source of restorations. Many repetitions occur in this epic, and the various recensions and copies offer variant forms of the same episodes. Thus restorations may be purely conjectural, plausible if taken from similar passages, or virtually certain if from exactly parallel passages. Only in special cases are notes given on particular passages indicating the source of the restoration, if any exists. For all other cases the glossary should be consulted, where the line-numbers of restored occurrences are put within square brackets, e.g. [25], alongside the line-numbers of surviving examples. Trivial orthographic variants, especially of words in the context, are not noted, nor are half-brackets used. The glossary is intended to aid study of the text, not to dispense with it. Words only found in the late copies are indicated by the appropriate manuscript symbol; otherwise the words are Old Babylonian. The letter 'n' is appended to the line-numbers of words discussed in the philological notes.

ʾ

**i** cohortative particle: *i ni-im-ḫu-ur-ma* I 41; cf. 44 46 58 60 62 214 II vii 38 J 1 2; *i tu-uk-t[a]-bi-it* I 295 S iii 16n

ʾ

**u** 'and': *mu-ši ù ur-ri* I 38; cf. I [10] [18] 127 139 151 [164] 206 210 212 221 225 275 276 288 300 301 364 367 II vi [12] [14] 22 vii 49 III i 31 43 ii 45 iii 31 42 46 v 46 vi 24 [26] 44 vii 7 11 𝕳 obv. 10 rev. 3 S iii 9 iv [20] v [30] 33 W 3 7 8 x rev. i [4] 5 8 9 12 40 ii 2 [3] 9 [10] ⟨16⟩ [17] 32 [33] y 4 9

ʾ

**yāʾû** 'mine': *ia-a-at-tum ni-is-sà-s[ú]* III v 48

**yâši** 'to me': *ú-ul i-pa-at-tu-ú a-na ia-a-ši* 𝕳 obv. 11; *qí-ba-a ia-a-š[i]* U obv. 12; *ia-a-ši-im-ma-a* (**F** *ia-ši-im-ma*) *it-te-né-e[p-pu-uš]* I 107

ʾʾ

**ay/ē** negative: *a-ií-il-li-ka* II i 12; cf. II i 17 20 III i 30; *ia iš-šá-a* S iv 45; cf. S iv 49 51; II i 22; *e t[a]-ap-la-ḫa* I 378; cf. I 379 [393] [394] II ii 9 10 viii 33 S iv 31 38

ʾʾ

**ayyu** 'who, which?': *a-iu-ú ša* III vi 26; ? *ia-a* S vi 20; ? *ia-e* S vi 25

**ayyānu** 'where?': *a-ia-a-nu ú-ṣi na!-pí!-iš-tum* III vi 9

**ēšā** 'where?': *e-ša-a a-nu il-li-kam* III iii 51 v 39

ʾʾʾ

**atmû** 'to speak': *i-ta-mu it-ti* I 366 [367] cf. S iv 19 20 (*i-ta-mu*) v 29 30

**awātu** 'speech': *iš-[me] a-wa-tam šu-a-ti* I 166; *[a-w]a-tam an-ni-[tam]* III i 46; *ša ú-ša-a[s]-sà-ku a-wa-at-ka* III vi 26; *i-x-ar a-wa-as-su* I 168; *iš-me-e-ma DN* [—] II iii [29]; *a-ma-te-šu-nu a-na ki-ik-ki-[ši] i-ša-an-[ni]* 𝕳 obv. 12

ʾʾʾ

**ewû** 'to become like': *ki-ma zu-ub-bi i-wu-ú* III iii 45

ʾʾl

**ālu** 'city': *i-na a-li ib-nu-ú bi-is-sú* I 401 II ii 20

ʾʾl

**awīlu** 'man(kind)': *šu-up-ši-ik ilim a-wi-lum li-iš-ši* I 191 197; cf. 212 328 II iii 31 III vi 10 viii 10 **G** ii [12] I 226 (O *à-wi-l[um]*); *a-[me-lu]* V obv. 3 [4]; *PN* lú S iv 17 v 27; x rev. i 29; *i-nu-ma i-lu a-wi-lum* I 1n; *šu-up-ši-ik-ka-ku-nu a-wi-[l]am e-mi-id* I 241 II vii [31]; *lu-u[l-la-a a-wi-lam]* **G** ii [9]

**awīlūtu** 'mankind': *ba-ni-a-at a-wi-lu-ti* I 194; cf. I 242 II vii [32]; *ri-gi-im* — I 358 II i 7 S iv 6 (*a-me-lu-te*) x rev. i [2] ([*a-me-lu-ti*]); *a-me-lu-tim* I 242 (P) 240 (P)

**''m**

**ūmu** 'day, weather': *$u_4$-mu-um li-id-da-i-*[*im*] III iii 34; *$u_4$-mu iš-nu-ú pa-nu-ú-šu* III ii 48; *aḫ-ri-a-ti-iš $u_4$-mi* I 214 [227]; 9/7 *$u_4$-mi* I 294 303 III iv 24 S iii 15 (ud.meš); *$u_4$-mi*(-)[ III vi 4n; see *šammu* and x rev. i 7n

**ūmišam** 'daily': [*$u_4$*]*-mi-ša-am-ma* II iii 4 x rev. i 13 (-šam-) y 11 (-šam-) **G** ii 5 I [178]

**''n**

**īnu** 'eye': *i-ni mi-na-a a-mu-ur* I 109

**''ṣ**

**âṣu** 'to be few': *e-me-ṣu šam-mu* S iv 53; *li-wi-ṣú ša-am-mu* II i 10 cf. S iv 43 (*li-me-ṣu*); S iv 14n

**''r**

**a'āru** 'grow': *šu-ú ia i-im-ru* S iv 49 cf. *i'-ru* 59 v [8]

**ūrtu** 'order': *ub-la pí-i-ni . . . ur-*[*ta-am*] II v [15] 29 vi [24] cf. vii 36; II vi 6

**tērtu** 'oracle, command': *te-er-ta* I 116 II iii 33; *il-qí-a te-er-tam* I 385 III i 38; *il-qu-ú ter-ta* x rev. ii 28; *te-re-et* II iv 22; *te-er-ti PN* S vi 18 cf. x rev. ii [8] [31]; *te-re-ti-iš-*[*ka*] III viii 12

**''r**

**urru** 'day': *mu-ši ù ur-ri* I 38

**'b**

**abu** 'father': *DN a-bu-šu-nu* I 7; cf. I [124] 136 S ii [12]; *ma-ru a-na a-bi-*[*šu*] I 330

**'b**

**abu** 'what?': *a-bu-ma-an* III iv 5n

**'bb**

**abūbu** 'flood': [*a-bu-b*]*u ki-ma li-i i-ša-ab-bu* III iii [15]; *il-li-ik . . .* [*a-bu-bu*] III iv [25]; [*it-ta-ṣa-a*] *a-bu-bu* III iii 11 cf. U rev. 18; *a-bu-bu . . . ma-an-nu šu-ú* II vii 44; *ú-ul-la-da* [*a-bu-ba*] II vii [46]; *iš-ku-nu a-bu-ba* III iii 53 v 42 cf. III vi 21 viii 9 𝕳 obv. 2; *a-bu-ba . . . ú-za-am-me-er* III viii 18; *ba-a-a' a-bu-bi* III i 37; *ri-gi-im a-bu-bi* III iii 23 U rev. 20; *la-am a-bu-bi wa-ṣe-e* 𝕵 rev. 4; *a-na ma-mi-tú a-bu-bi* x rev. ii 46; III iii 20

**'bk**

**abāku** 'to bring': *i-bi-ik l*[*àḫ-mi*(?) x rev. i 28; *ib-bak me-ḫ*[*u-ú*] U rev. 4; *DN ib-bi-ku-nim* I 100 cf. II v 26; *li-ib-bi-ku-nim* I 98n cf. II v 24; I [133] 145

**ubbuku** 'overthrow': *ma-ru-šu ub-bu-ku* III iii 26 cf. U rev. 22; 𝕵 rev. 5

**'bl**

**abālu** 'to carry': *ub-la pí-i-ni . . . ma-mi-tam* III vi 8 cf. I 152 165 II v 15 29 vi [24] III v 44; [*ub-l*]*a-ma li-ib-ba-ku-nu u*[*r-ta*] II vii 36; *la-ap-nu* [*ḫi-šiḫ-ta ub-la*] III ii [14]; *ub-lu du-ul-la* I 2; [*ub-lu*] *e-pí-tam* I [408] II ii [26]; *ú-ub-ba-al qá-ti a-na n*[*i-ši-ia-ma*] II vii 43; II vii 35; III ii 29; *bi-la e-pí-ta* I 381 [396] II ii 12; *li-bi-$il_5$ ab-ša-nam* I 195 196 *li-bi-il* — **G** ii 10 11 V obv. 5 6; II iii 19; [*k*]*u-up-ru ba-bi-il* III ii 51; [*ib-ba-b*]*i-il ar-ḫu* III ii 39; *pa-ar-ṣa-am ta-ba-al-ma* I 171(KL); ? *bi-la* S vi 25

**'bl**

**ebēlu** see b'r

**'bn**

**abunnatu** 'umbilical cord': *a-bu-un-na-ti* I 260 (P); *ba-*RI*-iq a-bu-un-na-te* S iii 7

**'bn**

**abnu** 'stone': *at-ku-up-*[*pu na-ši a-ba-an-šu*] III ii [12n]

**'br**

**ibratu** 'outdoor shrine': I 275

**'bš**

**abšānu** 'yoke': *ab-ša-nam li-bi-il* I 196 cf. 195 **G** ii 10 11 16 V obv. 5 6

**'bt**

**abātu** 'to destroy': *ú-bu-ut bi-ta* III i 22

**'gbb**

**ugbabtu** 'a kind of priestess': *ú-uk-ba-ak-ka-ti* III vii 6n

**'gṣ'**

**egiṣītu** 'a kind of priestess': *e-gi-ṣi-a-ti* III vii 7n

**'gr**

**ugāru** 'field': *ṣa-al-mu-tum ip-ṣú-ú ú-g*[*a-ru*] II iv 7 cf. S iv 47 57 v [6] (a.gàr); *im-lu-ú ú-ga-ra* II vi 11

**'gr**

**igāru** 'wall': *i-ga-ru ši-ta-am-mi-a-an-ni* III i 20; [*i*]*-ga-ru-ma ši-m*[*e*] 𝕳 obv. 14

**'d**

**adi** 'so long as': *a-di-ma-mi* I 370

**'d**

**idu** 'side': *it-ba-a id-šú šu-tu* U rev. 9; [*i*]*-zi-qù a-na idi-šú* U rev. 10: *li-qí id-ka* I 171 (M)

**'d'**

**idû** 'to know': *i-lu ú-ul i-di* I 71 73 cf. II vii [45]; *i-$de_4$ mil-ká* 𝕳 obv. 9 cf. 10; [*w*]*u-ud-di-a* III i 13; [*ú-ul*] *ú-te-ed-du-ú i-na ka-ra-ši* III iii 14; *ba-al-ṭa it-ta-šu ú/li-še-di-šu-ma* I 216n 229

**mūdû** 'knowledgeable': *er-še-te mu-te-ti* S iii 8n

**adannu** 'set time': [*ú-ṣur*] *a-dan-na* W 5

**'dl**

**edēlu** 'to close': *i-di-il ba-ab-šu* I 89; *iš-tu-ma i-di-lu* — III ii 52; *e-di-il ba-ab-ka* I 87; *li-te-ed-di-li-ir-ta-ša* II i 19n; *ed-lu-tum/tim* II v 3 7 9 (?)

**'dr**

**adāru** 'to become afraid': *mi-in-šu ta-du-ur* I 94 96; *ul-ta-dar* U rev. 21

**na'duru** 'to be disturbed, become dark': *i-lu it-ta-a'-da-ar* I 355 II i 4 (Q *it-tar-du*) S iv 2 (*it-ta-'-[dar]*); *at-ta-a-*$^{di-ir}$*dar* S iv 7 40; *el-lu-tu[m] z[i]-mu-ši-na i'-a-ad-ru* III v 45

**'dr**

**idrānu** 'salt': *ṣe-ru . . . ma-li id-r[a-na]* II iv 8 cf. S iv 48 58 v 7

**'dš**

**eššu** 'new': *ḫi-pí eš-šú* U obv. 11 rev. 4

**'zb**

**ezēbu** 'to leave': *i-zi-ib* II ii 2′ (Q); *[i-t]e-zi-ib-ši-na-ti* I 412 II ii 34

**'zz**

**ezēzu** 'to be savage': *ša-ru uz-zu-zu* III ii 54; *[i]-te-te-zi-zu DN ù [DN]* III i 43

**'zḫ**

**ezēḫu** 'to gird': *[q]á-ab-li-ša i-te-zi-iḫ* I 286

**'zn**

**uznu** 'ear': *[uz-na] i-ša-ak-ka-na* II iii [8] [10]; geštu-*šú pi-ta-at* S iv 18 v 28

**'ḫ**

**aḫu** 'brother': *[ú-ul] i-mu-ur a-ḫu a-ḫa-šu* III iii 13; *ana a-ḫi-šu* I 168 169 (M); *i-li aḫ-ḫi-šu* I 48 175 (M) **G** ii 2 II vii [41] J 4 (*aḫ-ḫe-e-šu*) cf. I 106 112 (L)

**'ḫz**

**aḫāzu** 'to seize': *[q]a-tam i-ḫu-zu qa-ti-ša* I 11; *i-ta-aḫ-zu-nim i-il-la-ku-nim* I 68

**tāḫazu** 'battle': *ta-ḫa-za i ni-ib-lu-la qá-ab-la-am* I 62; — *e-ep-pu-uš* I 108; *[ta-ḫ]a-zi* I 129 141

**'ḫr**

**aḫriātiš** 'for ever': *aḫ-ri-a-ti-iš* $u_4$*-mi* I 214 227

**'ṭ'**

**eṭūtu** 'darkness': *[ša-pa-at e]-ṭú-tu* III iii 18

**'ṭl**

**eṭlu** 'young man': *eṭ-lu a-na ar-d[a-ti]* R 9; *li-it eṭ-li* I 274

**'ṭm**

**eṭemmu** 'ghost': *e-ṭe-em-mu li-ib-ši* I 215 217 (**E** PI-*ṭe-em-mu* I 215n) 228 230

**'k**

**iku** 'canal': *i-ki ib-nu-ú ra-bu-t[im]* I 338

**'kb**

**ikkibu** 'taboo': *lu-ú ik-ki-bu ši-na-ma* III vii 8

**'kl**

**akālu** 'to eat': *ṣi-iḫ-tum i-ku-ul-šu* II vi 16 18; *i-ku-lu ni-qí-a-am* III v 36; *i-ku-la la-a[r?-da?]* II iv 9; *[a-ki-l]u i-ik-ka-al* III ii 43; *[mur-ṣu] . . . e-kal māt*$^{tu}$ S iv 24 26; *i-ik-ka-lu ka-ar-ṣi* I 39; *kar-ṣi-šú-nu n[i-i]k-ka-al* I 176 (M) **G** ii 3; *[la tu-ša]-ka-la-nim* II vi 13

**'kl**

**ekēlu** 'to be dark': $u_4$*-mu-um . . . li-tu-ur li-ki-[il]* III iii 35

**'l**

**ul** 'not': *ú-ul i-di* I 71 73; cf. I [352] [405] [406] 416 II i 1 ii 23 [24] iv 2 4 5 6 vii [45] III i [42] [47] 48 ii 46 iii [13] [14] vi 15 (?) 𝕳 obv. 10; *ul* S iv [1] 55 59 61 v [4] [8] [9] [19] vi 8 W 13 x rev. i 43 (?)

**'l**

**ila** 'as soon as' (?): *i-la iš-mu-ú* III ii 50n

**'l**

**allu** 'hoe': *al-li ma-ar-ri* I 337

**'l**

**ilu** 'god': *i-lu ú-ul i-di* I 71; cf. I 173 (K) 355 II i 4; *[i-lu]-ma* II vi 15; *i-lu-um-ma ù a-wi-lum* I 212 (**E** dingir-*ma*); *i-lam ta-aṭ-bu-ḫa* I 239 II vii [33]; cf. I 208 (dingir); *ši-i-ir i-li* I 215 (**E** dingir) 228; cf. II iii 7 V obv. 3; dingir I 191 197 **G** ii 12; *it-ti i-li-ku-nu i-li ú-[ul ma-gi-ir]* III i 42 cf. 49; *il-šu* I 367 cf. 365 y 10 (dingir-*šu*); *i[t-ti i-li-šu]* I [366]; cf. II iii 2 11 S iv 19 v 29 31 (dingir-*šu*); *i-lu . . . ub-lu du-ul-la* I 1; cf. I 12 63 233 II viii 34 III iii 30 52 iv 15 v 34; dingir.meš I 209 𝕳 obv. 1; *a-na i-li aḫ-ḫi-šu* I 48; cf. I 3 43 45 57 59 [106] [122] 134 [146] [151] [159] 164 175 (MN) 232 236 247 (P) [339] 357 II i 6 vi 16 18 21 vii [41] III iii 24 33 36 vi 17 viii 11 cf. J 4 (*i-lu*); dingir.meš I 193 199 205 **G** ii 2 𝕳 obv. 9 rev. 1 4 S ii 10 iv 5 26 37 U rev. 12 [21] x rev. ii 45; *ú-ul ip-la-ḫu i-[li-šu-un]* I [405] II ii 23; *e ta-ap-la-ḫa i-li-ku-un* I 378 393; - — *e-li-ku-un* II ii 9 (Q); - — dingir.meš-*ku-un* S iv [31]

**iltu** 'goddess': *il-tum i-ba-ak-ki* III iii 32; *il-ta-am is-sú-ú* I 192

**'l**

**ali** 'where': *a-li a-li-it-tum ú-ul-la-du-ma* I 291

**'l'**

**el** 'over': *li-ša-sí-ik el-ni* I 42

**eli** 'over': *e-li ni-ši* III iii 12 U rev. 19 (ug]u); *e-li-ši-na ab-ki* III iv 10; ugu *ṭí-iṭ-ṭí-šá* S iii 4

**elu** 'over': *e-lu ṭi-iṭ-ṭi* I 234; *[e]-lu DN* I 20; *e-lu ni-qí-i pa-aḫ-ru* III v 35

**eliš** 'above': *e-li-iš ù ša-ap-li-iš* III i 31 W 3 (*e-liš*); *e-liš* S iv 44 54 v 3

**elênu** 'above': *e-le-nu-um* II iv 1; *e-le-nu-ia* III iii 44; 'upper regions': *iṣ-ṣú-ur DN e-le-e-nu* II v [16] 30 vi 25 x rev. i [4] [8] ii [2] 9 16 32

**ullîš** 'presently': *ul-li-iš* III i 34

**elû** 'to ascend': [*iš-tu DN*] *i-lu-ú ša-me-e-ša* I 17; *DN i-te-li* — I 13; *e-te-el-li-i-ma a-na ša-ma-i* III iii 48; [*ul-l*]*u-ú re-ši-šu* I 32; [*šu-li ana*] *lìb-bi-šá* W [7]

**'ld**

**alādu** 'to beget, bear': *ú-ul ul-da er-ṣe-tum re-e*[*m-ša*] II iv 4; *ul-da g*[*al-la-ta*] *ti-a-am-ta* III iv 5; *a-li a-li-it-tum ú-ul-la-du-ma* I 291 S iii 18 (*ú-la-du-ma*); *ú-ul-la-du* I 238 (P); *a-na-ku-ma ú-ul-la-da* [*a-bu-ba*] II vii 46; *a-la-da-am pu-ur-si* III vii 9n; *ṣēru . . . ú/lu-li-id id-ra-na* S iv 48 58 v 7

**ālittu** 'bearing woman': *a-li-it-tum* I 291 S iii 18 (*-tu*); *a-li-it-tum-ma la a-li-it-tum* III vii 2; *i-na bi-ir-ku a-li-it-ti* III vii 5; *i-na bīt a-li-te* S iii 15

**lillidu** 'offspring': *ki-ma zu-ub-bi i-wu-ú li-il-li-du* III iii 45

**'lk**

**alāku** 'go': *il-li-ik DN* I [134] cf. I 154; *ú-ul il-li-ik-ma* 600.600 mu.ḫi.a I [352] 416 II i 1; *il-li-ik ra-du* III iv 25; *a-ša-ar DN* [*il-li-ku-ma*] II v [18]; *eš-ru arḫu il-li-ka-am-ma* I 281: cf. II iv 11; *e-ša-a DN il-li-kam/ka-am* III iii 51 v 39; *a-ii-il-li-ka mi-lu* II i 12; *ú-ul i*[*l-li-ka*] *mi-lu* II iv [2] cf. S iv [1]; [*i-il-li-i*]*k-šu ma-as-ḫa-tum* I 409 II ii 27; [*il-li-k*]*u-ma* x rev. ii 30; *li-il-li-ik ša-ru* II i 14; — *DN* II vii 52; *li-il-li-ik-šu ma-as-ḫa-tum* I 382n 397 II ii 13; *li-il-li-ku* II vii 50; *a-ša-ar at-ta ta-al-li-ku-ma* II v 32 vi 27; *al-l*[*i-ik*] I 156; [*i*]*l-la-ka di-ma-šu* I 167; *qá-ad-di-iš i-il-la-ka* II iv 16; [*il*]*-lak DN* U rev. 14; *i-il-la-ku-nim* I 68; *al-ka-ma* II iii 33; *al-ka-nim* I 44 46 58 60; *al-ka-ni ka-la-ni* x rev. ii 46; *a-la-ki* II ii 3′ (Q); *qa-da-niš i*[*t-ta-n*]*a-la-ka* S v [17] vi 6

**'ll**

**ullu** 'yoke': *ap-ṭú-ur ul-la* I 243 cf. II v 19 [1′] vi 28

**'ll**

**elēlu** 'be pure': *ú-ul-la-*[*a*]*l ka-la-ma* I 202; *li-te-el-li-lu* dingir.meš I 209

**ellu** 'pure': *el-lu-tu*[*m*] *z*[*i*]*-mu-ši-na* III v 45; *el-lu-ti* III ii 32

**tēliltu** 'cleansing': *te-li-il-tam ú/lu-ša-aš-ki-in ri-im-ka* I 207 222

**'lp**

**eleppu** 'boat': [*e*]*-le-ep-pu ša ta-ba-an-nu-ú-*[*ši*] III i 25; *bi-ni e-le-ep-pa* III i 22; giš.má *ra-bí-tam* 𝕴 rev. 6; *e-le-ep-pa ip-ṭú-ur* III ii 55; giš.má *ul e-pu-uš* W 13 cf. 15; [giš.má] *e-ru-um-ma* ká giš.má *tir-*[*ra*] W 6; *ip-ḫa-a* gi[š.má] U rev. [3] cf. W [4]

**'m**

**ummu** 'mother': ama *a-na* dumu.SAL S v [19] vi 8; *zi-ba-ni-it* dumu.SAL *i-na-ṭal* ama S v 21 vi [10]; — ama dumu.SAL — S v [20] vi 9; *e-reb* ama dumu.SAL *i-da-gal* S v 18 vi 7; *um-mi še-er-ri* I 292 S iii 19 (ama)

**'m**

**emu** 'father-in-law': *bi-it* [*e-mi ra-bé*]*-e* I [302n]

**'m**

**amu** 'raft': *ki-ma a-mi-im* III iv 8n 9

**'m'**

**māmītu** 'oath': *ma-mi-tú* II ii 12′ (Q); *a-na ma-mi-tú a-bu-bi* x rev. ii 46; *ub-la pí-i-ni . . . ma-mi-tam* III vi 8; *i-*$de_4$ *ma-me-et-šu-nu* 𝕳 obv. 10

**'m'**

**ummânu** 'workman': dumu.meš *um-m*[*a-ni*] W 8

**'mbr**

**ibbaru** 'mist': *ib-ba-ra ú/li-ša-az-ni-in* II ii 16 30

**'md**

**emēdu** 'to put on, in to': *i-mi-da a-na ki-ib-ri* III iv 9 cf. 8; *šu-up-ši-ik-ka-ku-nu a-wi-*[*l*]*am e-mi-id* I 241 II vii [31]; *šèr-ta e-mi-id* x rev. ii 27 43; *mu-ur-ṣa i-im-mi-du-ni-a-ti* I 371

**'mḫl**

**imḫullu** 'evil wind': *im-ḫul-lu* U rev. 8

**'mm**

**umāmu** 'wild animals': *ú-ma-am ṣe-rim* 𝕴 rev. 11 W 9

**'mn**

**imittu** 'right-hand': *a-na i-mi-it-t*[*i*] I 257 (P) S iii 5 (zag)

**'mq**

**emūqu** 'strength': *e-mu-qá šu-ur-ši* III i 33

**'mr**

**amāru** 'to see': *i-mu-ur-ma* I 334; *a-ii-i-mu-ur* III i 30; [*ú-ul*] *i-mu-ur a-ḫu a-ḫa-šu* III iii 13; *i-mu-ur-ma il-tum* III iii 32; *li-mu-u*[*r*] II iii 22 x rev. i 21 (*li-mur*); *i-ni mi-na-a a-mu-ur* I 109; *a-mu-ur-ma* III iv 10; *lu-mur-ma* W 15; *ma-qú-ra i-ta-ma-ar* III vi 5; *a-ta-mar pa-ni-k*[*a*] U obv. 11; *a-am-ru* II iii 17; *ar-qú-tum am-ru pa-n*[*u-ši-in*] II iv 15; *ni-šu ú-ul am-ra-*[(*a*)*-ma*] II iv 6

**'mr**

**amurru** 'west wind': *a-mur-ru* U rev. 10 cf. 6

**'mr**
**immeru** 'sheep' *ki-ma im-me-ri* III iv 19
**'n**
**ana** 'to, for': *a-na* I 16 [18] 81 83 84 98 100 110 117 [134] [155] 170 200 242 249 (P) 257 (P) 258 (P) ⟨301⟩ 330 [371] 381 386 [396] 408 II i 9 10 ii [12] 26 iii 21 28 30 v [20] 25 [2′] vi 2 29 vii [32] 37 42 43 viii 33 35 III i 39 ii 41 iii 27 48 54 iv 8 9 15 v 30 41 43 46 vi 48 viii 18 R 7 9 S iii 20 iv [18] [34] 39 42 50 52 60 v [9] [19] 22 [23] [28] vi 8 12 U rev. 10 22 x rev. i 26 38 44 ii 6 8 31 46 ℌ obv. 11 12; *ana* II ii 5′ (Q) S iii 5 6 vi 11 W [7] x rev. ii 13; *issaqar a-na* I 48 86 92 106 112 119 [169] 199 205 236 357 369 373 388 II i 6 iii [18] v 23 vii 41 viii 37 III i 2 12 16 41 vi 12 17 42 46 S iv 5 22 29 37 x rev. i [1] 18 ii 45 **G** ii 2 U obv. 14; — *ana* I 168 (M) 175 (LMN) J 4 S ii [8] x rev. ii 15 W 12
'at the discretion of': *a-na ra-ma-ni-ia* III iii 42n
**aššu** 'so that': *aš-šu la mu-uš-ši-i* I 217 230
**'n**
**ina** 'in, at' : *i-na ka-la-ak-ki* I 40; cf. I 44 46 58 60 122 [132] 144 148 161 206 209 210 213 215 218 221 224 225 228 [259] (P) 290 299 302 305 355 [359] 377 383 392 398 401 [404] 410 II i 4 8 ii [14] 16 17 20 22 28 30 31 iii [3] [6] 8 10 16 24 27 iv 12 14 16 v 5 [21] [3′] vi 16 [18] 19 30 vii 50 III i 44 47 [48] ii 49 53 54 iii [7] 14 31 36 43 47 50 iv 9 11 18 22 45(?) vi 1 10 18 44 vii 1 2 3 viii [10] ℌ obv. 2 3 7 S ii 10 iii 6 15 iv [2] [3] [7] [8] 30 [40] [41] 43 53 v [12] [13] [14] [15] 17 [18] [22] [26] 32 vi [1] [2] 3 4 6 7 11 15 U rev. 5 16 x rev. i 24 25 42 ii 47; *in* II ii 8 (Q); *ina* II ii 3′ (Q) ℌ obv. 5 S iii 17 W [14] 16 x rev. i 3 22
'from': *i-na ma-ia-li ú-še-et-[bi-šu]* I 79; *i-na na-aq-bi* II i 13 iv 3 S i 8 iv 45 55 v [4] cf. I [27]; *i-na né-el-m[e-ni]* III v 50; *i-na bi-ir-ku a-li-it-ti* III vii 5
**inūma** 'when': *i-nu-ma i-lu . . . ub-lu* I 1; I 301; *e-nu-ma* ℌ obv. 1 x rev. i 15 y 13
**inanna** 'now': *pa-na-mi . . . i-na-an-na* I 247
**'n**
**entu** 'a kind of priestess': *e-ne-ti* III vii 6
**'n**
**annu** 'yes': *i-pu-lu a-an-na* I 218
**'n'**
**annû** 'this': *an-nu-ú-ma* II iii 32 cf. x rev. i 30; *-d]u-uk an-ni-a-am* I 162 (**G**); *an-ni-a-am qá-ba-ša* I 244; cf. III viii 15; *an-na-a* x rev. i 40; *[a-w]a-tam an-ni-[tam]* III i 46; cf. III i 50; *an-ni-tam . . . i-ip-pu-uš* III vi 13; *zu-ub-bu-ú a[n-nu-tum]* III vi [2]
**annumma** 'now': *a-nu-um-ma ti-si-a tu-qú-um-tam* I 61
**'n'**
**unâtu** 'tackle': *lu-ú du-un-nu-na ú-ni-a-tum* III i 32
**'nṭ**
**uṭṭatu** 'barley': *[šu-li]* . . . še.bar-*ka* W 7
**'nk**
**anāku** 'I': *i-ni mi-na-a a-mu-ur a-[n]a-ku* I 109; cf. I 203 289 II iii 24 v 17 31 vi 26 vii 45 46 III i 34 iii 36 46 x rev. i 22 ii [19] [35]; *PN a-na-ku-[ma]* ℌ obv. 6
**'nn**
**enēnu** 'to punish': *[iš]-tu-ma e-ni-nu-šu-nu-ti* x rev. ii 26 42; *e-te-nin-šu-nu-ti* x rev. ii 25 41
**'nš**
**aššatu** 'wife': *aš-ša-tum ù mu-sà* I 276 300; dam-*ka* ℌ rev. 2 W [8]
**aššūtu** 'wifehood': *⟨a-na⟩ aš-š[u-ti] ù mu-tu-ti* I 301
**tēnišū/tēnišētu** 'mankind': *te-ni-še-šu* II vi 13n; *ut-ta-za-ma ta-ni-še-ti* S iv 23 25
**'nt**
**atta, atti** 'thou': *[at-t]a ù ši-i* III vi 44; *šu-uṣ-ṣi-ir at-ta* III i 19; cf. II v 32 vi 27 III viii 11 S ii 3 x rev. i 37 ii [5] [12]; *at-ti-i-ma šà-as-sú-ru* I 194 III vi [47]
**'sk**
**asakku** 'pestilence': *iš-šá-kín-ma . . . a-sa-ku* S iv 50 60 v [9]; cf. S iv 12 16 28
**'sm**
**simānu** 'moment': *si-ma-nu ši-im-ti* I 305 cf. I [280]
**'sq**
**isqu** 'lot': *is-qá-am id-du-ú* I 12
**'p**
**uppu** 'drum': *up-pa i ni-iš-me* I 214n cf. [227]
**'p'**
**epītu** 'cake': *bi-la e-pí-ta* I 381n [396] II ii 12 cf. I 408 (*e-pí-tam*) II ii 26
**'p'**
**appūna** 'moreover': *[a]p-pu-na ša-lu-uš-tum li-i[b]-ši* III vii 1
**'pl**
**apālu** 'to answer': *i-pu-lu a-an-na* I 218
**'ps**

**apsû** 'the Apsû': *[a]p-sa-a* I 29; *[a-na a]p-si-i [i]-ta-ar-du* I 18 cf. II iii 28 S vi 27 (?) x rev. i 26 38 (zu.ab); *šar-ri ap-si-i* I 102; *[k]i-ma ap-si-i* III i 29; *[ma-li-k]u-ut ap-se-e* S i 2

**'pr**

**apāru** 'to cover the head': *u'-pu-ur ka-aq-qá-as-sà* I 284

**appāru** 'hair'(?): *ap-pa-ri* S iii 7

**'pr**

**epēru** 'to supply with food': *[la t]e-ep-pí-ra-nim* II vi 14

**'pš**

**epēšu** 'to do, make': *la na-ṭú a-na e-pé-ši* I 200 cf. 180 (M); *ša-ab-su-ta-am i-pu-uš* I 285; *ši-ip-ra le-em-na . . . i-pu-uš* II viii 35; *pâ i-pu-ša-am-ma is-sà-qar* I 47 85 91 105 111 118 174 (K) 204 [368] 372 [387] II v [22] vii 40 viii 36 (**D** *i-pu-ša-ma*) III i 1 11 15 40 vi 11 16 41 45 **G** ii [1] J 3; *pâ* dù-*ša* S ii 8 iv 21 [29] U obv. 4 13; *pâ* dù-*ma* W 11 x rev. ii 14; *pâ i-pu-uš-ma* x rev. i [1] ii 44; *pâ te-pu-ša-am-ma* I 198 235; *ša DN i-⟨pu⟩-šu-ma* III v 47n; *[lu-ú e]-pu-uš* III vi 18; giš.má *ul e-pu-uš* W 13; *a-na-ku lu-pu-uš* I 203; cf. W [15]; *i-pu-ša qá-ta-ia* I 289; *ma-an-nu . . . i-ip-pu-uš* III vi 14; *ta-ḫa-za e-ep-pu-uš* I 108; *te-ep-pu-šu* 𝕴 rev. 10; *ia-a-ši-im-ma-a it-te-né-e[p-pu-uš]* I 107

**nēpišu** 'tool': *i-ša-tam ne-pí-ši-šu-nu id-du-ú-ma* I 64

**'ṣ'**

**aṣû** 'to go out': *ú-ṣi na!-pí!-iš-tum* III vi 9: *ša-am-mu ú-ul ú-ṣi-a* II iv 5 S iv 49 59 v [8] (*ú-ṣa-a*); *ki-i ú-ṣa-an-ni* x rev. ii 20 36; *i-ir-ru-ub ù ú-uṣ-ṣí* III ii 45; *li-ṣi-ma* I 115; *[it-ta-ṣa-a] a-bu-bu* III iii [11] U rev. 18 (*i-ta-ṣa-a*); *la-am a-bu-bi wa-ṣe-e* 𝕴 rev. 4; *li-še-ṣa-an-ni-ma i-na né-el-m[e-ni]* III v 50

**'ṣl**

**eṣēlu** 'to be stiff': ? *i-ta-aṣ-ṣú-la* I 336n

**'ṣn**

**eṣēnu** 'smell': *[i-ṣi-nu i-l]u e-re-ša* III v [34]

**'ṣr**

**eṣēru** 'to design': *i-ṣi-ir qé-ma* I 288; *e-[ṣir ú-ṣur-tú]* W [16]; *e-ṣir ú-[ṣur-tu]* W 14 (imptv.); *ú-ṣu-ra-te šá nišī*$^{meš}$ *ú-ṣa-ar DN* S iii 14 cf. R 5

**uṣurtu** 'design': *[ú-ṣur]-tu lu-mur-ma* W [15]; see also under *eṣēru*

**'q'**

**uteqqû** 'to observe': *ú-te-eq-qí* I 74; *[ú-t]e-qí-ma šikna* U obv. 2 6 8

**'q'**

**tēqītu** 'slander': *te-qí-ta* II vi 19n

**'ql**

**eqlu** 'field': a.šà . . . *šu-a (li)-iš-ši* II ii 19 [33]; *iš/li-šur* a.šà *iš-pi-ke-e-šu* S iv 46 56 v 5 cf. II i 18

**'qn**

**uqnû** 'lapis lazuli': *uq-ni ki-ša-di-i[a-a-ma]* III vi 3

**'qr**

**aqāru** 'to be rare': *DN zu-un-na-šu ú/lu-šá-qir* S iv 44 54 v [3]

**'r**

**irtu** 'breast': *i-ir-ti-ša* I 272; *li-te-ed-di-li-ir-ta-ša* II i 19n; *i/li-né-'* gaba-*šá* S iv 47 57 v [6]

**'r'**

**erû** 'to be dry': *ka-aq-qá-ra li-e-er-ri* II i 15n

**'rb**

**erēbu** 'to enter': *[i-ru-u]m-ma ip-ḫa-a* gi[š.má] U rev. 3; *i-ir-ru-ub ù ú-uṣ-ṣí* III ii 45; *i-te-er-bu* I 249; *e-tar-bu-ma* S vi 17; [giš-má] *e-ru-um-ma* W 6; *ki-im-ta-šu uš-te-ri-ib* III ii 42 cf. [34] 38; *li-[še-ri-b]u-ni a-na ma-aḫ-r[i-ia]* II v 25; *e-reb* ama dumu.SAL *i-da-gal* S v [18] vi 7; *e-re-ba-ka áš-me-ma* U obv. 1 5 7

**'rd**

**arādu** 'to descend': *[a-na a]p-si-i [i]-ta-ar-du* I 18; *e-tar-du* S i 1; *lu-ri-id* S vi 27; *iš-pu-ur DN ú-še-ri-[du-ni-i]š-šu* I 99; cf. *li-še-ri-du-[nim-m]a* I 97; *-r]i-du* S i 3

**'rd**

**ardu** 'slave': *is-sà-qar a-na ar-di-šu* I 373 III i 16

**ardatu** 'young woman': *ar-da-tum* R 8 cf. [10]; *eṭ-lu a-na ar-d[a-ti]* R 9 cf. 7; S iii [20]

**'rḫ**

**arāḫu** 'to consume': *bītu il-ta-nu šanû*$^{ú}$ *i-re-ḫa-ma* S v 24 vi 13

**'rḫ**

**arḫu** 'month': *[ib-ba-b]i-il ar-ḫu* III ii 39; *eš-ru* iti *il-li-ka-am-ma* I 281 cf. 280; *i-na ar-ḫi* I 206 221; *[i-ma]-an-nu ar-ḫi* I 279

**'rk**

**arku** 'long': *ar-ku-tum ma-az-za-zu-ši-na [ik-ru-ni]* II iv 18 S v [15] vi [4]

**'rk**

**arku** 'after': *pu-ra-na-ta ar-ki-šá* S i 7

**'rm**

**armānu** 'pomegranate': ? *ar-ma-na* II v 12

**'rn**

**arnu** 'crime': *[be-el ar-n]im* III vi [25]

**'rp**

**erpetu** 'cloud': *er-pé-e-tum li-iḫ-ta-an-ni-ba* II i 16; [*er*?-*p*]*é*?-*tum ú-ka-la-la* II vi 12; *i-na er-pé-ti* III ii 49 53

**'rṣ**

**erṣetu** 'earth': *er-ṣe-tum* II iv 4 S iv 49 58 v [7] (ki); *er-ṣe-tam* I 14; — *ša-ap-li-tam* II v 17n 31 vi 26; *er-ṣe-tim qab-li-tim* x rev. i [5] 9 ii 10 rev. ii 3 (ki-*tim*) 17 (ki-*tú*) 33 (*er-ṣe-tú*); *er-ṣe-et DN* III i 48

**'rq**

**arqu** 'green': *ar-qú-tum am-ru pa-n*[*u-ši-in*] II iv 15

**urqētu** 'grass': *ma-la* ú.šim *me-er-*[*'i-sun*] W 9

**'rr**

**arāru** 'to suffer cramp': *i-na bu-bu-ti i-ta-na-ar-ra-ar-ru* III iv 23

**'rš**

**erešu** 'smell': [*i-ṣi-nu i-l*]*u e-re-ša* III v 34

**'rš**

**eršu** 'bed': *na-de-e e-er-ši* I 299 (**E** P giš.ná)

**'rš**

**eršu** 'wise': *e-riš-tu DN* I 250 (P); *e-ri-iš-tam DN* I 193; *e-ri-iš-ta DN* III iii 33n; *e-riš-ta DN* S iii 16; *er-še-te mu-te-ti* S iii 8

**'š**

**išātu** 'fire': *i-ša-tam*/*ta-am* I 64 65

**'š**

**išû** 'to have': *ša i-šu-ú ṭe₄-e-ma* I 223; *mi-im-ma i-š*[*u-ú*] III ii 30 31; ᵈ*šamaš la-aš-šu* III iii 18

**'š'**

**ešû** 'to be confused': *ú-te-*[*ši*] I 74; ? *i-šu-ma* III v 47n

**'šb**

**ašābu** 'to sit': *a-šar uš-bu i-na bi-ki-ti uš-bu-ma* III iv 18–19; [*u*]*š-ša-ab ib-ta-ak-ki* II iii 12 14; *ú-ul ú-uš-ša-ab* III ii 46; *ú-ul ú-uš-ša-ab* III i 47; *it-ta-aš-bu-ma* I 332; [*ta-at-t*]*a-aš-ba-ma* II vii 34; *wa-ši-ib* I 101; *a-ši-ib* I 254 (P); *wa-aš-ba-at* I 189 [278] **G** ii 8; *áš-bat* S ii 6 V 1; *tu-ša wa-aš-ba-a-ku* III iii 49; *aš-ba-*[*ku*] 𝕳 obv. 7; [*w*]*a-aš-bu* I 103 cf. III iii 31; *aš-bu* I 172 (K); *áš-bu-ma* S ii 5; *i-ta-šu-uš a-ša-ba-am* II vi 15 17

**aššābu** 'tenant': *ki-i a-ša-bi i-na bi-it di-im-ma-ti* III iii 46

**šubtu** 'dwelling': *i-na šu-ub-ti-šu* I 44 46 58 60; *a-na* — I 84

**mūšabu** 'dwelling': *zu-uk-ki mu-ša-*[*ab*] I 329 (?)

**'škr**

**iškaru** 'task': [*iš-k*]*a-ra-a-tu* I 181 (M)

**'šn**

**šittu** 'sleep': *la i-ṣa-ba-su ši-tu* S iv [3] 8 41; *ú-za-am-ma ši-it-ta* I 359 II i 8 x rev. i [3]

**šuttu** 'dream': [*ša šu-ut-ti w*]*u-ud-di-a qí-ri-ib-ša* III i [13]; [*uz-na*] *i-ša-ak-ka-na i-na šu-na-a-ti* II iii 8 10

**'šp**

**šiptu** 'incantation': *ši-ip-ta it-ta-na-an-di* I 253 (P) cf. S iii 3; *ig-mu-ru ši-pa-as-s*[*a₆*] I 255 (P); *tam-nu-ú ši-pa-sa* S iii 3

**'šr**

**ašar** 'where': *a-ša-ar DN il-li-ku-ma* II v 18f 32 vi [27] ([*a-ša*]*r*); *a-šar uš-bu* III iv 18; III iv 26

**'šr**

**ešertu** 'shrine': *ib-nu-ú eš-*[*re*]*-ti* I 337

**'šr**

**ešēru** 'be straight': *rēmu . . . ul*/*ia ú-še-šèr šèr-ra* S iv 51 61 v [9]

**'šr**

**ešru** 'tenth': *eš-ru*/*ra arḫu*/*a* I 280 281

**'šr**

**mīšertu** 'abundance': *ú-ma-aš-še-er . . . mi-še-er-tam* II v [20n] [2′] vi 29; cf. *mi-šèr-tú* x rev. ii 6 13 (*me-šèr-tú*)

**'šš**

**ašāšu** 'to be pained': *i-ta-šu-uš a-ša-ba-am* II vi 15 17

**'št**

**išti** 'with': *iš-ti-ka* I 170 (K)

**ištu** 'after': *iš-tu-ma ib-lu-la ṭi-ṭa* I 231; cf. I [17] 255 (P) II iii 25 III ii 52 v 36 S iii 3 vi 26 x rev. i 23 ii [26] 42 'since': [*iš*]*-tu-ma ap-ta-na-a*[*l-la-ḫu DN*] III i 45; — *te-eb-nu-na-ši-ma* S iv 27

**'št**

**ištēn** 'one': *i-lu*/*lam iš-te-en* I 173 (KLN) 208 S ii 7 (diš); III iii 5n (?); *bītu il-ta-nu* S v 24 vi 13; *iš-ti-ta ša-at-tam* II iv 9

**ištēniš** 'together': *ub-la pí-i-ni iš-ti-ni-iš* II v 15 29 vi 24 III vi 8; *ka-la ni-ši iš-te-niš i-ṣa-bat* 𝕴 rev. 3

**iltānu** 'north wind': *il-ta-nu* U rev. 6

**'štr**

**ištaru** 'goddess': *iš-ta-ar-ku-un* I 379 394 II ii 10 S iv 31 (ᵈu.dar-*ku-un*); *iš-tar-šu-un* I [406] II ii 24

**'t**

**itti** 'with': *it-ti* I [152] 165 201 [366] II vii 47 III i 42 49 S iv 19 v 29; *it-ti-ia-ma* I 200; *it-ti-šu* I 367 S iv 20 v 30 (*-šú*) x rev. ii 48 (*-šú*); *it-ti-ša* III iv 15; *it-ti-šu-nu* III iii 38

**'t**

**ittu** 'sign': ? [*it*]*-ta* S vi 20; *ba-al-ṭa it-ta-šu ú*/*li-še-di-šu-ma* I 216 229

**'tkp**

**atkuppu** 'reedworker': *at-ku-up-[pu na-ši a-ba-an-šu]* III ii 12n

**'tl**

**etellu** 'noble': *e-te-el-li* I 170

**'tm**

**atmānu** 'residence': *ba-bi-ša-at-ma-ni DN* I 69n

**'tr**

**atāru** 'to be more': *a-na šá pa-na i-ta-at-ra* S iv 39

**atru** 'excessive': *šu-up-ši-ik-ku at-ru* I [149] 162; *at-ra-am* I 37

**b''**

**bâ'u** 'to go along': *i-ba-a' ka-šu-šu* III iii 12 U rev. 19 (*i-ba-a*); *i-ba-'* U rev. 11; *ba-a-a' a-bu-bi* III i 37n

**b'b**

**bābu** 'door': *i-di-il ba-ab-šu* I 89 cf. III ii 52; *ši-a ba-ab-šu* I 380 395 [407] II ii 11 25; *i-pé-eḫ-ḫi* — III ii 51; *ul i-pa-te* ká-*ša* S v 19 vi 8; *e-di-il ba-ab-ka* I 87; *pí-te* — I [120] S ii 9 (ká-*ka*); *i-na-aṣ-ṣa-ru* ká-*k[a]* W 10; ká *ili-šu* S v 31; ká giš.má W 6; *ú-pa-aḫ-ḫi-ir a-na ba-bi-šu* I 386 III i 39; *i-ru-ṣa a-na ba-bi-ia/ka* I [81] 83 110; *il-mu-ú ba-bi-iš-ka* I 114; *ba-bi-ša-at-ma-ni* I 69n

**b'd**

**būdu** (*pūdu*?) 'shoulder': *ra-ap-šu-tum bu-da-ši-na* II iv 17; *rap-šá-tu [bu-da]-ši-na* S v [16] vi 5

**b'l**

**bēlu** 'lord': *DN id-de-ki be-[el-šu]* I 78; *be-el ṭe$_4$-mi* III iii 51 v 40; [— *ar-n]im* III vi [25]; [en *t]a-ši-im-ti* S iv [17] v [27]; en S iv 23 25 vi 19; cf. U obv. 1 [5] [7]; *is-sà-qar a-na be-lí-šu* I [369] II viii 37 III i 2 12; cf. II ii 4′ (Q); — — *DN be-lí-[šú]* W 12; cf. en-*šu* S iv [18] 22 v [28]; *be-lí* I 80 93 155; W 17; *i-na bīt DN* en-*ia aš-ba-[ku]* 𝕳 obv. 7

**bēltu** 'mistress': *be-el-tum ra-bi-tum* III iii 28; *be-le-[et]* (P *-l]et*) *ka-la i-li lu-ú š[u-u]m-ki* I 247

**ba'ūlātu** 'subjects': *ba-ú-la-tu-uš-šu* I 14

**b'l**

**būlu** 'cattle': *bu-ú-[ul*? III ii 36; [*bu-ul*] *ṣēri* W [9]

**b'r**

**bâru** 'to be firm' or 'to rebel': *i-ba-a-ar* II v 10

**b'r**

**bâru** 'to snare' *i-bi-ir-[ma]* III ii 34n (or from *ebēlu*)

**b'r**

**bêru** 'to choose': *li-ib-te-ru* (**D** *li-ib-te-e-r[u]*) *šu-ú* II vii 48

**b'š**

**bâšu** 'to be put to shame': *i/li-ba-aš-ma i-na ka-at-re-e* I 383 398 [410] II ii 14 28

**bīšu** 'shameful speech': *ú-ša-aq-bi bi-i-[ša]* III iii 39n; *ú-ša-as-ḫi bi-i-š[a]* III iii 41

**b't**

**bītu** 'house': é *la-wi* I 71; é *il-ta-nu* S v [24] vi 13; *ú-bu-ut bi-ta* III i 22; *qí-ri-ib bi-ti* I 375 390 II ii 14′ ([*qí-rib bi-tu]m* Q); é *ši-im-ti* I 249 (P); *bi-it qá-di-iš-ti* I 290; — [*e-mi ra-bé*]*-e* I 302; — *i-li-šu* II iii 11; — *di-im-ma-ti* III iii 47; — *na-ak-ma-ti* III iii 50; é *DN* 𝕳 obv. 7; é *a-li-te* S iii 15; é *ḫa-riš-ti* S iii 17; *ib-nu-ú bi-is-su* I 402 II ii 20; *la-wi bi-it-ka* I 80 82

**bb'**

**bubūtu** 'hunger': *i-na ṣú-mi ù bu-bu-ti* III iii 31; *i-na bu-bu-ti* III iv 22 II iv 12 (*-tim*) S v [14] vi [3] (*-te*); *a-na bu-bu-ti-ši-na* II i 10; *bu-bu-ti-iš ni-ši* I 339

**bdr**

**budūru** 'profusion': *bu-du-ri nu-ni* III i 35n

**bk'**

**bakû** 'to weep': *ib-ki-i-ma* III iv 12; *e-li-ši-na ab-ki* III iv 10; *i-lu it-ti-ša ib-ku-ú* III iv 15; *il-tum i-ba-ak-k[i]* III iii 32; [*u*]*š-ša-ab ib-ta-ak-ki* II iii 12 14; *ib-ta-a[k-ki]* x rev. i 13; *ib-ta-na-ak-ki* II iii 4

**bikītu** 'weeping': *i-na bi-ki-ti uš-bu-ma* III iv 18

**bkr**

**bukru** 'son': *a-la-da-am bu-ur-⌜ra⌝* ? III vii 9n

**blḫ**

**bulḫītu** 'feverishness': [*bu-u*]*l-ḫi-ta ú-ka-la-la ša-ap-ta-ša* III iii 29n; *ṣa-mi-a ša-ap-ta-šu-nu bu-ul-ḫi-ta* III iv 21

**blṭ**

**balāṭu** 'to live': *ki-i ib-lu-uṭ a-wi-lum* III vi 10; cf. III viii 10 (*ib-lu-ṭ[ú]*); *i-na ši-it-ku-ki na-pí-i[š-ti ba-al-ṭa]* II iv [14]; cf. S v 26 vi [15] (*bal-ṭa-at*); *na-pí-iš-ta bu-ul-li-iṭ* III i 24

**balāṭu** 'life': *ba-la-ṭá lu-ú* [ 𝕳 rev 4 cf. 1

**baṭlu** 'living': *ba-al-ṭa it-ta-šu ú/li-še-di-šu-ma* I 216n 229

**blkt**

**nabalkutu** 'to rebel': *ib-bal-kat erṣetu re-em-šá* S iv 58 v [7] cf. S iv 49 (*li-bal-kat*)

**bll**

**balālu** 'to mix': *iš-tu-ma ib-lu-la ṭi-ṭa* I 231; *ta-ḫa-za i ni-ib-lu-la qá-ab-la-am*

I 62; *ú-ba-li-il ṭi-iṭ-ṭa* I 226 cf. I 211 (*li-ba-al-li-il*, *li-ba-li-il*); *i-lu-um-ma ù a-wi-lum li-ib-ta-al-li-lu* I 212

**bn'**

**banû** 'to build': [*iš-t*]*u-ma te-eb-nu-na-ši-ma* S iv 27; *a-na-ku-mi ab-ni* I 289; *ib-nu-ú eš-*[*re*]*-ti* I 337; *i-ki* — I 338; — *bi-is-sú* I 401; II ii 20; [*e*]*-le-ep-pu ša ta-ba-an-nu-ú-*[*ši*] III i 25; *bi-ni e-le-ep-pa* III i 22; cf. 𝕴 rev. 6; *bi-ni-ma lu-ul-la-a* I 195 cf. **G** ii 9 (*li-ib-ni-ma*) V [2] 4; I 190; *ba-ni-a-at a-wi-lu-ti* I 194; — *ši-ma-ti* III vi 47; *ba-na-at ši-im-tu* S iii 11; *šà-su-ra-ti . . . ú-ba-na-a* S iii 9 10

**binu** 'son': *bi-nu bu-nu-ka* I 93n 95

**bunu** 'son': *a-na kurummate*$^{te}$ *bu-na il-tàk-nu* S v [23n] vi 12

**binûtu** 'structure': *qá-ne-e gáb-bi lu bi-nu-us-sà* 𝕴 rev. 7

**bunu/būnu**?: *bi-nu bu-nu-ka* I 93n 95

**bsr**

**bussuru** 'to report': *il-šu DN ú-ba-*[*as-sa-ar*] I 365

**bql**

**buqlu** 'malt': *ki-ma bu-uq-li* II iv 13n; *ki-i* še.DIM$_4$ *me-te* S v [25] vi 14

**br'**

**bīru** 'between': [*i-na b*]*i-ri-šu-nu* I 259 (P) S iii 6 (*be-ru-*)

**brk**

**birku** 'knee': *i-na bi-ir-ku a-li-it-ti* III vii 5n

**bš'**

**bašû** 'to be': *e-ṭe-em-mu* [*ib-ši*] I [228] [230]; *šu-ru-pu-u ib-ši* S iv 13; *a-ii-ib-ši-ši-na-ši ri-iš-t*[*um*] II i 20; *mu-šum i-ba-aš-ši* I 70 72; *it-ti DN* — *ši-ip-ru* I 201 cf. II vii 47; **G** ii 7; *i-ba-aš-šu-ú* 𝕴 obv. 3 5; *ma-la* — 𝕴 rev. 5; [*i*]*b-ba-š*[*u*?-*ú*?] III viii 8; *li-ib-ši-ma . . . pa-ši-it-tu* III vii 3; cf. I 215 217 360 III vi 50 vii 1 S iv 9 (*lib-ši*); *ú-ša-ab-ši qá-a*[*b-la*] III viii 13

**bušû** 'goods': [*šu-li ana*] *lìb-bi-šá . . .* níg.šu-*ka* W 7

**btq**

**batāqu** 'sever': *ba-*RI*-iq a-bu-un-na-te* S iii 7n

**gb**

**gabbu** 'all': *qá-ne-e gáb-bi lu bi-nu-us-sà* 𝕴 rev. 7

**gzl**

**guzalû** 'chamberlain': *gu*$_5$*-uz-za-lu-šu-nu* I 9n 126 [138] (*-ku-nu*); gu.za.lá *i ni-im-ḫu-ur-ma* I 41; gu.za.lá *la-bi-ru-tim* I 49 J 5 (gu.za.lá-*e*)

**gl**

**gallû** 'sheriff': *gal-lu-šu-nu* I 10n 127 [139] (*-ku-nu*)

**gll**

**gallatu** 'rolling': *g*[*al-la-ta*] *ti-a-am-ta* III iv [5]

**gmr**

**gamāru** 'to complete': *iš-tu-ma ig-mu-ru ši-pa-as-s*[*a*$_6$] I 255 (P)

**gamertu** 'total destruction': *i-lu iq-bu-ú ga-me-er-t*[*am*] II viii 34n; cf. III iii 38 (*-ta-am*); *ub-la pí-i-ku-nu ga-me-er-tam* III v 44

**gn**

**gana** 'come!': [*ga-na sa-a*]*s-sú-ra DN ši-si-ma* III vi [43]; x rev. i 31

**gpš**

**gapāšu** II 'to collect': ku$_6$.meš *ú-gap-pi-šam-ma* x rev. ii 22 38

**gr'**

**gerû** 'to provoke war': [*ig-ra-am t*]*u-qú-um-tam* I [130] [142]; *ni-ig-ra-am tu-qú-um-tam* I [146] 160

**d'**

**di'u** 'sickness': [*mur*]*-ṣu di-'u šu-ru-pu-u a-sa-ku* S iv 12 16; *mur-ṣa di-'a* etc. S iv 28

**d'k**

**dâku** 'to kill': *šu-up-ši-ik-ku . . . id-du-uk-ni-a-ti* I [149n] 162; *ad-du-ku ma-aṣ-ṣa-ru tam-ti* x rev. ii 24 40 (*ad-du-ka*); *i-da-ak i-da-áš* U rev. 13

**d'm**

**da'āmu** 'to be dark': *u*$_4$*-mu-um li-id-da-i-*[*im*] III iii 34

**d'r**

**dāru** 'age': *a-*[*na da-ri*] I [371]

**d'š**

**dâšu** 'to thresh': *i-da-ak i-da-áš* U rev. 13

**dbb**

**dabābu** 'to complain': [*i-da-bu*]*-bu-ma i-ik-ka-lu ka-ar-ṣi* I 39

**dgl**

**dagālu** 'to watch': *e-reb* ama dumu.SAL *i-da-gal* S v 18 vi 7

**dk'**

**dekû** 'to rouse': *DN id-de-ki DN* I 76 78

**dll**

**dullu** 'toil': *du-ul-lu-um ka-bi-it* I 4; cf. I 177 (N *dul-la-šú-un*) G ii 4; *du-ul-lam ú-ša-az-ba-lu* I 6 cf. 38; *ub-lu du-ul-la* I 2; *ka-ab-tam du-ul-la-ku-nu* I 240; — *du-ul-la-ni* I 42; *du-ul-la-ni-ma* I 150 163

**dm**

**damu** 'blood': *i-na ši-ri-šu ù da-mi-šu* I 210 225

**dm'**

**dīmtu** 'tear': [*i*]*l-la-ka di-ma-šu* I 167

**dmm**
**dimmatu** 'moaning': *i-na bi-it di-im-ma-ti* III iii 47; *ú-qá-at-ti di-im-ma-ti* III iv 11
**dnn**
**danānu** 'be strong': *lu-ú da-a-an* III i 33 W 3 (*da-an*); *lu-ú du-un-nu-na* III i 32
**dannu** 'strong': *ṣú-lu-la dan-na* 𝔍 rev. 9
**dpr**
**dapāru** 'to be sated': *DN id-pí-ra* III iii 39
**drr**
**nadarruru** 'to move freely': *id-da-ar-ru-ma* I 245
**andurāru** 'freedom': *an-du-ra-[ra aš-ku-u]n* I 243; cf. II v [19] [1′] vi 28
**z'z**
**zâzu** 'divide': *is-qa-am id-du-ú i-lu iz-zu-zu* I 12
**z'z**
**izzuzzu** 'to stand': *mu-šu i-zu-uz-ma* x rev. i 16; *iz-za-az-zu-ma* II iv 21; *it-ta-zi-iz ma-ḫar DN* I 90; *i-ta-zi-iz* U obv. 3; *i-zi-iz ma-aḫ-ri-ia* I 88; *ki-mi-is i-zi-iz* I 123
**mazzāzu** 'leg': *ar-ku-tum ma-az-za-zu-ši-na* II iv 18n S v [15] vi 4 (*ma-za-zi-šu-nu*)
**z'm**
**zīmu** 'face': *zi-mu-ši-na [it-ta-ak-ru]* II iv 12 S v [14] vi 3; *el-lu-tu[m] z[i]-mu-ši-na* III v 45
**z'q**
**zâqu** 'to blow': *[ki-m]a me-ḫe-e i-zi-qa-ši-na-ti-ma* S iv 15; *[i]-zi-qù . . . a-mur-ru* U rev. 10; *[ki-m]a me-ḫe-e li-zi-qa-ši-na-ti-ma* S iv 11; *si-qu-šú* U rev. 7n
**ziqziqqu** 'gale': *siq-si-qu* U rev. 7n
**z'r**
**zêru** 'to hate': *ma-ak-ku-ra zé-e-er-ma* III i 23
**zbb**
**zubbu** 'fly': *zu-ub-bu-ú a[n-nu-tum]* III vi 2; *ki-ma zu-ub-bi* III iii 44 cf. 19 (*su-ub-bi*) v [35]; *su-bé-e ra-bu-ti* III v 46n
**zbb**
**zibbatu** 'tail': *lu-uš-te-e si-ib-ba-as-sà* III i 14n
**zbl**
**zabālu** 'to bear': *iz-bi-lu šu-up-ši-[i]k-ka* I 2; *[du]-ul-lam iz-bi-lu* I 38; *[m]u-uš-ša-ak-ki i-za-ab-bi-il* II iii 5 cf. y 12 x rev. i 14 (*i-zab-bi-*x); *i-za-bi-lu* S i 10–13; *DN du-ul-lam ú-ša-az-ba-lu DN* I 6
**zbn** (?)
**zibānītu** 'scales': *zi-ba-ni-it* ama dumu.SAL *i-na-ṭal* S v [20] vi 9 cf. v [21] vi 10
**zk'**
**zakû** 'to be clean': *zu-uk-ki mu-ša-[ab]* I 329
**zkr** (see also sqr)
**zikaru** 'male': *zi-ka-ru a-na [ardate]* S iii 20; R 6; *ú-ba-na-a* nitá.meš S iii 9
**zm'**
**zummû** 'to lack': *ú-za-am-ma ši-it-ta* I 359 II i 8 x rev. i [3]
**zmr**
**zamāru** 'to sing': *a-bu-ba . . . ú-za-am-me-er* III viii 19
**zamāru** 'song': *an-ni-a-am za-ma-[ra] li-iš-mu-ma* III viii 15
**znn**
**zanānu** 'to rain': *ib-ba-ra ú/li-ša-az-ni-in* II ii 16 30; *ú/li-ša-az-ni-in na-al-ša* II ii 18 32; *[ú-ša-az-ni-i]n DN zu-un-ni-šu* II vi [10]; *ú-ša-az-na-na-ak-ku ḫi-iṣ-bi iṣ-ṣú-ri bu-du-ri nu-ni* III i 34n
**zunnu** 'rain': *zu-un-ni-šu DN li-ša-aq-qí-il* II i 11; cf. S iv 44 54 v [3] (*zu-un-na-šu*); see also *zanānu*
**znn**
**zanānu** 'to provide food': *i-za-an-nu-un* III v 32
**zqn**
**ziqnu** 'beard': *zi-iq-nu* I 273
**ḫ'ṭ**
**ḫâṭu** 'to watch': *i-ḫi-iṭ* I 75
**ḫbl**
**naḫbalu** 'bar': *[ši-ga-ra n]a-aḫ-ba-lu ti-a-am-tim* I 15 cf. x rev. i 6 10 ii [4] 11 18 34 y 1 7 S v [1]
**ḫbr**
**ḫubūru** 'noise': *i-na ḫu-bu-ri-ši-na ú-za-am-ma ši-it-ta* I [359] II i 8 S iv 3 8 41 x rev. i 3; — — *i-lu it-ta-a'-da-ar* I [355] II i 4
**ḫd'**
**ḫadû** 'to rejoice': *[n]a-am-ru-ma ḫa-du-ú pa-nu-ša* I 283; *ša-[ab]-sú-tum . . . li-iḫ-du* I 290 S iii 17
**ḫidūtu** 'rejoicing': *[li-iš-š]a-ki-in ḫi-du-tum* I 303
**ḫlp**
**halūpu** 'lapse (of time)': *[ḫ]a-lu-up pa-le-e* I 282n
**ḫlq**
**ḫalāqu** 'to disappear': *ana ḫa-la-qí* II ii 5′ (Q); *ú-gap-pi-šam-ma iḫ-liq-ma* x rev. ii 22 38
**ḫnb**
**ḫanābu** 'to grow full': *er-pé-e-tum li-iḫ-ta-an-ni-ba* II i 16n
**ḫss**
**ḫasāsu** 'to remember': *lu-uḫ-sú-ús-sú* III vi 4
**ḫp'**
**ḫepû** 'to break': *[r]i-gi-im-ša iḫ-pí* III iii 10; *ḫe-pí-i-ma li-ib-ba-šu* III ii 47

**ḫīpu** 'break (in tablet)': *hi-pí* II i 12 U obv. 11 rev. 4 9
**ḫṣb**
**ḫiṣbu** 'abundance': *ḫi-iṣ-bi iṣ-ṣú-ri* III i 35
**ḫr'**
**ḫarû** 'to sever' (?): *um-mi še-er-ri ú-ḫ[a-ar]-ru-ú ra-ma-an-ša* I 293n; cf. *lu-ḫar-ri-šá* S iii 19n
**ḫr'**
**ḫerû** 'to dig': *i-ḫe-er-ru-nim* I 21 23; [*i-ḫer*]*-ru-ú* S i 5
**ḫrš**
**ḫarištu** 'woman in confinement': *a-li-te ḫa-riš-ti* S iii 15 17
**ḫrš**
**ḫurūšu** (?): *lu pu-ut-tu ḫu-ru-šu* 𝔍 rev. 5
**ḫšḫ**
**ḫišiḫtu** 'necessities': *la-ap-nu* [*ḫi-ši-iḫ-ta ub-la*] III ii [14]
**ḫšḫš**
**ḫašḫašu** 'feeble': *ú-ṣé-mi ḫaš-ḫa-*[*šá*] U obv. 10
**ṭ'ṭ**
**ṭiṭṭu** 'clay': *ṭi-iṭ-ṭa-am* I 203; *ú*/*li-ba*(*-al*)*-li-il ṭi-iṭ-ṭa* I 211 226; [*ṭi-i*]*ṭ-ṭa i-kab-ba-sa-am* I 252 (P); *iš-tu-ma ib-lu-la ṭi-ṭa ša-ti* I 231 (O [*ṭ*]*i-ṭa-a-š*[*a*]); *e-li ṭí-iṭ-ṭí-šá* S iii 4; *li-ib-ta-al-li-lu . . . i-na ṭi-iṭ-ṭi* I 213; *ru-u'-tam id-du-ú e-lu ṭi-iṭ-ṭi* I 234
**ṭ'm**
**ṭēmu** 'personality': *ša i-šu-ú ṭe₄-e-ma* I 223n; *i-lam ta-aṭ-bu-ḫa qá-du ṭe₄-mi-šu* I 239 II vii 33 cf. I 243 (P *ṭè-mi-šu*)
'mind': [*i*]*š-ta-ni ṭe₄-e-em-šu* III iii 25
**bēl ṭēmi** 'president': *be-el ṭe₄-mi* III iii 51n v 40 (*ṭe₄-e-mi*)
**ṭb'**
**ṭību** 'dipping': *li-te-el-li-lu* dingir.meš *i-na ṭi-i-bi* I 209
**ṭbḫ**
**ṭabāḫu** 'to slaughter': *i-lam ta-aṭ-bu-ḫa* I 239 II vii 33; *ilam iš-te-en li-iṭ-bu-ḫu-ma* I 208; *i-na pu-úḫ-ri-šu-nu iṭ-ṭa-ab-ḫu* I 224
**ṭḫ'**
**ṭeḫû** 'to approach': *iṭ-ḫi-a a-na qú-ut-ri-ni* III v 41; *iṭ-ḫe-e-ma a-na su-bé-e ra-bu-ti* III v 46
**ṭrd**
**ṭarādu** 'to send': [*iṭ*]*-ṭa-ar-du-ni-in-ni* III i 44
**k**
**kī** 'how?': *ki-i aq-bi* III iii 37; *ki-i ib-lu-uṭ a-wi-lum* III vi 10
**kī** 'like': *ki-i a-ša-bi i-na bi-it di-im-ma-ti* III iii 46; *ki-i* dingir.meš 𝔋 rev. 4; *ki-i* 7 mu.m[eš] U obv. 9; *ki-i buqli me-te* S v [25] vi 14

**kī/akkī** 'when': *ki-i ú-ṣa-an-ni* x rev. ii 20 36; *ak-ki a-li-it-tu ú-la-du-ma* S iii 18
**kīma** 'like': *ki-ma li-i i-ša-ab-bu* I [354] II i 3 III iii 15; *eqlu ki-ma ša-ar-ra-qí-tu šu-a* (*li-*)*iš-ši* II ii 19n [33]; *ki-ma im-me-ri im-lu-nim ra-ṭa-am* III iv 19; cf. II iv 13 III i 29 iii [10] [12] 16 19 40 44 iv 6 8 9 v [35] S iv 11 15 U obv. 2 6 8 rev. 17 [19] W 2
**kīma** 'that': *ki-ma ni-iš-ku-*[*nu a-bu-b*]*a* III viii 9
**k'l**
**kâlu** 'to hold': *ka-i-la pár-ṣi-šu* S iv 32
**k'n**
**kânu** 'to be firm': *lu kin ub-bu-ku* 𝔍 rev. 5; *uš-ta-ka-an* III iii 24
**kbs**
**kabāsu** 'to tread': [*ṭi-i*]*ṭ-ṭa i-kab-ba-sa-am* I 252 (P)
**kbr**
**kabru** 'fat': *ka-ab-ru-ti* III ii 33
**kbr**
**kibru** 'shore': *i-mi-da a-na ki-ib-ri* III iv 9; *i-na* DI*-ib-ri* II iii 27
**kibrātu** 'world regions': *a-bu-ba iš-ku-nu i-na ki-ib-ra-ti* 𝔋 obv. 3
**kbt**
**kabātu** 'to be heavy'; *ik-ta-ab-ta ri-gi-im a-wi-lu-ti* I [358] II i 7 x rev. i 2 S iv 6 (*ik-tab-ta-m*[*a*]); *du-ul-lu-um ka-bi-it* I 4 150 [163] 177 (K) **G** ii 4; *tuk-ku* — I 179 (N) **G** ii 6; *i tu-uk-t*[*a*]*-bi-it DN* I 295 (**E** *-t*]*ab-bi-it*) S iii 16 (*tùk-ta-bit*)
**kabtu** 'heavy': *ka-ab-tam du-ul-la-ni* I 42 cf. 240
**kk**
**kakku** 'weapon': *ka-ak-ki-šu il-qí* I 90 [153]; *ka-ak-ki-ka li-qí* I 88 121; giš.tukul.meš*-ka* [—] S ii 9
**kkš**
**kikkišu** 'reed wall': *ki-ki-šu šu-uṣ-ṣi-ri ka-la sí-iq-ri!-ia* III i 21; *ki-kiš* U obv. 15; [*iz-za-ka*]*r a-na ki-ki-ši* U obv. 14; *a-ma-te-šu-nu a-na ki-ik-ki-*[*ši*] *i-ša-an-ni* 𝔋 obv. 12
**kl**
**kalû** 'all': *ka-la i-li-ma* I [122] 134 [146] [151] [159] 164 247 (P) x rev. ii 45; [*k*]*a?-la ša-di-i* I 33; *ka-la sí-iq-ri!-ia* III i 21; *ka-la ni-ši iš-te-niš* 𝔍 rev. 3; *ú-ul-la-*[*a*]*l ka-la-ma* I 202; *ra-bu-tum DN ka-lu-ni* II v [14] 28 vi [23] III vi 7; *al-ka-ni ka-la-ni* x rev. ii 46
**kullatu** 'the whole': *ku-ul-la-at ka-la i-li-ma* I 146 151 159 164; *a-na ku-ul-la-at ni-ši* III viii 18
**klk**

**kalakku** 'excavation': *i-na ka-la-ak-ki* I 40 [148] 161

**kll**

**kullulu** 'to complete': *ši-na-šàm*$^{šá-na}$ *ú-ka-la-la-ši-na* S iii 12n 13; [*ši-i*]*p-ra* . . . *ú-ša-ak-li-il* I 238

**kullulu** 'to cover': [*er?-p*]*é?-tum ú-ka-la-la* II vi 12; [*bu-u*]*l-ḫi-ta ú-ka-la-la ša-ap-ta-ša* III iii 29

**kll**

**kulīlu** 'dragon-fly': *ki-ma ku-li-li* III iv 6

**klṣ**

**kalāṣu** 'to contract': [*li-š*]*ak-li-ṣi ri-gim-ši-na nam-tar* S iv 10 cf. 14n, see p. 172

**km**

**kimtu** 'family': *ki-im-ta-šu uš-te-ri-ib* III ii 42; *ki-mat-ka sa-lat-ka* W 8

**kms**

**kamāsu** 'to consign': *ni-ši ik-mi-su a-na ka-ra-ši* III iii 54 v 43

**kms**

**kamāsu** 'to kneel': *ik-mis uš-kín i-ta-zi-iz* U obv. 3; *ú-ul ú-uš-ša-ab ú-ul i-ka-am-mi-is* III ii 46; *ki-mi-is i-zi-iz* I 123 S ii 10 (*ki-m*[*is*])

**kmr**

**kamāru** 'to heap up': *ku-um-mi-*NI 𝕵 rev. 12

**kpp**

**kippatu** 'circle': *ki-ma kip-pa-ti* W 2

**kpr**

**kupru** 'pitch': *ku-up-ru lu-ú da-a-an* III i 33 W [3]; [*k*]*u-up-ru ba-bi-il* III ii 51; *ku-up-ra* [*it-ta-ši še-er-ru*] III ii 13

**kṣr**

**kaṣāru** 'bind': *rēmu* (*lu*) *ku-ṣur-ma* S iv 51 61 v [9]

**kr'**

**katrû** 'gift': *i*/*li-ba-aš-ma i-na ka-at-re-e* I 383 398 410 II ii 14 28; S iv 36

**kr'**

**karû** 'to be short': *ar-ku-tum ma-az-za-zu-ši-na ik-ru-ni* II iv [18] S v 15 vi 4

**krb**

**karābu** 'to bless': *i-ka-ar-ra-ab* I 287; *kat-ra-ba-ma* S iv 35

**krm**

**kurummatu** 'food': *a-na* ŠUK-*te bu-na il-tàk-nu* S v [23] vi 12

**krp**

**karpatu** 'pot': [*ki-ma ka-ar-pa-ti r*]*i-gi-im-ša iḫ-pí* III iii [10]; cf. U rev. 17 (dug)

**krṣ**

**karāṣu** 'to pinch off', **kirṣu** 'piece': [*k*]*i-ir-ṣi* 14 *uk-ta-ar-ri-i*[*ṣ*] I 256 (P) cf. 257–58 (P) and S iii 5–6 (*kí-ir-ṣi, tàk-ri-iṣ*)

**karṣu** 'slander': *i-ik-ka-lu ka-ar-ṣi* I 39; *mi-nam kar-ṣi-šú-nu n*[*i-i*]*k-ka-al* I 176 (KN) **G** ii 3

**krš**

**karāšu** 'disaster': *ni-ši ik-mi-su a-na ka-ra-ši* III iii 54 v 43; *i-na ka-ra-ši* III iii 14 vi 10 viii [10]

**krš**

**karšu** 'stomach': *i-na kar-ši-ši-na e*/*li-me-ṣu šam-mu* S iv 43 53

**kšd**

**kašādu** 'to arrive': (2) *šattu i-na ka-šá-di* S v [12] 13 [15] [18] [22] vi [1] [2] [4] 7 11

**kšd**

**kišādu** 'neck': *uq-ni ki-ša-di-i*[*a-a-ma*] III vi 3

**kšš**

**kašūšu** 'power': *e-li ni-ši i-ba-a' ka-šu-šu* III iii 12 cf. U rev. 19

**ktm**

**katāmu** 'to cover': *ki-ma bu-uq-li ka-at-*[*mu pa-nu-ši-in*] II iv 13 cf. S v 25 vi [14] (*kat-mu*)

**l'**

**lā** 'not': *aš-šu la mu-uš-ši-i* I 217 230; cf. I 200 III iii 53 v 42 vii 2; [*la tu-ša*]-*ka-la-nim* II vi [13]; cf. II vi [14] S iv 3 8 39 41; *la-aš-šu* III iii 18

**ša lā** 'apart from': *ma-an-nu an-ni-tam ša la DN i-ip-pu-uš* III vi 14

**l'**

**lū** (asseverative particle): [*lu-ú e*]-*pu-uš* III vi [18]: *ba-la-ṭá lu-ú* [ 𝕳 rev. 4; III v 49

**lū** (precative particle): *lu-ú du-un-nu-na ú-ni-a-tum* III i 32; cf. I 248 (P *lu*) II i 21 III i 31 33 v 52 vi 3 vii 8; *lu* W 1 3 S iv 51 𝕵 rev. 5 7 8; joined to verb as in *li-ša-sí-ik* I 42; passim

**l'**

**lû** 'wild ox': *ki-ma li-i i-ša-ab-bu* I 354 II i 3 III iii 15

**l''**

**lawû** 'to surround': *il-mu-ú ba-bi-iš-ka* I 113; S i 14; *bītu la-wi* I 71 73 80 82

**l''**

**lītu** 'cheek': *li-it eṭ-li* I 274

**lbb**

**libbu** 'heart': *ḫe-pí-i-ma li-ib-ba-šu* III ii 47; *li-ib-ba-ša ú-na-ap-pí-iš* III iv 12 cf. vi 40 (*li-ib-bi*); *li-ib-ba-ka* III vi 23; [*ub-l*]*a-ma li-ib-ba-ku-nu* II vii 36; *DN ina* šà-*š*[*u*] 𝕳 obv. 5; [*šu-li ana*] *lìb-bi-šá* W 7

**libbātu** 'anger': *li-ib-ba-ti ma-li* II v 13 III vi 6

**lbn**

**libittu** 'brick': *li-in-na-di li-bi-it-tum* I 294 (P *li-bit-tum*); *li-bi-it-ta id-di* I 288; *it-ta-di li-bit-ti* I 259n (P) cf. S iii 6 15 (sig$_4$)

**lbr**

**labirūtu** 'old time': gu.za.lá *la-bi-ru-tim* I 49 cf. J 5

**lgm**

**ligimmû** 'offspring': *li-gim?-ma?-a li-ib-ni-ma* I 190n

**lḫm**

**laḫmu** 'water monster': *a-na la-aḫ-mi* II iii 30n; *l[àḫ-mi]* x rev. i 28 (?)

**ll**

**lullû** 'man': *bi-ni-ma lu-ul-la-a* I 195; **G** ii 9n; lú.u$_x$.lu V obv. 2 4

**ll'**

**lalû** 'emotion': *la-la-ša iṣ-ru-up* III iv 14 cf. U rev. 23 (*la-lu-šá*)

**lm**

**lāma** 'before': *la-am a-bu-bi wa-ṣe-e* 𝔍 rev. 4

**lmn**

**lemnu** 'evil': *ši-ip-ra le-em-na* II viii 35

**nelmēnu** 'distress': *li-še-ṣa-an-ni-ma i-na né-el-m[e-ni]* III v 50

**lpn**

**lapnu** 'poor': *la-ap-nu [ḫi-šiḫ-ta ub-la]* III ii 14

**lpt**

**lapātu** 'to touch': *il-pu-ut si-ik-ku-ra* I 75

**lq'**

**leqû** 'to take': *ka-ak-ki-šu il-qí* I 90 153; *il-qí-a te-er-tam* I 385 III i 38 cf. x rev. ii 28 (*il-qu-ú*): *ši-ip-ru il-qú-ú* II iv 19 S vi 16; *ka-ak-ki-ka li-qí* I 88 121; cf. S ii 4 [9] I 171 (LM); *li-il-qí a[r-da-tum]* R 10; cf. II iii 19; *lil-qé-e-ma* x rev. i 19

**lrd**

**lardu** 'couch grass' (?): *i-ku-la la-a[r?-da?]* II iv 9n

**ltk**

**maltaktu** 'water-clock': *ip-te ma-al-ta-ak-ta šu-a-ti ú-ma-al-li* III i 36

**m**

**-ma** (copula appended to verbs in sequence): *li-id-di-nam-ma . . . lu-pu-uš* I 203; passim

**-ma** (emphatic particle): *it-ti-ia-ma la na-ṭú* I 200; passim

**ma** (particle introducing direct speech): *ma bēl* S iv [23] vi 19 U obv. [5]

**-mi** (particle appended to word of direct speech): *a-di-ma-mi* I 370; cf. I 128 [129] [130] [140] [141] [142] 159 246 289 376 II v 14 28

**m'**

**mātu** 'land': *ma-tum ki-ma li-i i-ša-ab-bu* I [354] II i 3; — *ir-ta-pí-iš* I [353] II i 2 S iv 1 (kur); *[m]a-ta-am* III iii 9; *ma-ta* III vii 26; [k]ur U rev. 17 S vi 19; *mur-ṣu e-kal* kur$^{tu}$ S iv 24 26; *i-na ma-tim* I 377 392 [404] II ii 22; *ma-ti* II ii 8 (Q) S iv 30 (kur$^{ti}$); *ib-ku-ú a-na ma-tim* III iv 15; *na-pí-iš-ti ma-tim* I 22 24 S i 6 (kur); *ma-tim* I 30; *i-na* kur.meš$^{ti}$ ℌ obv. 2

**m''**

**mâ'u** 'to vomit': *i-ma-a' ma-ar-ta-am* III ii 47

**m'd**

**mâdu** 'to be much': *ni-šu im-ti-da* I 353 II i 2 S iv [1]; *ma-a-ad ša-ap-ša-qum* I 4 [150] 163 177 (M) **G** ii [4]

**m't**

**mītu** 'dead': *ki-i buqli me-te* S v [25] vi 14

**mgr**

**magāru** 'to agree': *it-ti i-li-ku-nu i-li ú-[ul ma-gi-ir]* III i [42]

**mdr**

**midirtu** 'canal': *me-ed-ra-tu šu-ḫu-rat* S v 33n; *mid-ra-tum?* x rev. i 15; *mi-id-r[a-x]* y 13

**mḫ'**

**meḫû** 'storm': *me-ḫu-ú* III iii 5; *ra-du me-ḫu-ú* III iv 25; cf. III vii 25 (?); *[ki-m]a me-ḫe-e (l)i-zi-qa-ši-na-ti-ma* S iv 11 15; U rev. 4 7

**mḫr**

**maḫāru** 'to face': gu.za.lá *i ni-im-ḫu-ur-ma* I 41; *mi-it-ḫ[u-ra-at]* III i 26

**maḫru** 'front': *li-il-li-ku i-na [ma-aḫ-ri]* II vii [50]; *ib-bi-ku-nim a-na ma-a[ḫ-ri]-šu* I 100; *ma-ru-šu ub-bu-ku* — — III iii 27; *a-na m[a-aḫ-ri-k]a* I 98; *i-zi-iz ma-aḫ-ri-ia* I 88; *a-na ma-aḫ-r[i-ia]* II v 25; *it-ta-zi-iz ma-ḫar DN* I 90; *aš-bu DN ma-ḫar-ka* I 172 (LM) S ii [5]; *ú-ka-la-la maḫ-ru-šá* S iii 13; *a-ši-ib ma-aḫ-ri-ša* I 254 (P) cf. 252 (P)

**miḫru** 'dam': *li-ir-[di mi-iḫ-ra]* II vii [53]; U rev. 14

**mṭ'**

**maṭû** 'to become less': *[ni-š]u la im-ṭa-a* S iv 39

**mkr**

**makkūru** 'goods': *ma-ak-ku-ra zé-e-er-ma* III i 23; *[šu-li ana] lìb-bi-šá . . . bušâ-ka u* níg.ga-[*ka*] W 7

**ml'**

**malû** 'to fill': *im-lu-ú ú-ga-ra* II vi 11; *im-lu-nim ra-ṭa-am* III iv 20; *im-la-a-nim na-ra-am* III iv 7; *im-la-ni* S v [24] vi 12; *ṣe-ru . . . ma-li id-r[a-na]* II iv 8; *li-ib-ba-ti ma-li* II v 13 III vi 6; *ma-al-ta-ak-ta . . . ú-ma-al-li* III i 36

**mala** 'as much as': *ma-la i-ba-aš-šu-ú* 𝔍 rev. 5; *ma-la urqētu me-er-['i-sun]* W 9

**mīlu** 'flood': *a-ií-il-li-ka mi-lu i-na na-aq-bi* II i 13; cf. II iv 3 S iv 45 55 v [4]

**mlk**

**malāku** 'to take counsel': *ša la im-ta-al-ku-ma* III iii 53 v 42 (*-ku-ú-ma*); *im-taš-ku mil-ká* ℌ obv. 1; [*at-t*]*a ù ši-i mit-it-li-ka* III vi 44

**malku/māliku** 'counsellor': *ma-li-ik i-li* I 43 45 57 [59] III viii 11; [*m*]*a-li-ik-šu-nu* I 8; *ma-li-ik-ku-nu* I 125 [137] S ii 13

**milku** 'counsel': *ni-a qí-ri-ib bi-ti mil-ka* I 375 390 II ii 14′ (Q); *im-taš-ku mil-ká* ℌ obv. 1; *mil-ká ša* dingir.meš ℌ obv. 9; *mi-lik-šá is-p*[*u-uḫ*] U rev. 17

**mālikūtu** 'rulership': ? [*ma-li-k*]*u-ut ap-se-e* S i 2

**mn**

**mannu** 'who?': *ma-an-nu-um-mi* I 128 129 130 140 141 142; *ma-an-nu šu-ú* II vii 45n; *ma-an-nu* III vi 13

**maššum** 'what?': [*m*]*a-šu-um-ma lu-uš-te-i* III i 17n

**mīnu/minû** 'what?': *mi-nam kar-ṣi-šú-nu* I 176 (K) **G** ii 3; *mi-nam* x rev. i 42; *i-ni mi-na-a a-mu-ur* I 109 (**F** *mi-na*); *a-na mi-nim* II vii 42

**mīnšu** 'why?': *mi-in-šu ta-du-ur* I 94 96

**mimma** 'whatever': *mi-im-ma i-š*[*u-ú*] III ii 30 31

**-man** (appended particle): *a-bu-ma-an* III iv 5n

**mn'**

**manû** 'to count': [*šanātim im*]*-nu-ú ša šu-up-ši-ik-ki* I 34 36; [*tam*]*-nu ši-ip-ta* S iii 3; *iš-tu-ma tam-nu-ú* — ibid.; [*i-ma*]*-an-nu ar-ḫi* I 279; *ú-šám*$^{\text{šá-am}}$*-na-ši* S iii 2 cf. I 254 (P)

**mqr**

**maqūru** 'boat': *ma-qú-ra i-ta-ma-ar* III vi 5

**mqrqr**

**maqurqurru** 'boat': *lu* giš.má.gur.gur*-ma* 𝔍 rev. 8

**mr**

**marru** 'shovel': *al-li ma-ar-ri* I 337; *ma-ar-ri-šu-nu i-ša-ta-am . . . it-ta-ak-šu* I 65

**mr'**

**māru** 'son': *ma-ru a-na a-bi-šu* I 330; dumu *šip-ri* x rev. ii 15; *ma-ru ra-ma-ni-ka* I 94 96; *ma-ru-šu ub-bu-ku* III iii 26 cf. U rev. 22 (dumu.meš*-šá*); *i-lu ma-ru-šu* III iii 52; dumu.meš*-šú it-ti-šú* x rev. ii 48; dumu.meš *um-m*[*a-ni*] W 8; dingir.meš dumu.meš*-šu* S iv 5 37; [*ilā*]*ni ma-re-e-šú* II i 6 (Q); *a-na ma-*[*ri-ka*] I 117

**mārtu** 'daughter': dumu.SAL *i-da-gal/i-na-ṭal* S v 18 [20] vi 7 9; *il-tàk-nu a-na nap-ta-ni* dumu.SAL S v 22 vi [11]; *zi-ba-ni-it* dumu.SAL S v [21] vi 10; *a-na* dumu.SAL S v [19] vi 8

**mrk'**

**nemerkû** 'to be present': *DN i-*[*me-re-e*]*k-ki* I 102n

**mrṣ**

**murṣu** 'illness': (*l*)*i-zi-qa-ši-na-ti-ma* [*mur*]*-ṣu* S iv 12 16; [*mur-ṣu*] *šá* dingir.meš *e-kal* kur*-tu* S iv [26] cf. 24 ([*mur--ṣ*]*i-ku-nu-ma*); *mu-ur-ṣa i-im-mi-du-ni-a-ti* I 371; [*ta-pa-ra*]*-sa mur-ṣa* S iv 28

**mrr**

**marta** 'gall': *i-ma-a' ma-ar-ta-am* III ii 47

**mš'**

**mašû** 'to forget': *aš-šu la mu-uš-ši-i* I 217 230

**mš'**

**mūšu** 'night': *mu-šum i-ba-aš-ši* I 70 72; *mu-šu i-zu-uz-ma* x rev. i 16; *mu-ši ù ur-ri* I 38; *i-na mu-š*[*i*] II iii 24 x rev. i 22; *i-na mu-ši-im-ma li-ša-az-ni-in na-al-ša* II ii 17 cf. 31; *ba-a-a' a-bu-bi* 7 *mu-ši-šu* III i 37n; 7 $u_4$*-mi* 7 *mu-š*[*i-a-tim*] III iv 24

**mšk**

**muššakku** 'oblation': [*m*]*u-uš-ša-ak-ki i-za-ab-bi-il* II iii 5n cf. x rev. i 14 y 12 (*maš-šak-ka*)

**mšl**

**mišlu** 'half': *mi-ši-il ma-aṣ-ṣa-ar-ti* I 70 72; [*ša ši-ga*]*-ru iš-bi-ru mi-šil-šu* x rev. ii 23 39

**mšr**

**muššuru** 'to let loose': *ú-*[*m*]*a-aš-š*[*e-er a-na ni-ši mi-še-er-tam*] II v 20n cf. II v [2′] vi 29 ([*tu-m*]*a-aš-še-er*) x rev. ii [6] 13 ([]*-šèr*)

**mt**

**mutu** 'husband': [*aš-ša*]*-tum ù mu-sà* (**E** *mu-us-sà*) I 300 cf. I 276 (*mu-us-sà*)

**mutūtu** 'husbandhood': ⟨*a-na*⟩ *aš-š*[*u-ti*] *ù mu-tu-ti* I 301 (P *-t*]*u-ú-tim*)

**mt'**

**matīma** 'ever': [*ma-t*]*i-ma-a . . . ul e-pu-uš* W 13

**n''**

**ne'û** 'to turn': *i-né-' irta-šá* S iv 57 v [6] cf. S iv 47 (*li-né-'*); *ni-a . . . mil-ka* I 375n [390] II ii [14′] (Q)

**n'd**

**na'ādu** 'to heed': *i-ta-'i-du iš-tar* I 302

**n'd**

**nâdu** 'to praise': *i-t[a-ad s]a-as-sú-ra i-ta-ad ke-ša* I 297–8

**tanīttu** 'praise': *ša-ni-it-ti-iš-[ka]* III viii 14n

**n'l**

**itūlu** 'to lie': *li-i'-ti-[lu aš-ša]-tum ù mu-sà* I 300

**maiālu** 'bed': *i-na ma-ia-li ú-še-et-[bi-šu]* I 79; *il-ta-kán ma-a-a-al-šu* S v 32

**n'n**

**nūnu** 'fish': *bu-du-ri nu-ni* III i 35; [k]$u_6$.meš I šár $ku_6$.meš . . . $ku_6$.meš x rev. ii 21 22 37 38

**n'r**

**nāru** 'river': *[li-b]i-il na-ru* II iii 19; *[idi]glat na-ra-am* I 25n; *im-la-a-nim na-ra-am* III iv 7; *[i-ḫer]-ru-ú* íd S i 5; *pu-ti-iš na-ri* II iii 26; *[i-n]a pu-ut* íd S v 32; cf. x rev. i 24; *na-ri* II iii 18

**n'r**

**namāru** 'to shine': *[n]a-am-ru-ma ḫa-du-ú pa-nu-ša* I 283

**n'r**

**nâru** 'to kill': *i ni-na-ra-a[š-šu]* J 1

**n'r**

**nīru** 'yoke': *i ni-iš-bi-ir ni-ra* J 2

**n'r**

**nâru** 'to roar': *[ki-ma p]a-ri-i na-e-ri* III iii 16

**n'š**

**nēšu** 'life': ? I 413–15 (Q *ne-e-ši*)

**nb'**

**nabû** 'to call': *lu-ú ši-im-ti i-ba-[a]* III v 49; *i-ta-ab-bi* I 296 (E *i-tab-bi*); *[l]i-ib-bu-[ú]* I 304 (P); *iš-tar [li-it-ta-a]b-bu-ú DN* I 304; *ú-na-ab-ba DN* III iv 4 13; [x-*t*]*a-ab-bi*-x I 306

**ngr**

**naggāru** 'carpenter': *na-ga-[ru na-ši pa-as-su]* III ii 11n

**ngr**

**nāgiru** 'herald': *(li-)is-su-ú na-gi-ru* I 376 391 [403] II ii 15′ 21 S iv 30 ([ni]gír)

**nd'**

**nadû** 'to put': *li-bi-it-ta id-di* I 288; II iii 13; *is-qá-am id-du-ú* I 12; *i-ša-tam ne-pí-ši-šu-nu id-du-ú-ma* I 64; *ru-u'-tam id-du-ú* I 234; *it-ta-di li-bit-t[i]* I 259 (P) S iii 6 (*i-ta-di*); III v 31; U rev. 2; *[qá-sa ta-at]-ta-di* S iii 4; *[l]i-id-du-šú tam-ta* I 173 (M); *i-d[i-šu tam-ta]* S ii 7; *na-de-e e-er-ši* I 299; *ši-ip-ta it-ta-na-an-di* I 253 (P); *[l]i-in-na-di li-bi-it-tum* I 294 S iii 15 (*li-na-di*)

**ndn**

**nadānu** 'to give': *[ši-ga-ra n]a-aḫ-ba-lu ti-a-am-tim [it-ta-a]d-nu a-na DN* I 16; *ṭi-iṭ-ṭa-am li-id-di-nam-ma* I 203

**nzm**

**nazāmu** 'to shout': *na-ap-ḫa-ar-šu-nu ut-ta-az-za-am* III v 38; *ut-ta-za-ma ta-ni-še-ti* S iv 23 25; *[ut-ta-az]-za-mu* I 40

**nḫš**

**nuḫšu** 'prosperity': *nu-ḫu-uš ni-ši nisaba* II vi 14

**nṭ'**

**naṭû** 'to be suitable': *it-ti-ia-ma la na-ṭú* I 200

**nṭl**

**naṭālu** 'to look': *zi-ba-ni-it* ama dumu.SAL *i-na-ṭal* S v 20 vi 9 cf. S v 21 vi 10

**nkm**

**nakkamtu** 'treasure': *bi-it na-ak-ma-ti* III iii 50

**nkm**

**nakāmu** 'to itch' (?): *ú-na-ak-ki-ma! na-ak-ka-am-t[a]* II iv 10n S v [12] vi [1] (*na-kám-t[a]*)

**nakkamtu** 'itch' (?): see *nakāmu*

**nkr**

**nakāru** 'to become strange': *zi-mu-ši-na [it-ta-ak-ru]* II iv [12] S v 14 vi 3 (*it-tak-ru*)

**nkš**

**nakāšu** 'to put': *šu-up-ši-ik-ki-šu-nu* $^{d}$*girra it-ta-ak-šu* I 67n

**nlš**

**nalšu** 'dew': *li-ša-az-ni-in na-al-ša* (**B** *na-aš-[ša]*) II ii 18 cf. 32

**nmš**

**nammaššû** 'wild animals': *na-[ma-aš-še-e]*(?) III ii [37]

**nsḫ**

**nasāḫu** 'to pull out': *ta-ar-ku-ul-li DN [li-na-si-iḫ]* II vii [51] cf. U rev. 15n (*ú-na-sa-ḫa*)

**nsk**

**šussuku** 'to do away with': *du-ul-la-ku-nu ú-ša-as-sí-ik* I 240; *ša ú-ša-a[s]-sà-ku a-wa-at-ka* III vi 26; *du-ul-la-ni li-ša-sí-ik el-ni* I 42n

**nss**

**nissatu** 'mourning': *iš-bi ni-is-sà-tam* III iv 16; *ia-a-at-tum ni-is-sà-s[ú]* III v 48

**npš**

**nuppušu** 'to give rest to': *li-ib-ba-ša ú-na-ap-pí-iš* III iv 12 cf. III vi 40

**napištu** 'life': *a-ia-a-nu ú-ṣi na!-pí!-iš-tum* III vi 9; *[ú-uš-t]a-ṣi-ra na-pí-i[š-tam]* III vi 19; III vii [11]; *na-pí-iš-ta*

**napištu** 'life' (*cont.*) *bu-ul-li-iṭ* III i 24; *šum-ša lu na-ṣi-rat na-piš-tim* 𝔍 rev. 8; *i-na ši-it-ku-ki na-pí-i[š-ti]* II iv 14 cf. S v 26 vi [15] (zi); *[n]a-pí-iš-ti ma-tim* I 22n 24 S i 6 (*[n]a-púl-ti*)

**nṣr**

**naṣāru** 'to guard': *iṣ-ṣú-ur DN e-le-nu* II v 16 30 vi 25 cf. *iṣ-ṣur* S v 2 x rev. i 11 ii 16 17; *aṣ-ṣú-ur er-ṣe-tam ša-ap-li-tam* II v 17 31 vi 26; cf. x rev. ii 19 (]-*ṣur*) 35 (*aṣ-ṣu-ra*); *iṣ-ṣu-ru DN e-le-nu* x rev. i 8 ii 32; cf. x rev. i 9 ii 33 y 6 8 (*iṣ-ṣú-ru*); *i-na-aṣ-ṣa-ru bāb-k[a]* W 10; *i-na-aṣ-ṣa-ru e-le-nu* x rev. ii 2 9! cf. 3 10 (*i-na-ṣa-ru*); *[ši-ga-ru n]a-aḫ-ba-lu tam-ti [at-ta ta]-na-aṣ-ṣa-ra* x rev. ii 5 12 (*-ṣa-ru*); cf. x rev. i 7 (*li-iṣ-ṣur*) y 2 (*li-iṣ-ṣú-ru*); *li-iṣ-ṣu-ru [DN e-le-nu]* x rev. i 4 5; *[ú-ṣur] a-dan-na* W [5]; *šum-ša lu na-ṣi-rat na-piš-tim* 𝔍 rev. 8; *[ú-uš-t]a-ṣi-ra na-pí-i[š-tam]* III vi 19; *ši-ip-ra . . . šu-uṣ-ṣi-ir at-ta* III i 19; *šu-uṣ-ṣi-ri ka-la sí-iq-ri!-ia* III i 21

**maṣṣāru** 'guard': *ma-aṣ-ṣa-ru tam-ti* x rev. ii 24 40

**maṣṣartu** 'watch': *mi-ši-il ma-aṣ-ṣa-ar-ti* I 70n 72

**nq'**

**naqû** 'to pour out': ? *iq-qú-ú* J 8

**niqû** 'offering': *ma-as-ḫa-tum ni-qú-ú* I 382 397 409 II ii [13] 27 S iv 33 (siskur); *i-ku-lu ni-qí-a-am* III v 36; *e-lu ni-qí-i pa-aḫ-ru* III v 35

**nqb**

**naqbu** 'the deep': *[i-na n]a-aq-bi* I 27 II i 13 (Q *-b]e*) iv 3 cf. S i 8 iv 45 55 v [4]

**nš**

**nišū** 'people': *ni-šu ú-ul am-ra-[(a)-ma]* II iv 6; *ni-šu im-ti-da* I 353 II i 2 S iv [1]; *[ni-š]u la im-ṭa-a* S iv 39; *qa-da-níš i[t-ta-n]a-la-ka ni-šu* S v 17 vi 6; *ni-šu . . . [zi-m]u-ši-na it-tak-ru* S v [14] vi 3; *ni-šu . . . bal-ṭa-at* S v [26] vi 15; *a-na ni-ši* II i 9 v [20] [2′] vi 29 viii 35 III vi 48 S iv 42 52 (*ni-še-e*) S iv 50 60 v [9] x rev. ii 6 13 (ukù.meš); *i-na ni-ši* III vii 1 2 3; *e-li ni-ši* III iii 12 U rev. 19 (*ni-še*); *ka-la ni-ši* 𝔍 rev. 3; *a-na ku-ul-la-at ni-ši* III viii 18; *nu-ḫu-uš ni-ši* II vi 14; *bu-bu-ti-iš ni-ši* I 339; *ni-ši ik-mi-su a-na ka-ra-ši* III iii 54 v 43; *ú-ṣu-ra-te šá* ukù.meš-*ma* S iii 14; *ú-ṣú-ra-at ni-ši* R 5; *ni-ši-šu iq-ri* III ii 40; *ú-ub-ba-al qá-ti a-na n[i-ši-ia-ma]* II vii [43]

**nš'**

**našû** 'to carry': *ul/ia iš-šá-a me-lu i-na na-aq-bi* S iv 45n 55 v [4]; *ku-up-ra [it-ta-ši še-er-ru]* III ii [13]; *šu-up-ši-ik ilim a-wi-lum li-iš-ši* I 191 197 **G** ii [12] V obv. [3]; *eqlu . . . šu-a (li-)iš-ši* II ii 19 33; *šu-ú na-ši* I 333; *na-ga-[ru na-ši pa-as-su]* III ii [11] cf. [12]

**nšk**

**niššīku, naššīku, ninšīku** 'prince': *ni-iš-š[i-ku]* I 250 (P [ᵈ*nin*]-*ši-kù*) cf. S iii [1]; II vii 39; *a-na DN ni-iš-ši-ki* III vi 42 cf. I 16n (*na-aš-ši-ki*)

**nšq**

**našāqu** 'to kiss': *ú-na-aš-ši-qú še-pi-ša* I 245

**nšr**

**našāru** 'to cut off': (*li-*)*iš-šu-ur eqlu iš-pí-ki-šu* II i 18 S iv 46 (*li-šur*) 56 v 5 (*iš-šur*)

**ntk**

**natāku** 'to drip': *ti-ku a-ii-it-tu-uk* II i 17n

**tīku** 'drop': see *natāku*

**s'q**

**sâqu** 'to be narrow': *ra-ap-šu-tum bu-da-ši-na [is-si-qá]* II iv [17] cf. S v 16 vi 5 (*is-si-qa*)

**sūqu** 'street': *qá-ad-di-iš i-il-la-ka i-[na sú-qí]* II iv [16] S v 17 (*su-qi*) vi 6 (*su-qí*)

**sb'**

**sibû, sibittu** 'seven': [7] *ù* 7 *šà-su-ra-ti* S iii 9 cf. 10; *ra-bu-tum DN si-bi-it-tam* I 5n; 7 *ki-ir-ṣi* I 257–8 (P) cf. S iii 5–6; 7 ud.meš S iii 15

**sebūtu** 'the seventh day of the month': *i-na ar-ḫi se-bu-ti ù ša-pa-at-ti* I 206 221

**sḫ'**

**saḫû** 'to rebel': *ú-ša-as-ḫi bi-i-š[a]*: III iii 41

**skp**

**sakāpu** 'to overthrow': *sa-ki-i[p]* III iv 27

**skr**

**sekēru** 'to block': *is-sa-kír šap-liš* S iv 55 v 4; *li-sa-kír šap-liš* S iv 45n

**sikkūru** 'bolt': *il-pu-ut si-ik-ku-ra* I 75 (K [*š*]*i-*)

**sl'**

**sullû** 'to pray': *ú-ul ú-se-el-lu-ú iš-tar-šu-un* I 406 II ii 24; *e tu-sa-al-li-a iš-ta-ar-ku-un* I 379 [394] II ii 10

**sl'**

**salātu** 'kin': *ki-mat-ka sa-lat-ka* W 8

**silītu** 'womb': *si-li-tam ip-te* I 282

**smn** (?)

**simanû**: *ši-bu-ti si-ma-ni-i* I 374n 389 II ii 13′ (*[si-ma]-né-e* Q)

**snš**

**sinništu** 'female': *ú-ba-na-a* SAL.meš S iii 10

**ssr** see **šsr**

**spḫ**
**sapāḫu** 'to scatter': *mi-lik-šá is-p[u-uḫ]* U rev. 17
**sp'**
**suppû** 'to pray': *e tu-sa-pa-a* ᵈu.dar-*ku-un* S iv 31
**spn**
**sapannu** 'edge': *i-mi-da a-na s[a-pa]n-[ni]* III iv [8]
**sqr/zkr** (see note on I 63)
**saqāru** 'to speak': *PN pí-a-šu i-pu-ša-am-ma is-sà-qar a-na PN* (or, *a-na PN is-sà-qar*): I 48 86 92 106 112 119 168 M 175 (MN ]-*aq-qar*) 199 205 236 369 373 388 II v [23] vii 41 viii 37 III i 2 [12] 16 41 vi 12 [17] 42 [46] **G** ii 2; cf. U obv. 14 ([*iz-za-k*]*ar*) W 12 ([*iz-zak*]-*kar*) x rev. i [1] 18 ii [15] (*iz-zak-kar*) x rev. ii 45 (*iz-za-kár*) S ii 8 iv [22] 37 (mu) S iv 29 (mu-*šu*) U obv. 4 (mu-*ár*) J 4; *is-sà-q[ar]* I 169 [357] II i 6 iii 18 S iii 1; [*iz-z*]*a-ka-ra* S iv 5; *is-sà-qar-šu-nu-ši* II v 27
**siqru** 'speech': *sí-iq-ra ša DN* I 113n; *ú-ša-ap-ta sí-iq-ra* III vi 15; *iš-mu-ú sí-qí-ir-šu* I 63n 400 III iii 52; *šu-uṣ-ṣi-ri ka-la sí-iq-ri!-ia* III i 21
**p'**
**pû** 'mouth': *ub-bu-ku a-na pi-šá* U rev. 22; *ub-la pí-i-ku-nu* III v 44; *ub-la pí-i-ni* I 152 165 II v 15 29 vi 24 III vi 8; *pí-a-šu i-pu-ša-am-ma* I 47 91 105 111 118 204 368 372 387 II v 22 vii 40 viii 36 III i 1 11 15 40 vi 11 16 41 45; *pa-a-šu* — I 85 111 (**F** cf. L) 118 (**FL**) 174 (KN) **G** ii 1; cf. J [3]; *pa-a-šú* W 11 x rev. i [1] ii 14 44 ka-*šu* U obv. [4] 13; ka-*šú* S ii 8 iv 21 [29]; *pí-a-ša te-pu-ša-am-ma* I 198 235
**p'**
**pūtu** 'front side': *pu-ut nāri* S v 32 x rev. i 24 25; *pu-ti-iš na-ri* II iii 26
**p'š**
**pāšu** 'axe': *na-ga-[ru na-ši pa-as-su]* III ii [11n]
**pgr**
**pagru** 'body, self': *a-na ra-ma-ni-ia ù pa-ag-ri-i[a]* III iii 42n
**pḫ'**
**peḫû** 'caulk': *ip-ḫa-a* gi[š.má] U rev. 3; *i-pé-eḫ-ḫi ba-ab-šu* III ii 51; *pi-ḫi* giš.[má] W 4
**pḫr**
**paḫāru** 'to assemble': *e-lu ni-qí-i pa-aḫ-ru* III v 35; [*pa*]*ḫ-ra-ma er-še-te mu-te-ti* S iii 8; *ši-bu-ti ú-pa-aḫ-ḫi-ir* I 386 III i 39; *š[à-a]s-su-ra-a-tum pu-úḫ-ḫu-ra-ma* I 251 (P) cf. 277
**puḫru** 'assembly': [*p*]*u-uḫ-ru* II ii 11′ (Q); *pu-úḫ-ra* II viii 32 III vi 27; *i-na pu-úḫ-ri* I 122 218; cf. I [134] II vi 16 18 III iii 36; *mi-it-li-ka i-na pu-uḫ-ri* III vi 44; *a-na pu-ḫur ka-la* dingir.meš x rev. ii 45; cf. I 122 (**F** *pu-ḫu-ur*) S ii 10 (ukkin); *DN il-ta-kan/kán pu-ḫur-šu* S iv 4 37; *pu-ḫur-šú* II i 5 (Q); *i-na pu-úḫ-ri-šu-nu* I 224
**puḫur** 'together': *li-ib-ta-al-li-lu pu-ḫu-ur* I 213n
**napḫaru** 'totality': *na-ap-ḫa-ar-šu-nu ut-ta-az-za-am* III v 38
**pṭr**
**paṭāru** 'to release': *ip-ṭú-ur ul-l[a]* II v 19; *e-le-ep-pa* — III ii 55; *ta-ap-ṭú-ur ul-la* II v [1′] vi 28; *ap-ṭú-ur* — I 243
**pl**
**palû** 'period': [*ḫ*]*a-lu-up pa-le-e* I 282
**plḫ**
**palāḫu** 'to reverence': *ú-ul ip-la-ḫu i-li-šu-un* I 405 II ii 23; *e ta-ap-la-ḫa i-li-ku-un* I 378 [393] II ii 9 S iv [31]; [*iš*]*-tu-ma ap-ta-na-a[l-la-ḫu DN]* III i 45
**plk'**
**palkû** 'extensive': *ṣe-ru pa-ar-ku* II iv 8; edin *pal-ku-ú* S iv 48 58 v [7]
**pn'**
**pānū** 'face': $u_4$*-mu iš-nu-ú pa-nu-ú-šu* III ii 48; *ḫa-du-ú pa-nu-ša* I 283; *ka-at-[mu pa-nu-ši-in]* II iv [13] cf. *pa-nu-ši-na* S v [25] vi 14; *ar-qú-tum am-ru pa-n[u-ši-in]* II iv 15; *a-ta-mar pa-ni-k[a]* U obv. 11; *pa-ni-ia li-ip-t[e]* III v 51
**ina pāni** 'in front': x rev. ii 47; *i-na pa-ni-ku-u[n]* III vi 18
**pāna** 'formerly': *pa-na-mi . . . i-na-an-na* I 246; *a-na šá pa-na* S iv 39
**pṣ'**
**peṣû** 'to become white': *ṣa-al-mu-tum ip-ṣú-ú ú-g[a-ru]* II iv 7 cf. *ip-ṣu-u* S iv 57 v [6]; *lip-ṣu-ú* S iv 47
**pqd**
**paqādu** 'to administer': *pa-qí-du ši-ma-ti* I 220
**pql**
**paqālu** 'to carry': *ša DN i-⟨pu⟩-šu-ma i-pa-an-qá-l[u]/a[l]* III v 47n
**pr'**
**parû** 'to cut': *ip-ru-u' ma-ar-ka-sa* III ii 55
**pr'**
**parû** 'wild ass': [*ki-ma p*]*a-ri-i na-e-ri* III iii 16; *ir-ta-kab pa-re-e-[šu]* U rev. 5
**prk'**
**naparkû** 'to be lacking': *i-na šu-par-ke-e napišti* S v [26] vi 15
**prs**

**parāsu** 'to cut off': *[ta-pa-ra]-sa mur-ṣa* S iv 28; *ip-t[ar-s]u a-na ni-še-e ti-ta* S iv 52; *[p]u-ur-sa* — — — II i 9 S iv 42 (*p[ur]-sa-ma*); *a-la-da-am pu-ur-si* III vii 9

**prṣ**

**parṣu** 'rite, authority': *par-ṣa-am ta-ba-al-ma* I 171 (K); *ka-i-la pár-ṣi-šu* S iv 32

**prš**

**mupparšu** 'winged': *mu-up-pa-a[r-ša iṣ-ṣú-ur] ša-ma-ií* III ii 35

**pš'**

**pešû** (?): *ba-*RI*-iq a-bu-un-na-te tep-te-ši* S iii 7

**pšṭ**

**pāšittu** (a demon): *li-ib-ši-ma i-na ni-ši pa-ši-it-tu* III vii 3n

**pšq**

**šapšāqu** 'distress': *ma-a-ad ša-ap-ša-qum* I 4 cf. [150] 163 **G** ii [4]; — *ša-ap-šaq-šu-un* I 177 (M)

**pšr**

**pašāru** 'to explain': *ip-šu-ur* I 135; *ap-šu-u[r]* I 157; *a-pa-aš-šar* 𝔍 rev. 2

**pt'**

**petû** 'to open': *si-li-tam ip-te* I 282; *ip-te ma-al-ta-ak-ta* III i 36; ama *a-na* dumu.SAL *ul i-pa-te* ká-šá S v 19 vi 8; *ma-me-et-šu-nu ú-ul i-pa-at-tu-ú* 𝔓 obv. 11; *uzun-šú pi-ta-at* S iv 18 v 28; *pa-ni-ia li-ip-t[e]* III v 51; *pí-te [ba-ab-ka]* I 120 cf. S ii 9; *lu pu-ut-tu ḫu-ru-šu* 𝔍 rev. 5; *ú-ša-ap-ta sí-iq-r[a]* III vi 15

**ptn**

**naptānu** 'meal': *il-tàk-nu a-na nap-ta-ni* dumu.SAL S v 22 vi 11

**ṣ'ḫ**

**ṣīḫtu** 'laughter': *ṣi-iḫ-tum i-ku-ul-šu* II vi 16 18

**ṣ'r**

**ṣēru** 'country': *ṣe-ru pa-ar-ku* II iv 8 cf. S iv 48 58 v [7] (edin); *ki-ma a-mi-im i-na ṣe-ri* III iv 9n; III ii 37; *ú-ma-am ṣe-rim* 𝔍 rev. 11; *ú-ma-am* edin W 9

**ṣ'r**

**ṣēru** 'over': *i-na ṣe-ri-ia-ma* III iii 43; *di-im-ma-ti i-na ṣe-ri-ši-in* III iv 11

**ṣurru** 'to extol': *li-iṣ-ṣí-ru na-ar-bi-ka* III viii 17n

**ṣbt**

**ṣabātu** 'to seize': *ka-la ni-ši . . . i-ṣa-bat* 𝔍 rev. 3; *la i-ṣa-ba-su [ši-tu]* S iv 3 cf. 8 41 (*i-ṣa-ba-ta-ni*); *pa-ši-it-tu li-iṣ-ba-at še-er-ra* III vii 4

**ṣḫt**

**masḫatu** 'sesame-meal': (*li-*)*il-li-ik-šu ma-as-ḫa-tum* I 382 397 409 II ii [13] 27 S iv 33 (*-ḫ]a-tu*)

**ṣll**

**ṣullulu** 'to cover over': *lu-ú ṣú-ul-lu-la-at e-li-iš ù ša-ap-li-iš* III i 31; *ṣú-lu-la dan-na ṣú-ul-lil* 𝔍 rev. 9; *[k]i-ma ap-si-i . . . ṣú-ul-li-il-ši* III i 29

**ṣulūlu** 'roof': see *ṣullulu*

**ṣlm**

**ṣalmu** 'black': *ṣa-al-mu-tum ip-ṣú-ú ú-g[a-ru]* II iv 7 S iv 47 57 v [6] (gi$_6$.meš)

**ṣm'**

**ṣamû** 'to be thirsty': *ṣa-mi-a-at ši-ik-ri-iš* III iv 17; *ṣa-mi-a ša-ap-ta-šu-nu* III iv 21; *ú-ṣé-mi ḫaš-ḫa-[šá]* U obv. 10

**ṣūmu** 'thirst': *i-na ṣú-mi ù bu-bu-ti* III iii 31

**ṣmd**

**ṣamādu** 'to yoke': *[i]ṣ-ṣa-am-du* III iii 6

**ṣpr**

**iṣṣūru** 'bird': *[iṣ-ṣú-ur] ša-ma-ií* III ii [35]; *iṣ-ṣur ša-me-e* 𝔍 rev. 11; *ḫi-iṣ-bi iṣ-ṣú-ri* III i 35

**ṣpr**

**ṣupru** 'claw': *[i-na ṣ]ú-up-ri-šu [ú-ša-ar-ri-iṭ] ša-ma-i* III iii 7 cf. U rev. 16 (*ṣu-up-ri-šu*)

**ṣṣ'**

**ṣuṣû** 'marsh': *ṣú-ṣi-a ra-bi-a* I 35

**ṣrp**

**ṣarāpu** 'to consume': *la-la-ša iṣ-ru-up* III iv 14n U rev. 23 (*la-lu-šá*)

**q'**

**qātu** 'hand': *[q]a-tam i-ḫu-zu qa-ti-ša* I 11n; *ú/li-ša-aq-qí-il qá-as-sú/su* I 384 399 411 II ii 15 29; *[il?-t]a?-kán*$^{ka-an}$ *qat-su* S iv 36; *[qá-sa ta-at]-ta-di e-li ṭí-iṭ-ṭí-ša* S iii [4n]; *i-ta-aṣ-ṣú-la qá-ti* I 336 (?); *ú-ub-ba-al qá-ti* II vii 43; *i-pu-ša qá-ta-ia* I 289 (P *qá-ta-a-a*); *i-na qá-ti-šu* II vi 19

**qb'**

**qebû** 'to speak, command': *[a-w]a-tam an-ni-[tam iq-bi]* III i [46]; *iq-bi-ma iṣ-ṣu-ru* x rev. i 8 cf. y 3; *ba-a-a' a-bu-bi . . . iq-bi-šu* III i 37; *[an-ni-ta]m iq-bi-a-a[m]* III i 50; *taq-bi-ma DN iṣ-ṣur* x rev. ii 16 32; *šá taq-ba-a* W 17; *ki-i aq-[bi]* III iii 37; *[aq-bi-m]a DN i-na-aṣ-ṣa-ru* x rev. ii [2] [9]; *iq-bu-ú* II v 2 viii 34; *iq-bu-ma* I 403 II ii 21 S iv 13; *[ši-i]p-ra ta-aq-bi-a-ni-im-ma* I 237; *DN pâ-šu dù-šá i-qab-bi* S ii 8 iv 21 29 U obv. 13 x rev. i [1] ii 14 44 W 11 (dug$_4$.ga); *[m]a-šu-um-ma lu-uš-te-i ta-qá-ab-bi* III i 17; *ša a-qá-ab-bu-ku* III i 18; *ša ta-qá-ab-b[a-ni-in-ni]* II vii 44; *qí-ba-ma(-mi)* I 376 [391] II ii [15′] x rev. i 4 cf. S iv 9 [30]; *qí-ba-a ia-a-š[i]* U obv. 12; *qí-ba-šu-nu-ti* S ii 11; *ú-ša-aq-bi bi-i-[ša]* III iii 39

**qabû** 'speech': *an-ni-a-am qá-ba-ša* (P *qa-ba-ša*) I 244
**qbl**
**qablu** 'battle': *qá-ab-lum i-ru-ṣa a-na [b]a-bi-ka/ia* I 81 83 110; *ta-ḫa-za i ni-ib-lu-la qá-ab-la-am* I 62; *ú-ša-ab-ši qá-a[b-la]* III viii 13; *qá-ab-lam* I [131] 143; *[qá]-ab-lim* I 128 140; *[ki-ma qá-ab-l]i e-li ni-ši* III iii [12] cf. U rev. [19]
**qablu** 'middle': *[q]á-ab-li-ša i-te-zi-iḫ* I 286
**qablû** 'middle': *er-ṣe-tim [qab-li-tim]* x rev. i [5] [9]; — *qab-li-tú/qa-ab-li-tim/qab-li-tum* x rev. ii 3 10 17 33
**qd**
**qadu** 'with': *i-lam . . . qá-du ṭe$_4$-mi-šu* I 239 cf. 243 P (*-d*]*u-um*) II vii 33; [*qá-du šam-me-šu*] S v [2] cf. x rev. i 7 ii 5 12 19 35; *qá-da* x rev. i 11
**qdd**
**qaddiš, qaddāniš** 'hunched': *qá-ad-di-iš i-il-la-ka* II iv 16; *qa-da-niš i[t-ta-n]a-la-ka* S v [17] vi 6
**qdm**
**qudmu** 'front': *bi-la e-pí-ta a-na qú-ud-mi-šu* I 381 408 II ii [12] 26; — — — *qú-ud-mi-ša* I 396n cf. S iv 34 (*qud-me-šá*); *qú-ud-mi-iš* II iv 20 23
**qdš**
**qadištu** 'prostitute': *i-na bi-it qá-di-iš-ti* I 290
**qm'**
**qēmu** 'meal': *i-ṣi-ir qé-ma* I 288
**qn'**
**qanû** 'reed': *qá-ne-e gáb-bi lu bi-nu-us-sà* 𝕵 rev. 7
**qqd** (qdqd)
**qaqqadu** 'head': *u'-pu-ur ka-aq-qá-as-sà* I 284
**qqr (qrqr)**
**qaqqaru** 'ground': *ka-aq-qá-ra li-e-er-ri* II i 15; *ina qaq-qa-ri e-ṣir ú-[ṣur-tu]* W 14 16
**qr'**
**qerû** 'to invite': *ni-ši-šu iq-ri* III ii 40
**qerētu** 'banquet': *a-na qé-re-ti* III ii 41
**qrb**
**qirbu** 'inside': *qí-ri-ib bi-ti* I 375 [390] II ii [14′]; *qí-ri-ib-šu* I 31; [*ša šu-ut-ti w*]*u-ud-di-a qí-ri-ib-ša* III i 13n; *a-ií-i-mu-ur* $^{d}$*šamaš qí-ri-ib-ša* III i 30
**qrd**
**qurādu** 'hero' (always Enlil, except once Anu: I 169): *qú-ra-du* I 8 [125] [137] II v 27 vi 32 III vi [5] S ii [13]: *qú-ra-dam* I 43 45 57 59; *qú-ra-di* I 69 92 112 169 III vi 12 x rev. ii 31 (*qu-*)

**qt'**
**qatû** 'to come to an end': *iq-te* II iii 16; *ú-qá-at-ti di-im-ma-ti* III iv 11
**qtr**
**qutturu** 'destroy': *lu-ú qú-ut-tu-ur* II i 21n
**qutrīnu** 'incense offering': *iṭ-ḫi-a a-na qú-ut-ri-ni* III v 41
**r''**
**ru'tu** 'spittle': *ru-u'-tam id-du-ú e-lu ṭi-iṭ-ṭi* I 234n
**r''**
**merītu** 'fodder': *ma-la urqētu me-er-['i-sun]* W 9
**r'd**
**rādu** 'downpour': *il-li-ik ra-du* III iv 25; aga[r$_x$] U rev. 7n
**r't**
**rāṭu** 'trough': *ki-ma im-me-ri im-lu-nim ra-ṭa-am* III iv 20
**r'm**
**rēmu** 'womb': arḫuš *lu ku-ṣur-ma* S iv 51 cf. 61 v [9]; *ú-ul ul-da er-ṣe-tum re-e[m-ša]* II iv 4; *ib/li-bal-kat erṣetu re-em-šá* S iv 49 58 v [7]
**r'ṣ**
**râṣu** 'to move': *qá-ab-lum i-ru-ṣa a-na ba-bi-ka/ia* I 81n 83 110
**r'š**
**rēšu** 'head': [*ul-l*]*u-ú re-ši-šu* I 32
**r'š**
**rīštu** 'rejoicing': *a-ií-ib-ši-ši-na-ši ri-iš-t[um]* II i 20
**rb'**
**rabû** 'to be great': *šu-up-ši-ik i-li ra-bi-[m]a* I 3
**rabû** 'great': *ṣú-ṣi-a ra-bi-a* I 35; [*e-mi ra-bé*]*-e* I 302; *be-el-tum ra-bi-tum* III iii 28; *ra-bi-tam* I 157; giš.má *ra-bí-tam* 𝕵 rev. 6; *ra-bu-tum DN* I 5 103 219 233 II v 14 28 vi [23] III iii 30 vi 7; *i-li*/dingir.meš *ra-bu-tim* I 106 199 205 232 (*-ti*) 236 357 II i 6 III vi 17 (*-ti*) viii [11] S ii 10 (gal.meš); dingir.meš *ra-ab-bu-ti* 𝕳 obv. 9; *i-ki . . . ra-bu-t[im]* I 338; *a-na su-bé-e ra-bu-ti* III v 46
**narbû** 'greatness': *li-iṣ-ṣí-ru na-ar-bi-ka* III viii 17
**rb'**
**erbû** 'four': im.limmu.ba U rev. 5
**rgm**
**rigmu** 'noise': *ri-ig-ma i-še-em-mu-ú* I 77 cf. 179 (M); *ta-aš-ta-'i-ṭa ri-ig-ma* I 242 II vii 32; *ri-ig-ma ú/li-še-eb-bu-ú* I 377 [392] 404 II ii 8 22 S iv 30 (KA); *ša-ḫu-ur-ru ri-ig-mi* III iii 47; *ri-gi-im a-wi-lu-ti* I 358 II i 7 S iv 6 x rev. i [2]; *ri-gi-im a-[bu-b]i* III iii 23

**rigmu** 'noise' (*cont.*)
cf. U rev. 20 (KA); *iš-mu-ú ri-gi-im-šu* III ii 50; [*r*]*i-gi-im-ša iḫ-pí* III iii 10; *iš-te-me ri-gi-im-ši-in* I 356 II i 5; *ri-gi-im-ši-na eš-me* III iii 43; *ri-gim-ši-na* I 413–15 (Q) cf. 360 ff. (V); [*li-š*]*ak-li-ṣi ri-gim-ši-na* S iv 10 cf. 14; [*i-na*] *ríg*$^{ri-gi}$*-me-ši-na at-ta-a-dar* S iv 2 7 cf. 40

**rd'**

**redû** 'to flow': *li-ir-*[*di mi-iḫ-ra*] II vii 53; *mi-iḫ-ra* [*ú-šar-di*] U rev. [14]; *ú-ša-ar-di a-na šu-ub-ti-šu* I 84

**rḫṣ**

**raḫāṣu** 'to overwhelm': [*i-r*]*a-ḫi-iṣ i-da-ak* U rev. 13

**rkb**

**rakābu** 'to ride': *ir-ta-kab pa-re-e-*[*šu*] U rev. 5

**rukūbu** 'chariot': *ru-ku-ub* dingir.meš U rev. 12

**rks**

**markasu** 'hawser': *ip-ru-u' ma-ar-ka-sa* III ii 55

**rm'**

**rummû** 'to let loose': *ru-um-mi* III vi 24

**rmk**

**rimku** 'washing': *te-li-il-tam . . . ri-im-ka* I 207 222

**rmn** (?)

**ramānu** 'self': *ú-ḫ*[*a-ar*]*-ru-ú ra-ma-an-ša* (P *-šá*) I 293 cf. S iii 19; *ma-ru ra-ma-ni-ka* I 94 96; *a-na ra-ma-ni-ia ù pa-ag-ri-ia* III iii 42

**rpš**

**rapāšu** 'to be wide': *ma-tum ir-ta-pí-iš* I [353] II i 2 S iv 1 (*ir-ta-pi*[*š*])

**rapšu** 'wide': *ta-ma-tú ra-pa-áš-tú* x rev. ii 7 29; *ra-ap-šu-tum bu-da-ši-na* II iv 17n S v [16] vi 5 (*rap-šá-tu*)

**rṣo** (?): *ir-ṣi-*x[ **G** ii 5 cf. I 178 (N)

**rqd**

**raqādu** 'to dance': *ur-*[*taq*]*-qù-da* U rev. 9n

**rš'**

**rašû** 'to have': *e-mu-qá šu-ur-ši* III i 33

**š**

**ša** (genitive particle): *i-na pu-úḫ-ri ša i-li* II vi 16 18 III iii 36; cf. I 34 36 77 108n (?) II ii 20 v [13] vi 21 III i [13] vi 6 𝔥 obv. 9; *šá*: S ii 10 iii 14 iv 26 39 x rev. ii [23] [39]

**ša** (relative particle): *DN ša i-šu-ú ṭe*$_4$*-e-ma* I 223; cf. I 113 II iii 31 vii 44 III i 18 25 iii 53 v 42 47 vi 26; *šá*: S vi 25 W 5 17 x rev. i 29 (For *ša lā* see *lā*.)

**š'**

**šû** (3rd person pronoun): *šu-ú-ma* I 202; cf. I 333 364 367 II vii 45 48 x rev. i 12 y 9; [*š*]*u* S iv 20 v [30]; *a-wa-tam šu-a-ti* I 166; *šu-a-ti ṣú-ul-li-il-ši* III i 29; *šu-a-ti ú-ma-al-li* III i 36; *ki-ma ti-ru-ru šu-a-t*[*i*] III iii 40; *ṭi-ṭa ša-ti* I 231; *šu-nu-ti* II vi 3 5 (verbal suffix?)

**šî** (3rd person pronoun): [*at-t*]*a ù ši-i* III vi 44; cf. I 253 (P) II vii 35 (?) 37 III iv 18 v 46 𝔍 rev. 8; *ši-a-ti* III vi 38

**š'**

**šu'u** 'grain': *šu-ú ia i-im-ru* S iv 49 59 v 8; *eqlu . . . šu-a* (*li-*)*iš-ši* II ii 19 33

**š''**

**še'û** 'to seek': [*i-še*] *bāb ili-šu* S v [31]; *i-ši-ú ba-ab-šu* I 407 II ii 25; *ši-a ba-ab-šu* I 380 [395] II ii 11; *lu-uš-te-e si-ib-ba-as-sà* III i 14; [*m*]*a-šu-um-ma lu-uš-te-i* III i 17

**š'b**

**šību** 'elder': [*ši-b*]*u-tum iš-mu-ú* I 400 cf. III ii 10; *ši-bu-ti si-ma-ni-i* I 374 389 II ii [13′]; — *ú-pa-aḫ-ḫi-ir* I 386 III i 39; *is-sà-qar a-na ši-bu-ti* I 388 III i 41

**š'ṭ**

**šâṭu** 'to drag': *ta-aš-ta-'i-ṭa ri-ig-ma* I 242 II vii 32, see p. 172

**š'l**

**šâlu** 'to ask': *il-ta-am is-sú-ú i-ša-lu* I 192; *ša-la* II iii 34 (?)

**š'm**

**šīmtu** 'fate': *bīt ši-im-ti* I 249 (P); *si-ma-nu ši-im-ti* I 305 280 (*ši-ma-ti*); *lu-ú ši-im-ti i-ba-*[*a*] III v 49; *pa-qí-du ši-ma-ti* I 220; *ba-ni-a-at ši-ma-ti* III vi 47 cf. S iii 11n (*ši-im-tu*)

**tašīmtu** 'understanding': [*bēl t*]*a-ši-im-ti* S iv 17 v [27]

**š'p**

**šēpu** 'foot': *še-ep-šu iš-ku-un* II iii 3; *ú-ul a-*[*ša-ak-ka-an še-pí-ia*] III i [48n]; *ki-ma šikin* gìr$^{\text{II.meš}}$*-k*[*a*] U obv. 2n 6 8; *ú-na-aš-ši-qú še-pi-ša* I 245 (P)

**š'r**

**šīru** 'flesh': *i-na ši-ri-šu ù da-mi-šu* I 210 225; *i-na ši-i-ir i-li* I 215 228

**š'r**

**šēru** 'morning': *i-na še-re-ti* II ii 16 30 iii 6

**š'r**

**šāru** 'wind': *li-il-li-ik ša-ru* II i 14; III iii 17 U rev. 4; *i-na* im.limmu.ba *ir-ta-kab* U rev. 5; *ša-ru uz-zu-zu* III ii 54; *te-bu-ú šārū*$^{\text{m}}$[$^{\text{eš}}$] U rev. 8; *a-na ša-a-r*[*i*] III v 30

**š'r**

**šērtu** 'penalty': *šèr-ta e-mi-id* x rev. ii 27 43; *šu-ku-un še-re-et-ka* III vi 25

**š't**

**šūtu** 'south wind': *it-ba-a id-šú šu-tu* U rev. 9; *šu-ú-tu* U rev. 6

**šb'**

**šebû** 'to be sated': *iš-bi ni-is-sà-tam* III iv 16

**šb'**

**šabû** 'to be loud': *ma-tum . . . i-ša-ab-bu* I 354 II i 3; *[a-bu-b]u* . . . — III iii 15; *na-gi-ru . . . ri-ig-ma ú/li-še-eb-bu-ú* I 377n 392 404 II ii [8] 22 S iv 30 (*lu-šá-bu-ú*)

**šbr**

**šebēru** 'to break': *[šá ši-ga-r]u iš-bi-ru mi-šil-šu* x rev. ii 23 39; *i ni-iš-bi-ir ni-ra* J 2

**šbs**

**š/tabsūtu** 'midwife': *ša-[ab]-šu-tum* (E *tab-sú-tum*) . . . *li-iḫ-du* I 290 cf. S iii 17 (*šab-su-tu-um-ma*); *tab-sú-ut* dingir.meš I 193n; *ta-ab-su-ut i-li* III iii 33

**šabsūtu** 'midwifery': *ša-ab-su-ta-am* (E RU-*ab-su-ta!-am*) *i-pu-uš* I 285n

**šgm**

**šagāmu** 'to roar': *i-ša-ag-gu-um i-na er-pé-ti* III ii 53; *iš-ta-ag-na DN i-na er-pé-ti* III ii 49n

**šgr**

**šigaru** 'bolt': *[ši-ga-ra n]a-aḫ-ba-lu ti-a-am-tim* I [15] cf. S v 1 x rev. i 6n 10 ii [4] [11] [18] [34] y 1 7 (xy *ši-ga-ru*); *[šá ši-ga]-ru iš-bi-ru mi-šil-šu* x rev. ii 23 39

**šd'**

**šadû** 'mountain': *[k]a?-la ša-di-i* I 33

**šadû** 'east wind': kur-*ú* U rev. 6

**šḫrr**

**šuḫarruru** 'to be quiet': *ša-ḫu-ur-ru ri-ig-mi* III iii 47; *ša-ḫu-ur-ra-at* II iii 15; *me-ed-ra-tu šu-ḫu-rat* S v 33n

**šk'n**

**šukênu** 'to bow down': *ik-mis uš-kín* U obv. 3

**škk**

**šakāku** 'to harrow': *i-na ši-it-ku-ki na-pí-i[š-ti]* II iv 14n

**škl**

**šukkallu** 'vizier': *a-na* sukkal *DN* I 86 [119] II v 23

**škn**

**šakānu** 'to put': *an-du-ra-ra iš-ku-un* II v [19]; *še-ep-šu* — II iii 3; II v 21; 7 *ki-ir-ṣi . . . iš-k[un]* I 258 (P); *iš-ku-nu a-bu-ba* III iii 53 v 42; *an-du-ra-ra ta-aš-ku-un* II v [1′] vi 28; II v [3′] vi [30]; 7 *ki-ir-ṣi . . . taš-ku-un* S iii 5 6; *an-du-ra-[ra aš-ku-u]n* I 243; *áš-kun-šu-nu-ti-[m]a* x rev. ii 25 41; *iš-ku-nu* III vi 39; dingir.meš *a-bu-ba iš-ku-nu* 𝔓 obv. 2; x-*ra-me e ta-áš-ku-na-ši-na-ti* S iv 38; *ki-ma ni-iš-ku-[nu a-bu-b]a* III viii 9; *ni-iš-ku-u[n]* I 147 [161]; *i-ša-ka-an* J 7; *[uz-na] i-ša-ak-ka-na i-na šu-na-a-ti* II iii 8 10; J 6; *a-[ša-ak-ka-an še-pí-ia]* III i 48; *il-ta-kan/kán pu-ḫur-šu* S iv 4 37; *il-ta-kán ma-a-a-al-šu* S v 32; *[il?-t]a?-kán*$^{\text{ka-an}}$ *qat-su* S iv 36; *[iš-t]a-ak-nu* I 28; S i 9 (*il-ták-nu*); *il-tàk-nu a-na nap-ta-ni* dumu.SAL S v [22] vi 11; *a-na kurummate*$^{\text{te}}$ *bu-na il-tàk-nu* S v 23 vi 12; *šu-ku-un še-re-et-ka* III vi 25; *šu-uk-ni ú-uk-ba-ak-ka-ti* III vii 6; *te-li-il-tam ú/lu-ša-aš-ki-in ri-im-ka* I 207 222; *iš/l[iš]-šá-kín-ma . . . a-sa-ku* S iv 50 60 v [9]; *[li-iš-š]a-ki-in ḫi-du-tum* I 303; x rev. i 20

**šiknu** 'placing': gar *ki-ma* gar *šēpē*$^{\text{II. meš}}$-*k[a]* U obv. 2n 6 8

**škr**

**šikru** 'beer': *ṣa-mi-a-at ši-ik-ri-iš* III iv 17

**šl'**

**šulû** 'street': *[ib]-ra-ti ù šu-li-i* I 275

**šlš**

**šaluštu** 'third': *ša-lu-uš-tum ša-at-tum* II iv 11; *ša-lu-uš-tum li-i[b]-ši* III vii 1

**šm**

**šumu** 'name': *šum-ša lu na-ṣi-rat na-piš-tim* 𝔍 rev. 8; *be-le-[et] ka-la i-li lu-ú š[u-um]-ki* (P *šum-ki*) I 248

**šm'**

**šamû** 'heavens': *[ú-ša-ar-ri-iṭ] ša-ma-i* III iii 8 U rev. 16 (an-*e*); I 19; *a-nu šar-ri [ša]-me-e* I 101; *[iṣ-ṣú-ur] ša-ma-ií* III ii 35; *iṣ-ṣur ša-me-e* 𝔍 rev. 11; *a-na ša-ma-i* (M *-m]a-mi*) I 170 III iii 48; *i-te-li ša-me-e-ša* I 13n 17

**šm'**

**šemû** 'to hear': *iš-[me] a-wa-tam šu-a-ti* I 166; *iš-me-e-ma* II iii 29; *iš-mé-ma* x rev. i 39; *iš-[m]é-e-ma* x rev. i 27; *ri-gi-im-ši-na eš-me* III iii 43; *e-re-ba-ka áš-me-ma* U obv. [1] 5 7; *i-la iš-mu-ú ri-gi-im-šu* III ii 50; *iš-mu-ma an-ni-a-am qá-ba-ša* I 244; *iš-mu-ú sí-qí-ir-šu* I 63 400 III iii 52; *[up-pa iš-mu]-ú* I [227]; *e ta-aš-mi-a a-na . . .* II viii 33; *up-pa i ni-iš-me* I 214; *i-še[m]-me* 𝔓 obv. 4; *ri-ig-ma i-še-em-mu-ú š[a . . .]* I 77; *[ni?-še-e]m-me ri-ig-ma* I 179 (M); *iš-te-me ri-gi-im-ši-in* I [356] II i 5; *an-ni-a-am za-ma-[ra] li-iš-mu-ma* III viii 16; *a-bu-ba . . . ú-za-am-me-er ši-me-a* III viii 19; *i-ga-ru ši-ta-am-mi-a-an-ni* III i 20 cf. U obv. 16 (*[ši]-ta-ma-ni*) 𝔓 obv. 14 (*ši-m[e]*); *ú-še-eš-m[e]* I 227 (O)

**šm'l**

**šumēlu** 'left (hand)': 7 *ki-ir-ṣi a-na šu-me-li iš-k[un]* I 258 (P) cf. S iii 6 (gùb)

**šmm**

**šammu** 'plant': *li-wi-ṣú ša-am-mu* II i 10 cf. S iv 43 53 (*šam-mu*); *ša-am-mu ú-ul ú-ṣi-a* II iv 5 cf. S iv 49 59 v [8] (*šam-mu*); *DN* (*li-*)*iṣ-ṣur qá-du šam-mi-šu* x rev. i [7n] 11 cf. ii 5 12 (*šam-mi-ka*) 19 (*šam-me-iá*) 35 (*šam-mi-iá*) cf. S v [2]

**šmn**

**šamnu** 'oil': *ša-am-ni* R 4

**šmš**

**šamšu** 'sun': *i-na aš-qú-la-lu ša-am-ši* II v [21] [3′] vi 30; see also Šamaš

**šn**

**šattu** 'year': *ša-lu-uš-tum ša-at-tum* II iv 11; *iš-ti-ta ša-at-tam* II iv 9; *ša-ni-ta ša-at-tam* II iv 10; 2, 4, 5, 6 mu *i-na ka-šá-di* S v [12] [15] [18] [22] vi 4 7 11; 3, 2, 3 mu.an.na — — S v [13] vi 1 2; 1 mu.an.na S vi 28; 600.600 mu.ḫi.a I 352 416 (Q *šá-na-a-tim*) II i 1 (Q —) S iv [1]; 40 mu.ḫi.a *at-ra-am* I 37; [mu.ḫi.a *im*]-*nu-ú* I [34] [36]; *ki-i* 7 mu.m[eš] U obv. 9

**šn'**

**šanû** I 'to change': *u*$_4$*-mu iš-nu-ú pa-nu-ú-šu* III ii 48; [*i*]*š-ta-ni ṭe*$_4$*-e-em-šu* III iii 25 II 'to repeat': *a-ma-te-šu-nu . . . i-ša-an-*[*ni*] 𝔥 obv. 13; [*ter-ti*] *DN . . . ú-šá-an-nu-ú* x rev. ii 8 cf. 30

**šanû** 'second, other': *bītu il-ta-nu* 2-*ú i-re-ḫa-ma* S v 24 vi 13; [*šá*]*-né-e i-ša-ka-an* J 7; *ša-ni-ta ša-at-tam* II iv 10

**šinašam** 'in pairs': *ši-na-šàm*$^{šá-na}$ *ú-ka-la-la*(*-ši-na*) S iii 12 13

**šs'**

**šasû** 'to call': *is-si* I 232; *il-ta-am is-sú-ú* I 192; *is-sú-ú eš-ra arḫa* I 280; — *na-gi-ru* I 403 II ii 21; *pa-na-mi DN ni-ša-si-ki* I 246 (P); [*a*]*l-ta-si* II ii 8′ (Q); *li-is-su-ú na-gi-ru* I 376 391 II ii [15′] S iv [30]; [*sa-a*]*s-sú-ra DN ši-si-ma* III vi 43; *i-lu iš-te-en ši-si-ma* I 173 (KLN) cf. S ii 7; *ti-si-a tu-qú-um-tam* I 61n

**šsr**

**š/sassuru** 'birth-goddess': *wa-aš-ba-at D*[*N šà-as-s*]*ú-ru* I 189 V obv. 1n (*sa-as-*[) **G** ii [8] S ii [6]; [*š*]*à-as-sú-ru li-gim?-ma?-a li-ib-ni-ma* I 190 cf. V obv. 2 (*sa-as-su-ru*); *at-ti-i-ma šà-as-sú-ru* I 194 cf. III vi 47; *i tu-uk-t*[*a*]*-bi-it DN sa-as-sú-ru* I 295 (P *-su-*); [*š*]*à-su-ru ba-na-at ši-im-tu* S iii 11; *i-t*[*a-ad s*]*a-as-sú-ra* I 297; [*sa-a*]*s-sú-ra DN ši-si-ma* III vi 43; *a-na DN sa-as-sú-ri* III vi 46; *š*[*à-a*]*s-su-ra-a-tum pu-úḫ-ḫu-ra-ma* I 251 (P); [*šà-as-s*]*ú-ra-tum* — I 277; [7] *ù* 7 *šà-su-ra-ti* S iii 9

**šp**

**šaptu** 'lip': [*bu-u*]*l-ḫi-ta ú-ka-la-la ša-ap-ta-ša* III iii 29; *ṣa-mi-a ša-ap-ta-šu-nu* III iv 21

**šp'**

**šapû** 'to be thick': [*ša-pa-at e*]*-ṭú-tu* III iii [18]

**špk**

**išpikū** 'crop': *li-iš-šu-ur eqlu iš-pí-ki-šu* II i 18 cf. S iv 46 (*iš-pi-ke-e-šu*) 56 (*iš-pi-ke-šú*) v [5]

**špl**

**šaplû** 'lower': *er-ṣe-tam ša-ap-li-tam* II v [17n] 31 vi 26

**šuplu** 'under part': *šu-pu-ul* [ x rev. i 20

**šapliš** 'below': *ša-ap-li-iš a-ii-il-li-ka* II i 12 iv 2; *is*/*li-sa-kír šap-liš* S iv 45 55 v 4; *e-li-iš ù ša-ap-li-iš* III i 31; cf. W 3

**špr**

**šapāru** 'to send': *iš-pu-ur* I 99; *iš-pu-ra-an-ni* I 124 [136] S ii 12; [*ta-aš-pu-ra*]*-an-ni* I 155; *ša a-šap-pa-rak-*[*ka*] W 5; [*a-šap*]*-pa-rak-kúm-ma* W 10; *šu-pu-ur* I 97

**šipru** 'task': *it-ti DN-ma i-ba-aš-ši ši-ip-ru* I 201; [*ši-i*]*p-ra ta-aq-bi-a-ni-im-ma* I 237; *ši-ip-ra le-em-na* II viii 35; *ši-ip-ra ša a-qá-ab-bu-ku* III i 18; *ši-pí-ir DN* I 196; *ši-ip-ru il-qú-ú* II iv 19 cf. S vi 16 (kin); *ši-pí-ir-šu* II vii 47; *šip-ra-ši-na* II ii 6′ (Q)

**mār šipri** 'messenger': [*iz-za-kar*] *ana* dumu *šip-ri* x rev. ii 15

**špšk**

**š/tupšikku** 'toil': *šu-up-ši-ik-*[*ku*] *at-ru* I 149 [162]; *iz-bi-lu šu-up-ši-*[*i*]*k-ka* I 2 cf. S i 10–13 (*i-za-bi-lu tup-ši-ka*); *ša šu-up-ši-ik-ki* I 34 36; *šu-up-ši-ik i-li* I 3; — *ilim a-wi-lum li-iš-ši* I 191 197 **G** ii 12 ([*šu-up-ši*]*-ku*) V obv. 3 (*tu-up-ši-ik-ku*); *šu-up-ši-ik-ka-ku-nu a-wi-*[*l*]*am e-mi-id* I 241 II vii 31; 'carrying basket': *šu-up-ši-ik-ki-šu-nu* $^{d}$*girra it-ta-ak-šu* I 66

**špt**

**šapattu** 'fifteenth day': *i-na ar-ḫi se-bu-ti ù ša-pa-at-ti* I 206 221

**šql**

**šuqqulu** 'to withhold': [*ú-š*]*a-aq-qí-il qá-as-su* I 411 II ii 29; *li-ša-aq-qí-il* — I 384n 399 II ii 15; *zu-un-ni-šu DN* — II i 11

**šqll**

**ašqulālu** (?): *i-na aš-qú-la-lu ša-am-ši* II v [21] [3′] vi 30

**šr**

**šāru** 'myriad': 1 šár ku$_6$.meš 1 šár$^{\text{ta.àm}}$ x rev. ii 21 37

**šrṭ**

**šarāṭu** 'to tear': [*ú-ša-ar-ri-iṭ*] *ša-ma-i* III iii [8] cf. U rev. [16n]

**šrp**

**šuruppu** 'plague': [*šu-r*]*u-up-pu-ú li-ib-ši* I 360 (V [*š*]*u-ru-up-pu-u*) cf. S iv 9 13 (*šu-ru-pu-u*); [— *i-te-z*]*i-ib-ši-na-ti* I [412]; [*mur*]-*ṣu di-'u šu-ru-pu-u a-sa-ku* S iv 12 16 28

**šrq**

**šarāqu** 'to act stealthily': (*li-*)*iš-ta-ar-ri-iq* . . . *li*/[*ú*]-*ša-az-ni-in na-al-ša* II ii 17n 31

**šarrāqû** 'furtive': *eqlu ki-ma ša-ar-ra-qí-tu šu-a* (*li-*)*iš-ši* II ii 19n 33

**šrr**

**šarru** 'king': *DN a-bu-šu-nu š*[*ar-r*]*u* I 7; *šar-ri* [*ša*]-*me-e* I 101; *šar-ri ap-si-i* I 102; SAR-*ru* I 413–415 Q

**šrr**

**šerru** 'child': *ku-up-ra* [*it-ta-ši še-er-ru*] III ii [13]; *li-iṣ-ba-at še-er-ra* III vii 4; *ul*/*ia ú-še-šèr šèr-ra* S iv 51 61 v [9]; I 351; *um-mi še-er-ri* I 292 cf. S iii 19 (*šèr-ri*)

**šš'**

? **šašû** 'to disturb': *i ni-iš-ši-a i-na šu-ub-ti-šu* I 44n 46 58 60

**št'**

**šatû** 'to drink': [*ša*]-*tu-ú i-ša-at-ti* III ii 44

**t''**

**te'ūtu** 'food': [*p*]*u-ur-sa* . . . *te-i-ta* II i 9 (**B** *te-i-tam*, Q *ti-wi-tú*) cf. S iv 42 52 (*ti-ta*); *ti-i-ti-iš* [*i-li*] I 339

**t'm**

**tâmtu** 'sea': *ta-ma-tú ra-pa-áš-tú* x rev. ii 7 29; *ul-da g*[*al-la-ta*] *ti-a-am-ta* III iv 6; [*ši-ga-ra n*]*a-aḫ-ba-lu ti-a-am-tim* I 15 cf. S v [1] x rev. i [6] 10 (*ta-am-ti*) ii 4 (*tam-ti*) 11 (*ta-am-ta*) 18 (*tam-tú*) 34 (*ti-am-ti*); *ma-aṣ-ṣa-ru tam-ti* x rev. ii 24 40; *ti-a-am-tim* II vi 1

**t'm** (?)

**tāmtu** 'destruction': [*l*]*i-id-du-šú tam-ta* I 173n (M); *i-d*[*i-šu tam-ta*] S ii [7]

**t'r**

**târu** 'to turn': *it-tu-ru* I 413 II ii 35; *u$_4$-mu-um* . . . *li-tu-ur li-ki-*[*il*] III iii 35; *ši-*[*i*] *li-tu-ur a-na up-*[ II vii 37; [*ú*]-*tir-ram-ma šèr-ta e-mi-id* x rev. ii 27 43; ká giš.má *tir-*[*ra*] W 6

**tb'**

**tebû** 'to rise': *DN it-bi-ma* I 104; *DN it-bé-e-ma* III v 37; *it-ba-a id-šú šu-tu* U rev. 9; *te-bu-ú* IM.meš U rev. 8; *i-na te-bi-šu* III ii 54; *i-na ma-ia-li ú-še-et-*[*bi-šu*] I 79

**tkk**

**tukku** 'lament': *tu-uk-kum ka-b*[*i-it*] **G** ii 6 cf. I [179n] (N)

**tkl**

**tukultu** 'help': *tuk-la-at* ℌ rev. 3

**tm'**

**tamû** 'to swear': *DN it-ta-mi* x rev. ii 48; . . . *i-li ta-mi-ma* II iii 7 9; *i-na pa-ni ta-mu-ni* x rev. ii 47; dumu.meš-*šú it-ti-šú ta-mu-ni* x rev. ii 48; *a-na mi-nim tu-ta-am-ma-n*[*i*] II vii 42; *i n*[*u-t*]*a-am-mu-ni* II vii 38

**tpšk** see **špšk**

**tqm**

**tuqumtu** 'war': *ti-si-a tu-qú-um-tam* I 61; *ma-an-nu-u*[*m-mi ig-ra-am t*]*u-qú-um-tam* I 130 142; *ni-ig-ra-am* — I [146] 160 (*tu-qú-um-ta-am*, **G** *tu-qum-tam*)

**trkl**

**tarkullu** 'mooring pole': *ta-ar-ku-ul-li DN* [*li-na-si-iḫ*] II vii 51 cf. U rev. 15 (*t*[*ar-kul-li*])

**trr** (?)

**tiruru** (a demon): *ki-ma ti-ru-ru šu-a-t*[*i*] III iii 40n

**tš**

**tūša** 'as if': *tu-ša wa-aš-ba-a-ku* III iii 49n

# LIST OF NAMES IN THE AKKADIAN TEXTS

Ni 2552+2560+2564
Obv. i

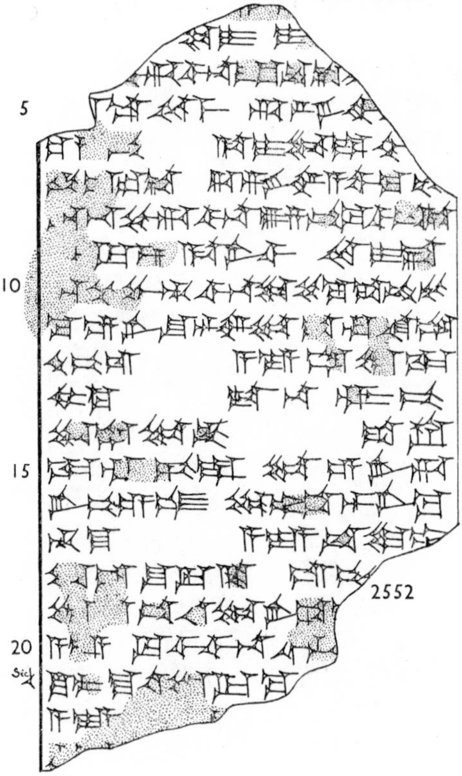

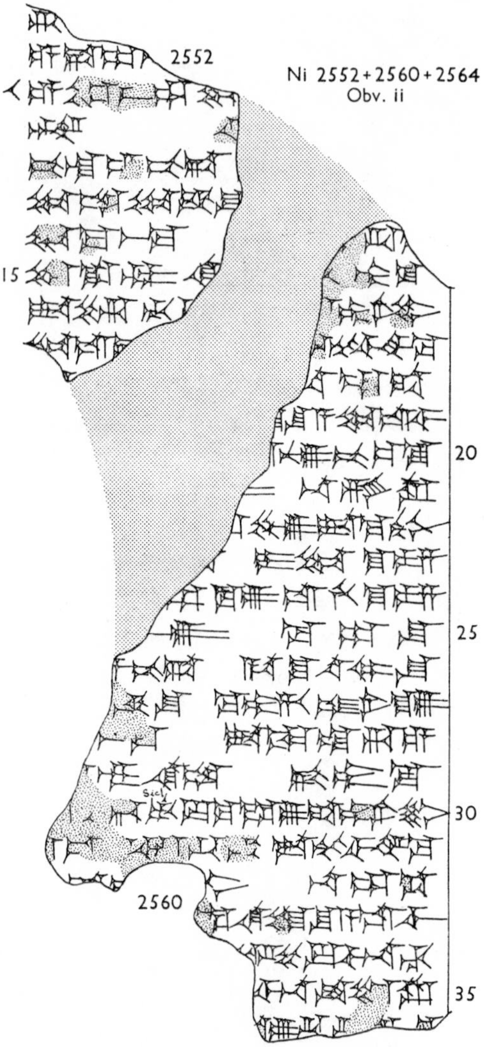


Ni 2552+2560+2564
Obv. ii

Ni 2552 + 2560 + 2564
Obv. iii

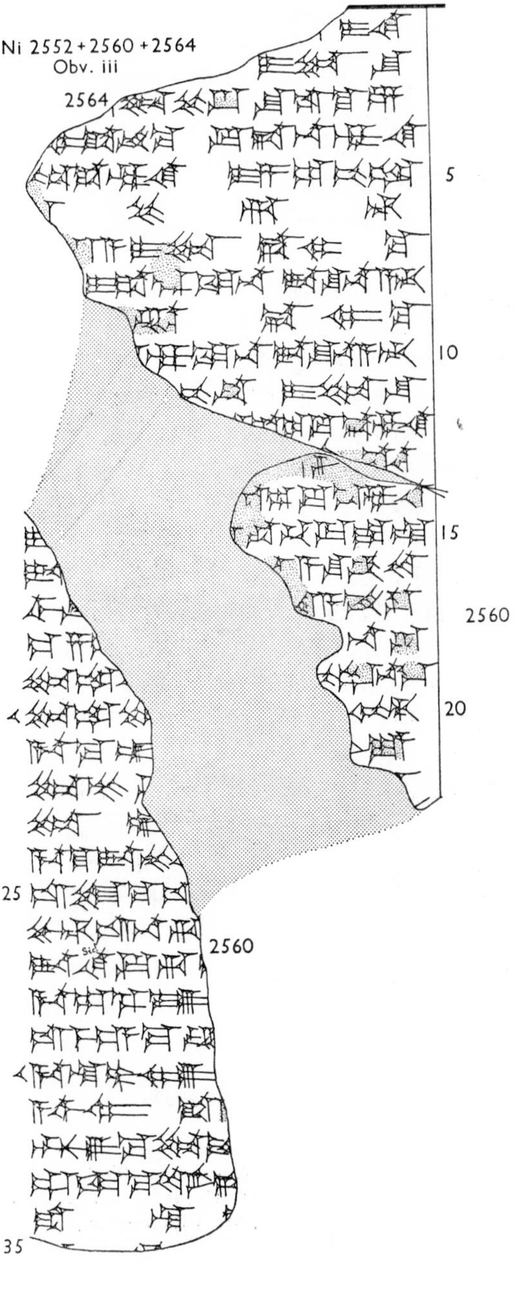


(3)

Ni 2552 + 2560 + 2564
Obv. iv

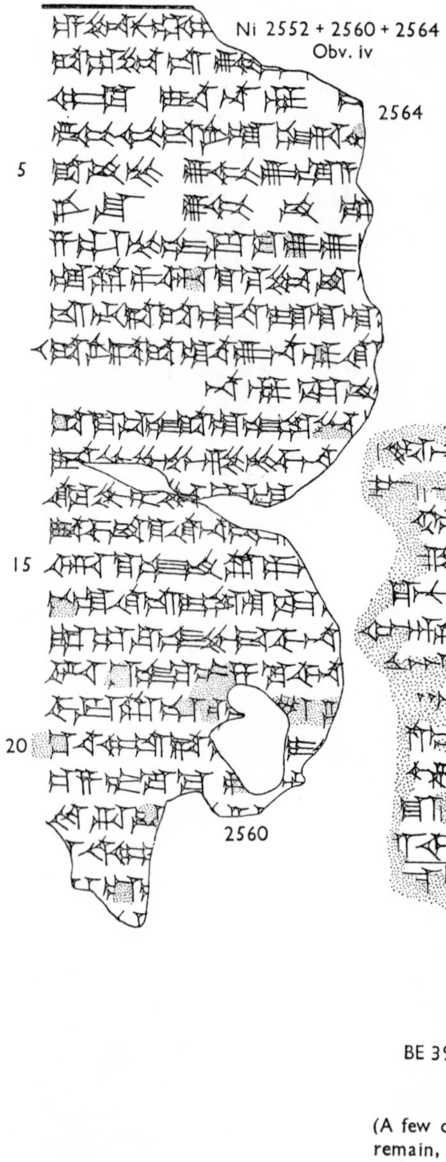


**Obv. i**
(Perhaps line 7 of column)

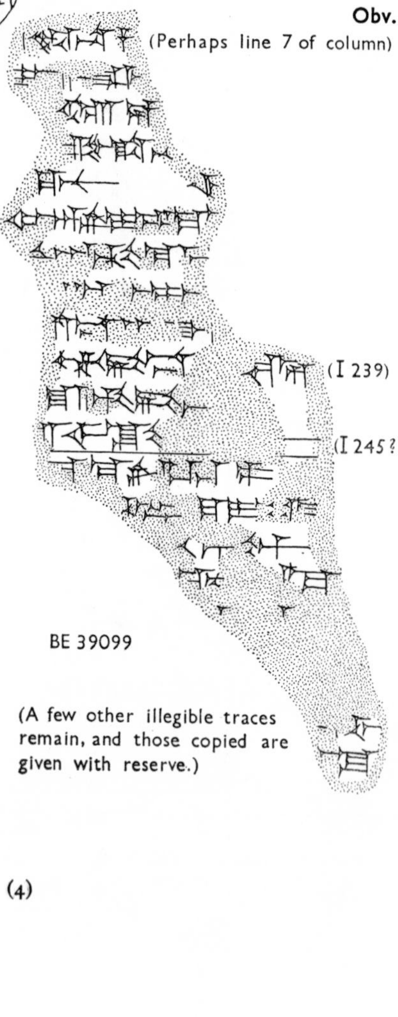


BE 39099

(A few other illegible traces remain, and those copied are given with reserve.)

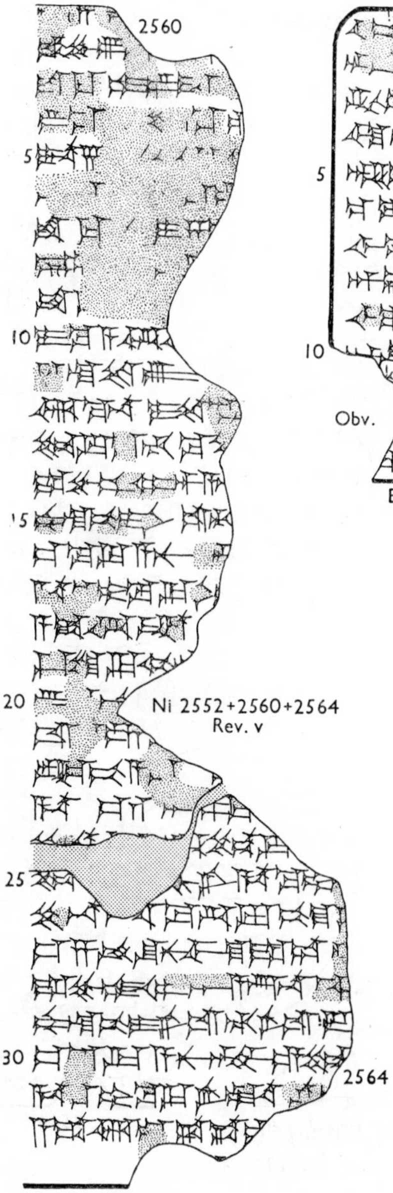


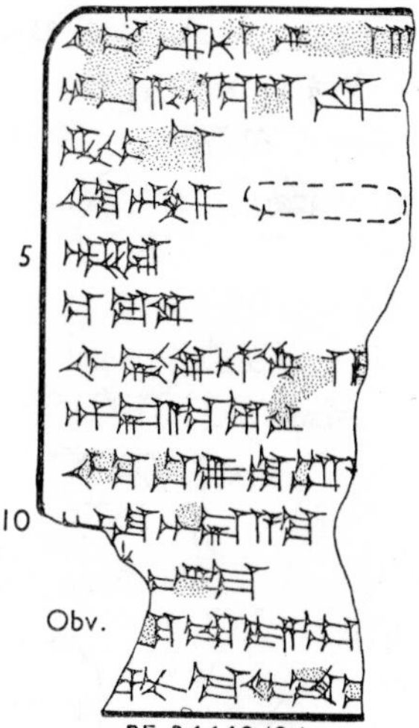


BE 36669/24 a

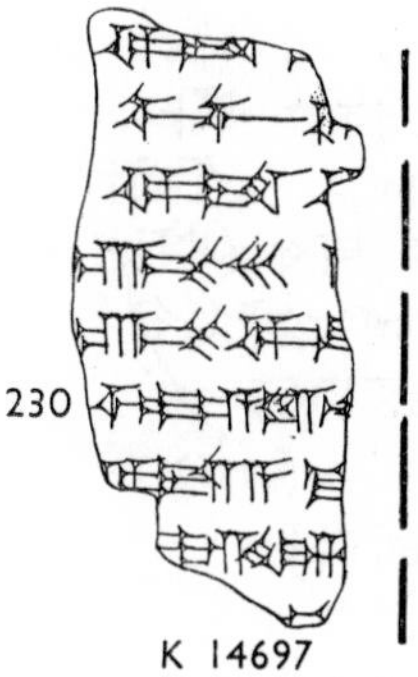


K 14697

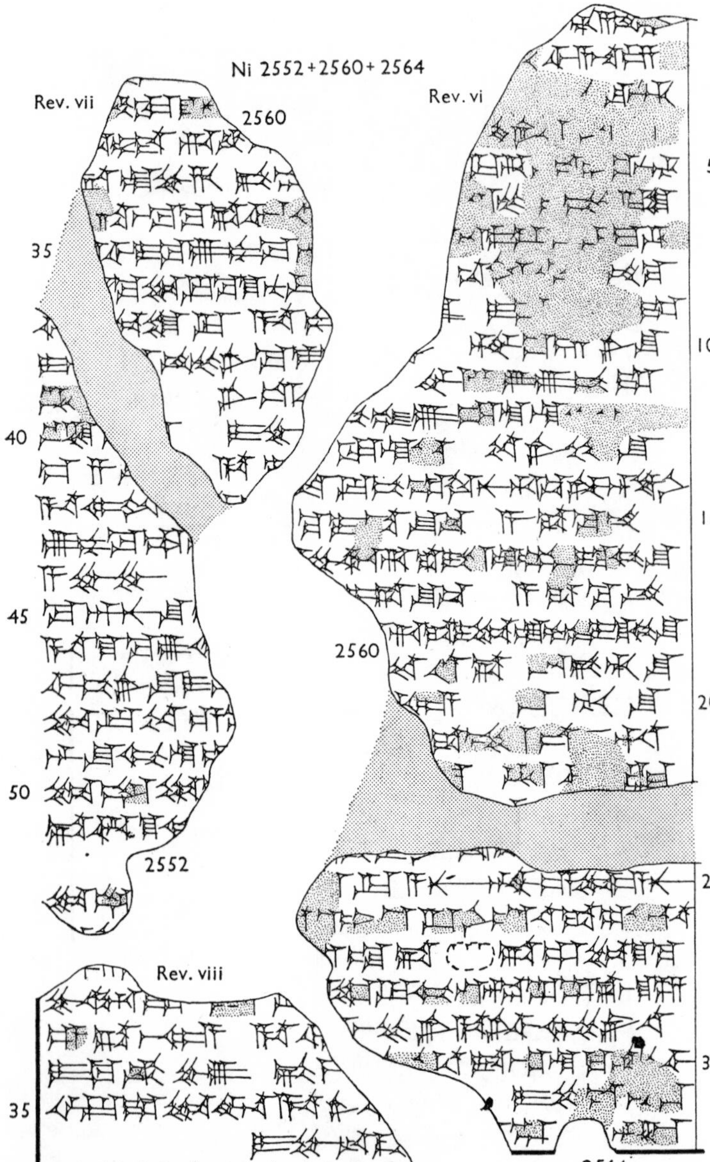
Ni 2552+2560+2564
Rev. vii
Rev. vi
Rev. viii
2560
2552
2564
(remainder uninscribed)

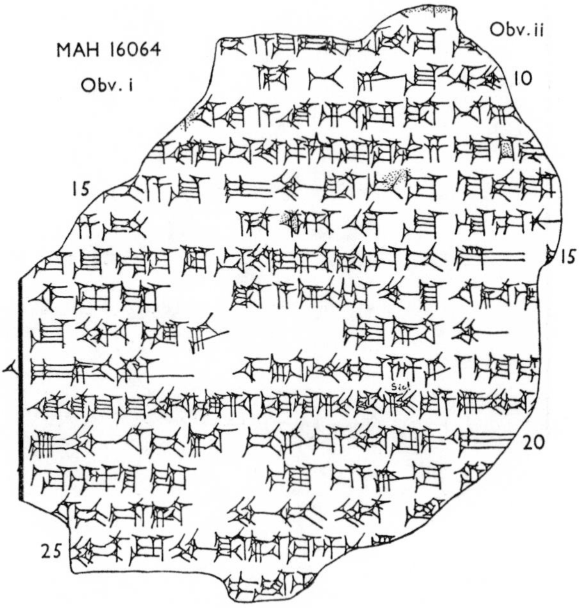
MAH 16064
Obv. i
Obv. ii
Sic!

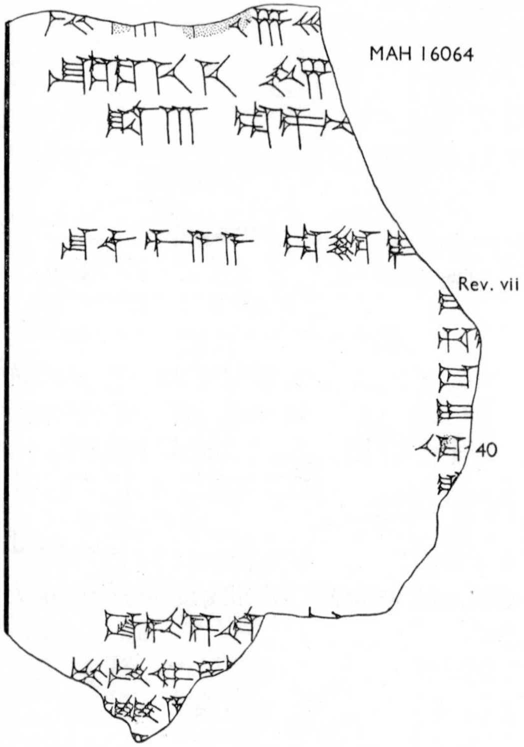
MAH 16064
Rev. vii
40

BE 39099

Rev. ii — Rev. i

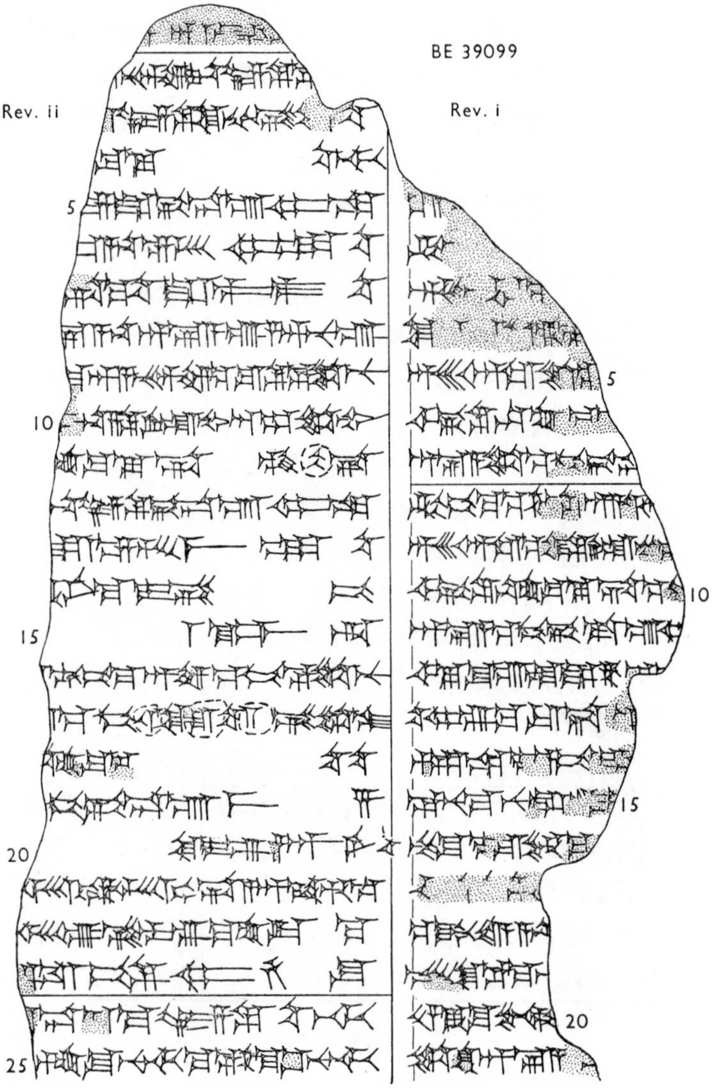

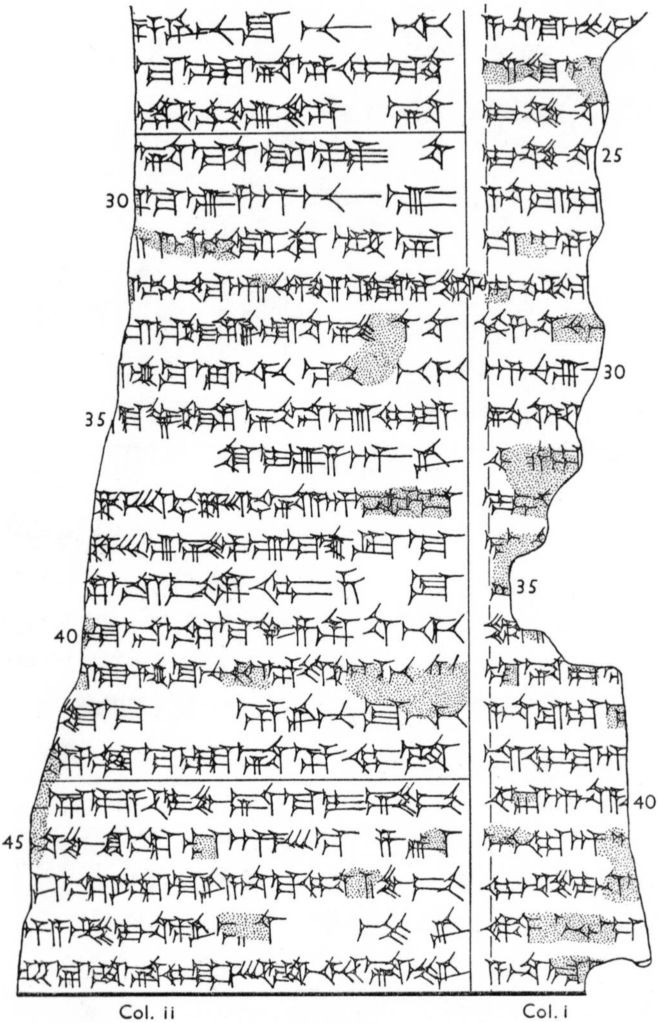


BE 39099 Rev.
(cont.)

Collations: numbered texts from *CT* 46; G = *CT* 44 20.

No. 1
14
16
26
47 or
52 fifth from bottom
58 al-
60
84 (tam sup. ras.?)
108 pu- (uš!)
129
130
155 a-n[a]
165 ⌜na⌝-
220
224
227 end
238
281
282
285 -ab
290 -[ab
302 i-ta--
307
320
336 -ti
346
361 ši-
369 a-na
371 ni-a-ti a-
374 si- -ni-
375 -[r]a

380 nam-ta-
389 -[m]a
413
414-5 No missing line

No. 3: i 46
i end: four or five lines missing
ii 32
ii 34 -ib
ii 35 -pa-
ii 36 (t]a?)
ii 39 ar-
iii 9
iii 16
iii 17
iii 21 Wider gap!
iii 33
iii 39 i-
iii 44 -ub-bi
iii end: probably one line missing
iv 8 a-na
iv 27 ki-
iv 41
iv 42
iv end: five or six lines missing
v 12
v 29
v 33
v 45 -mu-
v 47 -qá-
v 52
v end: probably no line missing

vi 4 ,
vi 6 -li
vi 15 ú-
vi 22 -ku-un
vi 26 -iu-
vi 27 pu-
vii 1 -pu
vii 10 ni- ,
vii 11
vii 12 Wider gap!
viii 3-9 (right-hand edge)
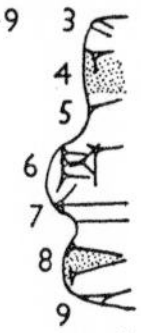
viii 7
viii 10 lu-

No. 10: Obv. 2
5 -ta

No. 12: Obv. 2 -ma, ni
4

No. 14: Obv. 1 x x (bu?)
2

No. 15: 1 lu-
5 [má]
18

G: i 3 ig-
i 8
ii 7
ii 9
ii 12
ii 17
ii 18

PRINTED IN GREAT BRITAIN
AT THE UNIVERSITY PRESS, OXFORD
BY VIVIAN RIDLER
PRINTER TO THE UNIVERSITY